SOCIAL WORK
PRACTICE
WITH
BLACK FAMILIES

FORDHAM
UNIVERSITY
AT
TARRYTOWN
LIBRARY

FORDHAM
UNIVERSITY
AT
TARRYTOWN
LIBRARY

SOCIAL WORK PRACTICE WITH BLACK FAMILIES

A Culturally Specific Perspective

FORDHAM
UNIVERSITY
AT
TARRYTOWN
LIBRARY

Sadye M. L. Logan

The University of Kansas
School of Social Welfare

Edith M. Freeman

The University of Kansas
School of Social Welfare

Ruth G. McRoy

The University of Texas at Austin
School of Social Work

Longman
New York & London

Social Work Practice with Black Families:
A Culturally Specific Perspective

Copyright © 1990 by Longman, a division of Addison-Wesley Publishing Co., Inc.
All rights reserved.
No part of this publication may be reproduced,
stored in a retrieval system, or transmitted
in any form or by any means, electronic, mechanical,
photocopying, recording, or otherwise,
without the prior permission of the publisher.

Longman, 95 Church Street, White Plains, N.Y. 10601
A division of Addison-Wesley Publishing Co., Inc.

Associated companies:
Longman Group Ltd., London
Longman Cheshire Pty., Melbourne
Longman Paul Pty., Auckland
Copp Clark Pitman, Toronto

FORDHAM
UNIVERSITY
AT
TARRYTOWN
LIBRARY

From *The Dream Keeper and Other Poems* by Langston Hughes, Copyright 1932
by Alfred A. Knopf, Inc. and renewed 1960 by Langston Hughes. Reprinted by
permission of the Publisher.

Executive editor: David J. Estrin
Production editor: Camilla T. K. Palmer
Cover design: Anne M. Pompeo
Text art: K & S Graphics
Production supervisor: Kathleen Ryan

Library of Congress Cataloging in Publication Data

Social work practice with Black families : a culturally-specific
    perspective / [edited by] Sadye L. Logan, Edith M. Freeman, Ruth G.
    McRoy.

      p.   cm.
    Includes index.
    ISBN 0-8013-0012-6
      1. Afro-Americans—Social work with. 2. Family social work—
United States. I. Logan, Sadye Louise, 1943-   II. Freeman,
Edith M. III. McRoy, Ruth G.
HV3181.S62   1990   88-34124
362.8′496073—dc19   CIP

ABCDEFGHIJ–MA–99 98 97 96 95 94 93 92 91 90

To those who have always been there—
   My mother and dad, sisters, brothers, friends,
   and beloved Gurumayi

Sadye M. L. Logan

To my family for their support, understanding, and contributions—
   Herby, David, Meredith, and Karen

Edith M. Freeman

To my family, Dwight, Myra, Melissa, and my father,
   for their love, patience, and encouragement—

Ruth G. McRoy

We dedicate this book to the continuing survival and growth of all
families.

We have tomorrow
Bright before us
Like a flame.
  —*Langston Hughes*

Contents

Foreword: Black Families in Perspective

Recent years have witnessed a revival of public and professional interest in the status of black families. Many of these discussions focus almost exclusively on the dysfunctional aspects of those families. Addressing this tendency in a commencement address at Spelman College in 1986, the poet Gwendolyn Brooks gently decried the focus on "the vanishing black family." It is not that these negative portrayals should be avoided altogether, she argued, but that one longs for a sense of "balance." She was echoing a theme advanced earlier by the novelist Ralph Ellison, who has remarked on the variety and complexity of the black experience. Without denying the problems of this experience or the crippling consequences, Ellison reminded us that black families are more than the sum of their dysfunctions. There is, he says, that "something else" which makes for our strength and our endurance.

Social scientists and social workers often have difficulty approaching the sensitivity and insight which these creative writers bring to the subject of black family life in America. We are often too bound up in our concepts, theories, and simplistic two-way comparisons to search for the complexity that is often exhibited by black families. Robert Hill has reminded us that there are certain strengths of black families and that without an understanding and appreciation for them it is difficult to fashion strategies for enhancing these families. It is difficult to help people based on their weaknesses, he argues. It is better to help them by reinforcing their strengths. It is a sad commentary on social science research and social work practice that this imbalance in perspectives on black families is perpetuated. It would not be immediately apparent from a regular reading of the literature that black families come in all shapes, sizes, colors, socioeconomic levels, levels of functioning, and types of family structure and that they evolve, grow, progress, and regress throughout the entire life span from the cradle to the grave. This book makes an important contribution to addressing this problem and to the search for the balance of which Gwendolyn Brooks speaks.

Many seminal ideas permeate this book. First, the black family is placed within the context of the larger society as a social and cultural subsystem of that society. These families, whatever their problems, can best be understood and treated within this social context. Second, the book argues that history plays an important role in the evolution of a people. Thus, it is imperative that social workers and other helping professionals know and understand the history of the Afro-American people within the context of the larger society. Third, the book argues the theme of complexity and cultural diversity. Fourth, the book connects theoretical and research findings with the imperatives and imprecision of professional practice. It is not enough, the authors seem to argue, to know the complexities of the Afro-American experience. The translation to practice requires practice itself with this knowledge base in hand. Fifth, in assessing what seems to work in efforts to help families function better, the authors have made a similar contribution. While it is generally true that there are positive and negative consequences to most complex social phenomena, these authors point up ways of enhancing the functional or of "accentuating the positive."

Finally, to take only a few of the remarkable contributions of this book, some of the most pressing problems facing black families (e.g., alcoholism, unemployment, aging, school failure) are clarified by these authors.

Readers of this book who truly absorb its contents will become more educated, more enlightened, and more competent as professional practitioners in a complex and culturally diverse society.

Andrew Billingsley, Ph.D.
Professor and Chair, Department of Family
and Community Development
University of Maryland, College Park, Maryland

Preface

Despite the advances made in understanding and working with black families, there are still many barriers to providing adequate and effective social work practice to this client population. Moreover, because much of the literature about various aspects of black family life is sociological in nature and difficult to translate into usable practice principles, there is no adequate primary reference for clinical practice with black families. This text was written to bridge this gap in the literature. Our primary goal was to provide a framework for understanding the needs of black families and to describe culturally relevant approaches to practice with black families. The framework accommodates direct as well as indirect practice and emphasizes how to assess and intervene with black families utilizing a strengths perspective. Included are original contributions from professional social workers and educators who are prominent scholars in the field of social welfare.

Case vignettes illustrate practice principles and strategies for areas of practice discussed. There is also a comprehensive discussion of the most pressing needs and issues that are currently having an impact on black family and community life. An ecological perspective frames our notion of a flexible, client-specific practice that emphasizes strengths, black self-help, and relevant life domains in both direct *and* indirect practice.

Given the focus on assessment and treatment of black families, the chapters establish a sequential framework for understanding historical and cultural issues relevant to the functioning of the black family, for collecting and analyzing assessment data, and for identifying appropriate interventive strategies. Part One establishes a conceptual framework for understanding and intervening with black families. Specific social and cultural issues that have an impact on the assess-

ment process are described in Part Two. Suggestions are made for reconceptual-
izing the problems and needs of black families. In Part Three the focus moves
from assessment of strengths and problems to specific intervention strategies
with black families. This part moves beyond conventional ideas about treating
black families to a new framework of effective and culturally relevant helping.
This framework incorporates an ecostructural approach that includes the family
as well as other social systems as contributors and agents of change in the
family's overall structure and functioning. Part Four addresses practice and
research issues and challenges and opportunities for the future.

This text is designed to assist social work practitioners, classroom and
practicum instructors, and students in developing knowledge and skills for practice with black families. The target audience includes students and practitioners
who already work primarily with black families from a broad-based ecological
perspective or those who want to expand the focus of their practice with such
families. Helping professionals in other disciplines, such as nursing, psychology,
and counseling, will also find this book useful. This book can therefore be used
in graduate social work programs as a primary text in courses on clinical
practice, family treatment, and the black family, or it can be used as a secondary text in courses on social policy, practice-based research, human behavior in
the social environment, and field instruction. It can also be used in graduate
training programs for other helping professionals and as supplemental reading in
continuing education, in in-service training programs, and in public school,
child welfare, public welfare, family services, and health and mental health
settings.

Ultimately this book represents what we have lived through in our own
practice and taught to our students. We offer it to the social work practice and
education community as well as to other helping professionals who are concerned about and committed to strengthening the quality of life for all families.

S. Logan
E. Freeman
R. McRoy

Acknowledgments

All the contributors put much time and effort into developing and writing the chapters, and their interest in making this book a reality is deeply appreciated. We must also thank Mary Cook and Darrell Burnette, graduate social work students, University of Texas, Jerry Joyce, Catherine Mazzotta-Rees, and Catherine Potter-Ossman, graduate social work students the University of Kansas, and Viola V. Logan, a social work practitioner who read and provided feedback on the chapter drafts. We also want to thank our typists, Marian Abegg and Alice Burg, and especially Crystal Cunningham, illustrator and typist, who patiently and skillfully worked with us throughout the numerous revisions. We are indebted to the University of Kansas and the University of Texas at Austin for the support services and in-kind resources. The encouragement and love of our families during the development of this work inspired us and has instilled in us an even greater appreciation for the strengths of black families.

PART 1

A Conceptual Framework for Practice with Black Families

Social work practice with black families is a specialized area of practice that requires an understanding of the historical and cultural background of blacks in the United States and a consideration of the influences these factors have on the contemporary black family system. Part One of this book presents a historical and conceptual framework for viewing and analyzing black family life.

Chapter 1 looks at the life-styles and culture of African families prior to being captured, separated, and transported as chattel to be enslaved in America. The helping tradition characteristic of African societies was the foundation for black helping networks during and after slavery in America. A glimpse of the contemporary life-styles of blacks and a discussion of the need for innovative approaches to social work practice with this population are also provided.

Acknowledging the unique characteristics of many black families and the similarities that blacks have to all other families, Chapter 2 discusses concepts that have an impact on black family life—race, ethnicity, culture, and social class—and examines how each influences the ecological realities of black Americans. The variability within black communities and black families is emphasized. Moreover, it is suggested that knowing about the unique aspects of black family life can help practitioners make services more relevant to black consumers.

A review of the traditional social work practice approaches that have been used with black families follows in Chapter 3. Noting that micro- and macro-level approaches for work with blacks often ignore the strengths of black families, use middle-class standards as criteria for success, and deny such factors as discrimination and institutional racism, which help create and maintain problems in black families, a culturally relevant theoretical framework is proposed for assessing and intervening with black families. This approach takes into consideration the critical relationships between past history and current problems of blacks in the United States. Practice principles derived from the conceptual perspective are also presented.

CHAPTER 1

A Historical Overview of Black Families

Ruth G. McRoy
University of Texas at Austin

To understand contemporary black family life and culture, it is necessary to examine the influence of African cultural patterns, slavery, and the ways in which black families adapt to segregation and discrimination in American society. This chapter reviews both the historical underpinnings of the black family and contemporary forces affecting family life. In addition, it provides an overview of how black families interact with formal social service systems and of the development of self-help social services in the black community. The impact of limited access to mainstream programs on family functioning is highlighted.

AFRICAN PAST AND AMERICAN SLAVERY

Between the sixteenth and nineteenth centuries, blacks were taken forcibly from their African homelands, and many were transported to America to serve as slaves. They came from long and honorable cultural traditions in African society in which the family was highly valued. Common to many African societies were masculine-dominated families that represented economic, political, and religious units. Children and elders were highly valued in these close-knit, well-organized families (Billingsley, 1968). In traditional Africa, nuclear families were a part of an extended family network that formed a clan, and several clans would comprise a tribe or community that was characterized by a feeling of unity and mutual aid.

Male dominance was one of the foremost traditions of African family life. Men served both as heads of families and as leaders and decision makers in the community, and women were expected to be submissive and respectful to their husbands. Although women were expected to perform all household tasks, as

3

well as some agricultural labor, the most important role for women was that of childbearing. Children represented the continuity of life, and women were expected to be fruitful (Martin & Martin, 1985; Billingsley, 1968). African children were taught to value and be proud to help family members and others in the community. Communal aid, religious rituals and celebrations, music, and art were all important parts of the expression of everyday life in Africa.

Slavery existed in Africa, but in much more moderation than in America. The typical slave in West Africa was viewed as a member of a household and had many rights—such as the right to marry, to own property, to own a slave himself, and to inherit from the master (Elkins, 1967). The writings of early European traders reveal that, up to the eighteenth century, Africans were viewed as trade partners not as inferiors. A very proud people, Africans also did not consider themselves inferior to Europeans (Bennett, 1982, p. 33).

The first black immigrants arrived in the United States in 1619. Like many other early blacks in this country, they were not slaves but indentured servants, who worked out the terms of their indenture and later often acquired land and servants of their own. These early blacks often worked together with whites and sometimes intermarried. Prejudice was based more on class differences than on race, creed, or color. In fact, the earliest colonists identified themselves as Englishmen or Christians rather than as whites. The term "white" did not become synonymous with superiority until late in the eighteenth century, as a result of slavery. Similarly, the term "Negro," the Spanish and Portuguese word for "black," did not come into general use until the latter part of the eighteenth century.

With the growing worldwide demand in the 1660s for sugar and tobacco, the early colonists recognized the need for a huge cheap labor force. Small farms were becoming huge plantations, and the owners felt that they needed a permanent involuntary labor force instead of indentured servants. After ruling out enslavement of whites and Indians, these colonists settled on Africans, a group of easily identifiable and unprotected people whose supply seemed to be unending. A system of involuntary servitude based on skin color was established, and in the mid-1600s laws that prohibited intermarriage and made blacks slaves for life were enacted (Lacy, 1972).

Coming primarily from the west coast of Africa, Africans were captured in large numbers, shackled, and forced to march hundreds of miles to the coast, where they were examined like cattle and packed tightly like parcels into the hull of ships for the dreaded Mid-Passage to the Americas. Those that did not succumb to malnourishment, unsanitary conditions, disease, suicide, or rebellions on board ship were branded like beasts and sold when they reached the New World. Considered bondsmen, or slaves for life, these blacks were considered "things" that were owned by the master and could be bought and sold like any property. They had no civil status and could not enter into legal contracts, so they could not legally marry, own property, sue, or be sued. Slave masters could separate members of the slave's family at whim and could commit adultery with or rape bondswomen (Berry & Blassingame, 1982). Educating slaves was prohibited, and slaves were forbidden from assembling, voting, and holding political office. Black parents had no legal responsibility for their children; the master provided for and held final authority over slave children and their parents (Lacy, 1972).

Most blacks lived on plantations located in seven states in the south, but an estimated 500,000 blacks worked in cities as domestics, factory workers, or skilled artisans. Other blacks were free, living in both the north and the south (Bennett, 1982).

FAMILY LIFE UNDER SLAVERY

Despite the roadblocks to the formation of stable families, positive affective familial and kin arrangements among slave families did emerge (Sudarkasa, 1981). The slave's survival depended in large part on the training and sustenance provided in the slave quarters. Slave parents provided their children with love and affection, helped them to understand their situation and how to avoid punishment by the master, and taught them to cooperate with other blacks. This early socialization served to bolster the child's self-esteem by providing love, positive feedback, and acceptance as a valued person.

Among slave masters, there was a great deal of variability with regard to attitudes toward slave families. Many slaves lived on plantations in which the master had to approve a slave's marriage partner. Some masters promoted social relationships on the plantation so the slave would have fewer excuses to leave the estate and would be more likely to marry and have children, who would also become the master's slaves. Some slave masters encouraged strong family ties in order to lessen the likelihood of slaves rebelling and running away. Slave-owners sometimes recognized the black male as head of the household, and some even promoted sexual morality and encouraged monogamous relationships by punishing slaves for adultery. It was thought that if the male slave were devoted to his family he would be unlikely to engage in activities that might cause him to be separated from them. Other masters sanctioned polygamy and promiscuity among slaves, hoping to insure a continuous labor supply as well as economic benefits accrued from the sale of surplus slaves (Bennett, 1982).

In African societies, patriarchy had been the predominant form of family decision-making, but on the majority of southern plantations the master was in charge. He determined when the slave and his wife would go to work, when and whether the slave wife would cook the slave's meals, and he settled family arguments. The master furnished food, clothing, and shelter for the family. The slave husband was unable to protect his wife and children from sexual advances of whites or from floggings, and he often lived in fear that the master would choose to sell his wife and children at will (Blassingame, 1979). Approximately 10 percent of slave marriages were ended by the master in an attempt to teach slaves a lesson. Such a breakup affected not only the immediate family but also their relatives and other slaves on the plantation (Gutman, 1976).

Bondswomen were generally expected to do the same work as men, as well as raise their children and do domestic chores. Women as well as men in the agricultural work force were expected to plow fields, drop seeds, hoe, pick, sod, mate cotton, harvest rice, plant sugarcane, and perform many other tasks. As few as 5 percent of all adult slaves served in the elite corps of house servants responsible for cooking, sewing, ironing, washing, dusting, sweeping, child care, and being on call to any white slave-owner or house guest.

Slaves were able to survive these dehumanizing experiences partly because of the positive interactions in the slave quarters, the support provided through the church, and inner strength. Within the slave quarters and no longer under the direct view of the master, the male slave could demonstrate affection and true feelings toward his family. There he could play the role of husband and father and teach his children how to survive. In the confines of the slave cabin the slave could receive nurturance, respect, love, and have fun. Many slaves were highly respected within the slave quarters, especially if they held jobs that took them away from the plantation or became involved in protests, had important positions on the plantation, or were skilled craftsmen. Respect in the slave community was also accorded slaves who had learned to read and write despite restrictions on education (Blassingame, 1979).

Black women were expected to perform tasks equal to those of the men and were punished just as brutally. Many slave masters chose to "defeminize" women by insisting that they dress like men, by treating them like sex objects, and by breeding them like animals. Also, many black women suffered from the psychological burden of being repeatedly sexually victimized, as well as from poor health resulting from having many children (Martin & Martin, 1985).

HELPING NETWORKS DURING SLAVERY

The church too provided support, solace, and sometimes protection for slave families. Many white clergy preached against the separation of slave families. Advocating that marriages were divine institutions not to be broken, some clergy strongly discouraged masters from separating families. However, the importance of making profits generally superseded any biblical injunction (Blassingame, 1979). Participation in the black church made slaves better prepared to resist the psychological assault of human bondage. Creating their own means of worship, which reflected a combination of West African beliefs and Christianity, slaves used metaphors, rhythmic chants and music, clapping, prayers and sermons, shouting, and stomping of feet as a means of religious expression and emotional uplift. Through worship services, slaves were able to release their pent-up feelings of despair, express their desires for freedom, and look forward to the hereafter. The songs reflected the day-to-day experience of slavery, but they were also used to spread news of upcoming slave rebellions or plans for escape (Blassingame, 1979).

Church gatherings also gave slaves a brief respite from the toils of the day and an opportunity to spread hope for the next life, for deliverance, and for relief from toils. Religious gatherings helped develop group solidarity and promote mutual aid among slaves. These meetings provided slaves with another frame of reference and a source of positive self-feeling, courage, and confidence (Blassingame, 1979). Their belief that God recognized them as equal to whites and that God was more powerful than the slave master proved to be one essential tool for psychological survival.

The helping tradition characteristic of African societies was reinforced and became essential for survival during slavery. Slaves had to cooperate with each other to escape some of the master's oppression as well as to ensure that their basic needs would be met. They worked together to supplement the meager rations provided by the slave-owner, took care of each other in sickness, and helped newly arrived Africans. Blood relatives as well as fictive kin (unrelated neighbors or friends) were all part of the slave family. Blacks felt a sense of obligation to support not only family members but also others. Sometimes such terms as "aunt" and "uncle" were used by children to refer to nonkin adults (or "fictive kin") who were close to the family. Orphan children as well as new slaves were frequently incorporated into the family unit. The elderly, often considered practically worthless to the slave master, also received much respect from younger blacks and even if unrelated were often incorporated into the family (Martin & Martin, 1985).

FREE BLACKS DURING SLAVERY

Not all blacks were slaves. The noted historian Lerone Bennett states that in the late 1780s there were 697,000 black slaves and 59,000 free blacks. All but 8 percent of the slaves lived in the south, and the free blacks lived primarily in the northeast, mostly in New York and Philadelphia (Bennett, 1982). By 1860 there were about 500,000 free blacks, and most lived in the southeast in such states as Maryland, North Carolina, and Louisiana. Free blacks—blacks who were born in a nonslave state or had been set free or had successfully run away or bought their own freedom—were free from physical bondage but not from oppression and prejudice. Their free status was constantly challenged by whites, and they found that their rights differed according to where they lived. For example, in some states (e.g., Maryland and New York) free blacks voted, but in most southern states blacks did not have the right to vote. Most were relegated to low-status and low-paying jobs. They found solace in the extended family as members helped one another emotionally, spiritually, and physically. Despite the numerous hardships, some free blacks become skilled artisans, acquired property, and lived comfortably. In fact, some became slaveholders themselves (Berry & Blassingame, 1982).

Wealthier free blacks often formed fraternal orders and benevolent societies through the black church—for example, the Black Masons. These groups provided burial for their members, sick pay for disabled members, pensions to the elderly, and education for homeless children (Martin & Martin, 1985). Such early social welfare institutions assisted the natural helping networks within the family in combating poverty and provided services not available to blacks because of segregation. In addition, many free blacks worked with antislavery organizations (Berry & Blassingame, 1982).

Education was emphasized among free blacks and was viewed as a means of mental enhancement and a vehicle for improving one's chances for occupational advancement. Because they were often barred from white schools or, if admitted, treated as inferiors, free blacks established private schools, sometimes aided by white philanthropists. One of the best known such schools was the Institution des Orphelins, built in New Orleans in 1846 (Berry & Blassingame, 1982).

SOCIAL SERVICES FOR BLACKS
AFTER SLAVERY

Before the Civil War, slave masters were responsible for the care of poor and sick blacks, and free blacks were responsible for their own care. After the war, however, controversy arose over who would assume responsibility for the welfare of the freedmen (Rabinowitz, 1974). In 1865, after much debate, Congress established the first federal social welfare institution, the Bureau of Refugees, Freedmen, and Abandoned Lands, known as the Freedmen's Bureau. This organization was responsible for providing military protection, clothing, housing, tools, and land, as well as for distributing rations, for establishing social agencies, hospitals, day schools, industrial schools, night schools, institutes and colleges, and for educating freed blacks. Between 1865 and 1871 the Freedmen's Bureau spent more than $5 million on education for blacks (Berry & Blassingame, 1982). The bureau also helped former slaves reunite with families that had been separated during slavery. The Freedmen's Bureau was underfunded and opposed by hostile white southerners, and by 1872 the agency was no longer in existence. Despite some of the successful programs made available by this short-lived federally funded agency, the bureau did not provide sufficient services to reach the majority of freedmen. One out of every four blacks died of disease and want after emancipation (Bennett, 1982).

Supporters of the slave system used such statistics to suggest that blacks had been better off living on the plantation and being cared for by their masters. Some claimed that "the high death rate among blacks was due to inherent weaknesses of the race" (Rabinowitz, 1974, p. 331) and failed to consider the real causes: poverty and overcrowding. Additional justification for the continued segregation of the races occurred in 1896. In the case of *Plessy v. Ferguson*, the U.S. Supreme Court upheld "separate but equal" accommodations for blacks, thereby formally sanctioning segregation.

At various times between 1865 and 1890, segregated services for blacks provided by missionary societies, among others, were an impetus for the continuation of segregated facilities provided by state and local governments. These segregated almshouses, insane asylums, orphanages, schools, hospitals, and other institutions were in no way equal to their white counterparts and were not funded equally. Blacks were usually given inadequate accommodations and less funding for services.

Welfare services were also dispensed on a segregated basis in the south after reconstruction. In Virginia, food and fuel were available to whites during specified morning hours on certain days and to blacks in the afternoon. This practice gave whites first choice of goods and further relegated blacks to a second-class status. Blacks were barred from institutions for the "deaf, dumb, and blind" in the south until the mid-1880s. Blacks experienced such inequities in death as well as in life. Cemeteries established for blacks were generally littered, overcrowded, dreary patches of land. These discrepancies were based on the belief that blacks were inferior, as well as on the paucity of available resources for establishing identical facilities for blacks and whites. "Separate" facilities therefore became synonymous with "unequal" facilities (Rabinowitz, 1974).

BLACK SELF-HELP STRATEGIES

Blacks continued to supplement these governmental services and to help provide services to blacks. The extended family came to the rescue of thousands of related and nonrelated black children, widows, and elderly people who had no means of support. Large extended families were considered an asset, a survival mechanism, as families engaged in sharecropping after emancipation (Martin & Martin, 1985).

Other self-help efforts, including day care centers, working girls' homes, kindergartens, and private services for poor children, were launched to reach both unserved and underserved populations of black children. According to W. E. B. Du Bois (1909), churches made monetary contributions as well. Church members were engaged in such benevolent work as visits, care of the sick, and adoption of children. Du Bois suggested that at the beginning of the twentieth century black churches had contributed more than half a million dollars annually for "uplift purposes" (Du Bois, 1909). Black ministers also played an integral role in developing services for black juvenile offenders.

Black lodges of Masons or Odd Fellows performed social welfare func-tions, such as aiding widows and orphaned children. Societies connected with local churches provided sick benefits and burial services for members. Special-ized branches of private relief groups were formed to aid blacks. For example, the Colored Ladies Relief Society, a branch of the Nashville Ladies Relief Society in 1886, investigated the needs of poor black applicants. Both societies were financed by individual donations and county court appropriations. How-ever, the "colored society" received only one-third the amount the county appropriated to the white group (Rabinowitz, 1974).

Many of the early orphanages were founded by individual black women who could not tolerate the deplorable conditions that many black orphans were forced to endure. Other concerned black women would gather children from streets and alleys and educate and train them in trades or industry so that they could become useful citizens.

Because no provisions were made for reformatories for black youth, black delinquents in the south as young as six years of age were generally placed in penitentiaries and jails with adult criminals. White youths were seldom sent to the penitentiary, because juvenile reformatories had been established for them. In Virginia, the black press, organizations of black women, and black churches expressed concern about these inequities in the treatment of black delinquents. Their lobbying eventually led to the establishment of a reformatory for black youths in Richmond, Virginia, in 1898 (Pollard, 1978).

State and local governments did little on behalf of elderly blacks. States that did offer such services at the turn of the century provided the aged with a very meager existence. Again, it was black men and women who made donations to provide relief for black senior citizens. This pattern of mutual aid and reliance on the black community for the provision and subsidization of social services for blacks continued until the depression of the 1930s.

By the beginning of World War I, more and more blacks were leaving the rural areas and moving to the cities, hoping to escape sharecropping and the oppressive conditions characteristic of the south. Many former agricultural and domestic workers found jobs as janitors, railroad workers, merchants, and mechanics, or work in shipyards, steel and iron mills, chemical factories, and coal mines. Blacks were restricted to the least desirable and lowest-paid jobs by a number of means, including trade union exclusion and limited opportunities for advancement. Hoping to obtain economic prosperity, many found that their rural values of mutual aid and self-help were not adaptable to big-city life. The extended family, a benefit in the rural areas, became cumbersome in urban, industrial settings in which small, geographically and occupationally mobile families were the norm (Martin & Martin, 1978). To survive, many black families often assimilated the individualistic values characteristic of the dominant society and urban life-styles.

Due to the limited employment opportunities available to blacks during this time and the continued racial segregation, however, the black community support systems—churches, schools, and benevolent societies—continued to assist black families. Many extended-family systems served as supports to newly arrived blacks in urban areas, providing housing and emotional support to kin and fictive kin who were now seeking a better life in the large urban area.

During the depression of the 1930s, blacks again tried to rekindle the self-support energies characteristic of slavery and postslavery days to protect their own against the economic hardships of the time, but families were finding it difficult to feed their immediate blood relatives and had to begin limiting their efforts to help the wider community. Social service agencies that had depended on the charitable donations of the black working poor found themselves having to cease operations because those families were devoting all their resources to their own sustenance (Martin & Martin, 1985).

Blacks were hardest hit by the depression because they were at the bottom rung of the economic ladder. As factories closed or reduced the number of employees, blacks were generally the first to be released. In 1932, approximately 50.6 percent of blacks were unemployed, and 39.0 percent of whites. With the passage of the Social Security Act and the New Deal programs of President Franklin D. Roosevelt, however, the government began to assume more responsibility for providing social welfare services. In 1935 there were 2 million blacks on relief (Grant, 1968; Lacy, 1972). Although assisting blacks in many ways, the New Deal legislation served to further confine blacks to a caste-like status. For example, the Federal Housing Administration programs favored racially homogeneous neighborhoods and gave legal sanction to residential segregation by practices that discouraged the guarantee of mortgages on homes in integrated areas (Lacy, 1972).

In the 1930s and 1940s, blacks continued to protest unequal treatment, campaigning against employment discrimination, disenfranchisement, and segregation in education, housing, and public accommodations. Such organizations as the National Association for the Advancement of Colored People (NAACP) and the Congress of Racial Equality (CORE) were instrumental in leading the movement. By the 1950s it was clear that segregation meant discrimination, and in 1954 the U.S. Supreme Court ordered the integration of public education. As a result of the civil rights movement of the 1960s, additional barriers to equality were disbanded. Voting restraints were outlawed, and discrimination in housing, employment, and public accommodations was prohibited by law. By 1968, blacks had finally been given the same legal rights as all other Americans (Lacy, 1972).

ISSUES IN SOCIAL SERVICE DELIVERY TO BLACK FAMILIES

Although some progress was made in the mid-1960s to mid-1970s, the late 1970s brought a return to the conservatism of the past, and minority issues were no longer given high priority in American society, especially in governmental agendas. Race relations became more polarized as competition for jobs grew more intense during the recessions of the 1970s (Heffernan, et al., 1988; McGhee, 1983). Throughout the 1980s, the nation's economic difficulties have taken precedence over black economic problems. Gaps between black and white earning power continue, and blacks are still disproportionately poor and more at risk than whites for problems related to low-income status.

In 1968, the National Association of Black Social Workers was founded to improve the provision of social services to blacks and to call attention to the need for more black social workers. The National Association of Social Workers has since established a National Committee on Minority Affairs to address some of the issues of practice with minority populations.

In order to make social work education more relevant to the needs of minority groups, the Council on Social Work Education established a Commission on Minority Groups in the 1970s, and a curriculum policy statement in 1972 mandated the development and inclusion of content on minorities in the social work curriculum (Dieppa, 1984). Moreover, in 1978 the National Institute of Mental Health issued a twofold mandate: (1) that minority content be included in all mental health training programs and (2) that public resources be targeted for the unserved and underserved populations that are disproportionately minority and more at risk for mental health problems (Bush, et al., 1983). There has been some progress from efforts to increase the number of black social service professionals and to enhance mental health training by including an emphasis on effective intervention with specific minority populations, but much more work is needed to change attitudes and to enhance commitment to the development and integration of a systematic body of knowledge about social work practice with blacks.

Despite special efforts to enhance social services to blacks, few blacks are being reached. There continues to be a need for mutual aid and informal helping networks, such as the black extended family and fictive kin networks (Martin & Martin, 1985). Both financial aid and emotional support are important features of the mutual-aid system. McAdoo (1978) found that neither socioeconomic status nor upward mobility decreased the amount of informal support received by urban blacks in her sample. Similarly, Taylor's (1986) study of black family support among a sample of blacks revealed that the majority received support from their extended family members. Urban blacks in this study reported that they had frequent interaction with family members, lived relatively close to family and relatives, and found family life to be a source of satisfaction and emotional support.

Neighbors and Taylor's (1985) study found that the majority of blacks did not use social services and that the majority of those who did (14.4 percent) had incomes of less than $10,000 and contacted public social services regardless of the type of problem. The highest percentage of social service utilizers sought help for economic problems. Using the same data, Neighbors (1984) found that few blacks experiencing personal problems seek help from mental health agencies. These findings suggest that natural helping and support within the black community should be considered a very important component in the planning of social services to reach black families. Other family members can be viewed as support systems and as potential resources to assist with problem resolution.

Although the black extended family is still a viable mechanism in rural and urban communities, the helping tradition that seemed to be institutionalized in the black community during earlier times has waned. The racial consciousness of the 1960s that served as an impetus for blacks to consider the well-being of all blacks, not just family members, seems to have taken a back seat to the desire of some blacks to obtain material goods, gain social status, and escape the stigma of being poor (Martin & Martin, 1985).

Some social service and religious organizations have had to continue to provide services to black individuals and families, primarily because the availability of and extent of governmental social service programs tend to fluctuate depending on the state of the national economy and presidential politics and policies. During the late 1970s, churches as well as professional and fraternal organizations in some cases collaborated with social agencies to address some of the social problems facing blacks. For example, in 1978 the Congress of National Black Churches formed a nonprofit coalition and has since instituted programs in child care, economic development, employment, and teen pregnancy prevention (McAdoo, 1987; Logan, 1980). Taylor and colleagues (1987) found that both historically and currently the black church is one of the few institutions that is black owned and controlled. It is still a viable community gathering place and source of material, emotional, and spiritual assistance.

CONTEMPORARY FORCES AFFECTING BLACK FAMILY LIFE

Currently, blacks constitute about 12 percent of the population of the United States. This represents about 29 million people and 15 million black families. McAdoo (1987) characterized the contemporary black population as being younger and having a higher fertility rate than nonblacks. The average age of blacks is 26.3 years, and black children represent 15.4 percent of all children in the United States. About 56 percent of black children live in central cities (Edelman, 1981). Moreover, in 1984 the black population consisted of about 1.4 million more women than men. Over the past two decades, the structure of black families has changed (see Chapter 5), with the number of female-headed households increasing, the number of children living with two parents decreasing, and the rate of poverty among blacks increasing.

Since the 1960s the percentages of children living in one-parent families significantly increased by more than fifteen percentage points. A closer look reveals that in 1986 some 18 percent of white children lived with one parent, and 53 percent of black children ("More Children," 1988). Increasing separation, divorce rates, and out-of-wedlock births are among the factors responsible for this trend toward single parenthood. Also, because of the sex-ratio imbalance between black men and women, it is less likely that divorced black women will remarry. The divorce rate among whites has increased by about 300 percent over the past twenty years, and the divorce rate among blacks has increased about 400 percent. Also, the high cost of divorce means that many more blacks just separate, and children are left in a single-parent household (McGhee, 1985).

Although single parenthood is not necessarily problematic, the loss of a wage earner creates economic hardships for the family and often plunges many families into poverty. Black married couples generally have two incomes, and the males usually have higher median incomes than females and therefore fare better economically. For example, in 1983 the median income of a black married couple with both spouses in the labor force was $20,586, but for a black female head-of-household, the median income was $7,999. These income differentials can be attributed to the higher earning power of the black male and the dual-earner capacity within the two-parent family (McGhee, 1985).

After the divorce, because many noncustodial parents refuse to or are unable to support their children, the single parent may be in a difficult financial situation. For example, in 1981 only 16.0 percent of the 23.9 percent black women with minor children who were awarded child support payments actually received them. When actually paid, these awards were usually less than $70 a month per child (Edelman, 1985).

Teen parenthood is another major issue in the black community today and a cause of single-parent families. By the age of 20, nearly 50 percent of all black females have been pregnant (Wallis, 1985). Religious beliefs serve to dissuade many from considering abortion to terminate the pregnancy, and many are reluctant to place children for adoption outside the extended-family network. If they choose to raise their children in a separate household from their parents, they are almost certain to be in poverty (McAdoo, 1987).

According to a 1987 census study, out-of-wedlock births are much more likely to occur in families with incomes below the poverty line across all racial groups. Because blacks have disproportionately low incomes, more black children find themselves living in impoverished single-parent households for longer periods of time than white children in the same circumstances. While the average white child may live in poverty for about ten months of his or her life, the average black child will remain in poverty for at least five years (Schaefer, 1988).

Although the national poverty rate was about 14.0 percent, the poverty rate among blacks in 1986 was 31.1 percent. The hardest hit by poverty are single black mothers and children. According to the Children's Defense Fund, more than half of all black infants born in 1982 were born into poverty. Also in that year, about 71 percent of black female-headed families with children at home were poor (Edelman, 1985).

Unemployment rates have continued to be disproportionately higher for blacks than the rate for whites. For example, in 1986 the average unemployment rate was 14.5 percent for blacks and 6.0 percent for whites. The unemployment rate for black teenagers was 39.3 percent and for white teenagers it was 15.6 percent (Swinton, 1988).

Consequently, a number of factors are responsible for the change in black family structures today. These include high rates of unemployment for young black men, increases in rates of separation and divorce, and earlier sexual activity followed by reluctance to consider abortion or adoption (McAdoo, 1987). Blacks are still experiencing income inequalities. In 1986 the average median family income for blacks was $17,604, compared to $30,809 for whites (Swinton, 1988).

There has been little gain in income equality between the races since the 1960s. Although the rates moderated slightly during the 1970s, they rose at the peak of the recession in the early 1980s. This suggests that black economic progress seems to be directly influenced by the status of the U.S. economy. The escalating budget, trade deficits, and a weak dollar have drawn the attention of the nation, while the plight of the black population has been placed on the back burner (Swinton, 1988).

Poor and working-class blacks have suffered because of the back-to-back recessions, high inflation, and technological changes that resulted in a shift from high-paying unionized manufacturing jobs to low-paying nonunionized service jobs, but in the 1970s and 1980s, middle-class blacks were particularly vulnerable to these economic shifts. Between 1969 and 1984 the percentage of middle-class blacks decreased from 39 percent to 32 percent. These families too have not escaped the impact of economic instability on family structure. During this period, the proportion of single-parent families actually rose almost ten times faster among college-educated blacks than among school dropouts who were black. Hill (1987) predicts that in 1990 black family strengths will continue to be tested as this decline in the percentage of middle-income blacks will continue—low-paying jobs, such as janitors and fast-food workers, will be plentiful, and relatively few newly created high-tech jobs will be available.

CONCLUSIONS

Despite the external economic forces that have taken their toll, black families have proven to be amazingly resilient. As Hill (1972) has reported, such strengths of the black family as strong kinship bonds, strong work orientation, flexible family roles, strong achievement orientation, and a religious orientation have helped the black family to survive. These factors have been responsible for increasing the number of blacks who have not experienced teen pregnancies, welfare dependency, children in foster care, and involvement in criminal and gang activities.

In addition, black religious organizations and grassroots self-help organizations have been responsible for developing prevention programs and for organizing the black community to address specific issues. Blacks in political power should continue to fight for systemic changes, but the mutual-aid tradition of the past must resurface in order to provide black youths with successful role models, educational and occupational opportunities, hope for a better life, and belief in themselves and in the future.

Social workers and other mental health professionals are urged to (1) take a closer look at the multitude of external factors (income inequality, racism, etc.) that have had a negative impact on black families and their resulting special needs; (2) develop an appreciation for the mutual-aid survival mechanisms as well as the internal coping strategies that blacks have utilized since slavery; (3) develop policies and programs that acknowledge the unique and viable aspects of the black family structure, and recognize and overcome systemic barriers to service utilization (e.g., agency fee structures; location); and (4) work through existing religious, community, and familial support systems in order to serve black families effectively.

REFERENCES

Bennett, L., Jr. (1982). *Before the Mayflower: A history of black America* (5th ed.). Chicago: Johnson.

Berry, M.F., & Blassingame, J.W. (1982). *Long memory: The black experience in America*. New York: Oxford University Press.

Billingsley, A. (1968). *Black families in white America*. Englewood Cliffs, NJ: Prentice-Hall.

Blassingame, J.W. (1979). *The slave community: Plantation life in the antebellum south*. New York: Oxford University Press.

Bush, J.A., Norton, D.G., Sanders, C.L., & Solomon, B.B. (1983). An integrative approach for the inclusion of content on blacks in social work education. In F.H. Kuramoto, R. F. Morales, F.U. Munoz, & K. Murase (Eds.), *Mental health and people of color* (pp. 97–124). Washington, DC: Howard University Press.

Dieppa, I. (1984). Trends in social work education for minorities. In B.W. White (Ed.), *Color in a white society* (pp. 10–21). Silver Spring, MD: National Association of Social Workers.

Du Bois, W.E.B. (1909). *Efforts for social betterment among Negro Americans*. Atlanta, GA: Atlanta University Press.

Edelman, M.W. (1985). The sea is so wide and my boat is so small: Problems facing black children today. In H.P. McAdoo & J.L. McAdoo (Eds.), *Black children: Social, educational, and parental involvements* (pp. 72–82). Beverly Hills, CA: Sage.

Elkins, S.M. (1967). The African culture argument. In G.L. Miller Duval (Ed.), *The black experience* (pp. 18–26). Washington, DC: Institute for Services to Education.

Grant, J. (1968). Depression and war: Introduction. In J. Grant (Ed.), *Black protest: History, documents, and analyses: 1619 to the present* (pp. 215–221). New York: Fawcett World Library.

Gutman, H. (1976). *The black family in slavery and freedom, 1750–1925*. New York: Pantheon.

Heffernan, J., Shuttlesworth, G., & Ambrosino, A. (1988). *Social work and social welfare: An introduction*. St. Paul, MN: West.

Hill, R. (1972). *The strengths of black families*. New York: National Urban League.

Hill, R. (1986, December). The future of black families. *The world and I*, 573–585.

Hill, R. (1987, August). The black middle class defined. *Ebony*, 32–33.

Jones, J. (1985). *Labor of love, labor of sorrow*. New York: Basic Books.

Lacy, D. (1972). *The white use of blacks in America*. New York: McGraw-Hill.

Logan, S. (1980). The black Baptist church: A social-psychological study in coping and growth. *Dissertation Abstracts International*, 41/06A.

Martin, E., & Martin, J. (1978). *The black extended family*. Chicago: University of Chicago Press.

Martin, E., & Martin, J. (1986). *The black extended family*. Chicago: University of Chicago Press.

Martin, J., & Martin, E. (1985). *The helping tradition in the black family and community*. Silver Spring, MD: National Association of Social Workers.

McAdoo, H. (1978). Factors related to stability in upwardly mobile black families. *Journal of Marriage and the Family, 40:*761–776.

McAdoo, H. (1987). Blacks. In A. Minihan, R.M. Becerra, S. Briar, C.J. Coulton, G.H. Ginsberg, J.G. Hopps, J.F. Longres, R.J. Patti, W.J. Reid, T. Tripodi, J.M. Atkins, & K.R. Greenhill (Eds.), *Encyclopedia of social work* (pp. 194–206). Silver Spring, MD: National Association of Social Workers.

McGhee, J. (1983). The changing demographics in black America. In J.D. Williams (Ed.), *The state of black America, 1983* (pp. 1–44). New York: National Urban League.

McGhee, J. (1985). The black family today and tomorrow. In J.D. Williams (Ed.), *The state of black America, 1983*. New York: National Urban League.

More children lead single-parent lives. (1988, January). *The Austin American Statesman*, 5.

Neighbors, H. (1984). Professional help use among black Americans: Implications for unmet need. *American Journal of Community Psychology, 12,* 551–566.

Neighbors, H., & Taylor, R. (1985, June). The use of social service agencies by black Americans. *Social Service Review, 59,* 259–268.

Pollard, W. (1978). *A study of black self help.* San Francisco: R & E Research Associates.

Rabinowitz, H. (1974). From exclusion to segregation: Health and welfare services for southern blacks, 1865–1890. *Social Service Review, 48,* 327–354.

Schaefer, R. (1988). *Racial and ethnic groups* (3rd ed.). Glenview, IL: Scott, Foresman.

Sudarkasa, N. (1981). Interpreting the African heritage in Afro-American family organization. In H.P. McAdoo (Ed.), *Black families* (pp. 37–53). Beverly Hills, CA: Sage.

Swinton, D. (1988). Economic status of blacks 1987. In J. Stewart (Ed.), *The state of black America, 1988* (pp. 129–152). New York: National Urban League.

Taylor, R. (1986). Receipt of support from family among black Americans: Demographic and familial differences. *Journal of Marriage and Family, 48,* 67–77.

Taylor, R., Thornton, M., & Chatters, L. (1987). Black Americans' perceptions of the sociohistorical role of the church. *Journal of Black Studies, 18,* 123–138.

Wallis, C. (1985, December 9). Children having children. *Time,* 78–90.

CHAPTER 2

Black Families:
Race, Ethnicity, Culture, Social Class, and Gender Issues

Sadye M. L. Logan
University of Kansas

Many assume that American society is made up of a mixture of people of different races, creeds, and religions whose differences are viewed in a positive context. William Graham Sumner (1906, p. 13), however, captured the experience of our common existence in the concept of ethnocentrism. He saw ethnocentrism as reflecting that area of things "in which one's own group is the center of everything, and all others are scaled and rated with reference to it." Ethnocentric thinking suggests that individuals may view their own culture as the most important way of life in the world and therefore as the context for measuring all other significant experiences and acts. It was such thinking from the majority groups in American society that fueled the black ethnic pride movement witnessed nearly three decades ago.

Ethnocentrism also fosters the myth of the great melting pot and the illusion of color blindness. These myths do not strive to equalize race relations in America, but instead are the hallmarks of racism. The mythological view of the American society as a monolithic whole perpetuates a color-blind dualist perspective and belief system about the social and economic relationships among the masses. The "we" and "they" paradigm is also an outgrowth of this system of thinking (Greely, 1971). This paradigm not only serves to define and refine the life changes among blacks and whites in our culture, but also perpetuates the confusion about the interrelationships between race, ethnicity, culture, and social class. According to Solomon (1976, p. 53), "in a racist society, race tends not only to transcend ethnicity in responses elicited from others in the social system, it tends even to shape the cultural content that defines the group's ethnicity." Despite the predominant influence of race on black American life, the complexity of black family life requires a close examination of the concepts of race, ethnicity, culture, and social class, as well as gender role and gender identity. This chapter defines these concepts, illustrates their interrelationships, and discusses their implications for assessing and working effectively with black families.

THE CONCEPTUAL DILEMMA

To understand fully the ecological and social realities of black family life, it is imperative to decipher concepts that have been used to both describe and explain the dynamics of the black experience. These concepts are race, ethnicity, culture, social class, and gender role and gender identity.

Race

When people think of black Americans, they immediately think of a racial group. The physical identity and social categorization that is the essence of race determines this predominant perception of blacks in America. Given the history of racial oppression and stigma attached to blackness in this country, this is understandable, but black Americans need to be understood in more than just racial terms. Although this understanding will not come easy, a primary step will be to begin by establishing a context for examining the concept of race.

Race is perhaps the most discussed and controversial of the concepts. It is a misunderstood concept that evokes deep feelings, and it has had the most pervasive effect on the overall functioning of black Americans. Anthropologist Ashley Montague (1964) tells us that few people have a clear and correct idea of what "race" or "a race" is. Definitions of race range on a continuum from denial that race exists to the attempt to define race on an exclusively morphological basis (Brace, 1964). Among those professionally interested in studying race relations—social, behavioral, and political scientists, as well as politicians—there is greater unanimity. For example, social scientists define race as "A group of mankind, members of which can be identified by the possession of distinctive physical characteristics" (Brace, 1964, p. 125). The word "distinctive" in the above definition is significant in that the importance of race is primarily in the perception, attitude, and action of the perceiver (Brace, 1964). It follows that unless differences are clearly and easily perceived, little if any consistency can be maintained in practice. Therefore, it becomes questionable whether the social scientist is studying what he or she actually believes is being studied. In many cases the difference that is perceived may be primarily cultural or historical. For example, culturally, the dress code or the language may be the only distinguishing feature of an East Indian or someone of Mediterranean origin. On the other hand, the slave history of an African American may have resulted in some family members with a white pigmentation, causing them to be indistinguishable from someone from the caucasoid group.

Because "race" is an emotionally laden word that triggers stereotypical, pejorative images about certain groups of people, and because of the inhumanity that has been practiced in the name of race, several scholars have advocated that the term be abandoned (Brace, 1964; Garbeck, 1961; Montague, 1964). In a more recent discussion of the concept, Green (1982) describes it as useless, that it "serves no purpose other than to make and justify invidious distinction between groups of people." In addition, Green (1982) and McAdoo (1987) argued that the term "minority," which along with race is often used to describe oppressed people, is equally inadequate for describing differences among human beings. Both authors point out that minority status refers to power and privilege, not to numbers. Green further asserts that the term also refers to "the degree to which the individuals who are identified with some group may be denied access to privileges and opportunities available to others" (p. 7). McAdoo's (1987) observation on apartheid in South Africa serves as a powerful illustration of the above points, as well as of how the term is used politically as well as psychologically.

An interesting analogue to these positions is the heated debate within the academic and social community on William Julian Wilson's *Declining Significance of Race* (1978). Numerous scholars believed that Wilson was remiss in his thesis that the vestiges of racial oppression were declining in American society (Pettigrew, 1979; Willie, 1980). But Wilson was not advocating that the concept of race be abandoned. He was making a distinction between the effects of past discrimination based on race and the current effects of race in the economic world. Wilson (1978, p. 11) contends convincingly that, although race was a significant deterrent to the life changes of blacks during the earlier periods of this country, "the economy and the states have shifted the basis of racial antagonisms away from black/white economic contacts to social, political and community issues." He points out: "The net effect is a growing class division among blacks, a situation in which economic class has been elevated to a position of greater importance than race in determining individual black opportunities for living conditions and personal life experiences" (p. 11).

Wilson's critics, especially Charles V. Willie, counterargue that "the significance of race is increasing and that it is increasing especially for middle-class blacks who, because of school desegregation and affirmative action and other integration programs, are coming into contact with whites for the first time for extended interaction" (Willie, 1978, p. 157). It is important to note, however, that others prior to Wilson also saw class oppression as more insidious and destructive than racial oppression in American society. This point could best be illustrated through Greer's observations on racism. For example, Greer (1974, p. 35) believes that racism has been used as a smokescreen to obscure the basic facts of stagnation in the American economic system. He asserts:

> Ethnic-centered analyses serve to perpetuate the illusion of classlessness and the legend of equal opportunity and mobility. It is a pernicious syndrome. In large measure these myths account for the rationalization of poverty in this country through the promise that everybody who is willing and able can eventually make it. In other words, a secular state of grace is instituted that

legitimates the existing pyramid of power, encourages competitive and oppressive relationships along the various ethnic horizontals on the pyramid, and diverts attention from the parallel oppression and exploitation of the larger class system.

Solomon (1976, p. 52) tends to disagree with those advocating that the term "ethnic group" should be substituted for "race," and she offers a point of view that is perhaps most useful to practitioners in attempting to understand the influence of stereotypes on policies, programs, and interactional processes. She believes that, in addition to serving as a categorical descriptor of the three major subgroups in the human population, the term has some usefulness in that it refers exclusively to the "physical" characteristics that distinguish the three (racial) subgroups. She further points out:

The influence of race in interpersonal relationships is almost entirely a function of social attitudes. Thus, demonstrated of the attitude, almost endemic in American society, that there is a connection between racial, i.e. physical characteristics and social behavior and that, in this regard, some races are inherently superior to others, reveals essentially what is meant by the term racism.

Ethnicity

The concept of ethnicity, while extremely popular today, is also confusing and often misunderstood (Isajin, 1974). This is especially so when referring to American blacks. For example, in a discussion on ethnicity, Staiano (1980) raises the following questions about black Americans:

Can they [blacks] be treated as an ethnic group, albeit one without a territorial base, occupying diverse econiches, and widely dispersed across the "opportunity structure"? [or] Can a group [blacks] which apparently has no unifying institutions, religious forms, customs, and, it can be argued, language, which is partially assimilated into the dominant institutions and centers of power, whose members exhibit a vast array of life styles and political philosophies, and which has evinced a variety of "adaptive strategies" in both rural and urban contexts be thought of in any sense as analyzable in terms of ethnicity? (p. 78)

Staiano (1980) concludes her questioning with the observation that "blacks do not seem to have the 'cultural and social distinctiveness' that is normally thought of as underlying ethnicity" (p. 28).

Staiano is thinking in what Isajin describes as objective terms about black ethnicity while attempting to engender a subjective point of view. According to Isajin (1974, p. 115), an objective approach describes ethnic groups in concrete terms and simply assumes the groups "to be existing as [if] it were 'out there' as real phenomena." On the other hand, "the subjective approach defines ethnicity as a process by which individuals either identify themselves as being different from others or belonging to a different group or are identified as different by others, or both identify themselves and are identified as different by others." Isajin (1974) attributes this feeling of differentness either to a person's membership in a group with a different background or to the various characteristics of one's background, social class, culture, religion, skin color, and so forth.

The *Social Work Dictionary* (1987) does not include a definition of ethnicity, but the *International Encyclopedia of the Social Sciences* (Sills, 1968, p. 167) gives a definition that combines both the subjective and the objective approach: "An ethnic group is a distinct category of the population in a larger society whose culture is usually different from its own. The members of such a group are, or feel themselves, or are thought to be, bound together by common ties of race or nationality or culture." Max Weber's (1968) definition of ethnicity most clearly reflects the European ethnic experience and might be classified as a subjective definition. According to Weber (1968, 1: 389):

> "Ethnic groups" [are] those human groups that entertain a subjective belief in their common descent because of similarities of physical type or customs or both, or because of memories of colonization and emigration: this belief must be important for the propagation of group formation: conversely it does not matter whether or not an objective blood relationship exists. Ethnic membership (*Gemeinsamkeit*) differs from the kinship group precisely by being a presumed identity, not a group with concrete social action, like the latter. In this sense ethnic membership does not constitute a group; it only facilitates group formation of any kind, particularly in the political sphere. On the other hand, it is primarily the political community, no matter how artificially organized, that inspires the belief in common ethnicity. This belief tends to persist even after the disintegration of the political community, unless drastic differences in the custom, physical type, or, above all, language exists among its members.

A major concern emerges if one were to apply Weber's definition to American blacks: Weber's definition assumes ethnicity to be a belief in common ancestry because of similarities of customs and above all language, and Weber believes that any social organization within an ethnic group is due primarily to the political factor, not to the factor of culture. One could argue that American blacks did not initially speak a common language; nor were they captured from one tribe or state on the continent of Africa and enslaved on one plantation in the United States. A question would therefore be: what accounts for and constitutes ethnic identification among American blacks?

Most subjective definitions, such as Weber's, do not assume that only the political factor accounts for a belief in common ethnicity. The general assumption is that psychological ethnic identification can be made on the basis of several attributes. These attributes may include religion, race, language, and same culture, but instead of standing alone, some attributes can be subsumed under culture or cultural traits—that is, religion or language and the like. On the other hand, race, which refers to physical characteristics, remains on a different level of analysis. If used subjectively, race may be considered a part of a person's culture. For example, subjective definitions refer to race as part of the individual's self-definition, and if self-definitions of a category of people remain the same over time and space, they become part of a people's culture. Further, if race is viewed in biological, genetic terms, it can be defined as referring to common ancestral origin and thereby included with it.

Ultimately, Isajin (1974, p. 119) argues that religion and race, like ethnicity, require independent definitions of their own and should not be included in the definition of ethnicity. He goes on to say that religion, race, and ethnicity could be subsumed under a more generic "notion of groups with a sense of peoplehood." The glue that ties these categories together is the concept of an involuntary group. This concept implies that a person is born into a group that shares certain cultural traits and becomes socialized into them (Breton & Pinard, 1960). According to Isajin (1974), the concept of involuntary group includes not only ethnicity but also religious groups, racial groups, and social classes. He offers the concept of ethnic culture as the distinguishing element between these categories, with the understanding that members of an ethnic group are not necessarily members of the same religion, class, or race, but would all share basically the same culture.

How, then, does this discussion bring some clarity to the question of whether American blacks constitute an ethnic group? It might be proposed that, while American blacks can be viewed as a group closely linked through the sharing of a common history and experience—in short, its sense of peoplehood—as a group it experiences ethnicity as an ongoing process with social, psychological, and political ramifications. Isajin (1974, p. 121) describes this process as the "emergence of ethnic rediscovery"—that is, the emergence of people from any consecutive ethnic generation who have been socialized into the culture of the general society but who develop a symbolic relation to the culture of their ancestors. Barth (1969) describes this process in a slightly different manner. He contends that people will be identified by others as belonging to one or another ethnic group even if they no longer actively share the cultural patterns with that ethnic group, as long as a link to their ancestors can be made.

Isajin (1974) offers an interesting definition of ethnicity that moves beyond mere descriptions of concrete ethnic group processes to a possible explanation of those processes by combining both the subjective and the objective approach. He states that ethnicity refers to "an involuntary group of peoples who share the same culture or to descendants of such people who identify themselves and/or are identified by others as belonging to the same involuntary group" (p. 122). Isajin's definition reflects what Green (1982) describes as a transactional view of ethnicity. In this view, ethnicity is not a permanent, concrete feature of one's identity, but fluid and to some extent manipulable. Green goes on to say that, therefore, "the degree to which a person is 'acculturated' is situational rather than absolute and can be modified to suit the needs of different cross-cultural encounters" (p. 13). This understanding of ethnicity has profound implications for the ethnic-sensitive practitioner. The practitioner must recognize that individual clients can be selectively "acculturated" depending on the situation. For example, a black client may selectively choose to speak black English or standard English, depending on the nature and quality of a particular relationship. For the effective practitioner, "individualizing the client would require an accurate perception . . . of how the individual manages the symbols of ethnicity in a variety of cross-cultural as well as same-cultural relationships" (p. 13).

Culture

The preceding discussion of race and ethnicity demonstrates that the concept of culture is intricately linked to both concepts. Further, as one examines the implication of the concept of culture for group dynamics among American blacks, an equal amount of confusion and controversy also exists. The central issue regarding black culture has focused on its existence. The debate has been whether or not there is a unique African-American culture.

The controversy apparently had its origin in Gunnar Myrdal's widely acclaimed study *An American Dilemma* (1944). Myrdal asserted that American blacks are "exaggerated Americans" whose roles are a "pathological" elaboration on general American values (pp. 927–930). However, E. Franklin Frazier (1957) is perhaps most quoted regarding his views that American blacks are "not distinguished by culture from the dominant group." Essentially Frazier believed that black culture in the United States was synonymous with "folk culture of the rural Southern Negro or the traditional forms of behavior and values which have grown out of the Negro's social and mental isolation. Moreover, many of the elements of Negro culture which have grown out of his peculiar experience in America, such as music, have become a part of the general American culture" (pp. 680–681). Despite the emergence of critical scholarship supporting the assertion of a positive black culture (see, e.g., Blauner, 1970), the theme reflected in the works of Myrdal (1944), Frazier (1957), Glazer and Moynihan (1963), and Berger (1967) that American blacks have no culture is still evident today (Staiano, 1980).

The issue of whether there is a distinctive black culture is further compounded by various misconceptions evident in American society about ethnicity and culture. Blauner (1970) sheds additional light on this by presenting a sociological model of ethnic group assimilation. The model essentially encompasses two variables: the traditional culture, and the American value and condition. Blauner (1970) describes the process as a one-way and usually nonreversible movement from immigrant extranational status to ethnic group assimilation. However, this model has little or no relevance to the cultural experience of black Americans in that blacks entered this country not as immigrants but as a group of enslaved strangers with different cultural experiences. Enslavement both mitigated against the social and economic progress that accompanied assimilation of other ethnic groups and did not permit group autonomy (see Chapter 1). More important, the enslavement process vitiated those traditional African attributes (see Park, 1950). Despite the spurious acculturation process rendered by slavery, an ethnic group identity and distinctive culture evolved (Blauner, 1972). The essence of such a culture is a more subtle human orientation to problems of existence as ways of being in the world, as ethos or philosophy of life (Blauner, 1972). Thus, culture must be viewed in the sense of the spiritual life of a people as well as material and behavioral aspects. According to this broad-base perspective, all people have a culture.

When we define culture as the essence and the ethos of a people as well as a way of life, it becomes difficult if not impossible to deny the reality of black culture. Within this context, black culture becomes a synthesis of many elements. It reflects what is shared in common with other Americans. As Blauner (1972) points out, it becomes in some ways like all human cultures in the world, and then in other ways is considerably diversified by differences in regions, social class, age, and sex. It is also uniquely ethnic in some other ways.

The essence of black culture is not that it is unlike other cultures. The essential idea here is that different cultures value their common elements differently, insofar as one puts the accent here, another there, and that it is the ordering and the relations of elements to one another that determines the differences between the cultures. Thus, culture is not a static entity, but ever-changing. The backdrop of this process is the continuous and unifying stream in black life which is a combination of Africa, the American south, slavery, poverty, migration, and racism. It is a stream expressed in music, family life, language, love, religion, and countless other manifestations of a people's orientation to the world that constitutes black culture.

The aforementioned broad-base perspective moves us beyond the common misconception that black culture is primarily an "underclass" phenomenon of black people in America (Blauner, 1972; Chestang, 1976; Valentine, 1968). In this negative, pejorative view, the lifeways of black people are seen not as cultural but as merely a reflection of an "underclass" world view. Moreover, it is important to emphasize that poverty and black culture are not to be viewed interchangeably (Valentine, 1968).

The intent here is not to explicate the content of black culture, but it is important to define what is meant by the concept. Essentially, black culture is being defined here as the totality of all the attributes that make up the way of life of a people at a given period in history. Culture can be formally defined as the system of values and meanings shared by a group or a society, including the embodiment of those values and meanings in material objects (Popenoe, 1980). It refers to the characteristic lifeways of a people—the way they think, feel, and behave (Chestang, 1976, p. 99). Yet culture is viewed also as the more subtle human orientation to the problems of existence, as ways of being in the world, as ethos or philosophy.

The Class Controversy

The "class" concept, like culture, is slippery and difficult to define and has been defined in a variety of ways. Generally, the concept is used to describe the social or economic status of a group (Parsons et al., 1961; Weber, 1947). As a social indicator, class most clearly described those members who were ranked according to social status, prestige, or privilege, based primarily on ancestry, values, and style of life. As an economic indicator, class described members who were stratified or ranked in a hierarchy based on property holdings and other types of economic acquisitions. These two important distinctions highlight two common errors connected to the use of the term "class": (1) the practice of equating "middle-income" with "middle class" and "low-income" with "lower class" and (2) equating "middle class" with occupational position or education. The error in these practices is that income indicates only how much money a person has, whereas social class refers to styles of life, living standards, values, beliefs, behavioral expectations, and communication styles. On careful examination, it becomes evident that the misuse of these concepts blurs the diversity and fluidity that exist within and between different social and economic groupings. For example, while many middle-income people may have "lower-class" values and life-styles, many low-income people may have "middle-class" values and life-styles. A similar analogy applies within the context of equating "middle-class" with occupation. Although occupational position or educational training may enhance one's social status, it does not necessarily relegate one to "middle-class" status. For example, though the common usage is to define white-collar, skilled craft, and operative jobs as "middle-class" jobs, evidence indicates that for many blacks and other minorities these jobs may produce earnings below the poverty level (Hill, 1972; Wilson, 1978).

At this point an important question is: What constitutes the black class structure in this society? Several social researchers have proposed a social class structure of the black community. For example, Hill (1978) and Billingsley (1968), utilizing census, education, occupation, and income data, provided a roughly demarcated social class structure, but they both point out the numerous difficulties connected with paradigms that attempt to describe social stratification in the black community. Both Hill and Billingsley stress that in describing behavioral dynamics in the black community, the class concept is not useful. They emphasize that the indicators of social class are different from those used in the white community, but the definition of social status is equally complex. An example of this complexity in terms of class is reflected in the fact that upper-class blacks comprise families of judges, businessmen, and physicians who would be middle class on the basis of criteria used by whites. Further, a black lawyer, judge, or physician may be rated higher in prestige than a black teacher, nurse, or high school principal in the abstract, but when it comes to community involvement and deference given to them by persons who have a lower social status, this functional social status becomes blurred (Solomon, 1976).

Wilson (1980) offers another point of view on this slippery concept. He defines "class" in economic terms, as a concept that includes "any group of people who have more or less similar goods, services or skills to offer for income in a given economic order and who therefore receive similar financial remuneration in the marketplace" (p. ix). Although he believes that the crystallization of a black class structure is fairly recent (Wilson, 1980, p. x), he utilizes E. Franklin Frazier's classification system to demarcate class structures, contending that on the basis of occupational distribution at the middle of the twentieth century, approximately one-third of the black population could have been classified as either working class or middle class. Wilson includes within this category blacks with white-collar jobs and craftsmen and foremen positions. Since the 1960s and the civil rights movement, the economic status of educated blacks with marketable skills has improved significantly. On the downside, however, statistical evidence and observation reflect a worsening condition for inner-city low-income black families that have few resources and lack education and skills. As Wilson indicates, the black community is increasingly becoming divided into two groups: a relatively prosperous middle class and a poverty-stricken underclass.

Thus, to operationalize a class structure within the black community, very broad lines are required. Anyone concerned with understanding black family life must be concerned with both social and economic stratification. Helping professionals who come in contact with black families would find it more effective to assess social status individually within the context of helping relationships, instead of fitting the family to current usage of the social class definition. Billingsley (1968, p. 45) notes that social class is "completely inadequate and inappropriate for describing behavior, or values, or preferences, or styles of life, or child rearing patterns in the Negro community." It is further believed that the class concept for blacks at this time is best defined in economic terms: income distribution, education, and occupation (Hill, 1978). More recently, Hill (1987) illustrates this point through the classification used by the Tax Reform Act of 1986. To ensure that the able, "average" taxpayer benefited from the reform, Congress classified all taxpayers with income between $20,000 and $50,000 as "middle class." Based on the classification schema offered by Congress, Hill (1987) described households with incomes of $50,000 and over as "upper class," those with incomes between 20,000 and 49,999 "middle class," and those with incomes between $10,000 and $19,999 as "working class," and those with incomes under $10,000 as "poor." Hill goes on to explain that, based on 1984 Census Bureau data, 5 percent of black households are "upper class," 29 percent are "middle-class," 25 percent are "working class," and 40 percent are "poor."

It is important to acknowledge the heterogeneous grouping within each of the four broad categories of income. The Smith family, which is a large extended family, best illustrates this point:

> Mr. and Mrs. Smith were the parents of ten children (five boys and five girls). They were both born and raised in the rural south. Mr. Smith worked for many years as a construction worker in the south before emigrating to the north in search of a better job to support his family. With little more than an elementary education, he worked until retirement in the steel mills of Ohio and Pennsylvania. However, Mrs. Smith was able to attend school sporadically. She eventually dropped out in the fourth year of high school. She was primarily a homemaker, but did some domestic work to supplement the family's income during extreme financial hardship. All of the children graduated from high school, and the six younger children

completed college and graduate school. Among the high school graduates is a postal employee, a bus driver, a disabled veteran, a janitor, and an auto mechanic. Of the six college graduates, one is a lawyer, two are business executives, one a college professor, one a high school principal, and another owns a catering business.

This family not only reflects a diversity of values and life-styles based on education, occupation, and income, but also illustrates the complexity of ascribed and achieved social status within black families. For example, the black community would attribute middle-class status to the Smith family based on prestige that comes with their visibility and standing in the community. The children, especially those with graduate degrees and prestigious occupations, would be considered "upper class," a status achieved through occupation and education.

Gender Role and Gender Identity

Gender role and gender identity are more recent concepts, but because the available literature on these concepts is written from a white, middle-class perspective, the emphasis is not on issues related to the sex-role development of blacks. However, a discussion of such concepts as race, ethnicity, culture, and social class must acknowledge the interrelationship of gender.

In distinguishing between the complex concepts of gender role and gender identity, Condry (1984) describes gender as a primary defining trait that cuts across the physical, cultural, and behavioral levels of development and is in many ways a central feature of identity. Generally, gender role refers to the public manifestations of gender identity. Within this context, a series of behavioral characteristics have been considered appropriate for members of one sex and inappropriate for members of the other sex. For example, women are considered to be emotional, unaggressive, unreliable, and person-oriented, while men are viewed as aggressive, adventurous, relatively unemotional leaders, and more interested in mechanical things than in people. The great extent to which society has internalized such behaviors as uniquely masculine or uniquely feminine has been demonstrated clearly by Boverman and colleagues (1972).

On the other hand, gender identity refers to an individual's personal awareness of himself or herself as either male or female (Money & Ehrhardt, 1972). Lamb and Urberg (1978) point out that because of the private nature of gender identity, measurement is extremely difficult. The process must be indirect, and projective techniques are frequently used. The examiners' interpretation of the subjects' responses raise serious questions about whether the examiner is measuring what he or she thinks is being measured. The point here is that it is extremely difficult, if not impossible, to assess gender identity accurately.

For black families, sex-role socialization is generally approached with the awareness that black children must learn to survive and grow not only in their interaction with mainstream America but also within black communities. Research and anecdotal evidence suggest that black parents communicate both general values and specific role responsibilities to their children. This dual socialization perspective provides the necessary prerequisite for coping with the range of stresses that inevitably face black families as a result of oppression and discrimination. For example, a substantial number of black husbands have indicated that they are capable of effectively carrying out tasks traditionally associated with women—cooking, washing, ironing, sewing, caring for babies, washing diapers, keeping house, and shopping, and so on (Billingsley, 1968; Logan, 1987; Scanzoni, 1971).

Although available evidence suggests a reciprocal task-sharing in black families, the evidence does not fully support the notion that this dual perspective screens out stereotypes and sexist notions about women that are directly related to sex-role socialization in our society. For example, Bell Hooks (1981, pp. 98–99) points out: "While the 60s black power movement was a reaction against racism, it was also a movement that allowed black men to overtly announce their support of patriarchy." Hooks goes on to say, "The strongest bonding element [during this time] between militant black men and white men was their shared sexism—they both believed in the inherent inferiority of women and supported male dominance" (p. 99). Although Hooks is referring to the militant black man, she also believes that some black men have historically been sexist but that today their sexist behavior has taken the form of misogyny (undisguised woman-hating). Hooks attributes this development to the social and cultural changes in attitude toward female sexuality in the larger society.

It is dangerous to generalize Hooks' observations to *all* black men. The practitioner and the educator must keep in mind that it is impossible to speak of "all black men," just as it is impossible to speak of "the black family." Many black men, like men of other ethnic groups, are becoming more sensitized to women's issues (Moore-Campbell, 1986). Moore-Campbell (1986, p. 208) contends, "As women must learn the skills of achieving power in the larger world, men must explore femininity within themselves and use it to improve their lives." Herb Goldberg (1983) points out that men and women have a responsibility to minimize the sexism in each other by working to change behavior that encourages the other person's sexism. Ultimately it is the partners who must create a climate of open communication and encouragement of self-growth.

With the recognition that few men or women have grown up in homes where sexual equality was the norm, it is important that practitioners and educators, regardless of ethnicity, be mindful both of the impact of gender in general on black family dynamics and of the interrelationships between gender and class.

THE INTERRELATIONSHIPS
BETWEEN THE CONCEPTS

An appreciation of the interrelationships between race, ethnicity, culture, social class, and gender as they pertain to black Americans can best be addressed from the perspective of intergroup relations. Within American society there are two major types of groups: dominant and subdominant. According to Willie (1983), dominant groups in different societies and during various periods in history have assumed a threefold role: (1) they control social organizations; (2) they oppress people by their control of social organizations; and (3) they seldom, if ever, voluntarily share their power and authority with those over whom they exercise control. Willie further argues that subdominant groups constitute the oppressed in a society. Historically, blacks have exclusively occupied a subdominant category in this society. As a result of skin pigmentation, culture, and socioeconomic status, blacks have been denied equal access to those valuable resources within the broader society.

The suppression of blacks by the dominant group occurred through a variety of ingenuous schemes of racial and sexual discrimination, exploitation, and segregation. In the past, these schemes were more blatantly reinforced by elaborate ideologies of racism, but in recent times racist and sexist acts have been more subtle. Most blacks who have benefited from desegregated opportunities have experienced a new type of prejudice that was not present under conditions of segregation.

The living conditions and personal life experiences of blacks illustrate the interrelationships between race, ethnicity, culture, social class, and gender:

1.   Regardless of socioeconomic status, they were prohibited from moving to higher-status neighborhoods, as was the norm for other ethnic groups in the total population (Gordon, 1971; Glazer & Moynihan, 1963). The observations of Taeuber and Taeuber (1969) that "the net effect of economic factors [in] explaining residential segregation [for blacks as compared with other groups] is slight" and that "improving the economic status of Negroes is unlikely by itself to alter prevailing patterns of racial residential segregation" (pp. 94–95) still apply today.

2.   Black and brown professional and managerial individuals received a median annual income that was 15 percentage points less than that for whites, and educated blacks often have to obtain doctoral degrees to get jobs that are similar to those that some whites obtained with only an undergraduate college education or a master's degree (Willie, 1980).

3.   Blacks have been and still are severely disadvantaged by the education system at all levels in this country (National Education Association, 1987; Willie, 1987; Lee, 1985; Staples, 1986; Willie & McCord, 1972). Racial discrimination is a serious hindrance to quality education for black children (*Barriers to Excellence*, 1985), and at colleges and universities blacks are shockingly underrepresented from administration to the faculty down to the lowliest freshman. The reasons cited for this declining trend include such factors as inadequate or nonexistent support for recruitment and retention of blacks in university settings. Charges of discrimination and feelings of a lack of acceptance are often voiced by students and faculty (Farrell, 1988).

4.   Because of their gender and race, black women are doubly oppressed,

but if they fall into the poverty category they are triply oppressed by race, sex, and class (*Fact Sheets*, 1986). The oppression of black women is most noticeable in the work force. Historically, black women have been in the work force in proportionally greater numbers than any other group of American women. Yet black women are relegated to the bottom of the pay scale in pink-collar positions, such as clerical workers and waitresses, or in household service positions. Further, for every dollar a white man earns, on average, a black man earns 70 cents, a white woman earns 59 cents, and a black woman earns 55 cents (Carter, 1983; Lewis, 1977).

The above examples are not intended to be inclusive of the range of life experiences that reflect the interrelationships between the concepts under discussion. They simply give the reader a general flavor of the impact these concepts have on the quality of black life.

COMMON STRENGTHS AND LIFE PROBLEMS

Thus, the concepts of race, ethnicity, culture, social class, and gender have a direct impact on the ecological realities (social, psychological, physical, and spiritual) of black Americans. These interrelated concepts have an impact on the life-styles of blacks ranging from the most subtle forces to the obvious. Some of the more obvious examples of these forces are reflected in the educational system, the job market, and the physical and social characteristics of the communities where black Americans live.

In American society, blacks have always viewed education as the vehicle most likely to ensure economic security and upward mobility (Comer, 1987; Hill, 1972), but educational systems not only have failed blacks in the past but also continue to do so (Robinson, 1987). Robinson paints a disconcerting picture of the plight of black students in the educational system: "The full and complex range of crucial issues involving black students, parents, and institutions [issues that are addressed fully in Chapter 7] cannot be overstated" (Robinson, 1987, p. 31). Despite what appears to be a hopeless situation, there is a potential storehouse of opportunities to be found. For example, although black parents are shunted aside by the educational systems, they still care deeply about the educational issues affecting their children and simply need to be tapped as a viable source for change (Hill, 1972; Robinson, 1987).

Employment discrimination against blacks continues across age and the socioeconomic spectrum (see Chapter 11). "Despite modest improvements in economic conditions of black Americans during 1985 and 1986, the Reagan recovery has had such weak impact on blacks that their current labor market conditions are still more depressed than they were at the bottom of all previous postwar recessions" (Swinton, 1987, p. 49). In short, during the Reagan administration black family income declined, poverty rates increased, and the labor market difficulties intensified. According to the geographic profile of employment and unemployment for 1981–1983, the economic status of blacks also differs regionally. For example, in 1985 the midwest region reported the highest unemployment rates (over 30.0 percent in the past five years, but averaging 23.7 percent) as compared with the south (15.6 percent), the west (15.8 percent), and the north (15.1 percent).

But what accounts for the lack of black economic progress? Is it a result of failure in motivation, competence, or behavior (see Swinton 1987)? Consistent with the discussion in Chapter 1, the answer to these questions lies in an understanding of the historical treatment of blacks in American society as well as the nature and functioning of the U.S. economy.

Several factors have contributed to current economic difficulties: (1) few businesses are black owned, managed, or controlled; (2) blacks have limited opportunities for accumulation of wealth; (3) blacks have been traditionally discriminated against in gaining equal access to nonblack owned, managed, and controlled job situations; (4) blacks have traditionally had lower levels of formal education and training; and (5) there is a lack of available jobs. These factors reflect some very serious and recalcitrant problems for the economic survival of black families. However, researchers analyzing labor market and economic trends believe that a strong national economic policy combined with concentrated black self-help and a renewed commitment from the federal government to support affirmative action will solve the economic difficulties of the black community.

Black families live in diverse neighborhoods ranging from the stately, affluent, and immaculate to varying stages of decay and deterioration. Black communities reflect a variety of life-styles that create different life experiences for the inhabitants based on their ability to gain access to and utilize resources. In other words, level of education and income influences the degree of stress experienced by community residents with respect to the community's economy, political power structure, social agencies, and educational system (Carmichael & Hamilton, 1967; Clark, 1965). In general black neighborhoods may be grouped into two types of spatial configurations: urban and suburban. The urban areas are made up of what Rose (1971) referred to as ghetto cores and fringes, in which blacks constitute a clear majority. Examples of such areas can be found in New York, Chicago, Newark, and Miami. It is important to note that the word "ghetto" evokes images of what is commonly referred to as "urban blight," but the word is often not interchangeable with "slum" and has been criticized as being insulting to black people and to cities (Murray, 1970). The suburban areas may or may not include blacks in the majority. Rose (1971, p. 7) delicately describes black occupation of such areas as sufficient to "hasten the future outmovement of the white population."

Despite the numerous environmental problems and a lack of community cohesiveness experienced by the residents of black communities, there are inherent strengths on two broad levels: (1) the tendency to adopt children informally and to incorporate nonkin into the family household (Billingsley, 1968; Hill, 1972), and (2) a pervasive assumption that people are doing the best they can. More generally, there are strong spiritual/religious, work, and high achievement orientations (Hill, 1972). In short, the community residents care about each other and will lend a helping hand, as is manifested by the number of black clubs, fraternal and other self-help organizations, and political groups ("The Black Middle Class," 1987). It is generally the less affluent residents, those who are candidates for or currently recipients of some form of social service, who are caught in the powerless web of urban life—a life in which businesses, programs, and policies are supervised and determined by people who do not live in these communities.

PRACTICE IMPLICATIONS

Ethnicity and class are important variables in service delivery and should not serve as barriers to effective client-worker relationships. This principle of practice is consistent with the thrust of the helping professions over the past two decades toward making clinical services more relevant to the needs of blacks and other ethnic-minority groups. Increased knowledge and sensitivity about the interrelationships between the concepts of race, culture, ethnicity, class, and gender will enhance and broaden educators' and practitioners' frames of reference and help them reformulate their assessment and treatment of the black client. This reformulation should include both the practitioners' willingness to work on their own personal issues related to these concepts, and an ability to differentiate between psychopathological conditions and culture-specific phenomena (see Mayo, 1974).

For example, a black male client from the inner city is referred to the nearest mental health center across town, whose staff is 95 percent white. He sits staring at the floor with a deadpan expression and chooses to "volunteer nothing" because he simply does not see how talking about his problems with a young white female could help. He answers some questions with grunts or monosyllabic colloquial expressions in a distinct regional accent. It is important that a worker in this situation respond by identifying what elements of the client's behavior may be attributed to living in a hostile environment, to a coping style, and what might be characterological. Instead, however, the young female worker in our example summarized the contact with the following impressionistic statement: "This client is hostile, angry, depressed, and possibly in need of hospitalization. His colloquialisms are something with which I am unfamiliar—for example, he uses the expression 'That's cheer,' apparently meaning 'that's good.' His lack of literacy is disturbing." Factors contributing to lack of communication between worker and client in this example are extremely complex. Not only is the worker's lack of knowledge and experience in working with clients who have a different background a factor, but there is also a pervasive attitude about certain groups of clients within this service-delivery system. Generally, staff view those clients as unresponsive to psychotherapeutic interventions, and they are simply written off as nonserviceable. The above example in no way negates the difficulty that a black female worker might also have with this client. In fact, the client may see the black worker as equally ineffective because of gender differences as well as privilege acquired through her social class status based on her educational and social background. The black worker may also be viewed as young and having lived an existence that is commonly referred to as ahistorical (see Williams et al., 1985) and could find it extremely difficult to establish rapport with this client.

CONCLUSIONS

Given the complexity involved in conceptualizing and understanding the black experience in America, it is imperative that helping professionals increase their knowledge and sensitivity about the various concepts that attempt to describe as well as organize the black experience. In the context of making decisions about family dynamics and treatment strategies, it is important to emphasize that such decisions are based not only upon the practitioner's understanding of the interrelationships between the concepts of race, ethnicity, culture, social class, and gender, but also on the practitioner's frame of reference. Optimal recognition, understanding, and application of the concepts in this chapter will enhance the practitioner's overall effectiveness and provide an arena in which the client would be able to feel understood, thereby connecting to the treatment process in a growth-producing way.

REFERENCES

Barriers to excellence: Our children at risk. (1985). Boston, MA: Coalition of Advocates for Students.

Barth, F. (1969). Introduction. In F. Barth (Ed.), *Ethnic groups and boundaries* (pp. 9–38). Boston: Little, Brown.

Berger, B.M. (1967). Soul searching: Review of *Urban Blues,* by Charles Keil. *Transactions, 4*(7), 54–57.

Billingsley, A. (1968). *Black families in white America.* Englewood Cliffs, NJ: Prentice-Hall.

The Black Middle Class, where it lives. (1987). *Ebony, 42*(10), 34–40.

Blauner, R. (1970). Black culture: Myth or Reality? In N.E. Whitten, Jr., & J.F. Szwed (Eds.), *Afro-American anthropology: Contemporary perspectives* (pp. 347–366). New York: Free Press.

Blauner, R. (1972). *Racial oppression in America.* New York: Harper & Row.

Boverman, I.K., Vogel, S.R., Boverman, D.M., Clarkson, F.E., & Rosencrantz, P. (1972). Sex-role stereotypes: A current appraisal. *Journal of Social Issues, 28*(2), 59.

Brace, C.L. (1964). A nonracial approach toward the understanding of human diversity. In A. Montague (Ed.), *The concept of race* (pp. 103–152). New York: Free Press.

Breton, R., & Pinard, M. (1960). Group formation among immigrants: Criteria and processes. *Canadian Journal of Economics and Political Science, 26,* 465–477.

Bureau of Labor Statistics. (1981–85). Geographic Profile of Employment and Unemployment, Table 1.

Carmichael, S., & Hamilton, C. (1967). *Black power.* New York: Vintage.

Carter, C. (1983, March). What the ERA means to us. *Essence,* 154.

Chestang, L. (1976). The black family and black culture: A study in coping. In M. Sotomayer (Ed.), *Cross-cultural perspectives in social work practice and education.* Houston, TX: University of Houston Graduate School of Social Work.

Clark, K. (1965). *Dark ghetto.* New York: Harper and Row.

Comer, J. (1987). Education is the way out and up. *Ebony, 42*(10), 51–65.

Condry, J.C. (1984). Gender identity and social competence. *Sex roles, 11*(5/6), 485–511.

Fact Sheets on Institutional Sexism. (1986). New York: Council on Interracial Books for Children.

Farrell, C.S. (1988). Black students seen facing "new racism" on many campuses. *Chronicle of Higher Education, 34*(20), A1.

Frazier, E.F. (1957). *The Negro in the United States* (rev. ed.). New York: Macmillan.

Garbeck, J.P. (1961). Review of *Human races and readings on race,* by Sim Gorn. *Annals of Human Genetics, 25,* 169–170.

Glazer, N., & Moynihan, D.P. (1963). *Beyond the melting pot.* Cambridge, MA: M.I.T. Press.

Gordon, M.M. (1971). Assimilation in America: Theory and reality. In N.R. Yetman & C.H. Steele (Eds.), *Majority and minority report* (pp. 261–283). Boston: Allyn and Bacon.

Goldberg, H. (1983). *The new male: From macho to sensitive but still all male.* New York: Morrow.

Greely, A.M. (1971). *Why can't they be like us?* New York: Institute of Human Relations Press.

Green, J.W. (1982). *Cultural awareness in the human services.* Englewood Cliffs, NJ: Prentice-Hall.

Greer, C. (1974). Remembering class: An interpretation. In C. Greer (Ed.), *Divided society: The ethnic experience in America* (p. 35). New York: Basic Books.

Hill, R.B. (1972). *Strengths of black families.* New York: Emerson Hall.

Hill, R.B. (1978). *The illusion of black progress.* Washington, DC: National Urban League, Research Department.

Hill, R.B. (1987). The black middle class defined. *Ebony, 42* (10), 30–32.

Hooks, B. (1982). *Ain't I a woman: Black women and feminism.* Boston, MA: South End Press.

Isajin, W.W. (1974). Definitions of ethnicity. *Ethnicity, 1,* 111–124.

Lamb, M.E., & Urberg, K.A. (1978). The development of gender role and gender identity. In M.E. Lamb (Ed.), *Social and personality development* (pp. 178–199). New York: Holt, Rinehart, and Winston.

Lee, V. (1985). *Access to higher education: The experience of blacks, hispanics, and low socio-economic status whites.* Washington, DC: Division of Policy Analysis and Research.

Lewis, D.K. (1977). A response to inequality: Black women, racism, and sexism. *Journal of Women in Culture and Society, 3*(2), 339–361.

Logan, S.L. (1987). The nurturing black father: Myth or reality? Unpublished manuscript, University of Kansas, School of Social Welfare.

McAdoo, H.P. (1987). Blacks. In *Encyclopedia of social work*—(18th ed.). Vol. 1 (pp. 194–206). Silver Spring, MD: National Association of Social Workers.

Mayo, J. (1974). The significance of socio-cultural variables in the psychiatric treatment of black outpatients. *Comprehensive Psychiatry, 15*(6), 471–482.

Money, J.W., & Ehrhardt, A.A. (1972). *Man and woman, boy and girl.* Baltimore, MD: Johns Hopkins University Press.

Montague, A. (Ed.). (1964). *The concept of race.* New York: Free Press.

Moore-Campbell, B. (1986). *Successful women, angry men: Backlash in the two-career marriage.* New York: Random House.

Moynihan, D.P. (1965). *The Negro family: The case for national action.* Washington, DC: Government Printing Office.

Murray, A. (1970). *The omni-Americans.* New York: Outerbridge and Dienstfrex.

Myrdal, G. (1944). *An American dilemma.* New York: Harper. Republished New York: McGraw-Hill, 1964.

National Education Association. (1987). *Black concerns study committee report.* Washington, DC: National Education Association.

Park, R. (1950). *Race and culture.* New York: Free Press.

Parsons, T. (1955). Family structure and the socialization of the child. In T. Parsons & R.F. Bales (Eds.), *Family socialization and interaction process.* New York: Free Press.

Parsons, T., Smith, A., Marx, K., Goblet, E., Simmel, G., Pareto, V., Veblen, T., & Sorokin, P. (1961). Stratification and mobility. In T. Parsons, E. Shils, K.D. Nalgele, & J.R. Pitts (Eds.), *Theories of society* (pp. 517–576). Glencoe, IL: Free Press.

Pettigrew, T.F. (1979). The changing but not declining significance of race. *Michigan Law Review, 77,* 917–924.

Popenoe, D. (1980). *Sociology.* Englewood Cliffs, NJ: Prentice-Hall.

Robinson, S.P. (1987). Taking charge: An approach to making the educational problems of blacks comprehensible and manageable. In J. Dewart (Ed.), *State of black America, 1987* (pp. 31–36). New York: National Urban League.

Rose, H. (1971). *The black ghetto: A spatial behavioral perspective.* New York: McGraw-Hill.

Scanzoni, J. (1971). *The black family in modern society.* Boston: Allyn and Bacon.

Sills, D.L. (Ed.). (1968). *International encyclopedia of the social sciences,* vol. 5 (pp. 167–172). New York: Free Press.

Social Work Dictionary. (1987). Silver Spring, MD: National Association of Social Workers.

Solomon, B.B. (1976). *Black empowerment: Social work in oppressed communities.* New York: Columbia University Press.

Staiano, K.V. (1980). Ethnicity as process. *Ethnicity, 7,* 27–33.

Staples, B. (1986, April 27). The dwindling black presence on campus. *New York Times Magazine, 46,* 50–54, 62.

Sumner, W.G. (1906). *Folkways.* Boston: Ginn.

Swinton, D. (1987). Economic status of blacks 1986. In J. Dewart (Ed.), *State of black America, 1987* (pp. 31–36). New York: National Urban League.

Taeuber, K.E., & Taeuber, A.F. (1969). *Negroes in cities.* New York: Atheneum.

Valentine, C.A. (1968). *Culture and poverty.* Chicago: University of Chicago Press.

Weber, M. (1947). *The theory of social and economic organization* (A.R. Henderson & T. Parsons, Trans.) (rev. ed.). New York: Free Press.

Weber, M. (1968). *Economy and society: An outline of interpretive sociology.* New York: Bedminster.

Willie, C.V. (1978). The inclining significance of race. *Society,* 10–15.

Willie, C.V. (1980). *Leadership development for minorities: An evaluation of a Rockefeller Foundation program.* New York: Rockefeller Foundation.

Willie, C.V. (1983). *Race, ethnicity, and socioeconomic status: A theoretical analysis of their interrelationship.* Bayside, NY: General Hall.

Willie, C.V. (1987). The future of school desegregation. In J. Dewart (Ed.), *State of black America, 1987* (pp. 37–48). New York: National Urban League.

Willie, C.V., & McCord, A.S. (1972). *Black students at white colleges.* New York: Praeger.

Williams, D.A., Jackson, T., Weathers, D., Joseph, N., & Anderson, M. (1985). Roots III: Souls on ice: A post-civil-rights generation struggles for identity. *Newsweek,* 82–84.

Wilson, W.J. (1980). *The declining significance of race: Blacks and changing American institutions.* Chicago: University of Chicago Press.

Wilson, W.J. (1978). The declining significance of race revisited but not revised. *Society,* 11–21.

CHAPTER 3

Theoretical Perspectives for Practice with Black Families

Edith M. Freeman
University of Kansas

Many authors have discussed whether generic approaches or culture-specific approaches are more useful for social work practice with black clients. Some assumptions and documentation have been presented in support of both sides, but many findings conflict and provide little empirical evidence to support one position clearly to the exclusion of the other (Bell & Evans, 1981; Jones, 1983). Equally important have been the following questions: What does a culture-specific approach consist of, if such an approach is necessary for work with black clients, and what barriers might there be to generalizing this type of approach to clients from other minority groups and to majority group clients as well (Jones, 1983; Chestang, 1979)?

In part, answers to these questions rest on the profession's ability to define and differentiate clearly between such concepts as practice theories, approaches, models, and techniques in terms of the general client population (Devore & Schlesinger, 1987). There has also been a failure to clearly operationalize and distinguish between each of a number of interventive approaches being used in social work practice, such as the task-centered approach, the life model, psychoanalytic psychotherapy, the problem-solving model, client-centered therapy, transactional analysis, reality therapy, Rational Emotive Therapy (RET), Gestalt therapy, and behavioral approaches (Corsini, 1979; Perlman, 1967). In addition, continuing concerns about whether evaluation should be an integral part of social work practice and about the quality of evaluation procedures and methodology being applied when evaluation is attempted also limit the profession's ability to answer questions about the efficacy of culture-specific approaches (Fischer, 1973; Rubin, 1984; Wood, 1978).

But the need to seek out effective interventive approaches for work with black clients is clear. Economic and other large-scale social changes have recently had a negative impact on the functioning of families from all racial groups, but in particular on black and other minority families (Hartman & Laird, 1983; Keefe, 1984). There is also evidence that black families are underrepresented in referrals for social services and overrepresented in dropout rates once services have been initiated (Jones, 1983; Willie et al., 1973). Furthermore, both individual and institutional barriers to those services exist—for example, practitioner biases, small numbers of available black professionals, economic discrimination through fee-scheduling procedures, other factors that contribute to inaccessible services, a focus on irrelevant issues, and the use of inappropriate interventive techniques (Moore, 1981; Pinderhughes, 1979; Shannon, 1970; Willie et al., 1973). This indicates that whatever the contributing circumstances may be, a gap in obtaining adequate and relevant social services exists for black families.

This chapter provides a review of the traditional approaches and the problems involved and discusses various recommendations for selecting or designing approaches. An integrated set of approaches for work with black families is then proposed, followed by a discussion of the generalizability of those approaches, ways to evaluate them, and the effects of certain limitations on their use.

REVIEW OF APPROACHES USED
WITH BLACK FAMILIES

Compton and Gallaway (1984) made a useful distinction between descriptive and prescriptive theories. Descriptive theories are bodies of knowledge and related assumptions about human behavior. They explain such behavioral phenomena as how individuals grow and develop; the dynamics and causes involved in problem-formation; and the structure and function of complex social systems, organizations, and communities. General systems theory is an example of a dynamic descriptive theory.

Prescriptive theories are used to prescribe how problems should be resolved or needs should be met and are said to operate in concert with underlying descriptive theories, but at a much more practical level. They are evaluated in terms of their usefulness—that is, their ability to implicitly or explicitly provide practice principles to guide actual interventions. They are also frequently evaluated according to how closely they fit with the value base of social work or can be described as social work approaches compared with approaches developed within other disciplines (Turner, 1979).

A prescriptive theory may be derived from several compatible descriptive theories rather than from only one theory. The task-centered approach, the life model, Gestalt therapy, and Rational Emotive Therapy are examples of approaches based on two or more descriptive theories. For example, the task-centered approach draws upon problem-solving, developmental, and social learning theories, while RET draws upon social learning and cognitive theories. Further, the task-centered approach and the life model are recognized as social work approaches, whereas Gestalt therapy and RET are examples of psychological approaches used by mental health professionals in many disciplines, including social work (Turner, 1979; Steiner & Devore, 1983).

This discussion of prescriptive and descriptive theories provides a useful foundation for reviewing approaches that have been used with black families. The generalizability of these approaches to the unique and common needs of black families is often determined by how rigidly underlying descriptive theories for a particular approach define normative and deviant behavior (Devore & Schlesinger, 1987). Conversely, their usefulness for black families is often determined by the availability of practice principles that build on, rather than discount, the unique strengths and cultural dynamics in black families.

Traditional approaches that have been used with black families are presented here in three major categories: (1) approaches with underlying theories that utilize psychologically based explanations of human behavior, (2) approaches involving explanations based on inequities in social structures, and (3) approaches involving explanations based on interrelated social and psychological factors.

Psychologically Based Explanations

Approaches involving psychologically based explanations include psychoanalytic psychotherapy, client-centered therapy, and rational emotive therapy (Devore & Schlesinger, 1987). There is little empirical evidence that such approaches are useful specifically with black families (Turner, 1979; Lavis et al., 1978).

Willie et al. (1973) noted two additional ways in which these approaches may be inadequate for work with black families. Their theoretical explanations about problem development support a pathological, individual-deficit perspective. Problems are viewed as developing primarily from each individual's unique conceptualization of reality. But these theories fail to take into account that behavior labeled abnormal, deviant, and irrational by the majority culture may within the black culture be considered normative, or at least tolerable, and they largely ignore the effects of various societal factors, such as institutional racism. Thus, using these theories can tend to reinforce negative stereotypes about blacks (see Willie et al., 1973).

Devore and Schlesinger (1987) note that these approaches, which emphasize the past as a major determinant of behavior in the present as well as the importance of unconscious phenomena, are inconsistent with the pressing "here and now" survival needs of many of these clients. Finally, Maluccio (1974) noted that these "talking therapies" are inappropriate for nonverbal or action-oriented clients because of the emphasis on insight.

Explanations Involving Inequities in Social Structures

Underlying theories for approaches based on social structure inequities assume that problems of disadvantaged individuals and groups develop through resource disparity, inadequate social provision, racial discrimination, and barriers in organizational arrangements. A focus on resolving such problems at the individual level is viewed as counterproductive. Organizational, race and culture, and community development theories are examples of descriptive theories in this category. Some approaches that build on these descriptive theories include social activism, social planning, and structural approaches (Harper & Dunham, 1959; Younghusband, 1964). In terms of their structural approach, Middleman and Goldberg (1974) have noted: "Many of those served by social work—minority groups, the aged, the poor—are neither the cause of, nor the appropriate locus for change efforts aimed at lessening the problems which they confront" (p. 55). Such macro-level approaches therefore typically target large-scale changes at community, organizational, and social system levels. Advocacy, education, lobbying, program planning and evaluation, policy development and implementation, and resource acquisition are major skills used within these approaches.

In the process of focusing interventions on the inadequacies of social systems, however, some individual factors, such as how the individual responds to adverse conditions and how some responses are culturally determined, are often overlooked, making it less likely that those factors will be changed even though the large-scale social changes occur. Empirical research indicates that minority group individuals have made significant gains in some social provision programs, such as Headstart and Operation Push, but that those gains sometimes disappear. Institutional barriers, such as negative stereotyping by educators and discriminatory hiring practices that were ignored or inadequately affected by change efforts, eroded the gains (Mason et al., 1985; Sherradan, 1985). For example, the educational and social gains some black children make in Headstart programs are lost by the time they reach the second and third grade in regular elementary school, because of labeling and inappropriate recommendations for special education placements based on biased labels (see Chapter 7).

Devore and Schlesinger (1987) indicated that such approaches view race and ethnicity largely as problematic and tend to ignore black families' sources of strength and coping emphasized through research by Hill (1972) and others (Jones, 1983). They encourage workers to ignore opportunities to facilitate mutual aid and self-support activities that could increase self-esteem and reinforce a positive racial identity with black families. In addition, these approaches may encourage unwarranted generalizations across different racial or ethnic groups because they do not provide the necessary practical suggestions about how such principles can be operationalized in work with *black* families and fail to indicate how workers can adapt these approaches to respond to *varied* cultural contexts and racially based needs (Devore & Schlesinger, 1987).

Explanations Involving Interrelated Social and Psychological Factors

Approaches based on the interplay between social and psychological forces in an individual's development are most likely to be consistent with the social work perspective and the needs of black families. These approaches take into consideration the interface between the person and his or her environment, and other factors.

Approaches within this category include the psychosocial model, the task-centered approach, the problem-solving model, and such systems approaches as the life model and family systems models. The psychosocial and task-centered approaches are less successful than systems approaches because in problem identification and in developing goals for change the focus is more on the individual than on the environment. The psychosocial approach tends to focus more on the role of individual pathology in social adjustment problems than on the role of larger systems. The task-centered approach and the problem-solving model use more of a dual focus on person-in-environment. Barriers to task implementation and to the problem-solving process, both individual and environmental, can be targeted for changes. An additional benefit for black families in terms of the task-centered approach can be its time-limited, structured process and its emphasis on the importance of the client's selection of concerns for work and the tasks necessary for handling those concerns. These important aspects, along with the dual focus of *both* approaches, make them consistent with the social work frame of reference (Perlman, 1967; Reid, 1978).

The task-centered approach emphasizes the need to be aware of the values and self-perceptions that develop from ethnic and social class membership (Devore & Schlesinger, 1987), but it does not identify any of the specific coping strategies that various cultural and racial groups have developed. Further, some of its potential benefits (e.g., its focus on time limits) may run counter to the perspectives on time held by some racial groups.

The life model and other systems approaches have provided the most effectively conceptualized integration of psychological and social factors by focusing on the interface between individuals and systems and between various systems. The underlying theories for these approaches postulate that a dynamic interdependence exists between resources, people, and varying informal and formal systems (Germain & Gitterman, 1980; Hartman & Laird, 1983; McGoldrick, 1982). Five main problems have been identified as occurring on the basis of this interdependence: (1) the absence of needed resources, (2) the absence of linkages between people and resource systems or between resource systems, (3) problematic interactions between people within the same resource system, (4) problematic interactions between resource systems, and (5) problematic individual internal problem-solving and coping resources (Devore & Schlesinger, 1987).

Intervention procedures and social work roles are focused on each of these areas. For example, resource development, linking people with existing resources, and advocacy are used when resources are a priority. These approaches, however, fail to operationalize related practice principles to clarify how those activities can be accomplished with black families and individuals. For example:

> The life model does *recognize* the impact of social class, ethnic group membership, life style, and culture to a greater degree than many other models, . . . but although significant issues in the black experience are highlighted . . . in cases, the relevance of such information is not presented (Devore, 1983, p. 530; emphasis added).

Thus, recognition of social and cultural factors by the life model related to black families does not go far enough. Further, research on the life model and other family systems approaches with black families have been limited primarily to case studies. Case studies illustrating family therapy approaches are characterized by clear descriptions of some of the poor and minority group clients involved, the interventions being used, and the outcomes. In most of these descriptions, however, because the dynamic ongoing intervention *process* between the workers and the families involved is not clear, conclusions cannot be drawn about unique aspects of the worker's role or how those interventions should be adapted for effective use with black families (Guerin, 1976; Gurman & Kniskern, 1981). This is particularly true with the life model, on which almost no research has been done.

The approaches reviewed above have a number of indicators of their inappropriateness for black families, which help clarify the limitations of these approaches for effective work with black families:

1. Labeling, stereotyping, and stigmatizing conditions and behavior within black families as deviant, based on norms determined by white middle-class standards
2. Ignoring unique strengths and the related cultural context associated with individual and group differences that have an impact on problems and their resolution within black families
3. Setting prerequisites for intervention and criteria for success based on white middle-class standards that exclude many black families (e.g., that clients must be financially stable, verbal, motivated, and insightful)
4. Ignoring environmental conditions, such as discrimination and institutional racism, which help create and maintain problems in black families
5. Failing to provide clear practice principles for changing those adverse conditions and for building on the unique coping patterns and strengths of black families, even when those adverse conditions and the strengths are acknowledged
6. Targeting areas of change identified by the worker that are based on an individual-deficit perspective, rather than targeting concerns identified by the client system that consider important environmental constraints
7. Overemphasizing a cultural-deficit perspective and focusing on family structure, function, and roles in black families as negative conditions, without generating research that examines the effectiveness and adaptability of various practice approaches with black families and the roles to be assumed by worker and client system (Devore & Schlesinger, 1987; Shannon, 1970; Willie et al., 1973)

A PROPOSED APPROACH

A combination of some existing practice approaches has the greatest potential for effectiveness. This combination of approaches includes family systems models, behavioral models, and task-centered models.

The Conceptual Base or Focus

This expanded and integrated approach to practice incorporates family systems, behavioral, and task-centered concepts. The approach should be adapted to particular circumstances of the individual family that have been identified through assessment. The underlying descriptive theories for this integrated approach include systems, communication, social influence, role, problem-solving, developmental, cognitive, and social learning theories. For the most part, these theories and the related approaches are focused on the individual-in-environment perspective, a particularly critical requirement for practice with black families, for whom the impact of cultural and other environmental factors have often been ignored.

Devore and Schlesinger (1987) and others (Chestang, 1979) have proposed a number of recommendations for an ethnic-sensitive model of social work practice. Such a model, according to these authors, should include a focus on group history, individual history, and group identity; biculturalism as a requirement for blacks; the importance of current problems at the micro- and macro-levels; and ethnic reality as a source of strength and strain. Attention to the effects of group history requires consideration of the unique history of black oppression and the various strategies, such as provision of group support, that black families have developed to cushion members from the effects of that oppression; the effects of slavery on how black families perceive and organize their lives and on how they are perceived by others; and institutional barriers to the transmission of culture, religion, and language that give meaning to the daily existence of many blacks (see Table 3.1).

Individual history and group identity serve to filter and determine which aspects of black history and identity remain an integral part of each individual's functioning (Devore & Schlesinger, 1987). Thus, group history can affect identity formation in individuals differently, according to personality and other factors. Systems theory and family systems approaches examine and draw inferences about individual history and the impact of family structure and functions through the use of the *genogram*. This tool and similar procedures can be adapted for practice with black families to examine the impact of the important aspects of group history and identity. (See Chapter 4 for more on the use of the genogram.) This approach can also be helpful in exploring familial and other large system dynamics that interact in filtering the effects of group history and identity on the family, and their effects on current problems. Communication and role theories, when suitably expanded, can include a focus on the unique function of verbal and nonverbal language among blacks in the bicultural context in which cultural and societal expectations are different and on the flexibility and expandability of roles in black families as an adaptive strength in an historically hostile environment (Chestang, 1979).

Devore and Schlesinger's (1987) emphasis on the importance of current problems at the micro- and macro-levels requires that an ethnic-sensitive approach relate the incidence and distribution of problems among blacks to ethnic reality. Maluccio (1974) noted that such an approach must focus on the current problems or concerns of clients instead of on the worker's concerns. The fami-

TABLE 3.1. AN EFFECTIVE APPROACH TO WORK WITH BLACK FAMILIES

Considers	As Manifested By:
The effects of group history or the unique history of black oppression in this country	• Various coping strategies among black families, such as group support • The organization and forms of black family life, such as fluidity of roles and extended family closeness • Institutional barriers to black cultural maintenance (e.g., an education system that does not acknowledge, value, or teach black history)
Individual history and group identity	• Influences on particular aspects of black history and identity that are maintained by individuals and families, such as black language, ceremonies and customs, and roles • Responses to conflictual cultural and societal expectations that may be positive (e.g., role-sharing) or negative (e.g., alcohol use for stress reduction)
Biculturalism as a requirement for blacks	• Differential use of resources from the nurturing environment (the black community) and the task environment (larger society) • Positive defining and heritage reminding, which are examples of resources provided by the unique role of significant others in the black community in contrast to that role in other racial or ethnic groups
The importance of current problems at micro- and macro-levels	• Current individual and familial problems that are the consequences of societal racism and discrimination (and that may be evident from a family's past) • Barriers to problem-solving and positive mental health within societal structures: past and present (e.g., mislabels and stereotypes about blacks in the mental health system or inequitable employment policies and opportunities for blacks)
Ethnic reality as a source of strength and strain	• Values about important aspects of black family life, language, religion, etc., resulting in, for example, group cohesion or racial stress • Dynamic balance in cultural maintenance (biculturalism) versus assimilation

ly's past is examined to determine the individual consequences of societal racism and discrimination, which may have both positive and negative outcomes.

Social learning, cognitive, and systems theories, when expanded to include an understanding of large systems, can in an integrated fashion help to address the critical relationships between past history and current problems and between micro- and macro-issues. The task-centered approach insures a central focus on the here-and-now concerns of black families (not on the worker's concerns) and on individual and environmental barriers to task completion. Further, its emphasis on direct client involvement addresses the preferences of many black families for action-oriented and practical strategies (Bell & Evans, 1981; Reid, 1977). Adapting the approach to fit with a black family's idiosyncratic pacing in terms of time limits and to consider cultural and institutional barriers to task completion should make the approach even more effective with black families.

Chestang's (1979) concept of biculturalism as a requirement for blacks is another important aspect of an ethnic-sensitive approach. Chestang supports Norton's definition of this concept, which involves a dual perspective:

> The conscious and systematic process of perceiving, understanding, and comparing simultaneously the values, attitudes, and behavior of the larger societal system with those of the client's immediate family and community system. It is the conscious awareness of the cognitive and attitudinal levels of similarities and differences in the two systems (Norton, 1978, p. 3).

Chestang (1979) indicates that workers must have knowledge of black clients' nurturing environment and its cultural context. This emphasis on an ecological and holistic view of clients is inherent in systems approaches and can facilitate ethnic-sensitive practice when bicultural aspects of the black existence are understood. The ecomap, the time line, the life history grid, and other graphic illustrations can help to provide this holistic view of a black family's circumstances and of any conflicts from biculturalism that can be affecting current problems (Dettoyos et al., 1986). Social influence theory, along with role theory, helps direct the focus to areas of an ecomap that could easily be ignored if workers are not aware of their existence and significance in the daily lives of blacks. Wilhelmina Manns (1981) emphasizes a similar focus on significant others as role models and introduces related concepts about symbolic interactionism to explain aspects of the socialization process in black families—for example, socialization in black families in terms of symbolic validation of self. The process can occur through positive defining in which significant others articulate a positive definition of the individual, such as "she is very bright." Another aspect of symbolic validation is heritage-reminding, which involves a significant other reminding the individual of his or her racial background through role modeling or the teaching of black history (Manns, 1981). Along with this emphasis on the ecology of black family life, task-centered and behavioral approaches encourage an examination of past problem-solving related to the current problems—that is, they focus on how blacks use their social supports to achieve social status and stability despite negative environmental constraints.

Finally, consideration of ethnic reality as a source of strength and strain is also an important part of ethnic-sensitive practice. Social influence and role theories help to identify significant client roles within both the cultural community and the larger society, and what kind of impact values about family life, education, religion, language, rituals and celebrations, physical attributes, and emotional functioning have on those roles and current problems. Family systems and behavioral approaches help to determine how changes in any of these areas can result in concomitant changes in some of the other areas. Devore and Schlesinger (1987) note that some of these values can provide cohesion, group identity, and strength, while others can cause role strain, role conflict, and strife.

Practice Principles

The integrated approach described above can help to generate a set of relevant practice principles. The principles begin with knowledge and attitudinal issues and shift to include specific skill aspects that are important for the worker to integrate into practice with black families. Based on the proposed approach, the theoretical underpinnings for each principle below are also indicated, with an emphasis on social work theories. Social workers should:

1. Attempt to identify and understand the world view of black families as being distinct from that of larger society, since the latter view distorts the behavioral patterns being observed and labels them diagnostically as deviant instead of viewing them as natural responses to institutional racism. *(Cognitive and social learning theories)*
2. Assume the existence of strengths identified by Hill (1972) and Jones (1983) for black families and explore with the client how those strengths can be used to handle current client concerns. Such strengths might include strong kinship bonds; a work orientation; a religious-spiritual orientation; the adaptability or fluidity of family roles; an achievement orientation; and a high tolerance for environmental stress, ambiguity, and ambivalence. *(Role, cognitive, problem-solving, social influence, and developmental theories)*
3. Enhance engagement and the helping process by risking a one-down position in which the worker asks sensitive, nonjudgmental questions that clarify the client's view and culturally determined perceptions about reality. *(Cognitive and communication theories)*
4. Explore the client systems ideas about the dual perspective (black culture and larger society) related to its biculturalism and its perceptions about the demands and supports involved. *(Cognitive, social learning, and developmental theories)*
5. Acknowledge obvious differences between worker and client and explore how the worker and client view those differences and whether they can block or facilitate understanding between them. *(Communication, role, and problem-solving theories)*
6. Identify less obvious similarities between worker and client and how

worker and clients view those similarities and their potential effects on the work. *(Communication and role theories)*

7. Ask specific questions to determine whom the client system includes in its decision-making unit among family members and nonblood relationships, since within black families these tend to be defined differently from those of workers from other racial backgrounds. *(Family systems and behavioral theories)*

8. Reframe assumptions about the predominance of matriarchal forms within two-parent families to the concept of shared decision-making and view it as a strength rather than a deficit for black families. *(Family systems approach and social influence theory)*

9. Distinguish between role strain in black families and fluidity of family roles based on individual cultural history, availability of role supports, and the client's assessment of the benefits versus the deficits involved in the roles assumed. *(Social influence and role theories)*

10. Explore the rich source of influence from significant others within black families, based on black group identity, to determine their ability to influence the family toward change and to provide role models and other forms of support. *(Social influence and symbolic interaction theories)*

11. Use specificity of focus with black families to achieve clarity between worker and client and to direct attention to concrete problems. For many black families, past negative experiences with the larger society have made them naturally suspicious of the vague and general as expressions of indifference or a lack of knowledge about what they see as real problems. *(Task-centered approach and problem-solving model)*

12. Emphasize social intervenor activities that (according to Chestang, 1979) involve a set of roles that are important within the cultural context of the dual perspective. These roles include provision of emotional support and guidance, interaction based on respect for the client, teaching specific steps and tasks in problem-solving, mentoring, modeling, and acting as an advocate/broker by aggressively helping to remove environmental barriers and translating caring into actions about concrete problems (Devore & Schlesinger, 1987; Draper, 1979; Hartman, 1979; Hill, 1972; Jones, 1983). *(Task-centered, systems, and behavioral approaches)*

Evaluation

In following the practice principles listed in the previous section, several opportunities for evaluation can be optimized. Overall, evaluation of the recommended approach with black families is facilitated by the task-centered emphasis on formulating concrete culturally relevant goals and the development of an explicit contract (Reid, 1977). The review of tasks (completed between sessions) at the beginning of each session provides opportunities for ongoing and immediate feedback from the client system and actively involves the clients in the evaluation process. Changes in problem definition, the goals, the intervention plan, and most important in the worker's understanding of the families' cultural context should occur as this feedback is processed.

Process evaluation is also enhanced through the use of such procedures as the ecomap, which, based on the systems approach, provides feedback on the family's external functioning. All areas of the environment external to the family can be examined and monitored for changes that may be a result of mutually agreed upon interventions between worker and clients or of activities by significant others in the environment. Included in evaluation of the external environment via the ecomap are the family's relationships with extended family members, neighbors, and other significant individuals and with various social systems and formal organizations (Germain & Gitterman, 1980). Family members and the worker can compare ecomaps of the family's life space prior to, during, and after intervention to evaluate changes resulting from the use of this practice approach.

Internal functioning within the family—a focus on collective as well as individual needs—can be evaluated in a similar manner. The genogram is a useful tool for before, during, and after intervention comparisons in terms of the family's cultural awareness, assessment of role complementarity and role strain, balance in role assignments, success in handling developmental tasks, methods for handling the presenting problem, and understanding how to prevent future stresses (Hartman & Laird, 1983). In addition, simple questionnaires and scales, such as those developed by Hudson (1982), can be used as additional pre- and postmeasurements of change as long as they are interpreted *with* the family in terms of its cultural context.

Limitations of the Approach

Many of the limitations noted in the introduction to this chapter are relevant to the practice approach offered here. First, the conceptualization of this approach is only a beginning step; a clearer description of its major skill and interactional aspects and the interrelationships between them is needed; attempts in this direction have been made (see Freeman, 1987; Freeman & McRoy, 1986; Freeman et al., 1987). This approach and other recommended approaches will be operationalized more fully in Part Three of this book.

Second, effective use of the proposed approach depends greatly on each worker's continued awareness and skill in expanding it to include a culturally relevant focus. As specific methods for achieving such a focus become more clear, additional practice principles can be developed to help workers maintain the focus on the family's cultural context and to identify the specific kinds of concerns for which the approach is more appropriate.

Finally, although the task-centered and behavioral approaches have been researched under varied conditions, family systems and social influence approaches have not. As the major interventive activities involved in this integrated approach are clarified, it will be possible to conduct future research on its effectiveness with black families.

GENERALIZABILITY OF THE APPROACH

A culturally relevant approach for blacks is one that includes the skills and awareness of the client's perspective important in all social work but that extends those skills to assist with culturally relevant needs (Chestang, 1979). Such an approach may be generalizable to members of other minority groups and to majority group individuals, but only if the conditions under which a culturally relevant approach is effective are clearly understood. It is not sufficient to demonstrate that a particular approach is effective; the conditions of its effectiveness (e.g., the type of problems, the clients, how the approach is used, and the circumstances) must be clearly understood if it is to be used again successfully with others (Wood, 1978; Blythe, 1985). Thus, the generalizability of the recommended approach depends on the manner in which the limitations discussed in the previous section are addressed by the profession.

CONCLUSIONS

Some theories and practice approaches with black families involve inherent biases toward blacks. Others fail to provide practice principles for resolving those stresses, even though they are potentially more useful in work with black families because they recognize the effects of environmental stresses. But few of these approaches illustrate how to build on the strengths of black families. The proposed approach attempts to address the deficits identified in this chapter—for example, it encourages the worker to have the client system identify its decision-making unit and the role models that are useful for helping to cope with stresses, rather than having the worker do so on the basis of societal expectations or his or her own experiences. Additional work is needed to clarify more of the interventions used in this approach, to examine the effects of those interventions with black families under empirical conditions, and to clarify the circumstances for which the approach is most appropriate.

REFERENCES

Bell, P., & Evans, J. (1981). Counseling the black client. *Professional Education, 5*. Minneapolis, MN: Hazelton Foundation.

Blythe, B.J., & Briar, S. (1985, November–December). Developing empirically based models of practice. *Social Work, 30*, 483–488.

Chestang, L. (1979). Competencies and knowledge in clinical social work: A dual perspective. In P.L. Ewalt (Ed.), *Toward a definition of clinical social work* (pp. 1–12). Washington, DC: National Association of Social Workers.

Compton, B., & Galloway, B. (1984). *Social work processes* (3rd ed.). Homewood, IL: Dorsey.

Corsini, R. (1979). *Current psychotherapies*. Itasca, IL: Peacock.

Dettoyos, G., Dettoyos, A., & Anderson, C.B. (1986, January–February). Sociocultural dislocation: Beyond the dual perspective. *Social Work, 31,* 61–67.

Devore, W. (1983, November). Ethnicity reality: The life model and work with black families. *Social Casework, 64,* 525–531.

Devore, W., & Schlesinger, E.G. (1987). *Ethnic-sensitive social work practice* (2nd ed.). Columbus, OH: Merrill.

Draper, B.J. (1979). Black language as an adaptive response to a hostile environment. In C.B. Germain (Ed.), *Social work practice: People and environments* (pp. 267–281). New York: Columbia University Press.

Fischer, J. (1973, January). Is casework effective? A review. *Social Work, 18,* 5–20.

Freeman E.M. (1987). Interaction of pregnancy, loss, and developmental issues in adolescents. *Social Casework, 68*(1), 38–46.

Freeman, E.M., & McRoy, R.G. (1986, January). Group counseling program for unemployed black teenagers. *Social Work with Groups, 9,* 25–34.

Freeman, E.M., Logan, S., & McRoy, R.G. (1987). Clinical practice with employed women. *Social Casework, 68*(7), 413–420.

Germain, C., & Gitterman, A. (1980). *The life model of social work practice.* New York: Columbia University Press.

Guerin, P.J. (Ed.). (1976). Family therapy: Theory and practice. New York: Gardner.

Gurman, A.S., & Kniskern, D.P. (1981). Family therapy outcome research: Knowns and unknowns. In A.S. Gurman & D.P. Knisker (Eds.), *Handbook of family therapy.* New York: Brunner/Mazel.

Hartman, A. (1979). Competencies in clinical social work. In P.L. Ewalt (Ed.), *Toward a definition of clinical social work* (pp. 33–41). Washington, DC: National Association of Social Workers.

Hartman, A., & Laird, J. (1983). The family today. In *Family-centered social work practice* (pp. 23–40). New York: Free Press.

Harper, E.B., & Dunham, A. (Eds.). (1959). *Community organization in action.* New York: Association Press.

Hill, R. (1972). *The strengths of black families.* New York: Emerson Hall.

Hudson, W. (1982). *The clinical measurement package: A field manual.* Homewood, IL: Dorsey.

Jones, D.L. (1983). African-American clients: Clinical practice issues. In F.J. Turner (Ed.), *Differential diagnosis and treatment in social work* (pp. 565–578). New York: Free Press.

Keefe, T. (1984, May–June). The stresses of unemployment. *Social Work, 29,* 264–269.

Lavis, M.H., Lynch, M.L., & Munger, P.T. (1978). The influence of ethnicity on necessary and sufficient conditions of client-centered counseling. *Journal of Non-White Concerns in Personnel and Guidance, 5,* 134–142.

Maluccio, A.M. (1974, January). Action as a tool in casework practice. *Social Casework, 55,* 30–35.

Manns, W. (1981). Support systems of significant others on black families. In H.P. McAdoo (Ed.), *Black families* (pp. 238–251). Beverly Hills, CA: Sage.

Mason, J., Wodarski, J.S., & Parham, T.M. (1985, May–June). Work and welfare: A re-evaluation of AFDC. *Social Work, 30,* 197–203.

McGoldrick, M. (1982). *Ethnicity and family therapy.* New York: Guilford Press.

Middleman, R., & Goldberg, G. (1974). *Social service delivery: A structural approach to practice.* New York: Columbia University Press.

Moore, E.K. (1981). Policies affecting the status of black children and families. In H.P. McAdoo (Ed.), *Black families* (pp. 278–290). Beverly Hills, CA: Sage.

Norton, D. (1978). *The dual perspective.* New York: Council on Social Work Education.

Perlman, H.H. (1967). *Social casework: Problem-solving process.* Chicago: University of Chicago Press.

Pinderhughes, C. (1973). Racism and psychotherapy. In C.V. Willie, B. Kramer, & B. Brown (Eds.), *Racism and mental health.* Pittsburgh, PA: University of Pittsburgh.

Pinderhughes, E. (1979). Teaching empathy in cross cultural social work. *Social Work, 24,* 312–316.

Reid, W.J. (1977). *A study of the characteristics and effectiveness of task centered methods.* Chicago: School of Social Service Administration.

Reid, W.J. (1978). *The task centered system.* New York: Columbia University Press.

Rubin, A. (1984, November–December). Practice effectiveness: More grounds for optimism. *Social Work, 30,* 469–476.

Shannon, B. (1970, May). Implications of white racism for social work practice. *Social Casework, 51,* 270–276.

Sherraden, M.W. (1985, September–October). Chronic unemployment: A social work perspective. *Social Work, 30,* 403–408.

Steiner, J.R., & Devore, W. (1983, Spring). Increasing descriptive and prescriptive theoretical skills to promote ethnic-sensitive practice. *Journal of Education for Social Work, 19,* 63–70.

Turner, F.J. (Ed.). (1979). *Social work treatment: Interlocking approaches.* New York: Free Press.

Willie, C.V., Kramer, B., & Brown, B. (Eds.). (1973). *Racism and mental health.* Pittsburgh, PA: University of Pittsburgh.

Wood, K. (1978, November). Casework effectiveness: A new look at research effectiveness. *Social Work, 23,* 437–458.

Younghusband, E. (1964). *Social work and social change.* London: Rinehart.

PART 2

Assessment of Black Families

Part Two establishes the necessary parameters for exploring the concerns of black families within an expanded ecological context. It integrates (1) the existing theoretical information about families in the social work assessment process and (2) the unique features and available knowledge necessary for assessing black family structures and function. Moreover, the chapters in Part Two emphasize the central theme of the book: how to build on the strengths of black families. Implications are drawn for how strengths and problems of black families should be assessed, and what kind of impact specific cultural issues have on the assessment process, treatment planning, and subsequent evaluations of treatment.

The chapters in this section describe how to assess the life cycle of the black family, the structure and functioning of black families, and the family and its cultural and racial identity. Chapter 4 describes the family life cycle in general within a cultural context and its social work implications. In Chapter 5, types of black family structures and processes, and a nonbiased and culturally appropriate framework for analyzing basic family functioning, are described. Chapter 6 addresses the influences of culture on individual and group identity development within the context of family dynamics. The focus includes racial identity problems and their manifestations within work, school, and familial situations. In all three chapters, social work implications are included.

CHAPTER 4

The Black Family's Life Cycle:
Operationalizing a Strengths Perspective

Edith M. Freeman
University of Kansas

In order to work effectively with black families, factors related to the black family's life cycle must be addressed. A family's life cycle provides the developmental conditions, and for black families the cultural context, in which significant life events unfold. Exploration of this context is consistent with the dual focus of social work (Gordon, 1979) and with the ecological perspective (Germain, 1979; Meyer, 1983; Hartman & Laird, 1983). This point of view can be useful when assessing the needs of black families because it can insure that related interventions are culturally specific and therefore more likely to be successful. But effective work in this area begins with an acknowledgment that there are both differences and similarities in the life cycle of black families and that of other minority and majority families. In some situations, those cross-cultural differences may be only a matter of degree, while significant within-group differences often exist across black families. Awareness of the many variations *and* similarities can help to sensitize workers to the unique and common circumstances involved in the black family's life cycle experiences.

SIMILARITIES IN FAMILY LIFE CYCLE STAGES

The family life cycle stages, which are discussed in detail in the literature, include the unattached young adult, the formation of the dyadic relationship, the family with young children, the family with adolescents, the family launching children, the family with older members, and the family in later life (Carter & McGoldrick, 1980; Rhodes, 1979; Goldenberg & Goldenberg, 1984). The tasks for each stage are similar for all cultural and racial groups. For instance, the tasks assumed to be critical to the formation of the dyadic relationship or the beginning family include (Carter & McGoldrick, 1980; Rhodes, 1979):

1. Developing competence in decision-making
2. Working out mutually satisfying and realistic rules for obtaining and spending the family income
3. Achieving a satisfactory way to deal with intimacy, including the sexual relationship
4. Developing a readiness for parenthood, if parenthood is desired
5. Deciding how to relate to relatives and friends as a married couple
6. Developing ways of expressing and accommodating differences in a flexible manner
7. Working out a cooperative and satisfactory plan for living as a pair and accomplishing household routines

A second similarity among families of all racial groups is that family life stages can overlap. This often occurs when a couple moves into two stages simultaneously; they may be forming the dyad and having their first child at the same time or over a very brief period. These two family life cycle stages have very different tasks that can conflict with one another (Goldenberg & Goldenberg, 1984)—for example, for the mother or father, bonding with and caring for an infant may be more threatening to a couple's beginning relationship if they have not had sufficient opportunity to address the tasks described above, including how they will handle the issues of intimacy. In contrast, "a couple who have achieved intimacy are in a position to make the necessary adaptations to a new family member who is both helpless and demanding" (Rhodes, 1979).

Third, in most racial groups there can be an inadequate needs/resource balance within the ecology of family life so that some life cycle needs are not met. A family with an adolescent requires the focus and problem-solving skills necessary for addressing the developmental needs of the youth and of the family in that stage. If the couple is older than the "typical" family with an adolescent (if they are in their sixties, for example), their focus may be on the regrouping stage of the family's life cycle or on themselves as a family with older members (Rhodes, 1979). That inattention to the adolescent's needs may inadvertently encourage rebellion that precipitates a premature launching stage.

Finally, families are similar across racial groups in that external conditions can have an impact on their ability to respond productively to a particular stage of the life cycle. The stage of the unattached young adult may be disrupted by adverse economic conditions, such as a recession, which can force some young adults to return to the family of origin for survival reasons. Similarly, external conditions can have an impact on later stages of the family's life cycle. The stage of the family in later life may involve an older couple being separated, with one living in a nursing home and the other living either alone or with adult children. The decision to separate may result not from the couple's wishes but from a policy of the retirement home where the able-bodied spouse lives or from family members' disagreements about what is best for the couple. Separation during this stage of the life cycle—from retirement to death—can block the couple's ability to provide mutual aid to one another and to ward off feelings of uselessness (Rhodes, 1979).

THE BLACK FAMILY'S LIFE CYCLE

Despite the above similarities, some factors related to the life cycle are unique to black families. Many represent functional adaptations that developed in response to adverse external conditions, which include a history of oppression, institutional racism, and the close relationship between economic deprivation among black families and economic affluence for a large percentage of the nation. Adaptations arising in response to those conditions have been reframed as strengths of black families (see Hill, 1972; McAdoo, 1981a; Martin & Martin, 1985). Three of those adaptations help to illustrate some of the unique characteristics of the black family's life cycle: fluidity of roles, the value placed on education, and the dual perspective (Hill, 1972; Chestang, 1979).

Fluidity of Roles

Sudarkasa (1981) notes that a couple who married in Africa became part of a co-resident extended family that included adult siblings of the same sex and their families. This extended family lived in a single compound. The oldest male in the sibling group was usually the head, with all men in his generation considered to be the elders of the group. However, women, as mothers and sisters of the elders, could influence decision-making, particularly about property issues, thus enjoying more equality than women in Western nations (Oppong, 1974). Socialization of the young involved the entire extended family, not only the separate conjugal families. Children were taught to identify themselves collectively as the sons and daughters of a particular lineage and compound (Sudarkasa, 1981).

Such kinship relationships provided a stability of family life after a marital bond was broken by divorce, and resulted in a fluidity of roles. Even during slavery, which attempted to destroy kinship ties, slaves adapted by broadening the kinship group to include nonblood relationships. As a consequence, the characteristic of fluid roles was adapted to the external barriers imposed by the system of slavery (Aschenbrenner & Carr, 1980; Blassingame, 1979).

This pattern of including pseudo-family members and other relatives in family roles continues among many black families even today. For instance, in some black families, relatives other than parents participate in childrearing. Family life cycle stages in those circumstances must be assessed with this pattern of role fluidity taken into consideration, emphasizing role fluidity as a strength rather than as a pathological response (Hill, 1972). In one instance, a 32-year-old client sought counseling to handle the grief she was still experiencing three years after her grandmother had died. During the assessment process she reminisced about their relationship:

I was raised by my grandmother. Oh, I knew she wasn't really my mother—my
real mother lived in New York and I would visit her every few years. But it was
my grandmother who was there when I needed her. Years later, I thought about
what it must have been like for her—starting over again with a young child at her
age. But, I don't think she ever saw it as a sacrifice. She said it needed doing and
she did it. For a while, I thought I shouldn't leave home, that I should stay there
and take care of her . . . like she had taken care of me.

This situation illustrates the impact of role fluidity on this family's life
cycle stages. First, the grandmother and grandfather had reached the stage of a
family with older members or, as Rhodes (1979) labels this stage, "regrouping
versus binding or expulsion." The decision to raise their granddaughter meant
that, in addition to addressing the tasks of that stage, they were required to
reexperience the family life cycle stages that precede the regrouping stage. What
makes this situation unique to black families, as distinguished from the example
of the older couple in the previous section, are the cultural supports that can
exist based on a history of fluidity and flexibility in role assumptions (Willie,
1981). That cultural history provides sanction for such role assumptions when
they occur and reduces the need for out-of-home placements beyond the resources of the kinship group.

Second, the impact of the grandmother's role assumption on the client's
sense of obligation and on her ability to be launched successfully from the
family must be recognized during assessment. While the client acknowledged
her ambivalence about leaving her family of origin, she also acknowledged
receiving clear messages from her grandmother that raising her granddaughter
was not a sacrifice and that the latter should get on with her life. It is from
within this cultural context, during assessment, that the worker must develop an
understanding of the client's current pain. The worker must also be cautious in
interpreting how these cultural factors can effect a family's life cycle issues,
since such generalizations may not always apply to similar circumstances with
other black families.

Fluidity of roles may be an important factor related to other stages of the
black family's life cycle. More women entered the labor force during the past
ten years than during any previous decade, but among many black women this
pattern of working outside the home is a long-standing one attributable to economic reasons and patterns of discrimination (Freeman et al., 1987). The stage
of the family with young children, or what Rhodes (1979) calls "replenishment
versus turning inward," requires roles that help to develop nurturing patterns
among family members. Black families have adapted to this stage of the family's life cycle by a process of role sharing. Children in the family, as well as
extended family members and nonrelatives, share in providing emotional nurturance and carrying out instrumental tasks. Such patterns tend to broaden each
child's role network and teach him or her responsibility for others in the
"group"—those within the same cultural context. In assessment, however, distinctions must be made between these normative cultural expectations within
black families, and dysfunctional circumstances involving child neglect or paren-

tified children. In the latter circumstances, the absence of adequate nurturing and role reversal may require an assessment that focuses on the adequacy of the parenting available.

The Value Placed on Education

A second area of normative expectations involves the value the black family places on education and its impact on life cycle stages. Such a value has always been linked to the unique economic circumstances of black families in this country in their "struggle to survive under tragic conditions of economic inequality" (Davis, 1981, p. 127), which is likely to continue (Sherradan, 1985). Some black families have acquired the education, skills, and achievements that allow them to be economically secure (McAdoo, 1981b), but many others have not. Blacks are in a double bind: significant barriers remain even when blacks become educated, but blacks recognize that education is the *only* road to getting ahead (Manns, 1981).

These external conditions may have a profound effect throughout the black family's life cycle. During the launching stage, one developmental task for families is to provide career-planning opportunities for youth. Freeman and McRoy (1986) found that functional independence at this stage is inevitably linked with opportunities to obtain financial independence. For many black youth the high rates of unemployment in that population group may make it seem more realistic to drop out of high school and/or enroll in a vocational program to move more readily toward both financial *and* functional independence. The families of these youths may value education highly, but they often hold out little hope for making that value operational because of external barriers.

In other black families, education becomes the ultimate goal despite barriers. This goal is often chosen in recognition of future racial inequities: (1) the income of the average black college graduate is comparable to that of the average white high school graduate (U. S. Bureau of the Census, 1986), and (2) black youth can obtain a college education only by prolonging the launching stage and postponing movement toward other stages, such as those of the unattached young adult and the formation of dyadic relationships.

Individuals who view themselves as having "missed opportunities" to get ahead in their youth experience a further impact on family life cycle stages. They may feel hopeless about their circumstances and anticipate a lifetime of failure. Once they become parents, they may seem to have unreasonable expectations and educational aspirations for their children. For example:

> A white high school coach decided to visit the home of his star basketball player to talk with the mother about college. After the team's undefeated season, the coach was pleased that Reggie had been offered full-tuition scholarships to several top-rated colleges. The problem, as he saw it, was Reggie's mother, Ms. Jacks. She was not so sure Reggie should take *any* of the offers for athletic scholarships. Reggie was the oldest of six children, his mother was a single parent on AFDC,

and some of the younger children had not done as well in school as Reggie had. Ms. Jacks admitted that her family was supportive of Reggie's going to college and eventually "getting ahead." In fact, her lifelong dream had been that he would not make her mistake of dropping out of school at age 15—that he would go to college. But the point, she said, is for him to get an education, not play basketball.

In this example, the mother's disappointment in not doing well educationally herself has narrowed her vision about other avenues, such as athletics, that are open to her son for acquiring an education. But her tenacity in holding out for what she considers to be the best for her son educationally is viewed by the coach as an inability to appreciate her son's athletic abilities. This type of family situation would not typically be referred to a social service agency for assessment and services. Instead, black families with normative concerns such as these might do their own informal assessment or utilize their natural support network for that purpose.

In the family circumstances described above, for example, Ms. Jacks first attempted to explore the major issues with Reggie. When they reached an impasse in trying to sort out the priorities, the family had a choice of utilizing Ms. Jacks' older brother or the family minister. Ms. Jacks' brother was a resource because of his membership in a black social organization, of which several professional athletes in town were also members. In addition, in exploring barriers to resolving the situation, he was able to point out that Ms. Jacks might be overinvolved in the decision-making for Reggie because she had not been able to achieve *her* own dream of going to college. Similarly, his analysis of the situation indicated that Reggie was the oldest child and the first to leave home. He wondered whether Ms. Jacks had mixed feelings about this major change in the family's life cycle circumstances.

The brother provided further assistance by recognizing how important it was for Reggie to actively assess his own needs and choices—since he was choosing not only a college but also a future career and life-style. More important, Ms. Jacks' brother was able to recognize her fears that in accepting an athletic scholarship Reggie might be exploited. The brother was able to convey Ms. Jacks' natural concerns to the high school coach in order to encourage him to stop pressuring the family. Then the brother was able to help the family assess the record of each college that had offered Reggie a scholarship in ensuring that its athletes' right to an adequate education was not secondary to playing basketball for the school.

The impact a high value on education has on the black family's life cycle stages can be also demonstrated by focusing on the stage of the family that has older members. During this stage, black families often address issues of generativity (Erikson, 1979) by supporting the educational aspirations of children in their kinship groups and in the general community. Providing supports for the educational attainments of other children is viewed by black families as a responsibility for "the group" and as a natural part of this stage of the life cycle. Manns (1981) found that among blacks who had achieved social status and a college education a larger number of relative and nonrelative significant others had influenced their success than in the situations of white achievers.

Professional helpers, on the other hand, may label such mentoring as detrimental to the family at later stages since the resources of elderly blacks are often very limited.

The Dual Perspective

Black parents may also experience conflicts in terms of their cultural adjust-ment and self-image. They are required to adapt to and function well in a larger society that often views their racial and cultural background in a derogatory manner. They must also attempt to retain a positive racial identity and meet expectations of their racial group that may be in conflict with expectations of the society. Meeting both sets of expectations functionally while also providing for cultural maintenance requires the adoption of a "dual perspective" (Chestang, 1979). The alternative of meeting only the expectations of the larger society can result in alienation from one's racial group and in marginality (Norton, 1978), but if only the expectations of the racial group are attended to, cultural immersion and a limited ability to funciton well in the larger society can be the result.

Logan and colleagues (1987) conceptualized a cultural identity continuum ranging from cultural immersion to biculturalism for individuals with mixed racial backgrounds. Such a continuum, when modified as in Figure 4.1, is also appropriate for viewing how concerns about cultural maintenance can have an impact on the black family's life cycle stages. In the launching stage, for instance, it is not uncommon for adolescents from any racial background to

X---X---X

Complete assimilation within the dominant society.	Biculturalism or adoption of a dual perspective	Cultural immersion within the black culture
BENEFITS: Greater acceptance by and blending in with larger society when assimilation is successful. Increased access to various resources in larger society and a decrease in conflicting demands from society and the black culture.	Increased ability to function effectively in the dominant society *and* in the black culture, access to resources in both environments, and provision of cultural maintenance and a positive racial identity.	Increased group support, opportunities for cultural maintenance, and likelihood of positive racial identity formation. Decreased experiences with racial discrimination and rejection.
LIMITATIONS: Loss of the black culture, traditions, and group support. Increased risk of marginality and rejection by larger society. Increased likelihood of a negative racial identity formation and a denial of self.	Emotional stress associated with adapting to two often conflicting sets of expectations from larger society and the black culture.	Limited access to resources available in larger society, and loss of opportunities to learn about the positive effects of cultural diversity.

Figure 4.1. The Cultural Continuum

question and reject family values. Rhodes (1979) noted that "the surfacing of separation themes arouses intense feelings for all family members . . . as precursors of later developments involving major alteration in parent-child relationships" (p. 36). There is also a shift in the parenting role from arbitrary authority to the negotiation of differences through mutual accommodation. This type of shift, ironically, provides the opportunity for youth to challenge the parents' world view, including their perspective about cultural maintenance.

In assessing the needs of black families that are experiencing such conflicts with their adolescents, it is important to explore the extent to which cultural adjustment issues should be addressed. In one family,

> The sixteen-year-old daughter disagreed with many of the family's values. They argued about her curfew, her friends, how she spent her money from a part-time job, and how she used her leisure time. Jan described the parents' interests as "bourgeois," while she was really just a regular black. Further exploration indicated that the parents had adopted a dual perspective: They had professional jobs and middle-class values and yet maintained their ties with relatives and other aspects of the black community. Jan, on the other hand, wanted to get back to her roots by finding out more about her family's origins, while her parents wondered if this was just another way for her to question their "blackness."

In such situations the "typical" stress of a family with an adolescent must be understood within this cultural context. The family's differing views on cultural maintenance are complicated by the daughter's developmental imperative to challenge and reject family values. The family's upward mobility from a working-class status to that of the middle class—and what that implies to the daughter—is an additional complicating factor that must be assessed *with* the family.

This family was referred to a mental health center by a friend and was assigned to a white social worker who had only limited experience in working with black families. Consequently, he decided to use a black worker as a cultural consultant to improve his assessment of the family's circumstances. The consultant pointed out that the family seemed to be experiencing a normative life cycle crisis and that the parents and their daughter had described their relationship as very close prior to the last nine months to a year. The consultant was able to help the worker plan how to explore this issue further with the family and to use education to improve their understanding of the natural stresses involved in their current life cycle stage.

The white worker was uncomfortable in addressing cultural factors during the assessment and in raising questions about their potential effects on the family's conflicts. He felt that bringing them up could make him seem racist and that responding when the family brought them up seemed presumptuous, given his lack of knowledge about black families. Moreover, the worker assumed that all ethnic groups should assimilate, just as his Italian-American grandparents and parents had. That bias affected his ability to see other options for each individual's cultural adjustment, such as biculturalism. The consultant was able to explore the worker's bias and to educate him about the cultural continuum (see Figure 4.1). The worker used the continuum to help the family assess where each member was in his or her own cultural-adjustment process. This resulted in an accurate and relevant assessment of this family's needs, which then guided the worker's interventions. An assessment that ignores the issue of cultural maintenance or labels it as anything other than a normative life cycle task among black families can exacerbate the situation.

ILLUSTRATING FAMILY LIFE CYCLE ASSESSMENTS

While the previous discussion highlights aspects of the cultural context in which the black family's life cycle is experienced, a more detailed example illustrates how that knowledge can be applied during assessment. In an earlier example, a 32-year-old client had sought counseling to handle her grief three years after the death of her grandmother. After five sessions with a white worker at a family service agency, this client dropped out of treatment. The worker's initial assessment indicated, in part, that the client, Ms. Lindley:

> . . . has a strong pathological attachment to her grandmother, while being emotionally cut off from her mother. As an example, she continually refers to her mother as Lillian and avoids talking about her in any detailed way.

When the client did not return after the fifth session, the worker added progress notes to the record, including the following:

> The client is obviously not ready to work on her problems. She is unwilling to confront her excessive guilt about having been a burden on her grandmother while growing up.

It was not clear from the worker's progress notes at termination whether the client's cultural background and the relevant family life cycle stage had been considered during assessment or during the subsequent treatment sessions. Moreover, the differences and similarities between the backgrounds of the worker and client apparently had not been explored.

Assessment Update

Six months later, Ms. Lindley returned to the family service agency when her 8-year-old son was referred by his school because of conduct problems. A black worker was assigned to the case. Having read the previous intake, social history, and progress notes, she wanted to avoid making the same mistakes that the previous worker had made. When she called the family to make the initial appointment, she clarified that Ms. Lindley was coming for help with her son

Tim's problems at school. When the client asked who else should come in for the first interview, the worker suggested that she bring everyone who was interested in and responsible for Tim.

Ms. Lindley showed up for the first appointment with four individuals in addition to Tim, Mr. Lindley, and Tim's two sisters (Trish, age 11, and Kay, age 10). The family minister, an older woman in the neighborhood who had provided child care for Tim when he was younger, Mr. Lindley's father, and Ms. Lindley's aunt were there for the interview. The worker was surprised that Ms. Lindley had taken her statement so literally, since at the time she was thinking only about immediate family members. But she was resourceful enough to realize that an opportunity had been provided for learning more than usual about this family's situation.

An Expanded Ecological Assessment

The worker first met with the whole group to obtain a clear picture of the relevant information each person had to contribute and how they had been, and could continue to be, a resource to the family. Then the immediate family was seen alone in order to complete the intake process. The family was asked to return the following week to continue the assessment, and the other people present were asked if they would be willing to return as needed for a future session. They agreed to do so if it was important to the immediate family.

From this session, the worker was able to develop an ecomap of the family's current significant relationships. The *ecomap* is a practical means for depicting the family in space in terms of its relationships with other systems. It is valuable because it can identify systems or relationships that could be missed in discussion and because all relationships can be illustrated by lines that connect the systems. A strong solid line illustrates a strong positive relationship, a broken line is for a tenuous relationship, and a line with small hatch marks across it is for conflictual relationships. The family is shown in a large central circle with smaller surrounding circles for other systems (Hartman, 1979a). Included in the ecomap for the Lindleys were the relationships with the four individuals who showed up for the interview and others whom the family discussed during the initial session. It seemed clear that Mr. Lindley had several close relatives and friends for support, as did the three children. Ms. Lindley, on the other hand, commented that she had only her aunt in the area, to whom she was very close. She had been surprised and gratified when the aunt and the other three individuals had agreed to come with the family to the session. This helped her and other family members to see that they were not alone in trying to resolve their problems.

For instance, the neighbor, Ms. Albritton, often served as an objective sounding board for Tim and Trish when they were upset. This emotional support for the children relieved the parents of some of the stress connected with their everyday concerns and conserved the parents' problem-solving skills for other family issues. In addition, the parents had attended a four-week family enrichment group begun by their minister for helping families to become a "spiritual unit." The ecomap indicated that some of the group members had continued to meet occasionally and that those contacts were a source of support to Mr. and Mrs. Lindley. The worker consulted with the minister to learn more about those enrichment groups. During the course of that discussion, he offered her space in the church for counseling sessions. The worker therefore asked if the Lindley family would like to meet at the church for future counseling sessions, and they agreed they would be more comfortable meeting there.

During sessions held over the next three months, the family worked toward resolving Tim's school problems and other issues. As part of the initial assessment, however, the worker helped the family first to identify the many demands on them as a family with young children. A family's ability to respond to those new demands while also meeting the unit's needs can determine whether serious problems develop. Within this context, Tim's school adjustment problem was reframed as a family life cycle problem. This led to an exploration of how the family was managing that problem as well as the usual tasks of this stage: individuation of each member, emotional support and mutual aid, meeting basic needs (food, shelter, and clothing), and socialization.

Because Tim's behavior at school seemed to be a problem in socialization, the family's pattern for addressing that task was identified and discussed. Each parent talked about how he or she had experienced this stage in the family of origin. Ms. Lindley began to realize that the immediate family's present experiences reminded her of her grandmother's assumption of the parenting role when she was a young child. Perhaps mourning over the loss of her own childhood made her less clear and consistent in her expectations for Tim's behavior. The family agreed to explore their family-of-origin issues related to current concerns through a *genogram*. The daughters, at 10 and 11 years of age, were more eager than Tim to learn about their parents' families.

A genogram is a diagrammatic tool for analyzing the family relationships intergenerationally. Three or more generations in a family may be depicted over time, with males symbolized by a square and females by a circle. Written notations can be used to indicate ages, relationships, roles, religious and cultural factors, and other variables (Hartman, 1979b). A genogram developed over the three sessions that followed the initial session was very useful in assessing factors that might be influencing the Lindley family's resources for addressing its current life cycle needs (see Figure 4.2). Ms. Lindley's aunt and Mr. Lindley's father returned for one session to fill in gaps in information for the genogram. For instance, Ms. Lindley was uncertain about how the decision that her grandmother should raise her had been made. She learned from her aunt that initially it was to be a temporary plan until her mother obtained a job in New York. Later, because her grandparents had become very attached to her, it was decided that she would stay with them permanently in the small southern city where they lived at the time. The Lindley family still lives in this town. Ms. Lindley was encouraged to check out this information with her mother, to whom she had never been close but from whom she was *not* emotionally cut off.

The paternal grandfather was able to talk about a lack of involvement with

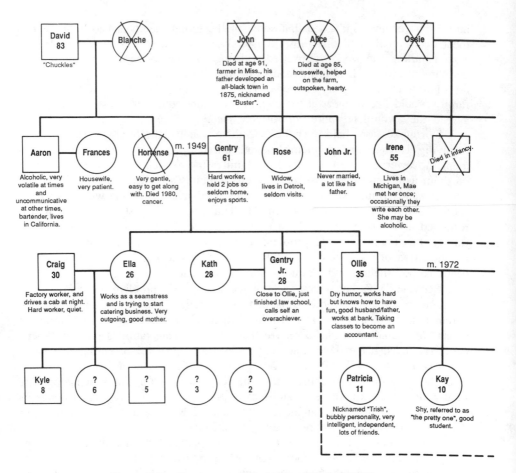

Figure 4.2. Genogram of the Lindley Family (1985)

his family at the same stage due to a lifelong pattern of having two jobs in order to support the family. The grandfather recognized the dilemma that this need often put black fathers in and helped Mr. Lindley talk more openly about his desire to be more involved with Tim. Mr. Lindley was working full-time *and* attempting to complete a training program in accounting. This usually left little time for being with his family, especially with Tim, who seemed to feel his absence more as the youngest and the only male child. Other contributing factors included Ms. Lindley's employment and preoccupation about her grandmother. Thus, neither parent had focused on Tim's socialization as much as they had with the two older children.

The genogram also helped family members see that Tim, the youngest child, viewed himself differently from the way the family saw him. When asked to write in the nicknames or labels used to characterize family members on the genogram, Tim was referred to as "last but not least." While the family used

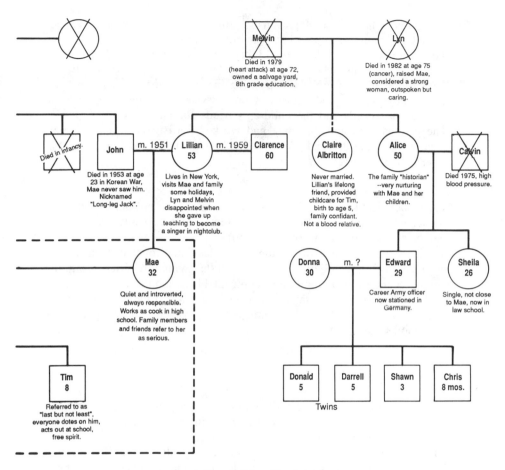

Figure 4.2. (*Continued*)

this term affectionately to indicate his "special place" as the youngest child, Tim saw the term as an indicator of a lower status.

The use of the church setting, the support provided by the minister and relevant others in some sessions, and the worker's knowledge about normative life cycle issues in black families guided an effective assessment. On the basis of this ecological assessment, the following conclusions were developed to guide the interventions with this family. (Because the focus of this chapter is assessment, the interventions are not discussed here):

Strengths

1. Family members cared deeply for one another, and the parents understood some of the necessary tasks of their current life cycle.
2. Mr. Lindley had a dry sense of humor that frequently relieved stressful situations at home.

3. The parents had a set of reasonable rules for family routines that involved the children appropriately in role sharing.
4. The parents valued education highly and were more than willing to cooperate with the school in resolving Tim's behavior problems there.
5. The sibling relationships were positive in spite of occasional conflicts.
6. The family had a good external support system that met their cultural maintenance needs and the children's needs for nurturance.
7. The parents indicated that they had worked hard to have a good marriage despite the demands from both of them being employed and Mr. Lindley being in school.

Problems
1. Tim's socialization, as a family life cycle task, was not being addressed adequately, as indicated by his perception that he had low status in the family and by his acting out at school.
2. Mr. Lindley and Tim both felt they spent less time together than desired because of Mr. Lindley's heavy schedule, which resulted from the unique economic conditions that confront black families.
3. The family's life cycle stage had reawakened Ms. Lindley's unresolved grief about her grandmother's death, which involved two losses: the loss of a mother *and* a grandmother.

Goals
The family will be able to:

1. Identify all of its life cycle tasks and develop a plan for each member's contribution to fulfilling those tasks, including increased role sharing by the family's external support system as needed.
2. Clarify Tim's status in the family and identify alternatives for meeting his socialization needs (including a closer relationship with his father).
3. Clarify expectations for Tim at school and ways to eliminate his inappropriate behavior there.
4. Help Ms. Lindley express and resolve her grief about the loss of her grandmother in culturally relevant ways and through the use of her support system.

In using the genogram to achieve a broad-base ecological assessment, the worker obtained information that she and the family agreed would *not* be the focus of their work. For instance, the genogram revealed examples of intergenerational alcoholism (see information about Irene and Aaron in Figure 4.2). Exploration of this issue with the parents indicated that alcoholism was not a problem in the current generation (neither the parents nor any of Mr. Lindley's siblings had alcohol problems). In addition, none of them seemed to have many of the problems that typically exist in alcoholic families, such as extreme rigidity or avoiding expression of feelings. Because alcoholism could potentially be a problem, however, the worker provided some education for the parents about the issue without making that part of their ongoing work. Similarly, the genogram made it apparent that Ms. Lindley knew little about her father and his family. The worker predicted that the loss of her father and the lack of information about his family might become a future life cycle issue, given Ms. Lindley's age. Part of the assessment process was therefore preventive: the worker explored how Ms. Lindley might use her natural support network to address those issues in the future if she chose to do so.

Second, the assessment of Tim's school problems was not confined to the family and neighborhood circumstances. It was necessary to help the family assess the impact of the conduct disorder label that the school had placed on Tim and what that might convey about their assumptions about black children. The worker's assessment with the school and with the parents supported the concept of a socialization problem that could be resolved by changing the expectations and consequences for Tim's behavior at school and at home. There was no evidence that there was a more serious conduct problem (see Chapter 7 for more on school adjustment problems).

PRINCIPLES OF SOCIAL WORK ASSESSMENT

The situation in the Lindley family involves a set of generalizable principles that can be used to guide assessments of other black families, for instance, in maintaining a person-in-environment focus. This expanded focus of assessment supports an ecological perspective as well as the professional value of beginning where the client is. In terms of the latter, where a family is at the point of assessment is often determined in part by its current family life cycle stage and the influence of the black cultural context.

Helping professionals need a broad understanding of family life cycle stages, integrated with substantive information about the cultural context of black families and variables relevant to that experience. Information about black family forms and cultural and racial identity can be found in Chapters 5 and 6, the references at the end of this chapter, consultation with experts on the black family, and a systematically monitored practice with black families. Supervisory or consultant-supported practice experiences with such families are essential for completing the knowing-understanding-doing paradigm.

Data collection during assessment should be guided by the social worker "going where the problem leads" (Hartman, 1979c). This principle requires being aware of factors that signal whether family life cycle issues need to be explored and addressed. For instance, the presenting problem may indicate that there are conflicts about which life cycle tasks should be a priority or how they should be addressed. In a previous example, the single parent who had dropped out of high school as a teenager understood her role in helping her son to do career planning but was in conflict with him and his coach about whether an athletic scholarship was the best way for him to achieve a college education. In other situations, family members may not be prepared for the tasks and demands of the new stage. When those new demands challenge a family's racial identity, as in the example of the middle-class teenager who viewed her parents as being bourgeois, the worker's assessment may verify that family members are unaware of how to address these demands while maintaining their dual perspective. Other indicators that family life cycle issues may need to be explored include a family's lack of knowledge about the normative stages that all families experience and the influence of culture on those stages, or a family's lack of resources for meeting particular life cycle needs. During assessment, workers can use these and other indicators to determine whether life cycle issues are relevant to a particular family's problem situation (McGoldrick, 1982).

In assessment of black families, the social worker should begin from a strengths perspective, that is, look at the cultural diversity implicit in the black versus white family's life cycle experiences as evidence of positive coping. Draper's (1979) concept of adaptive responses to a hostile environment is useful here, because many of the black family's life cycle patterns have developed in response to internal needs *and* to external forms of repression. Role fluidity, for example, should be assessed in terms of its value to the particular black family in carrying out its life cycle tasks. The worker should explore with the family additional ways to build on this strength if unmet needs are identified or if the family will soon be confronted with a new stage for which new resources are needed. The family should be encouraged to participate in the assessment of strengths with the worker because the unit's creative resources may identify strengths that are not readily apparent to the worker. In the example of the Lindley family, the parents' efforts toward cultural maintenance included making a collection of pictures and other memorabilia about a relative who helped to found the only all-black town in their state in 1875. During assessment, it was determined that working on this collection could be a useful way for Tim and Mr. Lindley to spend time together and enhance Tim's socialization by increasing his cultural and family pride.

A final principle involves the conceptual framework and the physical and emotional setting for effective assessments with black families. Engagement and assessment may be more effective in some circumstances, where the presenting problem is reframed positively in terms of the family's life cycle tasks. For instance, Ms. Lindley and other family members seemed more motivated to help with assessment and problem resolution when the problem was reframed as a need to increase Tim's socialization. This perspective was consistent with their value of education and sense of family pride. Moreover, they were more comfortable meeting in their church and including individuals in the sessions whom they identified as relevant to their family life. In contrast, when Ms. Lindley was first referred to the family service agency because of the stress she was experiencing as a result of her grief, the worker's failure to explore cultural factors and her framing of the problem negatively as a dysfunctional attachment to the grandmother led to the client's early termination of treatment. The assessment process and subsequent treatment sessions did not meet either the client's needs or her view of the problem. With other black families too, the worker should explore their view of the problem from within the cultural and life cycle context in which it is experienced.

CONCLUSIONS

Assessment of black families must be done in a manner that captures their internal view of the problem situation and conveys the worker's awareness of the unique and common life cycle issues that may be confronting them. During assessment the social worker should also be aware both of significant within-group differences *and* of similarities with other racial groups. The practitioner can facilitate exploration of life cycle issues if he or she has adequate knowledge about the family life cycle and a respect for the strengths of black families.

REFERENCES

Aschenbrenner, J., & Carr, C. H. (1980, November). Conjugal relationships in the context of the black extended family. *Alternative Lifestyles, 3,* 463–484.

Blassingame, J.W. (1979). *The slave community.* New York: Oxford University Press.

Carter, E.A., & McGoldrick, M. (1980). *The family life cycle: A framework for family therapy.* New York: Gardner.

Chestang, L. (1979). Competencies and knowledge in clinical social work: A dual perspective. In P.L. Ewalt (Ed.), *Towards a definition of clinical social work* (pp. 8–16). Washington, DC: National Association of Social Workers.

Davis, F.G. (1981). Economics and mobility: A theoretical rationale for urban black well-being. In H.P. McAdoo (Ed.), *Black families* (pp. 127–138). Beverly Hills, CA: Sage.

Draper, B. (1979). Black language as an adaptive response to a hostile environment. In C. B. Germain (Ed.), *Social work practice: People and environments* (pp. 267–281). New York: Columbia University Press.

Erikson, E. (1979). Life cycle. In M. Bloom (Ed.), *Life span development* (pp. 19–29). New York: Macmillan.

Freeman, E.M., Logan, S., & McRoy, R. G. (1986). Group counseling program for unemployed black teenagers. *Social Work with Groups, 9*(1), 73–90.

Freeman, E.M., McRoy, R. G., & Logan, S. (1987). Clinical practice with employed women. *Social Casework, 68,* 11–24.

Germain, C.E. (1979). Introduction: Ecology and social work. In C.B. Germain (Ed.), *Social work practice: People and environments* (pp. 1–22). New York: Columbia University Press.

Goldenberg, I., & Goldenberg, H. (1984). *Family therapy: An overview.* Monterey, CA: Brooks/Cole.

Gordon, W. (1979). Knowledge and value: Their distinction and relationship in clarifying social work practice. In B. Compton & B. Galaway, *Social work processes* (pp. 52–59). Homewood, IL: Dorsey.

Hartman, A. (1979a). Diagrammatic assessment of family relationships. In B. Compton & B. Galaway, *Social work processes* (pp. 299–310). Homewood, IL: Dorsey.

Hartman, A. (1979b). The extended family as a resource for change: An ecological approach to family-centered practice. In C.B. Germain (Ed.), *Social work practice: People and environments* (pp. 239–266). New York: Columbia University Press.

Hartman, A. (1979c). Competencies in clinical social work. In P.L. Ewalt (Ed.), *Towards a definition of clinical social work* (pp. 33–41). Washington, DC: National Association of Social Workers.

Hartman, A., & Laird, J. (1983). *Family-centered social practice.* New York: Free Press.

Hill, R. (1972). *The strengths of black families.* New York: Emerson Hall.

Logan, S., Freeman, E.M., & McRoy, R. G. (1987). Racial identity problems of biracial clients: Implications for social work practice. *Journal of Intergroup Relations, 25*(2), 11–24.

Manns, W. (1981). Support systems of significant others in black families. In H.P. McAdoo (Ed.), *Black families* (pp. 238–251). Beverly Hills, CA: Sage.

Martin, J.M., & Martin, E.P. (1985). *The helping tradition in the black family and community.* Silver Spring, MD: National Association of Social Workers.

McAdoo, H.P. (Ed.). (1981a). *Black families.* Beverly Hills, CA: Sage.

McAdoo, H.P. (1981b). Patterns of upward mobility in black families. In H.P. McAdoo (Ed.), *Black families* (pp. 155–169). Beverly Hills, CA: Sage.

McGoldrick, M. (1982). *Ethnicity and family therapy.* New York: Guilford.

Meyer, C. (1983). The search for coherence. In C. Meyer (Ed.), *Clinical social work in the eco-systems perspective* (pp. 5–34). New York: Columbia University Press.

Norton, D. (1978). *The dual perspective.* New York: Council on Social Work Education.

Oppong, C. (1974). *Marriage among a matrilineal elite: A family study of Ghanaian senior servants.* Cambridge: Cambridge University Press.

Rhodes, S.L. (1979). A developmental approach to the life cycle of the family. In M. Bloom (Ed.), *Life span development* (pp. 30–39). New York: Macmillan.

Sherradan, M.W. (1985). Chronic unemployment: A social work perspective. *Social Work, 30,* 403–408.

Sudarkasa, N. (1981). Interpreting the African heritage in Afro-American family organization. In H.P. McAdoo (Ed.), *Black families* (pp. 23–36). Beverly Hills, CA: Sage.

U.S. Bureau of the Census. (1986). *Current population reports.* Washington, DC: Author.

Willie, C.V. (1981). *A new look at black families.* Bayside, NY: General Hall.

CHAPTER 5

Diversity among Black Families:
Assessing Structure and Function

Sadye M. L. Logan
University of Kansas

The controversy over whether or not black families are in crisis has received more public attention than almost any other social issue. It is important to note that a little more than two decades ago the dynamics of black family life were also the focus of widespread attention after the publication of Moynihan's report on the black family (1965). This report advanced several erroneous ideas about the functioning of black families, most particularly that various systemic problems—crime, school failure, drug dependency—experienced by the black community were an outgrowth of black life-style. These problems were viewed not only as being perpetuated by the structure of black families but also as causing pathological or ineffectual family functioning. In recent years, however, there have been some attempts in the literature to move beyond this pejorative perspective of black family life (Gutman, 1976; Hill, 1972; Stack, 1974). Despite these attempts at presenting a perspective that taps into the diversity and richness of black life-style, there is an abundance of confusion for those in the helping professions who are working with a black clientele. This confusion is due in part to the contradictory nature of existing literature on the dynamics of black family life.

Those helping professionals who work with black families must not only have an appreciation for and understanding of the black experience, but also possess a high level of competence in assessing black families. This chapter provides the framework for assessing black families effectively, addresses the rich diversity of family structures and interactional processes, suggests conceptual tools for use in family assessment, and considers important practice implications.

PERSPECTIVES ON BLACK FAMILIES

Black families represent a diverse mixture of ethnic groups and cultures. Although the majority are descendants of the enslaved Africans from West Africa, blended within this majority are Native Americans, Europeans, Caribbeans, and Hispanics. From this perspective, our focus will be on the diversity that exists among black families in terms of values, personal characteristics, and life-styles, intersected by geographic regions, religious influences, socioeconomic status, level of acculturation, and age. Within this context at least three major perspectives provide a better understanding of the complexity of black family life and the various family structures. Included are the traditional view, the revisionist view, and the contemporary view.

The Traditional View

The traditional view of black family life is reflected in literature extending from approximately 1870 to 1975. This body of literature defined almost all aspects of black life in pathological terms (Guthrie, 1976; Jones, 1973; Kamin, 1974; Newly, 1965). The only disagreement among the social scientists studying black family life centered on whether the underlying cause of this so-called pathology was a function of genetic factors or environmental factors. The biogenetic perspective extended from approximately 1870 to 1930, to be replaced by the environmental perspective (Frazier, 1937; Park, 1936) or an ecological orientation after 1930 (Jones, 1973). In an attempt to refute Melville Herskovits' (1941) thesis that most black Americans' social and cultural patterns were African in origin, E. Franklin Frazier (1957) produced the definitive social history of black families and black life. He also agreed with his contemporaries that the personal lives of poor blacks were characterized by pathology.

The Revisionist View

Robert Hill's research on the strengths of black families is perhaps the first well-publicized indication that scholars had begun the process of revisiting the established pathological theory on black family life (Hill, 1972). Extending the thesis of Hill's research, the work of Blassingame (1972), Fogel and Engerman (1974), Genovese (1974), and Gutman (1976) collectively seemed to dispel the notion that slavery destroyed the black family. These "revisionist" historians are credited with affirming a black family kinship system that was strong, intact, resilient, and adaptive in both rural and urban environments from slavery until a few years before the Great Depression, when all families—especially black families—were devastated by the economy.

The Contemporary View

Contemporary studies on black family kinship patterns continue to describe viable functional systems (Billingsley, 1968; Gary et al., 1983; Geismar, 1973;

McAdoo, 1977; Stack, 1974), but this observation is in no way a denial that the black family is currently experiencing a great deal of external as well as internal stress. This increasing stress, implicit in an array of social problems from crime to school failure, has helped to create diversified family systems that are referred to in the literature as "changing" or "dying" family systems.

Many theories have been offered to explain the "problems" encountered by the contemporary black family/kinship system despite the strengths and resiliency of black families (Geismar, 1973; Harrison, 1972; Stack, 1974). The common theme that runs through these theories is that problems arise and are exacerbated by a differential social and opportunity structure for blacks. Others have argued that there is more to this complex situation than social and economic opportunity (see Murray, 1984). Murray contends that many of the devastating systemic problems in the black community are directly tied to public policy and program implementation and that the combination of stigma-free public assistance and the financial penalty imposed when an AFDC family secures employment mitigates against responsible behavior. Utilizing a similar line of reasoning, Loury (1986) believes that the lack of virtuous behavior among some inner-city poor is at the heart of the matter. It is obvious from the points of view offered by Murray and Loury that no simple explanation exists for the problems black families encounter. However, it is clear that internal and external factors play a major role in perpetuating systemic problems, and further that despite these stressors black families are viable systems in constant interaction with the environment. This constant interaction serves to transform the structure and functioning of black families.

BLACK FAMILY STRUCTURES

As a result of responding adaptively to daily stressors, several types of black families emerged. These family types also include multiple family structures (see Figure 5.1). Here the family is being viewed as a social unit consisting of individuals usually related by blood and is confronted by a series of developmental tasks related to survival and growth.

Billingsley (1968) came up with twelve types of family structures among blacks in the United States. These structures have been reorganized in Figure 5.1 to reflect the present author's conceptualization of black family structures. Accordingly, there are three types of nuclear or primary families in which the spouses and their children have no other person living with them. These households are *incipient* when there are no children, *simple* if composed of husband and wife and their children, *attenuated* if there is a single parent with no other adult parent-figure present. Further, there are extended families in which other relatives or in-laws of the husband and wife share the same household with the primary family. Extended families may also be incipient, simple, or attenuated, depending upon whether children are present or whether there is only one parent. Finally, there are augmented families, which include nonrelatives in the household. There are at least six possible types of augmented families, depend-

TYPES OF HOUSEHOLDS:

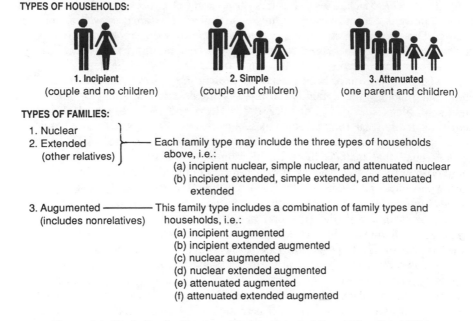

1. Incipient	**2. Simple**	**3. Attenuated**
(couple and no children)	(couple and children)	(one parent and children)

TYPES OF FAMILIES:

1. Nuclear ⎫
2. Extended ⎬——— Each family type may include the three types of households
   (other relatives) ⎭   above, i.e.:
                      (a) incipient nuclear, simple nuclear, and attenuated nuclear
                      (b) incipient extended, simple extended, and attenuated
                            extended

3. Augumented ——————— This family type includes a combination of family types and
   (includes nonrelatives)   households, i.e.:
                      (a) incipient augmented
                      (b) incipient extended augmented
                      (c) nuclear augmented
                      (d) nuclear extended augmented
                      (e) attenuated augmented
                      (f) attenuated extended augmented

Figure 5.1. Black Family Structure (*Source:* Adapted from Billingsley, 1968.)

ing on whether there are children present, whether the family includes relatives as well as nonrelatives, and where there is only a single parent as head of household (Billingsley, 1968).

Black families have experienced even greater diversification within these twelve family forms since Billingsley's formulation in 1968. For example, over the past two decades family structure has changed significantly. The most recent statistics indicate that married couple families that constituted 78 percent of all black families in the 1960s decreased to 53 percent in the 1980s. This decline parallels an increase in female-headed families. During the same period (the 1960s), when married couple families constituted a large majority of all black families, single-female-headed families accounted for only 22 percent of all black families, but by 1987 that figure had increased to 44 percent. A variety of social and environmental factors account for this dramatic increase in single-parent families—for example, high unemployment rates, an increasing divorce rate, high separation rates, a high rate of unmarried parenthood, and the early death rates of black men (Billingsley, 1987).

Single-parent families may be described as the fastest-growing structure among black families. Significant among this group are teenage parents (Logan et al., 1986; Moore et al., 1986). The vast body of research on single-parent families profiled these families as living in nonnurturing environments (Schultz, 1969) where the children lacked masculine or effective role models (Clark, 1965), displayed negative self-images and low self-esteem (Proshansky & Newton, 1968; Rainwater, 1970), were severely delayed in cognitive, affective, and intellectual development (Glasser & Glasser, 1970; Olim et al., 1967; Whiteman & Deutsch, 1970), and were sexually active at an early age (Clark, 1965; Rainwater, 1970). The research generally focused on those families that were both at the lowest end of the socioeconomic strata and experiencing severe stresses in coping with everyday problems in living. Further, this body of research rarely relied on the participants' description or interpretation of their experiences.

A different picture emerges when children and families are allowed to describe in their own words what it means to live in a single-parent household (Morris, 1977; Thompson, 1978). For example, what is viewed as "pathology" by researchers becomes a strength, the "matriarch" becomes a strong, secure force against a hostile world, and a "broken home" becomes a network of best friends, neighbors, uncles, and aunts. A broader perspective for viewing single-parent families will allow for a more realistic interpretation of the family's overall functioning (Logan, 1987). Single-parent families are indeed at risk for numerous stresses and the possibility of producing dysfunctional children, but many factors converge to help produce a dysfunctional family system. Underemployment or unemployment, family instability, limited personal resources, little or no education, and poor family support are major contributing factors to the quality of life and interpersonal processes in single-parent families (Billingsley, 1987; Logan, 1987; Savage, 1978).

INTERACTIONAL PROCESSES

The interactional processes within families in all racial groups are an outgrowth of the family's structure and functioning. The family structure reflects the invisible sets of demands that govern the manner in which family members interact or organize themselves (Minuchin, 1974). The consequences of particular kinds of family organization for responding to the needs of its members are known as "family function." These functional demands are commonly referred to as nurturer, protector, provider, and decision maker. The family's interactional processes reflect the relationship patterns and communication styles families use to achieve their goals (Pinderhughes, 1982).

Family interactional processes may be viewed on a continuum, and for our purposes we will not only view these concepts on a continuum (see Table 5.1) but also discuss them in the context of how the needs of all families are met.

The basic needs of family members are defined as emotional and physical (Foley, 1984). The present author believes that the physical needs are more obvious than the emotional needs. Emotional needs are defined in terms of intimacy, meaning, and power. These areas may be expressed in a variety of ways for different people, but for many the family as a social unit serves that purpose. Within this context all families are expected to provide for the physical, cognitive, emotional, and spiritual development of their members. This means that an income must be established, a household must be maintained,

TABLE 5.1. INTERACTIONAL PROCESSES (AND CONTINUUM OF FUNCTIONING) WITHIN BLACK FAMILIES

Life Domains	(Stable) Nurturing or Functioning Well	(Less Stable) Mid-range Functioning	(Severely Unstable) Dysfunctional or Non-Nurturing
Recreation/ Socialization	People feel loving. People feel free to talk about inside feelings. All feelings are okay and members can play together. Strong parental coalition.	People have difficulty putting feelings into words. Most feelings are okay and can be talked about. Children are sometimes triangulated by a parent.	Hurt and disappointment are typical reaction in the family. People compulsively protect inside feelings. Only "certain" feelings are okay. Coalitions exist across generations.
Self-image	Individual differences are accepted. Members are considered more important than performance. Each member likes self and respects others. People have high self-worth.	Some conformity is encouraged. Some ambivalence re person vs. performance. Most times individuals like self and are respectful of others. People's self-worth fluctuates.	Everyone must conform to strongest person's ideas, values. Performance is considered more important than the person. People have low self-worth.
Guidance	Each person responsible for own actions. Respectful criticisms and appropriate consequences for actions. There are very few shoulds for other members. Rules are clear, flexible.	Some control over action of others. Sometimes guilt is activated as the consequence for actions. There are some shoulds for other members. Rules are sometimes ambiguous.	Lots of control, criticism. Punishment and shaming are typically used as consequences. Lots of shoulds for members. Unclear, inconsistent, and rigid rules.

TABLE 5.1. (continued)

Life Domains	(Stable) Nurturing or Functioning Well	(Less Stable) Mid-range Functioning	(Severely Unstable) Dysfunctional or Non-Nurturing
Family *Cooperation*	People are planful. Decisions are shared. Roles are easily reversed and shared. People compromise easily.	People are usually planful. Decisions are often shared. Roles are somewhat flexible. People compromise.	Everything is spur-of-the-moment. Decisions are not shared. Roles are rigidly defined. People do not compromise.
Health (mental and physical)	All subjects open to discussion. Atmosphere is relaxed and joyous. The system faces and works through stress. People have energy. Growth is celebrated.	Some subjects are not open to discussion. Atmosphere sometimes tense and stressful. People are usually energetic. Growth is encouraged in most areas.	There are many taboo subjects, lots of secrets. Atmosphere is tense. Lots of anger, fear. The system avoids stress. People feel tired. Growth is threatening and thus discouraged.
Economics	People feel financially secure. People are gainfully employed. There is support for training or studying for job promotion or change in careers. Adequate living arrangements.	People are financially solvent. People are employed or in training programs. Living arrangements may be crowded, but adequate.	People feel financially insecure. People are not gainfully employed. No thoughts of training or study for job promotion or career change. Inadequate living arrangements.

food must be provided, and individual members must feel valued and loved. In addition, constructive social and emotional ties are expected to be established at work and in the community (Logan, 1987).

The family interactional processes are expressed in terms of the manner in which family members work toward meeting the needs of its individual members and the family as a whole. These processes are conceptualized here on a continuum and discussed in the context of the nurturing or well-functioning family, the less disturbed (or mid-range functioning) family, and the chaotic or dysfunctional non-nurturing family (see Table 5.1). A major advantage of conceptualizing black families on a continuum is that it alerts the practitioner to the fluidity of family functioning and to the characteristic manner of role-sharing within black families (Scanzoni, 1971). A family may experience one predominant mode of functioning on the continuum, but it may also fluctuate in and out of other modes of functioning. Even though the emphasis here is on variations that exist in the way all families organize to meet needs, it is imperative to be ever mindful of those factors related to cultural and social diversity and of the impact such variables have on black family functioning.

Nurturing or Well-Functioning Families

Nurturing families are at the high end of the continuum of functioning and can be found at any level of the socioeconomic strata. Viewed as a three- to four-generational whole over space and time, they seldom seek help outside of the family (Gary et al., 1983; Logan, 1980). Not only does the family system relate to a prototypical or intrapsychic family of three or more generations, but transactions within the extended family are related to this sense of their historical ethos (Whitaker & Keith, 1981).

Nurturing families have clear and flexible boundaries. Family interactions are not expressed in a formal manner. As Whitaker and Keith (1981) indicate, family interactions are expressed in the transaction rather than in words—for example, the dinner table is set at a certain time every evening, the children are never late for dinner unless previously excused, the family waits until all the members are home before dinner is served. The family's internalized and unspoken rule was: The entire family eats together and tardiness or absence is not tolerated. In another family, the parents have been divorced since their daughters were preschool age. The girls are now teenagers and have expressed interest in dating. Although the father shares custody with the mother, she has been primarily responsible for the girls' care. She is also very concerned about the issue of the girls' developing sexuality and the general increase in adolescent pregnancy. This concern has shaped the mother's social life and her relationship with the opposite sex. Although she has dated the same man since the girls were latency age, she has gone to great lengths to avoid sleeping overnight at his home or to have him sleep over at hers. The family's unspoken rule: Sex outside of marriage is unacceptable. Rules and regulations are utilized in all families to organize the way members develop healthy outside relationships as well as to move in and out of the family without creating a family crisis. For this to happen, however, the families must have a strong sense of identity, and for black families this sense of identity is in part linked to their historical past and a shared feeling of peoplehood (ethnicity). But such families are also quite comfortable being intimately connected through their experiences with mainstream America.

The nurturing family reflects an interactional pattern based on an "as if" quality (Whitaker & Keith, 1981). This "as if" quality allows not only for a separation of the generations but also for playful metacommunication. The television situation comedy "The Bill Cosby Show" provides an excellent example of this "as if" quality in maintaining separation between the generations as well as allowing for periodic role reversal among the family members through a form of play. A popular example of this on the Cosby show is the Thanksgiving skit in which the father finally agrees to let the son carve the family's Thanksgiving turkey—a role that was proudly assumed by the father as "head" of the family as well as part of the family's Thanksgiving tradition.

Because nurturing families are in touch with their feelings and are not afraid to express them, problem-solving is done within a context, based on the facts, and resolved through compromise and methods proven effective in past problem situations. The power structure of the nurturing family is flexible, and power is shared. Within some nurturing families, leadership is generally allocated to the father, with the mother as the most influential person in the hierarchy. Though the children are viewed as having less power than their parents, their input into family matters is encouraged and respected (Beavers, 1976; Minuchin, 1974). Each family member is encouraged to express himself or herself and to respect the uniqueness of the other person.

A most significant and often overlooked characteristic of all families, especially nurturing families, is the need for intimacy and sexual expression. According to Whitaker and Keith (1981), passion and sexuality are the voltage in a family system. When the flow is free, things go well. When the flow is impeded, the system heats up, and there is always the possibility of damage, such as one of the children beginning to exhibit behavior unacceptable to the parent—failing school subjects and staying out late without permission (Whitaker & Keith, 1981, p. 192).

Change and growth occur not only in the nurturing family through the search for new experiences but also through identity crises. Whitaker and Keith (1981) describe these crises as self-doubt, illness, and struggling with the children. Nurturing families function as a therapeutic unit in their role within the family system and the subsystems. Over time, as a social system, the nurturing family becomes increasingly strong, and there is strength and support in the interdependence between the system as a whole and its component parts.

Mid-Range Functioning Families

Mid-range functioning families are midway on the continuum between the nurturing family and the dysfunctional or non-nurturing family. Mid-range families can also be found at any level of the socioeconomic strata, but some are more likely to be less financially solvent than some nurturing families, because many black families at the mid-range of functioning suffer from inadequate job skills or the unavailability of jobs. In times of stress these families would seek assistance outside of the family system. Their boundaries are clear but rigid, making it difficult to adapt to change. Parents exert undue pressure to make the children obey or conform. Beavers (1976) points out that *control* seems to be a distinguishing feature of less stable families and may be manifested in a variety of ways.

In the mid-range functioning family, the members are told what they can think, feel, and do on the basis of whether it would be good for the family or how it would look to others. Instead of compromising when the family reaches an impasse, the members bicker and blame one another or someone or something outside of the family. This same rigidity is reflected in terms of expressing feelings. Expressions of anger, sexuality, and passion (struggles) are usually viewed as threatening to the family interactional pattern.

The power structure in mid-range families is tenuous. A basic leadership style is dominance by either the father or the mother. Although each style of parenting appears to have positive as well as negative effects on the children, some mother-dominated families appear to be generally less capable than father-dominated families in producing well-adapted children (Biller, 1970; Hetherington, 1965; Hetherington, 1972). It appears that the regular presence of the father is related to the performance of both boys and girls in quantitative skills and sex-typed characteristics (Huston, 1983). In an illustration of the impact of mother-dominated families on children, Huston refers to "a study conducted of 4-year-old, predominantly black Head Start children where girls' assertiveness was associated with maternal control and a tendency to use negative feedback in a teaching situation" (1983, p. 443). The study concludes with the observation, however, that both maternal warmth and maternal control were positively correlated with socially outgoing behavior.

In mid-range functioning families, any lack of separation between the generations is a covert matter. For example, relatively impotent triangles exist between a parent and child which sometimes result in manipulative and exploitative behavior. The rigid and sometimes inconsistent structure of these families often produces children who have behavior disorders and use blame to avoid responsible behavior. The Stillman family is descriptive of the mid-range level of functioning:

> Bob Stillman, 45 years old, and his wife Marva, age 32, have been married for thirteen years. This couple has three children: Dawn, 13 years old, Gloria, 12, and Crissie, 11. Bob, an electrician with two years of college, grew up in a large intact family in the south where parental roles were clearly though rigidly defined. There were five brothers and sisters. Bob was the eighth child in the family. Marva, a high school graduate, is employed as a teacher's aide in a day care center. She grew up in the north in a family of five where roles were loosely defined. She was the second oldest of one brother and sister. She was pampered by her family and grew up expecting things always to go her way.

Bob is helpful in sharing some of the family chores with Marva but insists that Marva shop, cook, and keep the house the way his mother did. Although the family is financially solvent, they manage on a very strict budget. They lived in an overcrowded, two-bedroom apartment in a slightly decaying neighborhood until the girls were in their late preschool years. Bob was anxious to move out of the neighborhood, but Marva told him that she didn't care whether they stayed or moved.

Bob and Marva did not plan the birth of their first child, Dawn. Both were inexperienced, and Marva was quite young. Assuming parenting roles was difficult for both, but especially for Marva. She frequently reminded Bob that Dawn was not her idea and that she was not ready to be a mother. She had a difficult time bonding with Dawn. After the birth of the last child, Marva underwent a tubal ligation.

Bob and Marva's marital and family life is mostly stressful. They infrequently do things together as a family. There are occasional family outings and contacts with extended family members. Some of the stress is exacerbated by financial difficulties, and especially their different ideas about how a family should live together.

The family problem is being expressed through Dawn's acting out behavior in school, which began in the third grade. Dawn has been described by her teachers as extremely bright, but she refuses to take direction and constantly disrupts the class. She is bossy and forever telling her classmates what to do. She hangs out at school and in the neighborhood with the younger children, who are easily dominated. The two younger girls are doing well in school and have many friends. Bob is very concerned about his family's reaction to Dawn's behavior and criticizes the school severely for Dawn's acting-out behavior. Whenever a note regarding Dawn's behavior at school is sent home, Marva would give it to Bob, saying that it had to do with his precious Dawn who was in trouble again. She refused to visit the school to discuss Dawn's problems, insisting that Bob attend alone.

Dysfunctional or Non-Nurturing Families

Non-nurturing families are at the low end of the continuum of functioning. Not unlike the nurturing or less stable families, these families can be found at any level of the socioeconomic strata. Although many of these families may be financially insolvent and receive some forms of social services, they are by no means all poverty-stricken, poorly educated, or unemployed. But these families include Minuchin's (1974) concepts of disengaged and enmeshed families, Whitaker and Keith's (1981) concept of craziness, and Bowen's (1978) concept of an undifferentiated family ego mass. As Beavers (1976) points out, it does not matter how the process is labeled because they are all describing different aspects of the same phenomenon: the family's inability to operate as a cohesive whole and to produce healthy children who are self-directed, clear about their identities, and capable of having and sustaining relationships outside of the family.

In non-nurturing families, the boundaries are blurred between the generations and easily permeated by external forces:

Negotiation becomes a senseless concept. Relationships are maintained unclear and unchanging. The members . . . behave as if human closeness is found by thinking and feeling just like one another; therefore, individuation is tantamount to rejection and exclusion. (Beavers 1976, p. 58)

The power structure in the non-nurturing family is extremely skewed. Where both parents are present, the father usually has little or no power. The father's power is further dissipated by a coalition between the mother and one of the children (Bowen, 1978; Minuchin, 1974). However, in single-parent families there is often a similar powerlessness that is attributable to the parent's overburdened physical, emotional, or spiritual condition. In such situations one of the children may assume a parentified role and the parent takes on a sibling-like role (Goldenberg & Goldenberg, 1980; Lidz et al., 1965; Minuchin, 1974). Consider the following example:

Immature and childlike in behavior, Ms. Moore is 31 years old and an alcoholic. She is the mother of three boys: Brian, age 11, Keith, age 9, and Craig, 5. Brian, who is physically the mirror-image of Ms. Moore, is also the parentified child. When involved with the boys' father, Ms. Moore relied completely upon him to make all the decisions. At an early age Brian assumed child care responsibilities for his younger brothers. Shortly after breaking off with the boys' father, Ms. Moore began referring to Brian as "her little man." Brian was 8 at that time. She views him as the family's protector, and on numerous occasions he lied to protect her from authorities—child protective workers and the police. Brian also assumes the role of family disciplinarian and nurturer to the younger boys.

According to Whitaker and Keith (1981), dysfunctional families are extremely resistant to change and growth. In fact, they are unable to tolerate any change in their myths and rituals. Because of their lack of confidence in their ability to confront and survive change, they cling to what is familiar.

UNDERSTANDING CAUSES OF BLACK FAMILY DYSFUNCTION

The psychodynamic aspects of family life are only one aspect of understanding family interactional processes. It is equally important to understand the transactions between the family and the external environment and how these sometimes influence the family's emotional health. Placing the family in the person-in-situation paradigm (see Figure 5.2 on p. 87) will help one to conceptualize not only how problems and needs occur but also how they are defined in terms of both internal and external factors.

The challenge for black families confronted with the residue of racial discrimination and other dysfunctional social attitudes is to seek and maintain a healthy emotional and social balance between family members and the external environment. However, the noxious effects of external forces on the overall functioning of black families help to create situations that are circular and reinforcing. These external forces include specific public policies that both directly and indirectly affect family functioning. Social policies having the greatest impact on black family life today include changes in the job market, the closing of major industrial plants, and the changes in eligibility requirements for public social services to needy recipients (Hill, 1987). Major technological advances are external forces that affect black families in some unique ways. The most devastating effect wrought by technology is reflected in extremely high unemployment rates. Bureau of Labor statistics predict that by 1990 there will be four times as many new jobs for janitors, 1.2 million jobs for fast-food workers and waitresses, and 250,000 jobs for computer analysts and programmers (Hill, 1987). The implications of this forecast are bleak for many black families, who will be inadequately prepared for scarcer, higher-paying technical jobs.

There is a positive correlation between unemployment or poverty and family instability, as reflected in such systemic problems as alcoholism, child and spousal abuse, and chronic depression. Adaptive and functional families and communities are dependent on each other for continued growth (see Pinderhughes, 1982), but as businesses and community services desert predominantly black communities, families requiring support from outside sources are further stressed because community resources are inadequate or unavailable. As a result, the community itself becomes non-nurturing or disorganized. External conditions seem to have a more devastating impact on families in the non-nurturing range because of combined social and psychological factors that are individually and environmentally related.

As a consequence, black families struggle to create family systems that can survive the impact of a hostile external environment and maladaptive internal transactions—impasses in the family growth caused by family transitions that create expected or unexpected crises: a death in the family, parents' loss of a job due to discrimination, arrival of a new baby, aging parents, a child's first direct experience with discrimination, a child leaving home, and cultural changes in the broader society. Some maladaptive family transactions develop from situational stress either anticipated or actually experienced: illness (mental or physical); accidents (blacks may work in more hazardous jobs); such natural disasters as fires; unemployment; school failure; separation and loss; and physical, verbal, and sexual abuse. Any one of these events can create family dysfunctioning, but it generally requires from three to four serious stressors within one year to impair a family's overall level of functioning seriously (Levy, 1982). Stressors attributable to discrimination have more impact because of the shared oral history that both records such events and teaches blacks how to cope with them. For example, racial discrimination is a perennial problem for blacks in this country. Recalling their formative experiences that parallel current experiences forces blacks to relive hurtful experiences, although this may serve as a catharsis. The process is a double-edge sword. Though extremely painful, talking about the experience provides valuable lessons in survival strategies for other blacks.

ASSESSING BLACK FAMILY FUNCTIONS

Assessment of black families must integrate an understanding of the family's unique dynamics with an understanding of environmental transactions. The person-in-situation paradigm (Figure 5.2), which allows us to make such linkages, is used here for three reasons. First, it depicts the interconnected factors within the family's life space—the social, cultural, political, economic, and broader environmental conditions that are often stressful and that create ambiguities in the day-to-day experience of black families and children. Second, it reflects six critical areas that are an integral part of the overall family assessment: the person, the social environment, the family life cycle, the family system, the parental subsystem, and the sibling subsystem. Third, it provides a broader view of the family transactional field that suggests that the problems and needs can be defined and assessed both within the individual or at the interface between families and numerous areas of transactions—for example, transactions between the school, peer groups, and the physical setting of the home and neighborhood, and interpersonal relations among and between members of subsystems.

The interactional processes illustrated in Table 5.1 (see page 76) will help the practitioner operationalize the person-in-situation paradigm. This assessment tool is to be used in conjunction with the social-emotional map in Figure 5.3, which also incorporates additional assessment tools, enclosed in parentheses. Essentially, Table 5.1 describes three levels of family functioning within the context of six life domains—recreation and socialization, self-image, guidance, family cooperation, health, economics—on a continuum from nurturing/well-functioning to dysfunctional and non-nurturing, described earlier.

The recreation/socialization domain addresses what the family does for fun, individually, as a couple, or as a family. This domain may also examine the nature and quality of the family support systems, as black families often identify activities with extended family members, friends, and "adopted" unrelated relatives.

The self-image domain examines how family members are feeling about themselves (see Chapter 6), individually and as a unit, as well as their perception of how others see them. A question to be considered is whether they are particularly harsh in their judgment about black people in general.

The domain of guidance is concerned with the family's values, attitudes, and beliefs. This domain also explores the family's religious and spiritual orientation. Are the black church and/or other cultural/spiritual organizations relied on as important resources in their lives (Logan, 1988)?

The domain that addresses family vocation and chores examines the level of cooperation within the family and allows for exploration of role conflict, role confusion, role reversal, and role overload. The family may be asked to describe their strengths, such as effective role sharing, as well as their concerns in this domain. This question may be used to assess other domains. It is an effective way of getting the family to describe how they live and work together.

The health (mental and physical) domain explores an often neglected and

THE PERSON → **TRANSACTION (process)** → **THE SOCIAL ENVIRONMENT**

- Racial self-identification
- Individual life cycle tasks
- Quality of self-image
- Coping style, including trust level and hope in life
- Developmental milestones
- Personality characteristics
- Boundaries
- Values, beliefs, attitudes

- School and other institutions
- Mass media
- Stresses and demands
- Quality and type of social networks
- Quality of the neighborhoods
- Societal and/or cultural norms, values and attitudes
- Historical milieu (experiences with oppression)

THE FAMILY LIFE CYCLE
- Stage
- Cultural factors
- Needs and problems

THE FAMILY SYSTEM
- Economic, social, and educational level of the family
- The extended family
- Culture, emotions, intellectual quality of the home
- Power structure
- Roles
- Communication (values, beliefs, attitudes)
- Boundaries
- Interpersonal relationship
- Degree of individuation
- Acceptance of separation and loss
- Problem-solving capacity

THE PARENTAL SYSTEM
- Life cycle needs
- Spousal or partner relationship
- Parent-child relationships
- Boundaries
- Personality characteristics
- Attitude, values, and beliefs

SIBLING SYSTEM
- Life cycle needs
- Personality characteristics
- Child-parent relationships
- Peer relationships
- Relationship to extrafamilial world
- Boundaries

Figure 5.2. The Person-in-Situation Paradigm

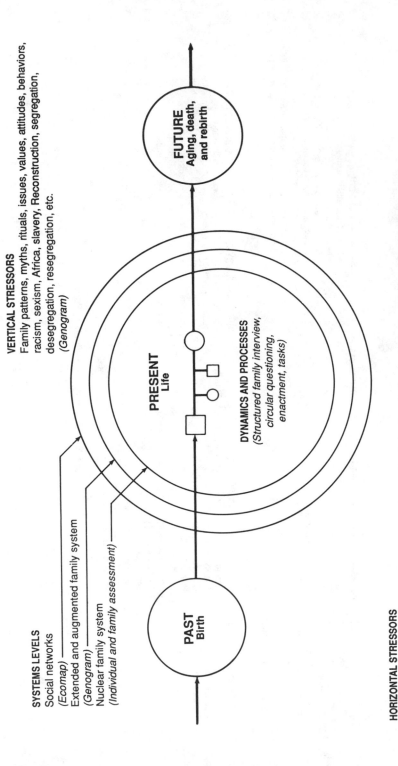

SYSTEMS LEVELS
Social networks
(Ecomap)
Extended and augmented family system
(Genogram)
Nuclear family system
(Individual and family assessment)

VERTICAL STRESSORS
Family patterns, myths, rituals, issues, values, attitudes, behaviors, racism, sexism, Africa, slavery, Reconstruction, segregation, desegregation, resegregation, etc.
(Genogram)

PAST
Birth

PRESENT
Life

DYNAMICS AND PROCESSES
(Structured family interview, circular questioning, enactment, tasks)

FUTURE
Aging, death, and rebirth

HORIZONTAL STRESSORS
Life cycle transitions, war, the economy, education, polity, lack of nurturing, early death, acute and chronic illness, etc.
(Time line)

Figure 5.3. Social-Emotional "Map" for Assessing Black Families (Diagram based on E. Carter and M. McGoldrick's (1980) depiction of horizontal and vertical stressors in the family.)

crucial area of family functioning. This domain not only provides some indication of the family's ability to maintain a balance between inner needs and outer
demands, but also is concerned with the family's attitude about and approach to
physical health.

The economic (housing and vocation) domain explores living arrangements
and financial pressures on the family. This domain looks at how satisfied the
family is with the physical setting of home and neighborhood, their values and
attitudes concerning their financial status, and how they choose to and would
like to use their income. Does the family externalize its social status through
material possessions or through some other form? Are needs prioritized in terms
of material possessions or in terms of major life necessities? To what extent
does economic discrimination or lack of opportunity affect the family's achievement orientation?

Complementing the continuum of functioning, the social-emotional map
(Figure 5.3) incorporates various aspects of the person-in-situation paradigm
(Figure 5.2). This "map" illustrates the influence of the vertical and horizontal
flow of black family dynamics. The vertical flow is transmitted across generations through a positive oral tradition as well as through emotional triangling
(Bowen, 1978). This flow includes values, attitudes, behaviors, racism, sexism,
slavery, segregation, African heritage, and other issues that have an impact on
the family's overall level of growth and development. The horizontal flow
includes a range of influences that create either supports for or stressors on the
family as it moves through space and time coping with the problems and needs
in the family life cycle. This flow includes predictable as well as unpredictable
life cycle events. Carter and McGoldrick (1980) point out that the emphasis of
this social-emotional map is at the intersection between the vertical flow of
family life and the horizontal flow of the various movements and transitions:

> The degree of anxiety engendered by the stress on the vertical and horizontal
> axes at the points where they converge is the key determinant of how well the
> family will manage its transitions through life. *It is imperative, therefore, for
> the family (worker) to assess not only the dimensions of the current life cycle
> stress, but also its connections to family themes, triangles and labels coming
> down in the family over historical time.* (Carter, 1978; quoted in Carter &
> McGoldrick, 1980, emphasis added.)

With black families, this historical overlay is further compounded by resi-
dues of slavery, racism, desegregation, and the like. Frequently, the interfacing
of this historical overlay with general life cycle events is the cause of a great
deal of family disequilibrium. To illustrate this, the case of Bob and Marva
Stillman, discussed earlier in this chapter, is useful:

> Bob and Marva married at a young age due to Marva's pregnancy *(life cycle
> event—horizontal flow).* Bob was reared in a large close-knit family where roles
> were clearly though rigidly defined. The father assumed only instrumental roles, the
> mother only expressive roles. Marva was reared in a small, loose-knit family where
> roles were unclear and everyone did mostly what they pleased. Bob had specific

ideas about the role of a wife and mother. Further, his expectations were that Marva should manage their household the way his mother did *(family patterns—vertical flow)*.

This case example reflects stressors that any young couple with similar life cycle issues would experience. However, the Stillmans' life experiences are uniquely tinged by their being black in a race-conscious society. Bob grew up in the south in a completely segregated environment. He remembers riding at the back of public buses, using separate facilities, and experiencing other indignities of living in a racist society *(racism—vertical flow)*. Despite the day-to-day interaction with whites on his job, there is still a feeling of mistrust. Marva, on the other hand, grew up in the north and experiences her white colleagues more amicably. She visits their homes and attends social affairs when invited. Bob refuses to accompany her on these occasions, but Marva insists on attending alone. Bob does not believe that a wife should attend social events unescorted *(life cycle—horizontal flow)*.

Essentially, the stress of becoming young parents to an unplanned baby was exacerbated by the unrealistic expectations they brought into their marriage about what are acceptable role responsibilities for a husband, wife, and parent. The impacts of intergenerational and historical influences were also precipitating factors.

In recognition of the complexity involved in understanding and viewing human behavior (such as that described in the Stillmans' case) as a product of the transition between the individual and the environment, the person-in-situation paradigm, the types of black family structures, the social-emotional map, and the following questions are being suggested as guides to assist the practitioner in the assessment process:

1. *The Person:* What specific life cycle tasks does each child and adult in the family face, and to what extent does the black experience influence the meaning assigned to these tasks? How well are the tasks being negotiated? Are any developmental difficulties interfering with task accomplishment? How is the accomplishment of life tasks influenced by ego capacities, coping mechanisms, personality characteristics, quality of self-image, and family patterns in coping with racial identity and cross-cultural contacts?

2. *The Environment:* What resources are available? What are the quality and type of social networks? What has been the quality and nature of the opportunity structure for black families? What is the nature and quality of the physical environment? What and where are environmental stresses, demands, rewards, values, mores, and attitudes, and how are they viewed by the resident families?

3. *The Family:* What are the specific life cycle tasks of the family, and how are these influenced by social and cultural factors? What is the nature of the parents' life cycle needs, personalities, and spousal or partner relationships? What are the nature and quality of parent-child relationships? Who has the power in this family? How does the family view its ways of being in and of the

world, its feelings of wholeness, connectedness, and openness to the concept of a universal consciousness or a supreme being? How does the family deal with separation and loss, and with individuation? What is the nature of family communication, roles, interpersonal relationships, and coping strategies, including those related to the black experience? Are there significant problems or conflicts in child-parent relationships? What are the nature and quality of sibling and extrafamilial relationships?

IMPLICATIONS FOR TREATMENT

If family intervention is indicated, treatment usually begins with the individual. In part, this has a lot to do with many black families' orientation toward interpersonal helping. There is a general belief among many blacks that the family is nobody else's business and that problems should be resolved within the family (Gary et al., 1983; Logan, 1980). In addition, many established service agencies are predominantly if not exclusively staffed and administered by non-black employees, which often gives the black client the impression that the agency is not interested in providing services to a black clientele (Logan, 1980). If blacks seek help outside of the family, the clergy are likely to be the primary source (Gary et al., 1983; Logan, 1980). Regardless of families' orientation to the service-delivery system, the manner in which the practitioner defines his or her intervention strategies is critical.

Using the person-in-situation paradigm to frame the assessment, practitioners must acknowledge the numerous situations in which individually oriented concerns give the impression that the problem is solely of an emotional nature. It may become clear, however, that the problem reflects interpersonal difficulties or a lack of fit between the needs of the individual and social resources. Regarding intervention, the critical point here is twofold. (1) The point of entry into the family system is varied and must be decided with skill and caution and (2) the practitioner can adopt a family-oriented stance and conceptualize the individual needs and problems in the context of the family and cultural dynamics, even if treatment can be sustained only with the individual instead of the entire family.

Given that problems and needs within the family may present either as an individual concern or as a concern among the person, family, and the environment, the treatment plan must include the following:

1. *Enhancement of individual growth and development.* Individual growth and development may be enhanced within a family context, but it is not always feasible or preferable to treat an individual concern with the entire family present. As an example, take the case of Donna.

Donna, a 14-year-old black teenager, was experiencing adjustment problems. Her mother had recently married her natural father and the entire family had moved to a new location. Donna resents both her father, who in the past had not assumed a parenting role with her, and the move away from her friends and extended family. Although very bright, Donna has a low self-image and self-esteem. She feels lonely and isolated in her new school and was making veiled suicidal gestures. Although the entire family was seen in the assessment, it was agreed that Donna should be seen alone. Contacts were to be continued with the mother, the father (who was adamant about not joining the treatment process), and Donna, as treatment indicated.

This situation, along with other types of interpersonal problems, dictates an individually oriented approach, which may be indicated when there are individuals who are struggling with issues of sexuality, self-identity, racial identity, self-esteem, and school- and job-related concerns.

2. *Increase differentiation among family members by enabling more growth-enhancing marital, parent-child, and family transactions.* Differentiation within the family may be enhanced by stimulating the family members to become involved in examining cross-generational issues, their thoughts, their feelings, and their experiences of being black in a race-conscious society. Differentiation may also be enhanced by encouraging the family to be explicit about family beliefs, rituals, rules for interaction, and acceptance of individual uniqueness. Boundary maintenance also allows for family differentiation—for example, in many families the members do not really recognize each other's boundaries. Through modeling, however, families can be helped to strengthen boundaries and to discover and correct such maladaptive and debilitating transactional patterns as over-protectiveness, authoritativeness, positivity, constriction, and passivity.

3. *Promote clear self-identity, self-esteem, mastery, and competence in the individual and the family.* Feeling good about self and others is intimately linked to mastery, competence building, and being able to make an impact on the environment in significant ways (White, 1959). Making an impact on the environment requires not only an action-oriented stance on the part of the practitioner but also the family's willingness to risk and challenge non-nurturing systems. These non-nurturing systems may include neighborhood schools, the extended family, the work environment, and social service agencies.

4. *Enhancing the fit among individuals, families, and the social environment by helping the family to cope effectively with the impact of racism and oppression in their daily lives, as well as by influencing external systems to be more responsive to identified needs.* This focus can be readily illustrated in the school context. Consider the case of Theo:

Theo is in junior high. He has twin sisters who are 5 years old. His parents have been divorced since he was 8. The family still resides in the predominantly white neighborhood where they lived prior to the divorce. Susan, Theo's mother, is in a training program and receives AFDC. Her ex-husband sends child support sporadically. Susan detests being dependent on public assistance, especially the stigma she feels during those periods when recertification is necessary. The school is aware of the family's involvement with public assistance, and Susan believes the school treats Theo differently because of their welfare dependency and because he is a black student in a predominantly white school.

Theo has been described as very bright and has always made good grades. This is his last semester in junior high; his grades are beginning to fall and he has become lethargic about school and life in general. Upon closer scrutiny, it was revealed that Theo has been getting discouraging signals from his teachers and the guidance counselors about his dreams of wanting to go on to college and become a doctor. He was told that it may be better for him to think more about a trade school or a junior college.

This situation requires not only an understanding of the public welfare system and its devastating impact on family lives, but also an understanding of the school system and its varied levels of response (see Chapter 7). With such understanding, a practitioner could more effectively help families negotiate the boundaries of public agencies better and engage school personnel creatively and collaboratively in motivating children's learning and growth.

CONCLUSIONS

Assessing the structure and functioning of black families by conceptualizing family structure and functioning as on a continuum allows the social worker to view and assess black families as growing, changing, and open systems. It also mitigates biases and stereotypical beliefs about past and present interactional patterns of black families. This new way of thinking about black families can move the practitioner and the educator beyond the illness perspective and provide a framework for both understanding and utilizing specific tools in assessing needs and problems of black families.

The major conceptual tool is the Social-Emotional Map for Assessing Black Families, which serves as the umbrella for two additional conceptual tools: an expanded version of the person-in-person paradigm, and the depiction of three types of family structures described along six life domains. The proposed conceptual framework emphasizes the interface between the family and the environment. This focus dictates an ecological orientation concerned with the integration of the family's inner and outer environments. The ultimate aim is to help practitioners and educators achieve a balanced perspective in thinking about how black families function and in selecting creative intervention strategies that would build on family strengths.

REFERENCES

Beavers, R. (1976). A theoretical basis for family evaluation. In J.M. Lewis, R. Beavers, J.T. Gossett, & V.A. Phillips (Eds.), *No single thread: Psychological health in family systems* (pp. 46–82). New York: Brunner/Mazel.

Blassingame, J. (1972). *The slave community.* New York: Oxford University Press.

Biller, H.B. (1970). Father absence and the personality development of the male child. *Developmental Psychology, 2,* 181–201.

Billingsley, A. (1968). *Black families in white America.* Englewood Cliffs, NJ: Prentice Hall.

Billingsley, A. (1987). Black families in a changing society. In J. Dewart (Ed.), *The state of black America, 1977* (pp. 97–111). New York: National Urban League.

Bowen, M. (1978). *Family therapy in clinical practice.* New York: Aronson.

Carter, E.A. (1978). Transgenerational scripts and nuclear family stress: Theory and clinical implications. In R.R. Sagar (Ed.), *Georgetown family symposia,* vol. 3, 1975–76. Washington, DC: Georgetown University.

Carter, E., & McGoldrick, M. (Eds.). (1980). *The family life cycle: A framework for family therapy.* New York: Gardner.

Clark, K. (1965). *Dark ghetto.* New York: Harper & Row.

Foley, V.D. (1984). Family therapy. In R.J. Corsini (Ed.), *Current psychotherapies* (pp. 447–490). Itasca, IL: Peacock.

Fogel, R.W., & Engerman, S.L. (1974). *Time on the cross.* Boston: Little, Brown.

Frazier, E.F. (1937). Negro Harlem: An ecological study. *American Journal of Sociology, 43*(July), 72–88.

Frazier, E.F. (1957). *The Negro in the United States* (rev. ed.). New York: Macmillan.

Gary, L.E., Beatty, L.A., Berry, G.L., & Price, M.D. (1983). Stable black families: Final report, Mental Health Research and Development Center, Institute for Urban Affairs and Research. Washington, DC: Howard University Press.

Geismar, L.L. (1973). *555 families: A social-psychological study of young families in transition.* New Brunswick, NJ: Transaction Books.

Genovese, E. (1974). *Roll, Jordon, roll.* New York: Pantheon.

Glasser, P.H., & Glasser, L.N. (Eds.). (1970). *Families in crisis.* New York: Harper & Row.

Goldenberg, I., & Goldenberg, H. (1980). *Family therapy: An overview.* Monterey, CA: Brooks/Cole.

Guthrie, R.V. (1976). *Even the rat was white.* New York: Harper & Row.

Gutman, H. (1976). *The black family in slavery and freedom, 1750–1925.* New York: Pantheon.

Harrison, B. (1982). *Education, training, and the urban ghetto.* Baltimore, MD: Johns Hopkins University Press.

Hetherington, E.M. (1965). A developmental study of the dominant parent on sex-role preference, identification, and imitation in children. *Journal of Personality and Social Psychology, 2,* 188.

Hetherington, E.M. (1972). Effects of father abuse on personality development in adolescent daughters. *Developmental Psychology, 7,* 313–326.

Herskovits, M.J. (1941). *The myth of the Negro past.* Boston: Beacon Press.

Hill, R.B. (1972). *Strengths of black families.* New York: Emerson Hall.

Hill, R.B. (1987). Building a future for black families. *American Visions, 2*(6), 161–25.

Huston, A.C. (1983). Sex-typing. In P.H. Mussen (Ed.), *Handbook on child psychology* (4th ed.), and E.M. Hetherington (vol. ed.), *Socialization, personality, and social development,* vol. 4 (pp. 388–467). New York: Wiley.

Jones, R.S. (1973). Proving blacks inferior: The sociology of knowledge. In J.A. Ladner (Ed.), *Death of white sociology* (pp. 28–33). New York: Random House.

Kamin, L.J. (1974). *The science and politics of I.Q.* Potomac, MD: Earlbaum.

Lidz, T., Fleck, S., & Cornelison, A.R. (1965). *Schizophrenia and the family.* New York: International University Press.

Levy, R. (1982). *The new language of psychiatry: Learning and using DSM-III.* Boston: Little, Brown.

Logan, S. (1980). The black Baptist church: A social-psychological study in coping and growth. *Dissertation Abstracts International,* 41/06A.

Logan, S. (1987). An ecological perspective on social work practice with single parent families. Unpublished manuscript, University of Kansas, School of Social Welfare.

Logan, S. (1988). The black church and self-actualization: Implication for social work practice. Unpublished manuscript, University of Kansas, School of Social Welfare.

Logan, S., Freeman, E., & McRoy, R. (1986). *A comprehensive ecological approach to pregnant teenagers, their partners, and their families.* Paper presented at the National Association of Social Workers National Conference on Clinical Social Work, San Francisco, California.

Loury, G.C. (1986). The black family: A critical challenge. *Journal of Family and Culture,* 1–15.

Malouf, R.F. (1979). *Social basis of power in single and two-parent families.* Paper presented at the annual meeting of the Western Psychological Association, San Diego, California.

McAdoo, H. P. (1977, December). *The impact of extended family variables upon the upward mobility of black families.* Final report, submitted to the Department of Health, Education, and Welfare, Office of Child Development, Contract No. 90-C-631(1).

Minuchin, S. (1974). *Families and family therapy.* Cambridge, MA: Harvard University Press.

Moynihan, D.P. (1965). *The Negro family: The case for national action.* Washington, DC: Government Printing Office (prepared for Office of Policy, Planning, and Research of the Department of Labor).

Moore, K.A., Simms, M., & Betsey, C. (1986). *Choice and circumstance: Race differences in adolescent sexuality and fertility.* New Brunswick, NJ: Transaction Books.

Morris, R.B. (1977). Strengths of the black community: An investigation of the black community broken homes. *Dissertation Abstracts International,* 38/04.

Murray, C. (1984). *Losing ground: American social policy, 1950–1980.* New York: Basic Books.

Newly, I.A. (1965). *Jim Crow's defense: Anti-Negro thought in America, 1900–1930.* Baton Rouge, LA: Louisiana State University Press.

Olim, E.G., Hess, R.D., & Shipman, V.C. (1967). Role of mothers' language styles in mediating their preschool children's cognitive development. *School Review, 75,* 414–424.

Park, R.E. (1936). Human ecology. *American Journal of Sociology, 42,* 1–15.

Pinderhughes, E.B. (1982). Family functioning in Afro-Americans. *Social Work, 27*(1), 91–96.

Proshansky, H., & Newton, M. (1968). The nature and meaning of Negro self-identity. In M. Deutsch, I. Katz, & A.R. Jensen (Eds.), *Social class, race, and psychological development* (pp. 178–218). New York: Holt, Rinehart, and Winston.

Rainwater, L. (1970). *Behind the ghetto walls: Black families in a federal slum.* Chicago: Aldine.

Savage, J.E., Adair, A.V., & Friedman, P. (1978). Community-social variables related to black parent-absent families. *Journal of Marriage and the Family, 40*(4), 779–785.

Scanzoni, J.H. (1971). *The black family in modern society.* Boston: Allyn and Bacon.

Schultz, D.A. (1969). *Coming up black: Patterns and ghetto socialization.* Englewood Cliffs, NJ: Prentice Hall.

Stack, C.B. (1974). *All our kin.* New York: Harper & Row.

Thompson, C.L. (1978). Perceptions of intrafamilial relationships in single parent lower-class families of male adolescent antisocial behavior. *Dissertation Abstracts International, 39*/04B, p. 1972.

Toffler, A., & Toffler, H. (1981, March 22). The changing American family: Welcome to the "electronic college." *Family Weekly,* 9–13.

Whitaker, C.A., & Keith, D.V. (1981). Symbolic-experiential family therapy. In A.S. Gurman & D.P. Kniskern (Eds.), *Handbook of family therapy* (pp. 187–225). New York: Brunner/Mazel.

White, R.W. (1959). Motivation reconsidered: The concept of competence. *Psychological Review, 66,* 297–333.

Whiteman, M., and Deutsch, M. (1968). Social disadvantages as related to intellectual and language development. In M. Deutsch, I. Katz, & A.R. Jensen (Eds.), *Social class, race, and psychological development* (pp. 86–114). New York: Holt, Rinehart, and Winston.

CHAPTER 6

Cultural and Racial Identity in Black Families

Ruth G. McRoy
University of Texas at Austin

Much of the research literature on identity formation has failed to consider the significance of ethnicity as a comparable component of overall identity among minority group members (Hauser, 1971; Phinney & Alipuria, 1987). Invisible bonds, stemming from historical identification with others of similar characteristics, link ethnic group members and separate them externally from others. Ethnic group membership becomes more salient in cases in which members and nonmembers can be easily distinguished as a result of physical characteristics or language. Moreover, a minority group member's world view is influenced by his or her identification with significant others within a cultural context (Rosenthal, 1987).

Thus, the influence of racial and cultural factors must be considered in any assessment of black families. Racial self-identity has been responsible for the survival of the black race in a discriminating society. In a nonhostile, nonracist environment, membership in a minority group would perhaps be less significant, but the type of categorical treatment that minority group members have received in this society makes it mandatory to consider how this social status affects their overall identity.

This chapter provides an overview of familial, social, psychological, and contextual factors that influence the development of individual and group identity among black children and adults in the United States, theories of how racial group identity develops are presented, and strategies to help social workers assess racial and cultural identity and determine appropriate counseling approaches are included.

RACIAL GROUP IDENTITY

The concept of racial group identity refers to one's self-perception and sense of belonging to a particular racial group. This perception includes not only how one describes and defines oneself, but also how one distinguishes oneself from members of other ethnic groups and the extent to which an individual has acquired behaviors specific to the particular racial group.

Blacks in the United States are considered to have a caste-like status, because their ancestors were brought to this country involuntarily and permanently incorporated into an existing social system (Ogbu, 1983). For American blacks, the term "racial group identity" is difficult to define. It is a feeling or attitude that goes beyond a specific racial classification—it encompasses a shared history of struggles and personal and cultural adaptations, including folkways, music, speech patterns, religion, and kinship bonds. These and many other cultural nuances are as significant as the physical attributes that are used to connote black racial heritage ("What Makes You Black," 1983).

There is no such thing as a genetically pure race, but there has been a historical, sociological, and psychological tendency to emphasize the domination of African heritage in the roots of blacks, even though blacks actually have a multicultural heritage (Spurlock, 1986). In the United States, persons who have only one black parent are still generally viewed by society as being black.

BLACK SELF-REJECTION HYPOTHESIS

According to Powell (1983), being white in a white society has little to do with self-concept development, but being black in a white society is crucial to the self-concept. Much of the pre-1960s literature emphasized the self-hate and self-rejection behavior of black children and suggested that black children had poor self-concepts because they belonged to a racial group that was perceived negatively in American society.

More recent research suggest that blacks, especially black schoolchildren, have relatively high levels of self-esteem (Cross, 1978; McRoy & Zurcher, 1983; Rosenberg & Simmons, 1971; Simmons, 1978). Some have attributed this change to the black pride movement of the late 1960s, to reinterpretations of the theories associated with self-concept development, and to differences in research methodologies.

The phenomenon of black self-hate developed as an attempt to duplicate earlier studies concerning Jewish minorities. Sarnoff (1951) reviewed and discussed the relationship between Anna Freud's (1946) theory of identification with the aggressor and Jewish anti-Semitism. Kurt Lewin (1948) presented one of the most influential early statements of this position in his paper "Self-Hatred Among Jews." He argued that a Jewish person "dislikes or hates his own group because it is nothing but a burden to him. . . . he will show dislike for those

Jews who are outspokenly so and will frequently indulge in self-hatred" (p. 164). Assuming that the position of blacks in America was similar to that of Jews, many researchers become convinced that the black who felt disdain or hatred for his own racial group expresses disdain and hatred for himself at some level. Thus, the black self-concept was assumed to be the consequence of the experiences of blacks in America (Nobles, 1973). Accordingly, although it was not empirically confirmed, scientists began assuming that there was a perfect correlation between reference group orientation and self-concept.

In 1979, Rosenberg challenged the theoretical assumption that group rejection results in self-rejection. He found that the self-esteem of black respondents whose racial attachment is relatively weak differs little from the self-esteem of those with strong race identification and pride. Thus, according to his data, not only are group self-hatred and individual self-hatred not identical, but the association is extremely weak.

An alternative theoretical justification for the black self-hate hypothesis has been based on the reference group theories of Mead, Cooley, Sullivan, and others. Many early researchers took for granted that the dominant white majority comprised the "significant others" whose values and reflected appraisals determined the self-regard and other aspects of self-concept in racial-ethnic groups (Wylie, 1979). However, the black child's significant others are to be found in the family and in the black community, not in the larger society of which his community is a part. Self-evaluations occur largely within a comparative or relativistic framework and grow out of the child's experiences in the immediate community (Taylor, 1976).

A third theoretical issue emerging from a review of the literature on black self-concept pertains to the possible impact of contextual dissonance on three aspects of the self-concept: self-esteem, stability of the self-concept, and group identification. Contextual dissonance refers to the discrepancy between the individual's social characteristics and those of the population by which he is surrounded (Rosenberg, 1977). This concept is of particular importance in understanding the findings of studies of the self-concept of black children in desegregated schools. For example, Rosenberg (1975) stated that one reason black children in predominantly white schools appear to have lower self-esteem, contrary to expectations, is that the desegregated school is a dissonant context. He also found that the more racially dissonant the black child's environment, the greater the likelihood that he or she had been teased, excluded, or called names because of race.

In addition to the dissonant communications which black children experience in desegregated schools, Rosenberg believes that the black child's self-esteem may be affected also by a dissonant comparison reference group. There is some evidence that low achievers in schools where the average performance is low have higher self-esteem than equally low achievers in high-performing schools. Thus, self-assessment is based upon the performance of the comparison reference group as well as on one's own performance. In situations in which the individual compares unfavorably with those of the dissonant context, self-esteem is likely to suffer (Rosenberg, 1977).

DEVELOPMENT OF RACIAL IDENTITY
IN CHILDREN AND ADOLESCENTS

The developing black child's self-perception is influenced by the behavior of others toward the child, on the conscious teachings of others, and on the child's observations of others' behaviors. His experiences as a black child and his comparisons of himself to others influence his evaluation of himself as a black person (Powell, 1983).

The Early Years

Black children develop an early awareness of ethnic differences. In early and middle childhood they choose peers not only based on ethnicity but also according to similarity in interests and the like. With age, however, there tends to be an increase in preference for members of one's own ethnic group. Aboud (1977), Goodman (1964), Katz (1976), and Porter (1971) have developed age-related models that suggest that children become aware of racial differences at age 3 or 4 and begin engaging in social comparisons; between 5 and 7 they are aware of their group affiliation; and between 8 and 10 they become curious about other groups. Some will choose to have a very strong racial group orientation, others will take a more pluralistic world view and take on the characteristics and beliefs of the majority group (Phinney & Alipuria, 1987).

Racial identity is acquired and maintained through interaction with significant others as well as with generalized others. Children learn about racial identity gradually. Morland (1972) found that preschool children respond differently to the colors white and black. White tends to be positively evaluated, black negatively evaluated; good things are associated with white, and bad things with black. Children are taught early to be receptive to messages regarding light and dark colors long before they evaluate the black-white symbolism racially (Williams & Morland, 1976).

By the age of 3, children are conscious of the differences between themselves and others (McRoy & Zurcher, 1983; Mussen et al., 1969; Proshansky, 1965). They are able to distinguish between skin color and hair texture and often pick up value-laden messages from playmates and significant others. For example, they often hear the words "good hair" associated with straight hair and "bad hair" associated with very curly hair (Allen, 1976).

Between the age of 3 and 7 the child becomes increasingly aware of racial differences and learns from many sources the labels and emotional responses associated with various ethnic groups, including his or her own ethnic group. Thus, racial identity formation in children involves two important steps: the child learns to make racial distinctions at a conceptual level, and then the child evaluates his or her own membership in a racial group (McRoy & Freeman, 1986). White children learn that they are members of a favored racial group and view their group membership positively (Williams & Morland, 1976), but black children quickly calculate the social mathematics of being black in a society in which their race is considered second-rate.

The child's attitudes toward his or her racial identity are influenced by the attitudes and behaviors of significant others. If the child is in a home in which the family is preoccupied with racial classifications, he or she learns to view race as being very significant. Lack of communication about race, or nonverbal cues that covertly communicate parental feelings about persons of different races, may suggest to the child that expressing feelings about race is not appropriate and that it is best to pretend that they do not exist. This denial or race-neutral emphasis tends to unduly burden the child as he or she enters a world of interracial relationships (Spencer et al., 1985; Williams & Morland, 1976). However, either extreme preoccupation with race or neglect of the subject may cause the child anxiety and possibly a preoccupation with feelings about the danger of being black. Black parents have an extra socialization task that white parents do not have. They have to help prepare their children for a bicultural existence in both a black world as represented by their home and family and a white world as represented by their school and work (Comer & Poussaint, 1975).

School-Age Children

The elementary school years are characterized by cognitive, psychological, and social growth. At this stage, children understand the concept of race and incorporate attitudes about their race and that of others into their personality (Comer & Poussaint, 1975). Experiences within the school setting can have a significant impact on a child's racial identity perceptions. The child may be exposed to elements of prejudice, but most are able to adjust and ward off threats to self-esteem. If parents and other significant others (teachers, clergy, neighbors) have taught the child to be secure with, comfortable, and proud of his or her blackness, they have provided a buffer for the negative messages the child might receive from wider society (Harrison, 1985; Harrison-Ross & Wyden, 1973).

Moreover, the black child's perceptions are generally filtered through a black frame of reference, and negative evaluations are resisted. According to Rosenberg and Simmons (1971), "blacks probably evaluate themselves relative to one another and relative to whites. Their own racial subgroup is probably their 'comparison reference group' serving individuals as their standard or checkpoint for self-evaluations" (p. 47). Thus, blacks may admire the appearance of whites and judge the attractiveness of other blacks to the degree that they approximate this model, but it is unlikely that they compare their own looks with that of whites (Cross, 1979).

Some studies (Davis et al., 1941; Johnson, 1941; Warner et al., 1978) have suggested that children with darker skin and children who have fewer "white" characteristics are likely to view themselves more negatively than those who are more "white-like," but this may not necessarily be the case. Rosenberg and Simmons (1971) found that darker-complexioned children may have levels of self-esteem that are just as high as those of lighter children.

During adolescence, youth begin to ask "Who am I?" and "Where do I belong?" The sexual, religious, and racial issues reappear for reexamination and new understanding. Cultural background influences one's striving to achieve a strong and stable sense of self. Black youth find themselves testing their social reality as they search for continuity and an integrated self (Erikson, 1968). The typically stormy years for adolescents in general may be intensified in black youth if they must also cope with experiences of overt exclusion. The high rates of unemployment and high school dropouts suggest that black teens are over-represented in exclusionary processes (Spurlock, 1986).

Adolescence

In adolescence, ideas and perceptions are often shaped by peers. Youth often begin to identify with a sense of "peoplehood" and "blackness" and to question the relevancy of using the white norm for self-measurement. In cases in which the black adolescent is rejected by white peers on the basis of racial background or is unable to discuss racial identity with peers or parents, this transition period can become even more difficult (Logan, 1981; McRoy & Freeman, 1986).

Many black children who have grown up isolated from other blacks experience difficult identity problems. They may experience a sense of marginality in which they do not feel they belong to either the black group or the white group and an uncertainty about appropriate behaviors and attitudes (Rosenthal, 1987). They may be confronted by blacks as being "different," as "oreos," or as "acting white." Some may challenge their parents for having isolated them. Others may want so much to be accepted and to identify racially that they change their style of dress, music, and speech to exhibit a new level of black awareness. Others experience such racial identity confusions that they become pimps, prostitutes, and drug addicts in an effort to identify with societal stereotypes about being black.

Some who have grown up in all-white communities, in families in which black identity was devalued, or who were raised as a "racial nonperson" may now find that they are unable to relate to other blacks. For example, mixed-race adolescents sometimes find that they are not accepted by either whites or blacks as potential dating partners. Some blacks, having grown up isolated from whites, may have developed extreme antiwhite attitudes and find themselves blaming whites for all the problems they (blacks) might experience (Comer & Poussaint, 1975).

A recent study by Phinney and Alipuria (1987) showed that, in contrast to white youth, blacks go through an exploratory process as they arrive at their racial group orientation. They are exposed both to their own culture and to the majority white culture, and they become aware of how the majority culture responds to them based upon their physical characteristics.

ADULT IDENTITY DEVELOPMENT

One's racial identity can be considered a part of the self-concept derived from membership in a particular racial group and influenced by the value and emotional significance one attaches to it (Aboud, 1987; Tajfel, 1978). According to Block (1973), a mature racial identity involves a twofold process: having a realistic identification of one's racial self, and having a secure racial identification, in which one accepts one's racial group and perhaps has a preference for one's own, but yet feels comfortable in adopting attributes, values, and so on, associated with another group (Aboud, 1987; Block, 1973).

Several models of adult minority identity development, similar to those racial identity models for children, have been proposed (see Table 6.1). Each model suggests a fluid development continuum reflecting experiences with members of their own group and the dominant group. Atkinson and colleagues (1983) suggested a five-stage minority identity development model (MID) to help counselors understand minority client attitudes. The first stage, Conformity, suggests that the individual follows the dominant group for his or her choice of role models, life-styles, and the like. If these individuals acknowledge their distinguishing cultural characteristics, they often view them with shame and view other members of their minority group and members of other minority groups according to the dominant society's perceptions. In the Dissonance stage the minority group member begins to question the attitudes and beliefs held in the conformity stage. A growing sense of loyalty to other oppressed people begins, and dominant members of the society are viewed with suspicion.

The third stage, Resistance and Immersion, occurs as the minority person expresses pride in his or her own history and culture and rejects the dominant society and culture. Personal problems are generally viewed as a product of

TABLE 6.1. ADULT RACIAL IDENTITY MODELS

Atkinson, Morten & Sue (1983)	Cross (1987)	Bell & Evans (1981)
		Traditional (neither accepts nor rejects black identity)
Conformity	Pre-encounter (views world as nonblack)	Acculturated (rejects black identity)
Dissonance (conflict)	Encounter (rethinks original beliefs about self and other blacks)	
Resistance and immersion	Immersion (responds to encounter by immersion in black experience)	Culturally immersed
Introspection	Internalization (more balanced basis for interactions with blacks and whites)	
Synergetic articulation and awareness	Internalization–commitment (conflicts resolved, new pluralistic perspectives)	Bicultural (relates to blacks and whites both)

oppression. In the fourth, Introspection, stage, individuals are beginning to engage in self-exploration and are often in conflict with their desire to gain individual autonomy. Self-fulfillment in cultural identity occurs in the Synergetic Articulation and Awareness stage. The individuals feel good about themselves, their minority group, and other minority groups and selectively like and trust members of the dominant group. The authors of this model suggest that these stages are process-oriented and do not represent any preferred hierarchy of development (see Atkinson et al., 1983).

Cross (1987) has suggested that ethnic identity development involves a conversion experience from being "Negro to being Black." This process, which he terms "Nigrescence" (meaning "to become black"), is the process of transformation from pre-encounter self to post-encounter self. In the Pre-encounter stage, a person is programmed to view the world as being nonblack or anti-black. One's self-view is dominated by white society. During the Pre-encounter stage, a person's ethnic identity is at a very immature level. The ideological, emotional, and philosophical meaning of their identity is unclear. Some educators believe that this is characteristic of preschool or early elementary school children (Gay, 1985). Others believe that this stage could occur at later phases of development or during adulthood and that it is reflective of the identity change experienced by black adults in the late 1960s (Cross, 1987).

The second stage, Encounter, usually involves a negative experience or event that shakes the original view and makes the person more vulnerable to a new interpretation of his or her ethnic self. The person moves from a position of ethnic innocence toward rethinking his or her beliefs about his or her relationship to white society. This encounter could have been a visual event (e.g., observing news tapes of the riots of the 1960s or the assassination of Dr. Martin Luther King, Jr.) or a personal experience (e.g., being overtly discriminated against or being the target for racial slurs).

Individuals respond to the encounter by generally immersing themselves in the world of blackness (Cross, 1987). In this Immersion stage, the individual experiences exaggerated ethnocentrism and may vacillate between feelings of rage and depression, and power and helplessness. The person may become totally absorbed in ethnic literature, adopt an African name, travel to Africa, and prefer to wear African clothing. He may tend to denigrate white culture and deify black culture. During the latter part of this phase, the individual begins to become clearer about black identity and gains greater personal control.

In the fourth stage, Internalization, black individuals acquire a more realistic perception of the value of their culture and achieve a feeling of inner security. These self-concept modifications allow them to see value in other cultures. Although blacks are still the primary reference group, the individuals can begin to reach out to whites as well.

In the final stage, Internalization–Commitment, the individual solidifies his identity and is committed to helping others deal with the disabling effects of racism on minority individuals. This "ideal" person attempts to go beyond rhetoric and to translate personal activities that are meaningful to the masses of black people (Cross, 1971).

Cross' identity transformation process suggests that black individuals may move from feeling very little ethnic pride to feeling very self-assured about their ethnicity and their ability to acknowledge and appreciate the ethnicity of others. Because one's level of ethnic identity development influences one's world view, it is essential to take this into consideration in assessing the attitudes and behavior of blacks (Gay, 1985).

Bell and Evans (1981) suggested four categories of black interpersonal styles that are somewhat parallel to Cross' developmental model and that can be useful in assessing black clients' racial and cultural identity. According to Bell and Evans, these styles are fluid, and as a person may exhibit attitudes, behaviors, and personality traits associated with more than one category simultaneously, Bell and Evans suggest that these styles represent a continuum of racial identity.

The Acculturated interpersonal style is in many ways similar to Cross' Pre-encounter stage. These individuals have chosen to assimilate into the white mainstream culture totally and have rejected black identity as inferior to the dominant culture's norms. Being confronted with being black can be uncomfortable and unpleasant for them. This style becomes problematic only when the rejection of one's culture also means rejection of one's self, or self-hatred.

Persons having a Bicultural interpersonal style have a great deal of pride in their racial identity but also tend to seek out racial diversity. They are comfortable in both predominantly black and predominantly white settings and encounters. Generally they are middle class and live in integrated neighborhoods, and they may be involved in interracial friendships, business arrangements, dating, or marriage.

The Culturally Immersed interpersonal style is most like Cross' Internalization stage. This style is characterized by a rejection of white values, norms, and culture. The black frame of reference is paramount and the individual is distrustful of whites. Individuals at this stage are often inner-city residents from poverty backgrounds.

The Traditional interpersonal style includes persons who have limited contact outside the black community. They may be elderly or from poverty backgrounds. The traditional black family norms and values regarding the church and extended family characterize these individuals. Being black is an innate part of the person, so the person does not actively accept or reject his black identity.

The value that one places on his or her racial identity may vary among blacks. For some, identity as black is a necessary component of a positive self-image; for others, black identity may be viewed very negatively; for others it is seen as less salient or equally salient than such factors as occupation, educational level, and religious affiliation (Solomon, 1983).

An assessment of a person's perceptions of his or her own racial identity, and their perceptions of how blacks and whites view them, yields much useful information for work with black families. Each of the aforementioned styles could be prevalent in one black family and may influence members' attitudes, behaviors, and communication patterns within the family as well as with the professional. Therefore, in order to effectively serve black clients, their interpersonal styles must be assessed.

ASSESSING RACIAL AND CULTURAL IDENTITY

A number of factors must be considered in assessing racial and cultural identity to determine appropriate treatment approaches. These factors are also useful in assessing whether the client is experiencing conflict related to his or her membership in the black racial group.

Racial Self-Identification

The individual's self-identification can provide initial clues about racial identity. A person who identifies himself or herself as a Negro or colored should probably be categorized as having a "traditional" interpersonal style. If the client were to describe himself or herself as "Afro-American," it is likely that the client is "culturally immersed." However, further examination of the following characteristics would provide additional information to substantiate or alter the initial assessment.

Physical Appearance. The individual's phenotypic characteristics, such as coloring and physical features, are all important in assessing racial self-perceptions. The congruence or incongruence between his or her physical appearance and racial self-identification may suggest whether there may be issues related to racial identity. For example, a medium-brown-complexioned, curly-haired young black man who indicates that his racial identity is part white may actually have one white birth parent but may also be uncomfortable with acknowledging his visible black heritage. This may suggest to the worker that further exploration regarding the client's racial identity issues is needed. Skin colors among blacks may vary from dark brown to white, and hair may vary from very kinky to very straight. Similarly, eye color and shape of nose and mouth may vary. In family treatment situations, it is particularly important to consider how easily the client blends in with other members of the immediate and extended family. In many black families, intergenerational characteristics related to race may not be visible in all family members.

Race of Mother and Father. The race of a client's mother and father is important in assessing whether the client is the offspring of an interracial marriage or perhaps a transracial adoption. An individual raised in either environment is at greater risk for the development of racial identity problems.

Economic Status and Occupation of Profession. Families who are middle to upper class and who are in professional occupations may be more likely to be acculturated and to be accustomed to working with whites on a regular basis. Some of these clients may identify more with whites, may prefer a white counselor, and may respond readily to intrapsychic approaches to treatment. However, the social worker must be aware that despite the client's acculturated status, his or her experiences with prejudice and discrimination may affect the current presenting problem. Some black clients who are in this category and who work mostly in white settings are more prone to on-the-job stress. They may have planned both their social and their professional lives around their work setting in an effort to become closer to their image of the successful business person (Campbell, 1982); despite this some may not have received the same rewards.

Education. The client's educational level, as well as the racial composition of the client's elementary, secondary, and university settings, will provide valuable clues about his or her level of acculturation. Clients who have attended all-black or mostly black schools may tend to be much more culturally immersed.

Church Membership and Other Social Affiliations. Attending predominantly black churches and/or belonging to black social or community organizations usually indicates that the client has a support network of black friends and associates and may value his or her black racial group membership. If the person belongs to a predominantly white church or has no black affiliations, it is further evidence that he or she may have a very acculturated coping style.

Relationship with Extended Family. The frequency and quality of contacts and support that a black client has with extended family is critical in understanding the client's racial identity. Very geographically mobile acculturated blacks who have severed contacts with the black community may also have limited contacts with their family of origin and find themselves emotionally isolated. On the other hand, some blacks who live and work in predominantly white areas and who have maintained strong ties with family and friends in the black community have a source of support that the social worker can help them assess for coping with the current concerns.

Language. The degree of acculturation to white patterns influences the language characteristics of blacks. Some blacks may use Ebonics, Black English (Dillard, 1983), while others use mainstream American English exclusively. Ebonics is an oral communication system that consists of phonology, syntax, morphology, semantics, lexicon, rate, rhythm, stress, and nonverbal communication (Wofford, 1979). Many blacks are skilled in the use of both language patterns and vary their communication styles depending upon the situation. The client's communication style will provide additional clues to level of acculturation. Persons communicating in Ebonics may be identified as traditional or culturally immersed.

Life-Style Factors. The Racial composition of the community in which a family resides may provide valuable information as to sources of stress or support that may be relevant to the problem situation. Very acculturated individuals are likely to live in mostly white communities, bicultural individuals often live in mixed communities, and culturally immersed and traditional individuals are more likely to reside in predominantly black or all-black areas.

Experiences with Racism. The degree to which clients have been directly victimized by racism and oppression, and the meaning attached to these experiences, provide additional clues about the client's racial self-feelings. The worker should also explore the meaning the client attaches to his or her experiences as a black person in general (Pinderhughes, 1982).

The Worker's Level of Acculturation

The worker's experiences with racism may be equally important in the assessment process. It is often assumed that black therapists are automatically aware of the cultural diversity of blacks and that they can work with all black clients, but the level of acculturation of the black worker can have a negative impact on interaction with a lower class black client. Extremely acculturated black workers may have accepted traditional white perceptions of the behavior of blacks and may view black clients just as stereotypically as some white therapists (Dillard, 1983). The white worker's experiences can also affect the process. White workers who believe that race should not be considered as a factor in working with clients are denying a very significant part of the black client's reality. Whites who overemphasize the significance of race and blame society for all a black client's problems are also doing a disservice to the client.

Data Collection and Analysis

Data on racial identity can be gathered by direct observation, by analyzing responses to interview questions, by observing nonverbal behavior and the level of comfort when racial identity issues are discussed, and by noting the degree to which the client attributes the current situation to racial problems. The ecomap and genogram are useful assessment tools. The genogram, usually used to examine the nature of relationships within the family, communication patterns, significant family events, and role assignments, can be expanded to help the client explore the racial background of siblings and parents; family members' attitudes toward racial differences; how the client is labeled racially within the family; life-style factors, such as economic conditions; occupational choices, and causes of stress and patterns of coping with stress (Logan et al., 1987). The ecomap can also be used to assess the availability of role models and other environmental supports or barriers related to positive racial identity formation. Data gathered from these assessment frameworks will help the worker plan intervention (Logan et al., 1987).

CONCLUSIONS

Social workers should be aware that racial identity issues could be the source of cultural or emotional pain that may be masked by other problems within black families. The assessment of racial identity should (1) assess actual and potential sources of conflict in racial self-perceptions; (2) assess the extent to which the client's racial self-feeling is influencing his or her overall self-concept; (3) assess the types of cultural defense mechanisms and rationalizations that the individual may be using to reconcile racial identity dilemmas; and (4) identify sources of support that may facilitate an understanding of racial identity dilemmas and may remedy some of the cultural pain.

REFERENCES

Aboud, F. E. (1977). Interest in ethnic formation: A cross-cultural developmental study. *Canadian Journal of Behavioral Science, 9*, 134 146.

Aboud, F. E. (1984). Social and cognitive bases of ethnic identity constancy. *Journal of Genetic Psychology, 145*, 227–229.

Aboud, F. E. (1987). The development of ethnic self-identification and attitudes. In J. S. Pinney & M.J. Rotheram (Eds.), *Children's ethnic socialization: Pluralism and development* (pp. 32–55). Newbury Park, CA: Sage.

Allen, W. E. (1976). The formation of racial identity in black children adopted by white parents. Ph.D. dissertation, The Wright Institute, Los Angeles.

Atkinson, D. R., Morten, G., & Sue, D. W. (Eds.). (1983). *Counseling American minorities: A cross cultural perspective* (2nd ed.). Dubuque, IA: Wm. C. Brown.

Bell, P., and Evans, T. (1981). *Professional education, counseling the black client: Alcohol use and abuse in black America*. Center City, MN: Hazeldon.

Block, J. H. (1973). Conceptions of sex role: Some cross-cultural and longitudinal perspectives. *American Psychologist, 28*, 512–526.

Butler, R. O. (1976). Black children's racial preference: A selected review of the literature. *Journal of Afro-American Issues, 4*, 169–171.

Campbell, B. M. (1982, December 12). Black executives and corporate stress. *New York Times Magazine*, 36–39, 104–107.

Clark, K. B., & Clark, M. P. (1947). Racial identification and preference in Negro children. In T. M. Newcomb & E. L. Harley (Eds.), *Readings in social psychology* (pp. 169–178). New York: Holt, Rinehart, and Winston.

Comer, J. P., & Poussaint, A. F. (1975). *Black child care*. New York: Simon & Schuster.

Cross, W. E., Jr. (1971). The Negro to black conversion experience. *Black World, 20*, 13–27.

Cross, W. E., Jr. (1978). The Thomas and Cross model of psychological nigrescence: A review. *Journal of Black Psychology, 5*, 13–31.

Cross, W. E., Jr. (1979). *Black families and black identity development: Rediscovering the distinction between self-esteem and reference group orientation*. Unpublished paper presented at Cornell University, Ithaca, New York.

Cross, W. E., Jr. (1987). A two-factor theory of black identity: Implication for the study of identity development in minority children. In J. S. Phinney & M.J. Rotheram (Eds.), *Children's ethnic socialization* (pp. 117–133). Newbury Park, CA: Sage.

Davis, A., Gardner, B. B., & Gardner, M. R. (1941). *Deep south: A social anthropological study of caste and class*. Chicago: University of Chicago Press.

Dillard, J. M. (1983). *Multicultural counseling: Toward ethnic and cultural relevance in human encounters*. Chicago: Nelson-Hall.

Erikson, G. H. (1968). *Identity: Youth and crisis.* New York: Norton.

Freud, A. (1946). *The ego and the mechanisms of defense.* New York: International University Press.

Gay, G. (1985). Implications of selected models of ethnic identity development for educators. *Journal of Negro Education, 54,* 43–55.

Goodman, M. E. (1952). *Awareness in young children.* Reading, MA: Addison-Wesley.

Goodman, M. E. (1964). *Race awareness in young children* (rev. ed.). New York: Collier.

Harrison, A. O. (1985). The black family's socializing environment: Self-esteem and ethnic attitude among black children. In H.P. McAdoo & J.L. McAdoo (Eds.), *Black children: Social, educational, and parental environments* (pp. 174–193). Beverly Hills, CA: Sage.

Harrison-Ross, P., & Wyden, B. (1983). *The black child: A parent's guide.* New York: Wyden.

Hauser, S. (1971). *Black and white identity formation.* New York: Wiley.

Johnson, C. S. (1941). *Growing up in the black belt.* Washington, DC: American Council on Education.

Katz, P. A. (1976). The acquisition of racial attitudes in children. In P.A. Katz (Ed.), *Towards the elimination of racism.* New York: Pergamon.

Lewin, K. (1948). Self-hatred in Jews. In K. Lewin (Ed.), *Resolving social conflicts.* New York: Harper & Row.

Lewin, K. (Ed.). (1948). *Resolving social conflicts.* New York: Harper & Row.

Logan, S. L. (1981). Race, identity, and black children: A developmental perspective. *Social Casework, 62,* 47–56.

Logan, S. L., Freeman, E.M., & McRoy, R. G. (1987). Racial identity problems of bi-racial clients: Implications for social work practice. *Journal of Intergroup Relations, 15*(2), 11–24.

McRoy, R. G., & Freeman, E. (1986). Racial-identity issues among mixed race children. *Social Work in Education: A Journal for Social Workers in Schools, 8,* 164–174.

McRoy, R. G., & Zurcher, L. A. (1983). *Transracial and inracial adoptees: The adolescent years.* Springfield, IL: Thomas.

Morland, J. K. (1972). Racial attitudes in school children: From kindergarten through high school. Washington, DC: Department of Health, Education, and Welfare.

Mussen, P. H., Conger, J., & Kagan, J. (1969). *Child development and personality* (2nd ed.). New York: Harper & Row.

Nobles, W. W. (1973). Psychological research and the black self-concept: A critical review. *Journal of Social Issues, 29,* 11–31.

Ogbu, J. (1983). Crossing cultural boundaries: A comparative perspective on minority education. In *Race, class, socialization, and the life cycle.* Presentation at a symposium in honor of Allison Davis, John Deney Professor Emeritus, University of Chicago.

Phinney, J. S., & Alipuria, L. L. (1987). Ethnic identity in older adolescents from four ethnic groups. Paper presented at the Biennial Meeting of the Society for Research in Child Development, Baltimore.

Pinderhughes, E. B. (1982). Family functioning of Afro-Americans. *Social Work, 27,* 91–96.

Porter, J. D. (1971). *Black child, white child.* Cambridge: Harvard University Press.

Powell, G. J. (1983). Self-concept in white and black children. In C.V. Willie, B.M.

Kramer, & B.S. Brown (Eds.), *Racism and mental health* (pp. 299–318). Pittsburgh, PA: University of Pittsburgh Press.

Proshansky, E. H. (1965). *Basic studies in social psychology.* New York: Holt, Rinehart, and Winston.

Rosenberg, M. (1975). The dissonant context and the adolescent self-concept. In S. Dragastin & G.H. Elder (Eds.), *Adolescence in the life cycle: Psychological change and social context* (pp. 97–116). Washington, DC: Hemisphere.

Rosenberg, M. (1977). Contextual dissonance effects: Nature and causes. *Psychiatry, 40,* 205–217.

Rosenberg, M. (1979). *Conceiving the self.* New York: Basic Books.

Rosenberg, M., & Simmons, R. G. (1971). *Black and white self-esteem: The urban school child.* Washington, DC: American Sociological Association.

Rosenthal, D. A. (1987). Ethnic identity development in adolescents. In J.S. Phinney & M.J. Rotheram (Eds.), *Children's ethnic socialization* (pp. 156–179). Newbury Park, CA: Sage.

Sarnoff, I. (1951). Identification with the aggressor: Some personality correlates of anti-semitism among Jews. *Journal of Personality, 3,* 199–218.

Semaj, L. (1981). The development of racial-classification abilities. *Journal of Negro Education, 50, 6,* 59–79.

Simmons, R. B. (1978). Blacks and high self-esteem. *Social Psychology, 41,* 54–57.

Solomon, B. B. (1983). Value issues in working with minority clients. In A. Rosenblatt & D. Waldfugel (Eds.), *Handbook of clinical social work* (pp. 866–887). San Francisco, CA: Jossey-Bass.

Spencer, M. B., Bookins, G. K., & Allen, W. R. (Eds.). (1985). *Beginnings: The social and effective development of black children.* Hillsdale, NJ: Erlbaum.

Spurlock, A. (1986, January). Development of self-concept in Afro-American children. *Hospital and Community Psychiatry, 37*(1), 66–70.

Tajfel, H. (1978). *Differentiation between social groups: Studies in the social psychology of intergroup relations.* London: Academic Press.

Taylor, R. (1976). Psychosocial development among black children and youth: A reexamination. *American Journal of Orthopsychiatry, 46,* 4–19.

Warner, W. L., Junker, B. H., & Adams, W. A. (1978). *Color and human nature.* Greenwood, MS: Negro University Press.

What makes you black. (1983, January). *Ebony,* 115–118.

Williams, J. E., & Morland, J. K. (1976). *Race, color, and the young child.* Chapel Hill: University of North Carolina Press.

Wofford, J. (1979). Ebonics: A legitimate system of oral communication. *Journal of Black Studies, 9,* 367–382.

Wylie, R. C. (1979). *The self-concept* (Vol. 2). Lincoln: University of Nebraska Press.

PART 3

Intervention with Black Families

Part Three builds on the integrated, culturally relevant knowledge base and the expanded assessments with black families presented in Parts One and Two. It focuses on how social workers can apply that knowledge in interventions with black families. The chapters discuss many of the pressing issues that affect black families (and other families, to a different extent). A common theme is the influence of other social systems on how black families are viewed externally, and the impact of those biases on how intervention with such families is designed.

Social systems and issues that affect the lives of black children more directly are addressed first, then other issues that affect children less directly or that affect the family as a unit. Chapter 7 discusses how factors related to public schools either facilitate or block school adjustment of black children. Strategies for social workers to use in helping black families who are confronted with inappropriate recommendations for special education, drugs, and violence in schools and the community are presented. Chapter 8 focuses on out-of-home placement, primarily foster care, and its impact on the preservation of black families. A more functional interactional system between the child welfare system, the courts, and the natural supports found within black families and communities is proposed. Chapter 9 addresses teenage pregnancy in the black community and the role of families in combating factors that contribute to the problem. Specific strategies and the social worker's role as a significant other are discussed.

Chapters 10, 11, and 12 focus on the impact of poverty, unemployment, and alcohol abuse on black family life. Each proposes culturally relevant approaches to helping black families and identifies subgroups that are at greater risk for problems. As an example, Chapter 12 identifies adolescents and older persons as high-risk subgroups for alcohol problems that require special intervention strategies, including the use of natural supports. The black older person is the central focus of Chapter 13, in which lifelong threats to well-being and the strengths of the extended black family are considered integral factors in interventions. The complex medical needs of the older person and other members of black families are described in Chapter 14. This is done in terms of chronic and acute illnesses, and the differential impact of particular conditions such as high blood pressure and AIDS.

CHAPTER 7

The Black Family and the School

Frances S. Caple,
University of Southern California

The purpose of education is to help socialize and prepare youngsters to assume successful adult roles in society. Yet the nation risks losing 30 percent of its high school population to educational failure, suicide, drug abuse, and teen pregnancy (Hare, 1987). School failure is an enormous and growing problem in the United States across all racial and socioeconomic groups. The difference in lifetime earnings between those who have a high school diploma and those who do not is approximately $200,000 (Pallas, 1986). The negative result is shared by the dropout's family, community, and society as a whole. The nation loses tax revenues even as it subsidizes basic needs of school dropouts.

Children who do not experience academic or behavioral success in their school years often become truant or drop out, and even if they finish school they are inadequately prepared for life tasks and are assured underemployment, long periods of unemployment, and dependency on public welfare or other subsidies. Those limitations are apt to become a standard expectation to be passed on to the next generation. The special nature of the black experience in America magnifies the problem with regard to black children. For example, about 40 percent of high school dropouts subsequently return, but underachieving black students in urban and rural areas generally are not among them (Pallas, 1986).

The problem of school failure tends to fall into the cracks of social work practice. Many school districts do not provide social work services but even when they do school social workers are constrained from dealing with the full range of issues that affect school failure. Therefore, this chapter is addressed not only to school social workers, but also to practitioners in other settings (e.g., family service agencies) who must take into account the critical role of the schools in the lives of black families and children.

The explanation for school failure is often sought in the child's personal characteristics, but when failure occurs among large numbers of children who have certain basic characteristics in common, such as black children, a broader search is indicated. Accordingly, this chapter discusses pertinent environmental, individual, and family issues common to black children. It considers areas of vulnerability to school failure and offers guidelines for social work practice.

RACISM: A CONTRIBUTOR TO SCHOOL FAILURE

Racism contributes to school failure among black children. Whenever the government supports educational services, it is done out of a need identified by and deemed beneficial to the public. Individual goals that are not in conflict with public goals have the blessing of the public. This has been the situation with regard to public education. Initially, greatest concern was for educating those who would run the country—white males (Ploski & Williams, 1983)—and this emphasis has had a lasting effect. Although after the Civil War legal prohibitions against educating of black people were gradually removed, that did not automatically promote educational opportunity. When public education was seen as possibly enabling black people to improve their personal status and to take full advantage of their freedom, new laws were enacted to keep white schools from including black students and to otherwise make public facilities and funds unavailable for black people (Ploski & Williams, 1983).

Society still seems to have ambivalent attitudes about the education of black people. Open discrimination has affected the quality of education provided black citizens—for example, educational facilities and instructional materials for blacks have often been outdated and inadequate, if available at all (Ploski & Williams, 1983). Legislation and informal agreements that block full access to funds and facilities have maintained racist practices in the public schools. For example, enrollment in neighborhood schools has often been controlled by informal agreements in the business community about which racial or ethnic groups will or will not be permitted to rent or buy homes in the community.

The issue of whether public education should be provided to black children had shifted to how it would be provided. During the one hundred years after the Civil War, schools that many states described as "separate but equal" were operated, but in 1954 the U.S. Supreme Court ruled that separate schools were inherently unequal, as evidenced by the condition of facilities, inadequate curricula, and lower qualifications and salaries of black teachers (*Brown v. Board of Education*). School districts were ordered to desegregate "with all deliberate speed" but over the next fifteen years there were no serious efforts to implement the Court's ruling, so in 1969 the Court ruled that dual school systems were to end immediately. The ruling was met by new tactics to evade it. Some states closed public schools and repealed compulsory education laws; others made class assignments that kept black children segregated by classrooms (Allen-Meares et al., 1986).

Although northern, eastern, and western states did not operate dual school systems, many urban areas relied on the social and economic reality that the segregated housing patterns for black and white families would make it difficult, if not impossible, to have totally desegregated schools. Maintaining the neighborhood school has been a valued philosophy in the United States. Racially isolated neighborhoods therefore automatically result, in such schools being racially segregated. Often, in the absence of voluntary action by local school districts, court cases have been filed to remedy the situation and effect desegregation. A common solution has been to realign school attendance boundaries and provide busing to achieve a racial balance. Mandatory busing has had equally strong supporters and detractors among all racial groups, but there is no overall national support for desegregation (Allen-Meares et al., 1986).

Despite all legal and voluntary efforts, in 1982 only 8.5 percent of teachers were members of racial minority groups (National Coalition, 1985), and 62.9 percent of black students still attended predominantly minority schools (Ploski & Williams, 1983). Within this historical context of overt and covert racism, black families and children have experienced a sense of exclusion, devaluation, alienation, and powerlessness with regard to public education.

BLACK CHILDREN IN SCHOOL: OTHER ISSUES AFFECTING VULNERABILITY

Even within this climate of racism, black Americans have been expected to develop and convey to their children the value of education. Indeed, black parents strongly desire to see their children get a good education (Hill 1973). A great many more black children achieve educational success than do not, but, vulnerability to school failure is still at a high level. This vulnerability is a function of continuing racism, but it is exacerbated by poverty, geographic location, child-school relationships, child-family relationships, and peer interactions, especially related to drug and alcohol abuse. In most cases of school failure among black children there is a complex interplay between all these factors.

Poverty

Poverty is both a contributor to school failure and a likely result of it. The quality and amount of education a child receives is determined in large measure by the income level of his or her family (National Coalition, 1985). Combining the factors of race *and* poverty intensifies the potential for difficulty. Many school districts still allocate fewer dollars to schools in poor and minority group neighborhoods. A vicious cycle is set in motion when teachers' expectations about student classroom performance are reflected in the standard outcome measures of the system. Teachers often adjust educational goals, teach different materials, and reward or punish behavior differently by class as well as by race (National Coalition, 1985).

Interpretations of these findings will vary. For instance, public officials are apt to attribute both low income and low school achievement to presumed deficiencies in black family life styles. The belief in the United States that any school failure is an automatic indicator of family dysfunction is common. Different life-styles are characterized as deficient and weak rather than recognized and appreciated for the strengths they may represent.

A combination of factors should be considered in assessing the effects of poverty on school achievement. Teacher and school attitudes play a major part. In the absence of reasonable expectations of success, children are likely to fail, but children are also likely to fail if schools set standards too high and communicate to students that they do not believe they can meet those standards (National Coalition, 1985). In addition, teacher attitudes can be affected when administrators allocate less money for equipment and supplies in certain schools. The message is that there are lower expectations for the children, and the absence of essential supports can be demoralizing for teachers.

Other effects of poverty on school achievement are observable in the child's personal situation. Health problems, a shortage of food and adequate clothing (particularly in inclement weather), and lack of a stable, secure place to live can affect both regular attendance and the ability to concentrate on school tasks. In addition, the home environment may not contain many supplements, such as educational toys, games, and books, or a quiet place to read or do homework, and the opportunity to learn through travel and recreational outings is likely to be unavailable.

The War on Poverty in the 1960s focused attention on the disproportionately high number of low-income white *and* minority children who were performing below grade level. The federal response was the passage of "Title I" of the Elementary and Secondary Education Act (ESEA) of 1965. Many provisions of this act were subsequently authorized as "Chapter I" of the Education Consolidation and Improvement Act (ECIA) of 1981. Federal funds were made available to local districts to provide "compensatory education" for schools that served large numbers of children from low-income families. Services included supplemental educational materials, health programs, breakfasts, counseling, and additional teachers, and they have been effective (National Coalition, 1985, p. 8; Ploski & Williams, 1983), but only about half of those eligible for the programs actually received services (National Coalition, 1985). A national policy of commitment to educational opportunity for all children must be maintained and kept current with needs, especially of children who are at risk for school failure because of poverty.

Geographic Location

Students in urban and rural areas are more likely to experience school failure than students in suburban areas. Again, a major association is economic: Few poor children live in suburban communities (Sher, 1977). In addition, the school years of some children may be marked by regular migration as their families search for employment, or by intermittent movement between urban and rural communities as families make alternate arrangements, often with extended kin. It is not uncommon for some black children to spend one or more of their school years with grandparents or other relatives far from the nuclear family. Such changes from one environment to another can cause considerable adjustment problems for some students (Sher, 1977).

In rural areas, black people comprise the largest racial minority group. Major problems for schoolchildren in rural areas are associated with nonenrollment and irregular attendance, which at times have been twice the rate of urban areas (Sher, 1977). Nonenrollment and irregular attendance may be caused by such factors as lack of transportation, or inclement weather, health problems, other priorities set by the family (such as helping with child care or meeting basic needs), or a parental attitude that school is a waste of time because many school activities have no immediate relevance to their life-style of poverty and isolation. In addition, resources in rural areas are apt to be sparse, resulting in an impoverishment of experiences for students that leaves them underprepared for college or advanced technical and vocational study.

On the other hand, rural schools may have the greatest opportunity for home and school exchanges. Teachers may live in the same neighborhoods, belong to the same churches, or may otherwise have access to sources of information that can help children succeed in school. Yet there is a lack of anonymity and privacy, and potential reluctance of school children and their families to discuss openly with social workers the true nature of their concerns.

In urban areas, interactions between home and school are likely to be more formal. Teachers and students are strangers, whose time together is geared to the specific purpose of education; little time is left to get to know the hopes, dreams, and concerns of children and their families. A recent study conducted by the National Education Association (1987) found that in urban areas:

1. Black parents participate little in school activities.
2. Schools in the black community tend not to have outreach programs for parents beyond traditional parent-teacher groups.
3. Black parents find it difficult to participate in school activities because of the times such activities are scheduled, the lack of child care, and sometimes the distance between home and school.
4. Few black parents feel comfortable visiting the school.
5. Black parents find it difficult to speak up for their children's needs and placements because they are provided limited information.

The social worker may be able to facilitate communication and activity between the systems. Schools often have expectations of parent involvement that are not realistic because they are based on experience with white and middle class parents who have more resources, including adequate time for involvement. To reduce school failure among black children, parents and school personnel must be able to communicate with each other effectively and have a level of involvement sufficient to address needs of both the child and the school.

Child-School Relationships

There are two prevailing points of view about how child-school relationships affect the number of school failures. One is that it is the child who is assessed and labeled and who bears the consequences even though the causes of school failure do not originate in the child. This perspective suggests that perhaps *schools* might be assessed and labeled "underachieving" in situations where children do not attain their full potential. Another view blames the child and family for school adjustment problems. But blaming either side is not productive for positive change. The interactive nature of child-school relationships must be explored, as illustrated by analysis of the facts that follow.

FACT: *The school achievement of black children tends to drop below expectations in elementary school and to fall further behind as the children get older* (National Coalition, 1985). Some of the reasons for this fact are within the child and some are within the family, but a major responsibility must rest with the school. Are black students being prepared at appropriate levels for the outcome measures that are applied? Studies of teacher expectancy have documented that children rise or fall to the level set by the teacher (National Coalition, 1985). A concept of "effective schools" has recently been developed, and some schools have had great success in improving student achievement (see, e.g., Brookover et al., 1982), including schools "in poor areas and with disadvantaged students" (*Report 99-630*, 1986). The characteristics identified as basic to an "effective school" are strong leadership, emphasis on both basic and higher level skills, a safe and orderly environment, a climate of expectations that all students can learn, and continuous assessment of students (*Report 99-630*, 1986).

FACT: *Disciplinary action toward black students is disproportionately higher than that against white students.* Black students are suspended three times as often as white students (National Coalition, 1985), and although black students constituted 16 percent of the U.S. school population in 1980, they constituted 28 percent of all expelled, suspended, and corporally punished students (Ploski & Williams, 1983). There is no evidence that these measures teach a child how to behave in a more disciplined, self-controlled manner. In order of prevalence, students receive such punishments for (1) fighting or physical contact; (2) truancy and tardiness; (3) behavior problems (e.g., disrupting classroom activities, "bad attitude," disobedience); (4) verbal confrontations (e.g., insulting or disagreeing with teachers); (5) miscellaneous (e.g., smoking, destruction of property, drug and alcohol abuse) (Children's Defense Fund, 1974).

School policies and practices regarding punishment vary from school to school (Freeman, 1985). Such offenses as weapons possession and physical assaults may call for specific consequences based on predetermined district policies, but most disciplinary action is the result of a judgment or based on a number of factors. The high percentage of such actions against black children suggests that race often may be an overriding factor. The logic of some school actions is not always evident. For instance, suspension for tardiness or truancy is a contradiction, yet it is often applied.

One school social worker described his and the parents' frustration when, after weeks of working to get a student back in class, the principal suspended him for having been truant. Suspensions have an insidious effect. They keep the child apart from the environment with which he or she needs to learn how to cope. They also label a child as a "discipline problem," so that school staff anticipate misbehavior. The slightest new difficulty may be seen as cause for another suspension. The child's absences from school can only have an additional negative impact on overall school achievement.

If suspensions are the primary means of addressing behavior problems, the child will soon be performing at some point much below grade level. The student is apt to get the message that school personnel do not care, do not consider her or him competent, and do not expect much except disruptive behavior—they cannot help but feel devalued and unwelcome. This kind of adverse child-school interaction is reflected in the fact that the national dropout rate for black students in high school is nearly twice that of white students (National Coalition, 1985).

FACT: *Black children are placed in classes for the educable mentally retarded at three times the rate of white children* (National Coalition, 1985). Many such placements are the result of misclassification and serve to resegregate black children from the mainstream of the school environment. In addition, black children are only half as likely to be placed in a class for gifted and talented students (National Coalition, 1985), and many handicapped black children do not receive the special education services they need (Edelman, 1980).

Some children in special education classes are there more because of behavior problems than education problems. While social work is identified in Public Law 94-142 as one of the "related services," for special education students, social work services for child and family may not be adequate. This may make the exceptional child at risk of not benefiting fully from special education programs. P.L. 94-142 requires that parents be fully involved in the process of classifying their child's handicap, but this does not always occur, especially when a child's problems are believed to reflect parental attitudes or problems.

The differences in experiences black students have in the school compared with white students are often explained by school personnel as a problem of black children or of black families or of black communities. Black families and black community leaders explain the differences as problems of the school and of society. Each perspective has some element of truth because no single factor produces success or failure. However, there is little acknowledgment of the interactive nature of child-school relationships and the fact that the child is continually in developmental transitions. Black child development and behavior appear to be poorly understood by some of the professionals charged with educating children. Instead, power and influence have often been applied more to authoritarian control of black children than to promotion of positive development.

Child-Family Relationships

Family and personal dynamics of all kinds are likely to affect the black child's vulnerability to school failure. The times in a family's life that may be most distressing are those that follow a crisis or are part of an extraordinarily stressful event. For example:

> Ron was a black high school student whose grade point average was 3.75 before his father died. His grades slipped in the weeks that followed, and when Ds and Fs showed on his report card he was devastated. He never regained his interest in better achievement.

Preventive outreach by health service workers during Ron's father's illness might have included direct intervention with Ron, or there might have been a referral to school personnel or a community agency for evaluation and intervention as needed for Ron's initially normative reaction to a major loss.

The loss of a family member can be intensified if it is accompanied by demoralization for the family or for one of its members:

> Laura also was a high-achieving black student. After she disclosed an incident of incest, her father was arrested as the perpetrator and subsequently left the home. Laura and her family were referred for mental health services at an outpatient clinic. Laura was seen individually by a social worker, and her progress in treatment was reported to be good. During the seven months she was being seen, however, no inquiry about school adjustment was made. Laura's mother finally expressed her concern during a family session that Laura was about to be expelled from her magnet school and returned to her neighborhood school because of poor attendance and poor grades. In addition to structural family changes, they had experienced considerable loss of income and had lived in virtual poverty the past seven months.

Children like Laura who require protective intervention for neglect and abuse, and children moving in and out of foster homes, have high vulnerability for school failure. These children's needs are particularly underaddressed by social agencies and by schools. Often the focus is so specific to the issues of protection that school adjustment is overlooked, as it was in the following situation:

> As a part of an investigation of neglect, a child welfare worker discovered a 5-year-old child was not regularly attending school. The mother indicated she had been embarrassed when school officials scolded her for forgetting to pick up her kindergartner on time, so the mother never returned the child to school. The social worker helped correct other issues of neglect in the case but failed to intervene regarding school attendance since attendance at kindergarten in that state was not compulsory.

Poverty and urban living were two points of vulnerability already operating against this child's success in school. Her nonattendance in kindergarten could only put her further behind her peers socially and academically and seriously increase her vulnerability to school failure. This child could have benefited from a successful early childhood education program, such as Head Start (U.S. Department of Education, 1987).

Peer Interactions and Drug and Alcohol Use

Important influences on school performance can be identified in peer interactions. From the time the child begins to spend time with children and adults in the neighborhood, at child care facilities, at church, and in educational settings, behavior-shaping ideas and attitudes are exchanged. As the child matures, the field of influence is apt to include both specific peers and certain adults. The attitudes and behaviors of these peers and adults, both in everyday life and as seen in the mass media, serve as models for the roles the child or youth might like to try out or to assume permanently. Children and youth tend to enjoy the opportunity to "act" grown up. For instance, drug use—a "grownup" activity that seriously affects the child's ability to perform or remain in school—is common in media presentations, if not in a child's daily life too.

The most immediate concern is the damaging psychological and physical effects of drugs that may interfere with learning and contribute to school failure: effects on mood, concentration, and cognitive functioning (Polich et al., 1984); interference with memory, sensation, perception, and motor skills; disturbance in the brain's ability to take in, sort, and synthesize information (USDE, 1986). Long-term use can result in permanent physical or psychological damage. In addition, much of the physical violence that happens to peers and school personnel may occur while students are under the influence of drugs or alcohol (USDE, 1986; McRoy & Shorkey, 1985).

In planning services to control the use of drugs among students, it is important to keep the child-community interactions in mind. The child's behavior is "self"-centered, but the influences and effects are "community"-oriented. Polich and colleagues (1984) noted that the process by which adolescents start using drugs involves peer modeling, peer support, and networking (see Spiegler et al., 1985, p. 10).

CONCEPTUALIZING SOCIAL WORK PRACTICE WITH FAMILIES AND SCHOOLS

To reduce the incidence of school failure among black children, social workers must acknowledge and recognize the insidious nature of the development of the problem of school adjustment and failure. On a broader level, the social worker must also be involved in the regular, ongoing collection of data from public sources that identify and assess issues affecting school failure and should participate in prevention efforts that go beyond work with the individual child and family.

The next step is to establish a clear means for understanding the essential relationships among child, family, school, and other systems and the factors that contribute to school failure. The complex elements must be conceptualized in a way that makes the tasks manageable and assures that school failure is indeed the target of whatever intervention is provided. An ecosystems perspective provides a framework for such understanding (see Chapter 3; Meyer, 1983; Winters & Easton, 1983). This perspective facilitates a view of all interacting systems that both contribute to and help reduce the problem. The challenge thus shifts from an individual practitioner operating alone, just as the focus shifts from looking solely within individual children, or families, or teachers and schools for the causes and solutions to school failure.

An excellent example of an ecosystems approach to school failure is the original Title I (now Chapter I) programs, which were effective largely because they took into account the many variables involved in school failure. The programs also recognized that there was a need for a differential application of knowledge and skill based on interprofessional expertise. An ecosystems perspective requires that the social worker keep the broad picture in mind but encourage the use of many strategies and the involvement of other professionals' identified strengths, as well as those of the family.

This perspective assumes that a growing, developing child generally will not fail at "learning"—cognitive, behavioral, or affective—unless there is not a good fit between what the child needs for success and what is provided toward that end. "Goodness of fit" is also relative to a child's particular developmental needs. Disturbed behavioral functioning occurs where there is excessive stress resulting from a poorness of fit and dissonance between environmental expectations and demands and capacities of the child at a particular level of development (Chess & Hassibi, 1978).

In the ecosystems perspective, the child, the family, and the school are always in reciprocal interaction with each other, notwithstanding the tendency to keep the school somehow separate as a system that merely receives children to provide the service of education. A perspective that views the school only as a professional organization that dispenses an expert service (education) overlooks critical details about the dynamic interchanges that occur there. It promotes evaluation of deficits in the child when any dissonance develops in the educational process, rather than considering the entire interactional field.

Practice Illustration

An example can illustrate the importance of this broader view of the entire field. Desegregated schools should take deliberate steps to incorporate the values, norms, and mores of black children and families (Powell, 1982). But poor, black children in both desegregated and racially isolated schools have often been expected to adopt the idealized middle-class mainstream white culture and adapt to its environment. As a result, the poor and minority child is described as "culturally deprived" (e.g., Amos & Grambs, 1968; Loretan & Umans, 1966; Riessman, 1962; Wight, et al., 1970) and the child's own culture is dismissed as nonexistent or inadequate. This narrow formulation of the "problem" inhibits the development of high self-esteem in black children and does not engender feelings of being accepted and valued that are necessary to promote motivation for success in school. It also causes professionals to ignore or fail to explore conditions in the school or larger society that can block motivation in black children. If the term "cultural deprivation" should have been applied at all, it should have been applied to both child *and* school, since each has a mediating task if goodness of fit is to be achieved. The black child and family, however, have been abandoned to work out the fit alone as best they can. Thus, when a black child fails, the "poorness of fit" has been blamed on the child and family.

School and child always represent two cultures. A goodness-of-fit model would remove the need for labels and the need to place blame. The question "Whose fault is it?" is replaced by "How can the situation be changed to ensure better fit between child and school and thereby promote the growth and development of each? What are the sources of excessive stress?" Such questions were pertinent to the exploration and intervention process utilized by the worker in this example:

> Robert, a rambunctious, strong-willed, sometimes defiant 9-year-old black boy, was observed by his teacher (who was inside the building) to hop onto a moving construction vehicle one day at recess. She had watched as he cavorted in the mound of dirt in the vehicle, making large impressions of his feet and body, and as he slid down the sides several times. Robert's teacher responded in horror to her observation of his vehicle ride. She reported the incident to the principal.
>
> Because Robert's behavior was dangerous, the principal asked the school social worker to contact Robert's mother and then pursue a possible referral for community-based services. The principal and Robert's teacher recommended family counseling; they felt the mother "spoiled" this child. Robert's strong will and defiance were viewed only in negative terms, rather than as containing elements critical to his survival.
>
> Robert's mother reported to the social worker that she was concerned about her son. She had tried to correct his school problems by using corporal punishment. She felt that their relationship was becoming severely strained by her constant punishment of him for things that happened at school. (She was also at risk for a report of child abuse in regard to her use of corporal punishment.) She had told her son what she expected of him and did not know why the school could not manage his behavior there. At home, her son was generally responsive to her directions without the need for punishment. This fact alone enlightened school personnel about one (black) family's childrearing dynamics.
>
> The social worker arranged a conference at school with parent, teacher, and principal. Robert's teacher exhibited hyperactive behavior throughout the conference; she constantly switched positions in her chair. She had an obvious and extensive skin rash on her hands, arms, and legs, which she rubbed continually. Her descriptions of Robert's behavior seemed to intensify her motor activity. Her excessive stress was evident. As details about the school incident unfolded, it was clarified that there was no adult supervision at the time. Robert and the other children had been left to their own devices. He had stated that he got on the vehicle because he thought it would be fun.

The social worker sought a balance in this conference. The developmental and behavioral needs of all 9-year-old children were related to Robert's behavior and personal characteristics, even as the teacher's needs were empathically addressed. As a result of the conference, the principal reassigned Robert to a classroom with a teacher who was under less stress. This was done in a way that did not place blame or lower the self-esteem of the teacher or further label Robert as "a problem." There was acknowledgment of functional difficulties in the entire system. A regular assignment was made for adult supervision at all recess times. A janitor who had a positive relationship with Robert was later engaged to help with developmental teaching and guidance of specific behaviors. An erroneous assumption had been operating that *this* 9-year-old, like most other 9-year-olds, should "know better" and that he could exercise control over his impulsive tendencies to seek out and have fun. The teacher's attitude had been to "watch and report" the misbehavior she knew was bound to occur, rather than to supervise and teach appropriate behavior. Changes in the situation produced an improved "goodness of fit" and resulted in a learning process for everyone involved about this family's culture and that of the school.

Powell (1982) studied the effects of school desegregation on the self-concept of black students and summarized what a cohesive school and community experience for such students would be like:

1. There is maximal participation of parents and teachers.
2. The mores and norms of the home are reinforced in the immediate community.
3. Afro-American culture and life-styles are presented as important and positive aspects of the school curriculum.
4. Children are accepted by peers and teachers.
5. Adequate counseling and career options are presented to the children.
6. The principal of the school provides clear educational leadership.
7. Academic achievement is encouraged regardless of family background.
8. There are readily identifiable adult models for youth to incorporate into their sense of self.

GUIDELINES FOR ASSESSMENT AND INTERVENTION

A broad range of social work services are appropriate here, and the ecosystems perspective is vital to the effective use of the following practice principles and procedures. The school or community-based social worker should:

1. *Obtain an overall perspective of the school district, assess its sociopolitical climate, and make the assessment specific to all schools where black children are enrolled* (Winters & Easton, 1983). This critical early step in combating failure among black children should be initiated as soon as practice in a commu-

nity begins and should be kept current with new data. Agency staff meetings might regularly include discussion of pertinent details and assessment of local schools. Understanding the school systems is as vital as understanding individual children and families before any interventive plan is set in motion. Most data about school districts will be available in the form of public records, newspaper articles, and parents' comments. The worker can also:

- Attend at least one school board meeting.
- Gather data on the number and percentage of black children and how black children are represented in special classes, in achievement scores, and in suspensions, expulsions, or other punishments. Assess attitudes of the district or specific schools about special classes and punishment procedures (e.g., assess whether placement is used "only in extreme cases").
- Review regulations relating to school attendance, suspensions, and expulsions to determine their appropriateness.
- Determine the district's (or school's) philosophy of education and the model on which it operates (e.g., fundamental, alternative, "effective school," open classroom).
- Determine what services are available to children through such school sources as clothing rooms, emergency food, dental health care, mental health services, and school social work services and determine how and when those resources can be made available to clients.
- Determine what federally funded programs (i.e., Chapter I and P.L. 94-142 programs) are provided in a district and at which schools. Determine the number of black children and whether they are underserved or overrepresented within those programs.

2. *Implement district and school-level interventions as appropriate:*

- Determine the racial composition of specific schools. If a desegregation plan is in effect, assess community and school attitudes and the need for social work services to prevent or mediate differences and to address specific needs for inclusion, acceptance, and valuing of black children.
- Determine which community social workers or agencies are likely to offer outreach services or whether self-help parent groups might best be mobilized, and how black churches and civic groups or local chapters of fraternities and sororities might be involved.

3. *Utilize multilevel interventions where indicated.* If there is an overrepresentation of black children in special education programs, it is important to determine the most effective strategies at federal, state, and local school levels. Strategies could include direct service interventions with families whose children may have been inappropriately assigned. Natural or peer support strategies may be effective and could include parents whose children are being considered for special placement. Black self-help advocacy groups might also be a referral source for parents.

4. *Assess school adjustment and intervene as appropriate on a case-by-case basis.* This would occur no matter what the presenting problem. Because the school is such a central system in the child's life, and because of the frequently subtle development of many problems that result in school failure, *every* encounter with a professional social worker should include an opportunity to promote positive school adjustment.

Prior assessment of the schools would also provide clues (see guideline 1 above) to possible resources at school, whether the child is experiencing difficulty there or not. For example, if the family is under stress about its own issues, if a couple is separating, if a parent is alcoholic, abusive, neglectful, or seriously ill, the school may have personnel and services available to help the child in a secondary living environment. Such services are critical because they occur while the family is already being seen for other concerns. Joint planning with the family and the school can promote current goals as well as model future negotiations between parents and school on behalf of their children. In treatment with families, the worker can:

- Help parents become empowered to deal effectively with schools on their child's behalf. This can include going with them to school conferences (if necessary and if requested to do so by the parents) and role playing or rehearsing what might go on at a school conference that the parents attend alone. Assertive advocacy can be modeled in a worker's telephone call to the school while the parents are in the office. In working with parents this way, include suggestions for future situations and ways in which parents might be involved in their child's school and remind the parent of resource persons (including family members and friends) who might be asked to go with them if they feel intimidated in the school setting.

5. *Provide outreach services to parents or to entire families whose children have not been referred but who may be vulnerable to school failure.* Practitioners may need to:

- Conduct discussion groups about school problems held at some location where black families would feel at ease. Black parents whose children have had many disciplinary actions or behavior problems need active follow-up or outreach. Many parents are labeled as "disinterested" or "unmotivated," when they may really be demoralized and feel powerless to change their child's situation. Poor families have survival as a primary stressor and, realistically, getting a child to behave in school may be a low priority. A parent-centered interview could help in assessing the situation. For instance, it would be important to elicit parents' feelings and thoughts about their situation and to formulate treatment plans within a problem-solving framework rather than to begin by being prescriptive about ways to meet needs of the child or the school.
- Schedule prevention groups focused on "adjustment" at certain transition

points, such as entry into kindergarten, elementary school, junior high school, and senior high school.

6. *Offer outreach services to schools.* Two outreach activities might be consultation about children's needs in general, or in-service sessions on child and family matters, ways to involve parents, and how to conduct parent conferences. Schools that do not have school social workers may not know what services a social worker can provide. The prior assessment of the district should provide clues as to needs as well as to how a social worker can best offer services. For example, the suspension rate among black students may suggest a need for information about how to deal with problem behavior without the routine use of suspensions. Therefore, the worker should:

- Focus on the *problem* of suspensions, not the causes of the problem, to avoid conveying an attitude of blame toward the school or placing the students in the position of scapegoat. Schools may resist such offers, fearing that social workers might be judgmental about what goes on in the school. Entry for outreach services can be facilitated as an extension of a specific case contact. A good working relationship with teachers or parents in one case may encourage a principal to make other referrals.
- Consultation is especially important for work with teachers. The social worker needs to: Convey empathy, concern and caring, and nonjudgmental understanding. The social worker brings professional expert knowledge but should recognize that teachers also bring professional expert knowledge to the sessions. The sessions can follow a problem-solving mode rather than a "teaching-preaching" mode. A goal in consultation and in-service sessions is to provide supportive assistance to teachers so that they in turn can be supportive to black children and their families.

7. *Offer outreach services or special program activities to family, school, and community, focusing on school violence, sexual behaviors, and drug use among young children.* These services could respond specifically to assessed needs in a community—for instance, preventive strategies, such as Project DARE (Drug Abuse Resistance Education) in Los Angeles or peer counseling programs.

8. *Use community organization strategies, such as political activity to elect school board members and keeping before them the pressing issues of black children.* Social workers may be able to:

- Plan sessions between parent groups and school personnel to facilitate communication about key issues and about the uniqueness of the black experience as something to value and preserve.
- Develop creative new ways to involve families with schools, and schools with families, on behalf of children.

9. *Develop a structure for collaboration with other social workers and with other professionals who can participate to reduce school failure.* School and community social workers can join together to:

- Organize working coalitions of social workers, representatives from related fields of psychology, psychiatry, nursing, counseling, and/or local citizens who have other professional or organizational bases, such as business groups, service clubs, and fraternal groups. These coalitions could influence the local, state and federal political process for public policy to promote school success. The influence of constituent groups is much more powerful than that of an individual or family, and groups that have a national structure and membership lend an even more potent force. The proposed coalitions might serve other purposes, determined by specifically assessed needs of the local black community. For example, as the black members of the coalitions gain visibility at public meetings and in media reports, they can be viewed as empowered and caring role models by children and their families.

CONCLUSIONS

Both the causes and the effects of school failure among black children are linked to all persons within the student's ecosystem and to factors in the larger society. Each of these persons affects and is affected by the child's experience, as is society in the long term. To reduce school failure, all these people must be engaged in the prevention and remediation process. The most direct social work interventions occur with the child's primary systems, such as the family and the school; extended services can influence other large systems. The full range of social work service activity must be utilized, including collaboration among various professionals, to achieve effective comprehensive service delivery. The ultimate goal should be development of a climate within the school and other parts of the ecosystem that will facilitate positive experiences for black children and ensure their school success.

REFERENCES

Allen-Meares, P., Washington, R.O., & Welsh, B. (1986). *Social work services in schools.* Englewood Cliffs, NJ: Prentice-Hall.

Amos, W.E., & Grambs, J.D. (Eds.). (1968). *Counseling the disadvantaged youth.* Englewood Cliffs, NJ: Prentice-Hall.

Brookover, W. B., Beamer, L., Efthim, H., Hathaway, D., Legatte, L., Miller, S., Passalacqua, J., & Tornatsky, L. (1982). *Creating effective schools: An in-service program for enhancing school learning, climate, and achievement.* Holmes Beach, FL: Learning Publications.

Brown v. Board of Education of Topeka (1954). 347 U.S. 483–493.

Chess, S., & Hassibi, M. (1978). *Principles and practice of child psychiatry.* New York: Plenum Press.

Children's Defense Fund. (1974). *Children out of school in America.* Cambridge, MA: Author.

Edelman, M.W. (1980). *Portrait of inequality: Black and white children in America.* Washington, DC: Children's Defense Fund.

Freeman, E.M. (1985). Analyzing the organizational context of schools. *Social Work in Education, 7,* 141–159.

Germain, C.B. (1982). An ecological perspective on social work in the schools. In R.T. Constable & J.P. Flynn (Eds.), *School social work: Practice and research perspectives* (pp. 125–132). Homewood, IL: Dorsey Press.

Hare, I. (1987). As quoted in Education Commission: Advocate for nation's school social workers. *NASW NEWS, 32,* 4.

Hill, R.B. (1973). *Strengths of black families.* New York: Emerson Hall.

Loretan, J.O., & Umans, S. (1966). *Teaching the disadvantaged.* New York: Teachers College Press, Columbia University.

Meyer, C.H. (Ed.). (1983). *Clinical social work in the eco-systems perspective.* New York: Columbia University Press.

McRoy, R.G., & Shorkey, C.T. (1985). Alcohol use and abuse among blacks. In E. Freeman (Ed.), *Social work practice with clients who have alcohol problems* (pp. 202–213). Springfield, IL: Charles C. Thomas.

National Education Association. (1987). Black concerns study committee report. Washington, DC: Author.

National Coalition of Advocates for Students. (1985). *Barriers to excellence: Our children at risk.* Boston, MA: Author.

Ploski, H.A., & Williams, J. (Eds.). (1983). *The Negro almanac: A reference work on the Afro-American* (4th ed.). New York: Wiley.

Polich, J.M., Ellickson, P.L., Reuter, P., & Kahan, J.P. (1984). *Strategies for controlling adolescent drug use.* Santa Monica, CA: Rand.

Powell, G. J. (1982). Six-city study of school desegregation and self-concept among Afro-American junior high school students: A preliminary study with implications for mental health. In B.A. Bass, G. E. Wyatt, & J.P. Powell (Eds.), *The Afro-American family: Assessment, treatment, and research issues* (pp. 265–316). New York: Grune and Stratton.

Report 99-630. (1986, June 16). House of Representatives, 99th Congress, second session. (Effective Schools and Even Start Act.)

Riessman, F. (1962). *The culturally deprived child.* New York: Harper & Row.

Rosenthal, R., & Jacobson, L. (1968). *Pygmalion in the classroom.* New York: Holt, Rinehart and Winston.

Sher, J.P. (1977). Pluralism in the countryside: A brief profile of rural America and its schools. In J.P. Sher (Ed.), *Education in rural America: A reassessment of conventional wisdom* (pp. 87–104). Boulder, CO: Westview.

Spiegler, D.L., Harford, T.C., & Freeman, E.M. (1985). An ecological perspective on alcohol use among adolescents: Implications for prevention. In E. Freeman (Ed.), *Social work practice with clients who have alcohol problems* (pp. 7–25). Springfield, IL: Thomas.

The problems of teenage pregnancy and parenting: Options for the legislature: A report. (1988, May). California Office of the Legislative Analyst.

U. S. Department of Education. (1986). *What works: Schools without drugs*. Washington, DC: Author.

U. S. Department of Education. (1987). *Schools that work: Educating disadvantaged children*. Washington, DC: Author.

Wight, B.W., Gloniger, M. F., & Keeve, J. P. (1970, January). Cultural deprivation: Operational definition in terms of language development. *American Journal of Orthopsychiatry, 40*, 77–85.

Winters, W.G., & Easton, F. (1983). *The practice of social work in schools: An ecological perspective*. New York: Free Press.

Zeff, S. B. (1981, October). Program for disadvantaged elementary school students. *Social Work in Education, 4*, 19–29.

CHAPTER 8

Black Children in Foster Care

Patricia G. Morisey
Fordham University

The persistence of poverty, discrimination, and institutional racism places black children at high risk for placement and drift in long-term foster care. This chapter examines institutional factors in the child welfare system that increase the likelihood that black children will experience prolonged and often inappropriate and unnecessary out-of-home placement. Practice principles and social work roles for achieving black family preservation are identified.

OVERVIEW OF THE PROBLEM

Foster care, the generic term for out-of-home placement, includes many forms of temporary, full-time substitute care, including foster family homes, group homes, and residential treatment institutions. In the last ten years, several studies have focused on black children in foster care (Children's Defense Fund [CDF], 1978, 1985, 1986; Jenkins et al., 1983; Gurak et al., 1982; Mayor's Task Force, 1980, 1985; National Black Child Development Institute, 1986). It is difficult to assess the total scope of this issue, because there are no current aggregate data at the national level and many states and counties have failed to keep current data. The available data categorize black children inconsistently, as black, mixed race, minority, or nonwhite. Based on the data available, the Children's Defense Fund (1980, 1985) found:

- Black children are three times more likely to be in foster care than white children. Some 157,000 of the 423,000 in foster care in 1978 were black; more than 100,000 were in foster care several years later.
- Black children of all ages were in care; 49,000 were under the age of 3, 59,000 were age 6 to 13, and 28,000 were 14 to 18.

- Black children are often removed from their homes for reasons of poverty and inadequate housing.
- Black children remain in foster care longer than white children. Almost one-third of black children have been in out-of-home placement for more than five years.
- Once in out-of-home placement, black children are more likely to become lost through "foster care drift."
- Black children are more likely to be inappropriately placed, as the type of out-of-home care tends to be related to race and ethnic background.
- Black children are twice as likely as white children to be living in institutions and four times more likely to be in correctional institutions.
- Black children living away from their families but not in institutions live in group quarters at four times the rate of white children.
- The legal ties of the parents of black children are likely to be terminated sooner than those of white parents. Once legal ties have been terminated, black children are less likely to receive adoption services.
- Black children account for only 10 percent of the children adopted. In 1973 an estimated 50,000 black children in foster care had been freed for adoption but only two-thirds of them would be placed. In 1979 there was no substantial increase in the number of adoptions for black children (National Urban League, 1979).

BLACK CHILDREN AND THEIR FAMILIES: AT RISK

Economic factors influence the growing numbers of black children entering the foster care system. The Children's Defense Fund (1985) reported that:

- Black children are more likely than ever to be born into poverty.
- Almost half of all black children are poor compared to one in six white children.
- Black children in two-parent homes are more than twice as likely as white children to have no employed parent and five times more likely to have an adolescent or single mother.
- More than 56 percent of all babies born to black women were out of wedlock.
- The proportion of black children living only with their mothers more than doubled between 1960 and 1983, and female-headed black families are the poorest. Between 1977 and 1982, the median income of these families dropped 28.3 percent (Children's Defense Fund, 1985).

The absence of black men "may be the key to the tremendous growth in black female-headed families in recent years and the accompanying rise in poverty among black families (Center for the Study of Social Policy, 1984, p. 2). In the mid-1950s, some 78 percent of all black men 16 or older had jobs. By 1983, only 56 percent were working, and the median income of black males was only two-thirds of that of white males.

Health factors and educational issues also put low income black children at risk. Many black women receive little or no prenatal care, and black infants are likely to have low birth weights and associated problems; many black children do not receive regular health care and immunizations, and the nutritional status of black youth is poor. Educational issues affecting black families include poor school attendance and high dropout rates and school failure. There has been a significant increase in substance abuse and in reports of child abuse and neglect among black families, but no increase in appropriate services. AIDS, too, has affected many young black families.

Poverty as well as racism make black children a particularly vulnerable population in our society. In 1972, Billingsley and Giovannoni pointed out:

> The system of child welfare services in this country is failing black children. It is our thesis that the failure is a manifest result of racism; that racism has pervaded the development of the system of services; and that racism persists in its present operation. . . .
>
> Racism manifests itself in the present system of services in three major ways. One, the kinds of services developed are not sufficient to the special situation of black children. Two, within the system that has developed black children are not treated equitably and three, efforts to change the system have been incomplete and abortive (p. 28).

THE DEVELOPMENT OF OUT-OF-HOME PLACEMENTS

America's provision of services for children has always reflected society's negative view of poor, "immoral" and dependent parents. This image was based on the English "Poor Laws." A residual approach to child welfare policies was taken; programs were designed to rescue children from failed family situations. Prior to the Civil War, black slave children were informally adopted or cared for by extended kin or other blacks on the plantation. Those who were not slaves lived in local almshouses, but because blacks were excluded from most private orphanages, separate facilities, such as the Philadelphia Association for the Care of Colored Children, were established (McGowan & Meezan, 1983). After the Civil War, black churches, schools, women's clubs, the Freedmen's Bureau, a few religious groups, and individual philanthropy aided dependent black children in the form of orphanages, financial asistance, home care, work, and the like.

By the end of the nineteenth century, leaders had begun to recognize the state's responsibility and the importance of instituting regulatory systems, service monitoring, and case accountability. Dependent children and child offenders were cared for in two different systems, but neighborhood-based programs (e.g., the Charity Organization Societies and settlement houses) complied in service delivery with the pattern of residential segregation in the neighborhood (McGowan & Meezan, 1983; Billingsley & Giovannoni, 1972).

The principle that children should not be separated from their parents by reason of poverty alone was enunciated at the first White House Conference on Children in 1909, but provision for children continued to be residual—intervention after problems in family functioning were exacerbated to the point of breakdown—rather than prevention. Substitute care became the major child welfare service.

The Children's Bureau, established in 1912 as the first federal agency representing children's interests, brought about establishment of public child welfare agencies, and state departments of welfare assumed responsibility for setting standards, licensing, and regulating public and voluntary child care programs. Protective services were established and shifted from the exclusive emphasis on law enforcement to providing services to parents to enable children to remain in their home. Orphanages, day nurseries, kindergartens, and homes for working girls were set up for black youth, because blacks were at least partially excluded from white private agency services. In 1923, some 711 of the 1,070 child placement institutions and agencies in the northern states accepted only white children. In 1930 the White House Conference on Children and Youth called for equitable standards of care for black children (Billingsley & Giovannoni, 1972).

The Social Security Act of 1935 had a major impact on out-of-home placement. The provision of financial assistance to children (AFDC) ensured that many children would not be placed in foster care by reason of poverty alone.

Psychoanalytic and child developmental theory contributed new insights to the debate about foster care versus institutionalization and led, in the 1950s, to the professional view that large custodial institutions did not provide optimum environments for the development of children. Group homes with salaried staff and specialized services began to be established, as well as agency-owned foster homes providing care for a maximum of six children. By 1959 there were more than 500,000 children in foster care. With the gradual shift from institutional care to foster boarding care and the shift to public agency services, black children were finally being reached by child welfare services, and the number of black institutions decreased. The shift to foster homes benefited blacks, because black adults and families had an opportunity as foster parents to participate in service provision for black children.

The institutional settings had generally been sponsored and controlled by whites. In 1959, Maas and Engler's landmark study entitled *Children in Need of Parents* called attention to the failure of the child welfare system to ensure permanency planning. The study found that black children were apt to enter care often unnecessarily and that once in care they are likely to remain in "foster care drift" until age 18. Maas and Engler also found that black children were more likely to receive foster care services than adoptive services. Helen Jeter (1963) reported similar findings.

The foster care system has since been the subject of intensive study and analyses (see Fanshel, 1976; Children's Defense Fund, 1978, 1980; Gurak, Smith, & Goldson, 1982). These studies identified some common issues:

- The failure of the foster care system to provide continuity of care
- The need to identify the children in care and to develop a permanent plan for each
- The failure to focus on the social conditions leading to placement, and the need for alternative services, particularly for parents and natural families
- Issues related to the role and training of foster parents
- Issues arising from turnover and burnout of workers
- The cost of foster care, and the irrationality of a system that could spend from $5,000 to $50,000 for the care of a child, in contrast to the payment in AFDC
- Legal issues related to the best interests of the child, the rights and duties of natural parents, and the foster parents

These issues contributed to the passage of Public Law 96-272, the Adoption Assistance and Child Welfare Act of 1980, which reversed the funding patterns in child welfare that encouraged foster care by funding services designed to prevent or shorten placement, while limiting state aid to foster care. P.L. 96-272 specifically mandated district-wide plans as well as individual child and family assessment; required each state to monitor efforts to move children through foster care and apply sanctions to counties that failed to provide required protections and services to children and families; mandated eighteen-month court review; required a data collection system; and for the first time, allocated monies for preventive services. Public Law 96-272 represented a national commitment to permanency planning. It stimulated states to begin to make legislative, fiscal, administrative, and services changes that can achieve permanence for a larger number of children.

However, the situation of black children in the foster care system has not been substantially changed. This problem is compounded because many child welfare policy makers, administrators, and direct service providers know little about the culture, history, experiences, and diverse life-styles of black families. Many are intolerant of cultural diversity and hold negative, dysfunctional, and stereotypical ideas about these families.

A FRAMEWORK FOR UNDERSTANDING BLACK FAMILIES

In permanency planning for black children, the impact of institutional racism on the social and economic status of black families and the impact of individual racism on the psychosocial development of black children and youth must be taken into account. Blacks have had to acquire the usual coping skills and strategies needed by any member of a complex society, but they also must be able to handle majority attitudes and behavior that may disparage their very existence (Goodman, 1973). Black parents must raise their children to be bicultural—to be both American and black.

Billingsley (1968) viewed the family as an adaptive and resilient mechanism for the socialization of its children. The black family is part of a black community system with distinct, but widely varied and diversified sociocultural attributes, variant family structures, flexible family function patterns. Members of the extended family often serve as substitutes for the short supply of resources and social services allocated to the black family. Hill (1971) challenged the tendency of researchers to focus on indicators of instability, disintegration, weakness, or pathology within black families and instead noted such strengths as strong kinship bonds, strong work orientation, adaptability of family roles, strong achievement orientation, and strong religious orientation. McAdoo (1978), Willie (1976), and Ladner (1974) support Hill (1971) and Billingsley (1968), and show that kinship relations tend to be stronger among blacks than whites. Stack (1974) found that strategies of survival included (1) mutual aid systems and extensive networks of kin and friends supporting and reinforcing each other and (2) alliances of individuals trading and exchanging goods, resources, and the care of children.

The child welfare system has not yet fully incorporated these insights in its knowledge base. It has not given systematic attention to understanding the relationship between the high incidence of family and social problems in the black community and the disproportionately high rates of unemployment and poverty, health and housing problems, and barriers to quality education and preparation for work. The tendency to blame poor black families for their condition has been reinforced by notions from Freudian psychology which posit that the individual is the cause of his or her problems. Attention has been diverted from the socioeconomic factors and their impact on and interaction with individual and family functioning of blacks. The foster care system tends to victimize the victim—vulnerable black families and children.

The lack of knowledge about black families and the black community has reinforced the foster care system's tendencies to function on generalizations about these families. Rather than developing an individualized assessment of unwed mothers, social workers tend to react negatively and often punitively. In discussing the cause for what appears to be an increase in the numbers of black children in foster care, social work administrators (and the media) focus on alcohol and especially "crack." However, many children are coming into care because their families are homeless or cannot cope with the increase and persistence of poverty and the increasing difficulty of securing health, mental health, and day care services.

The child welfare system also tends to label children in care as disturbed, but many children enter care because of the problems in the family and the family situations rather than their own problems. Inappropriate placement and frequent replacement and isolation from families causes many of these children to develop emotional problems (Community Council, 1979). These problems are exacerbated by inequitable distribution of appropriate services to the poor, and especially poor minorities. The black community also is blamed for problems in service provision. Black families have been criticized for not providing adoptive homes, but Herzog and colleagues (1971) found that when black families are compared with white families with the same education, income, and social status, the proportion of black families adopting was as high as that of white families. There was also some indication that agency procedures and rules and workers' lack of knowledge about the families under study negatively affected the adoption process. Hill (1977) demonstrated the interest of the black community in their children and the viability of informal adoption as a resource for black children. These studies identified certain factors as deterrents to black adoptions: limited and inappropriate recruitment efforts; agency forms, requirements and questions, protracted family study process, and orientation process; and economic factors and responsibilities for children in the extended family.

The Role of the Social Worker

Social workers with a caseload of black children face the challenges of reducing the number of inappropriate placements and returning children to their families in a timely fashion, or of achieving permanence through adoption. These goals cannot be achieved unless social workers understand the current life situation of black families. This understanding can best be accomplished by adopting an ecological perspective through broadening the knowledge base of practice and developing new approaches to assessment and treatment planning. The intervention strategy should give priority to working with the strengths of the black family, the extended family, and community systems, and on a broader level, to addressing the broad systemic problems that have such a negative impact on the life of black families.

Morisey (1976) found that relationships among residents of Central Harlem were characterized by the prevalence of self-help and mutual help responses and behavior, and that one of the most prevalent mutual help systems is the informal child care system. Morisey observed that the child welfare system must enter into a planning coalition which should include all sectors—consumers, paraprofessionals, and representatives of both informal and formal organizations and of the middle and upper classes.

Meyer (1976, 1979) addresses the need to redefine the psychosocial approach in social work practice and move toward the ecological perspective. In the current context of social work practice and the way people live, critical factors are the urban environment, the particular and often disadvantaged situation of blacks and Hispanics who have moved to the nation's major cities, and issues related to employment and unemployment, money, poverty, changes in the role of the family, and the increasing bureaucratization of service systems.

The life model of practice develops from the ecological perspective (Germain, 1973; Pincus & Minahan, 1973). Germain (1973) discusses how the life model defines problems as problems in living, not as emotional disturbances. This model can be useful because the child welfare system often defines the presenting problems—such as juvenile delinquency, alcoholism, unwed pregnancy, child abuse and neglect, and strained emotional ties—without looking at the contributing factors, such as poverty or housing or the family's difficulty in finding and using services. This perspective opens up a view of a wider range of structural interactions, rather than focusing on dysfunctional responses. It can help differentiate families who are disengaged and families in which there are issues of role reversal or family functioning, from families who are enmeshed and alienated in the trap of hopelessness.

This perspective also suggests a treatment orientation that includes the family social network, which directs attention to the informal, family, and extended family networks and community supports as well as to problems. It includes crisis-oriented counseling as a positive treatment modality, and it permits no hierarchy in values, whether the goal is for intervention in a community system for rehabilitation, or prevention. An important issue growing out of this perspective is the specific role of the social worker and the importance of a team that not only includes persons with specific functions (e.g., providing home services, day care, respite services, parent education, and advocacy) but also focuses on the dynamic interactions of members of the team.

The life model builds on both the progressive forces and the adaptive potentialities within the family and related systems. It sees positive value in mobilizing the environmental processes. Altering the elements of the environment widens the arena of health and expands the role of the case worker. The life model also expands the role of the team and focuses on the interdependence of all the actors and systems, and it can effectively utilize the horizontal rather than the vertical model. The child and family system can be positively viewed as participants in this team effort.

The social worker must pay specific attention to professional values—his or her attitudes toward black families as well as toward families with problems in functioning. The tendency to adhere to the outmoded "rescue" model of a child welfare worker is reinforced when the social worker holds generalized stereotyped views about families, about single parents, and about individuals involved with such problems as substance abuse, unwed pregnancy, and family violence. The social worker must recognize the viability of varied family forms, the extent to which black families have coped, and adaptive trends that have developed in the extended family and community systems. The social worker also needs to make a major commitment to family-focused treatment rather than to the traditional focus on the child. This means making a broad assessment of the family situation and taking affirmative steps to prevent out-of-home placement.

An illustration of a preventive service is provided in the following case study. The local public child welfare agency referred this case to a private child care agency for foster care or preventive services.

> Ms. Jones was a 29-year-old divorced black mother of two children aged 3 and 4. Her former husband had recently died in a car accident. Before her ex-husband's death, Ms. Jones had not been employed, and Mr. Jones had been providing some child support. The loss of support forced Ms. Jones to live in her mother's house.

A long-standing poor relationship had existed between Ms. Jones and her family. At the time of the referral, Ms. Jones and her two children were living with six other family members in her mother's two-bedroom home. The agency worker determined that Ms. Jones was severely depressed and she was at a point of serious crisis. Ms. Jones felt helpless and wanted to give up her children.

Intervention strategies included support, direction, and modeling. The worker helped Ms. Jones contact the Social Security office and found that she and her children were eligible to receive benefits that would enable them to live independently. The agency team included the case worker, the family worker, and the job training developer, as well as a volunteer who was able to identify with this severely depressed mother, help her with her day-to-day management problem, serve as an outlet for ventilation of her problems with her family, and begin to help her identify positive short-term goals for herself.

The 3-year-old, who was a very disruptive, acting-out child, was placed in a specialized day care program and given speech therapy. In addition to receiving counseling for depression, the mother was helped to deal with her specific parenting problems. Time-limited tasks were identified rather than generalized parenting education. An important objective was to help develop goals for Ms. Jones and to help her become independent. She received help in enrolling in a GED program, to better enable her to get a job in the future. Her relationship with her children improved and for the first time in her life she was feeling that she could make it on her own.

Although the mother did have adjustment problems, priority was not given exclusively to psychological counseling. Efforts were made to help the mother with *all* aspects of her life, and in fact her outlook and her functioning improved as she began to be able to handle some of the problems which had frustrated her in everyday living.

This kind of family-oriented approach can effectively reunite children who are already in placement, as noted in the following case:

The local child welfare services unit received several referrals for malnutrition and medical and physical neglect of John Gerald, age 4. The protective services worker investigated the case and found insufficient evidence to justify the allegations. Several weeks later, the police department was called in to investigate the same family. A neighbor of Ms. Latasha Gerald, the children's mother, reported that Ms. Gerald's three children (Mary, 2; John, 4; and Jennifer, 5) had been left unattended for two days and nights. The children were dirty and in need of food. Ms. Gerald returned home just as the officers and protective services worker were preparing to remove the children. She explained that she had left the children with a friend while she worked during the past two nights and that she had been with the children during the day. She reeked of alcohol, and the officers believed that she had been on a drinking binge. The children were taken into custody and placed in a foster home. After a couple of weeks, the foster mother indicated that she could no longer take care of all three children, so the 2-year-old was placed in a different home about twenty miles away.

The child welfare services worker learned that the mother had dropped out of high school in the ninth grade and became pregnant with John at age 15. Although John's father, Sam Jenkins, expressed an interest in marrying Ms. Gerald, she refused because he was not working. Sam Jenkins and Latasha Gerald subsequently had two other children and lived together sporadically. At the time of the referral they were not living together, and Ms. Gerald was receiving AFDC. She is now 20 and feels overwhelmed. She fears that her children will be taken away from her permanently and is suspicious of the child welfare worker. Ms. Gerald has no family support, but she admits that the children's father sometimes helps her.

The protective services worker began to identify strengths and weaknesses in this family situation. She realized that the longer the children remained out of the home, the less likely the family would be reunited. The worker scheduled two visits between Ms. Gerald and her children at the agency. Although the foster mothers brought in the three children, their mother missed each appointment. The worker began to think that the mother was not interested in parenting the children. However, during a home visit, the worker discovered that the mother had become so depressed over the loss of her children that she had begun drinking heavily. The worker convinced her of the importance of maintaining contact and developed a plan to help her keep her children.

The worker realized that a team effort would be needed to identify resources that might enable the mother to become a better parent and to be reunited with her children. The agency worker contacted another social worker at an alcohol treatment center to identify alcohol programs that might meet Ms. Gerald's needs. She arranged for the mother to participate in a treatment program for women with alcohol problems and encouraged her to join a newly formed black Alcoholics Anonymous group at a neighborhood church. The worker also referred Ms. Gerald to a parent support group located in a neighborhood center. The worker arranged for Ms. Gerald to take GED preparatory classes offered in a high school located only ten blocks from Ms. Gerald's home. Weekly visits were planned with her children. The first visits took place at the agency and later were scheduled in Ms. Gerald's home. After the children had been in care about six months, the case was reassessed and it was determined that Ms. Gerald should be allowed to keep the children on weekends.

After several unsuccessful attempts, the worker was finally able to get the children's father involved in counseling and also helped him to obtain a job on a local construction crew. He gradually became more involved with the children during visits and occasionally attended parenting classes with Ms. Gerald. Ms. Gerald received her GED about a year after the children came into care, and began working as a teacher's aide in a day care center. Subsequently, the children were returned.

The cases of Ms. Jones and Ms. Gerald illustrate the utility of an ecological perspective and the life model of practice. The individualized assessments identified strengths and coping skills, as well as problems and needs. The family and the community systems were included in the assessment and treatment planning. Prevention of placement was achieved, in Ms. Jones' case, in part by establishing short-term task-centered goals and providing practical assistance and support. The team approach was of critical importance. The team included the social workers, foster parents, service providers in other systems, and members of appropriate groups in the black community, as well as family members. The period of placement was shortened in Ms. Gerald's case, and reunification was achieved, also due to a team effort and to the worker's ecologically based treatment plan.

Multilevel Intervention Strategies

The social worker's role and child welfare practice are affected by legislation, public and administrative policies, the role and function of the family court, the organization and administration of the child welfare system, funding patterns, and service strategies. Because black children are overrepresented in foster care, intervention strategies must focus on structural and institutional issues to prevent unnecessary placement, to strengthen families, to promote timely family reunification, and, when necessary, to promote permanence through adoption.

The commitment requires multifaceted efforts directed at policy change, program restructuring, increasing resources or changing patterns of funding, and new personnel and service strategies. Children should not be shunted to the child welfare system as a result of the failure of other systems to target their resources and helping these families.

For instance, social workers should examine the performance of the state and local mental health departments when children enter the foster care system with severe emotional problems. These departments are apt to allocate the major portion of their funds to programs serving middle-class, "treatable" populations rather than the poor ethnic minority populations with multiple problems. And if infants are coming into care because they appear to be suffering from the mothers' abuse of drugs during pregnancy, the foster care system must make the medical system responsible for study and follow-up of the infants and for providing treatment—particularly for mothers. The foster care system cannot assume full responsibility for meeting goals for these children in a timely and appropriate manner, particularly if the other systems have failed to assume their responsibilities, but it can help refer clients to and coordinate its services with those provided by these other essential agencies.

Social workers in the child welfare system should also bring these issues to public attention and enlist professional and public support to address them. One strategy would be to encourage (and/or force) the state and local governments to establish a coordinating and planning action committee that includes the key departments of the public and private agencies as well as identified community leaders and consumers. The black and ethnic minority community should also be represented on these committees at each level. Mechanisms should be established to respond to the issues presented in task force reports, research studies, critiques of policies and programs, and evaluation of the effectiveness of the foster care program.

A restructuring and/or diversifying of the agency's service system may be required (see Billingsley and Giovannoni, 1972; National Urban League, 1979). This should include involving the relevant black community and developing community based services—at least a formal, well-established neighborhood office. Ideally, the child welfare system might collaborate with another agency and work with the black community organizations to establish a local black-oriented agency. Within the agency itself, key elements of modern organizational technology, information systems, and management should be utilized, and patterns of communication and decision making, staff roles, and the development of a team approach should be examined (Sobey, 1977; Madison, 1977).

A broader knowledge base and a training and educational plan for every level of staff, as well as for foster parents and child care workers, is needed. The culture-variant perspective will provide insight into the black family's experience, values, coping mechanisms, and adaptive behavior. Staff need to be aware of the larger contextual problems of black families and the relevant systems and become sensitive to racism. They must also understand that a humanistic, color-blind approach is dysfunctional—that black and white families exist in different socioeconomic and cultural environments. Increased sensitivity through a broader knowledge base can contribute to more appropriate and effective assessment and interventions.

Black children are often placed in nonblack foster homes. It is imperative that the foster parents understand the significance of a positive racial identity for the black child. Special efforts should be made to nurture the child's black identity and to allow the child to talk about his or her feelings and experiences regarding life in a family that is racially different from the child's foster family (McRoy & Zurcher, 1983).

In their zeal to "rescue" children from what appears to be a problem-ridden family situation, social workers often make decisions about placement without fully understanding that children may feel strong bonds not only with the parents involved but also with the extended family and community. Children do not gain stability just by moving from a difficult home situation. As they are moved from one care facility to another, they become increasingly isolated from their immediate family and other important ties. Families of origin cannot be disregarded because they are poor or have a variety of personal and social functioning problems. An explicit as well as implicit base for a decision to remove a child from the home must be developed. Children should not be removed from their homes without considering, on an individual basis, the suitability of the resources available.

Even where there seem to be substantial grounds for removing a child from the family, the emotional ties between parent and child are not cut. The parents still love their children and are interested in their children's development. The Children's Defense Fund (1978) found that the parents who need the most help to sustain the relationship with their children often want to maintain close contact with children in placement but get little help with this. Funds to pay transportation costs are limited, and parents are not routinely informed about their children's progress and sometimes do not even know where their children are. This lessens the likelihood of reunification and weakens the parents' own sense of self-worth and competence.

When a valid assessment of the parents' problems in functioning has been made, there must be a commitment to long-term treatment, the treatment must not only include psychological counseling but also be based on an understanding of the strengths of the parents and the extended family, and a variety of modalities must be used. Because of institutional racism, oppression, and denial of opportunity, many black families have common problems, but the patterns of coping and adaptation are varied. Often, there are functioning, competent family members who are ready to be helpful.

There need to be innovative approaches utilized to prevent placement or to work towards reunification. Many parents cannot be full-time parents and at the same time complete their education, learn parenting skills, and resolve interpersonal problems. Needs for homemaker services, day care, special education for children, and respite care should be recognized.

There has been a significant increase in allegations of child abuse and neglect. While there is no aggregate data on race and ethnicity, reports establish that black children are overrepresented in both allegations and valid referrals. Nearly half the reported cases are unfounded, but the fact remains that the family still has needs that if met would be truly preventive. Again, such services as twenty-four-hour homemaker care, respite care, and day care are particularly important. Allegations of abuse and neglect are often the result of problems the parents were experiencing—incipient substance abuse, poor health, strained interpersonal relations—or a result of problems the child may be having at school (see Chapter 7).

The likelihood of adoption is remote for black children referred to the out-of-home placement system as young adolescents. This is true also for many younger children who have been freed for adoption for many years. These children are beginning to experience severe emotional problems and to question what permanence means to them. Creative community-based recruitment programs utilizing foster parents and local residents who have worked with children on an informal basis can open up adoption opportunities for many more children.

For many other children, prolonged adoption planning leads to long-term drift into unplanned foster care. Agencies should explore permanent foster care and home care arrangements. One component of these arrangements might be a kind of modification of open adoption. In most black communities—urban or rural—the residents utilize the same resources: church, social and fraternal groups, schools, shops, and health and social services. Long-term foster home placement may be possible without isolating the child from the parents, the extended family, and the community, even with termination of parental rights. For decades, black families have raised children without insisting on cutting the ties to the natural family and with recognition that at certain points in the life of the young person, such as graduation or marriage, the natural parents may be the key actors.

A social worker must make a shift in thinking about the role of the foster parent in long-term foster care, and this will require administrative changes in the agency. The foster parents' role must be clarified, and their strengths must be evaluated. Training and supervision will enable foster parents to participate more effectively as part of the team.

CONCLUSIONS

Social workers in the foster care system and in other agencies need to acquire skills in both case advocacy and systems advocacy. The team concept can energize and help complement the permanency planning. The social worker's role is critical. The staff's commitment to permanence must be strengthened, their sensitivity to the needs and problems of black children and their families must be increased, and their knowledge base needs to be expanded.

REFERENCES

Billingsley, A. (1968). *Black families in white America*. Englewood Cliffs, NJ: Prentice-Hall.

Billingsley, A., & Giovannoni, J. (1972). *Children of the storm: Black children and American child welfare*. New York: Harcourt Brace Jovanovich.

Children's Defense Fund. (1978). *Children without homes: An examination of public responsibility to children in out of home care*. Washington, DC: Author.

Children's Defense Fund. (1985). *Black and white children in America: Key facts*. Washington, DC: Author.

Children's Defense Fund. (1986). *A children's defense budget: An analysis of the fiscal federal budget and children*. Washington, DC: Author.

Community Council of Greater New York (1979). *Children, families, and foster care: New insights from research in New York City*. Unpublished manuscript, New York, New York.

Fanshel, D. (1976, March). Status changes of children in foster care: Final results of Columbia University Longitudinal Study. *Child Welfare, 55*(3), 143–171.

Germain, C. (1973, June). An ecological perspective in casework practice. *Social Casework, 54*(4), 12–18.

Goodman, J. (Ed.). (1973). *Dynamics of racism in social work practice*. Washington, DC: National Association of Social Workers.

Gurak, D.T., Smith, D.A., & Goldson, M. (1982). *The minority foster child: A comparative study of Hispanic, black, and white children*. New York: Fordham University, Hispanic Research Center.

Herzog, E., Sudia, C., Harwood, J., & Newcomb, C. (1971). *Families for black children: The search for adoptive parents*. Washington, DC: Government Printing Office.

Hill, R.B. (1971). *The strengths of black families*. New York: National Urban League.

Hill, R.B. (1977). *Informal adoption among black families*. New York: National Urban League.

Jenkins, S., Diamond, B. E., Flanzraich, M., Gibson, J. W., Hendricks, J., & Marshood, N. (1983, Winter). Ethnic differences in foster care placements. *Social Work Research and Abstracts, 19*,(4), 41–45. Silver Springs, MD: National Association of Social Workers.

Jeter, H.R. (1963). *Children, problems, and services in child welfare programs*. Department of Health, Education, and Welfare Administration. Children's Bureau Publication No. 403-1963.

Ladner, J. (1971). *Tomorrow's tomorrow: The black woman.* Garden City, NY: Doubleday.

Maas, H., & Engler, R.F. (1964). *Children in need of parents.* New York: Columbia University Press.

Madison, B.Q. (1977). Changing directions in child welfare services. In F. Sobey (Ed.), *Changing roles in social work practice* (pp. 31–71). Philadelphia: Temple University Press.

Mayor's Task Force on Foster Care Services. (1980). *Redirecting foster care: A report to the mayor of the city of New York.* New York: Author.

McAdoo, H.P. (1978). Factors related to stability in upwardly mobile black families. *Journal of Marriage and the Family, 40*(4), 761–776.

McGowan, B.G., & Meezan, W. (Eds.). (1983). *Child welfare: Current dilemmas, future directions.* Itasca IL: Peacock.

McRoy, R. G., & Zurcher, L.A. (1983). *Transracial and inracial adoptees: The adolescent years.* Springfield, IL: Thomas.

Meyer, C.H. (1976). *Social work practice: The changing landscape.* New York: The Free Press.

Meyer, C.H. (1979, July). What direction for direct practice? *Social Work, 24*(4), 267–281.

Morisey, P.G. (1976, December). Policy implications of recent foster care research. In Community Council of Greater New York, *Children, families, and foster care: New insights from research in New York City.* New York: Author.

National Black Child Development Institute. (1986). *The status of black children in 1980.* Washington, DC: Author.

National Urban League. (1979). *Final report, Interagency Adoption Project.* New York: Author.

New York State Council on Children and Families. (1984). *Characteristics of children in out-of-home care.* New York: Author.

Pincus, A., & Minahan, A. (1973). *Social work practice: Model and method.* Itasca, IL: Peacock.

Sobey, F. (Ed.). (1977). *Changing roles in social work practice.* Philadelphia: Temple University Press.

Willie, C. (1976). *A new look at black families.* Bayside, NY: General Hall.

Zeff, S.B. (1981, October). Program for disadvantaged elementary school students. *Social Work in Education, 4,* 19–29.

CHAPTER 9

Treatment Considerations for Working with Pregnant Black Adolescents, Their Families, and Their Partners

Sadye M. L. Logan, *University of Kansas*
Edith M. Freeman, *University of Kansas*
Ruth G. McRoy, *University of Texas at Austin*

Teen pregnancy is an issue about which our entire society should be alarmed. Second only to Hungary, the United States leads nearly all developed nations in its adolescent birth rate (Taborn, 1987). The majority of these births are to white adolescents, but for black adolescents the birth rate is disproportionately high in comparison to their representation in the population. For example, although black adolescents represent about 15 percent of the teenage population in the United States, they account for 29 percent of births in that age group. It should also be noted that birth rates for black adolescents are declining faster than white adolescent birth rates. Between 1980 and 1985, the birth rates for blacks declined 31 percent, while white rates declined only 25 percent (Children's Defense Fund [CDF], 1988).

Twenty years ago, the teenage birth rate was actually higher than it is today; many teenage mothers were married, and adolescent parenthood was not considered such a major problem. Now that the stigma of illegitimacy is largely removed, pregnant adolescents are less likely to make adoption plans for their babies. In the early 1960s, about 35 percent made adoption plans, and now only 5 percent do so (Stengel, 1985). As more and more young parents choose to raise their children outside of marriage, the costs to society become greater. These youths are often unskilled and unable to obtain a job, and they are at great risk for poverty, welfare dependency, health problems, and additional pregnancies.

Insufficient attention has been given to the unique issues of black adolescent parents (Battle, 1987). In many low-income black areas of the United States, teen pregnancy rates have reached epidemic proportions. Further, nearly 50 percent of black females in the United States are pregnant by the age of 20.

They have the highest fertility rate of any teenage population in the world in terms of percentage rates. According to the Children's Defense Fund (1988), black youth under 15 are particularly at risk for early childbearing, and almost 60 percent of all births to teenagers younger than age 15 were to black adolescents. Moreover, close to 90 percent of all black teenage parents are not married (Stengel, 1985).

These young women and their offspring are also at great risk for health problems related to early childbirth. Only one in five girls under the age of 15 will receive prenatal care during the first few months of pregnancy (Stengel, 1985). Black infants born to these mothers are also almost twice as likely to die than infants born to white teenage mothers (Taborn, 1987). Further, teenage mothers in general are more likely to have poor diets and inadequate medical care, and they are at great risk for premature delivery (Stengel, 1985). Black adolescent mothers are more likely to be single and often have to rely on their parents and additional significant others to help them deal with the financial and emotional responsibilities of a child. Also, black adolescent mothers are more likely than white counterparts to have a repeat pregnancy during their teens (CDF, 1988).

Thus, statistics suggest that special attention be given to the causes and effects of black adolescent parenting so that effective interventive and preventive programs that take into account the unique race and class issues related to the problem can be designed. This chapter examines the issue from the perspective of black adolescent parents and their families and proposes specific social work strategies.

POVERTY AND ADOLESCENT PREGNANCY

Poverty is often viewed as one reason for the disproportionately high numbers of poor adolescents who, regardless of race, become pregnant. According to John Jacob of the National Urban League, black teen pregnancy is related more to poverty factors than to racial factors. High rates of adolescent pregnancy are found in both the poor white community and the poor black community (Stengel, 1985). Since black families are overrepresented among the poor population, disproportionately higher numbers of black adolescents are at risk for pregnancy. Many feel that their lives are circumscribed; they feel trapped and see little hope of ever getting out of poverty. Some have been deprived, neglected, and abused. This sense of loss of control leads some of them to deliberately become pregnant to obtain (as they think) some control over their lives. With pregnancy many gain recognition, acceptance, and status among their peers, in the community, and within the family for their children. Their role as mothers provides them with a sense of security and nurturance. (Olson 1980).

The role models of many poor black adolescents are often adults who were teenage parents themselves, some of their peers may already be teenage parents, and many believe their life chances for educational achievement are slim. Boxill (1987) conducted clinical interviews with twelve black adolescent mothers that shed some additional light on their perceptions of their life chances. Boxill found that they generally perceived their parents to be powerless to make changes in their own lives and the family unit; had poor, distrusting relationships with peers and others; felt a lack of control over their lives and their children because of their ambiguous position of being very young but having adult responsibilities; and had a desire to be better parents than their own. Coupled with this poor self-image and sense of no control, the adolescent has a great deal of difficulty making decisions and taking on adult-like responsibilities.

FACTORS INFLUENCING DECISION-MAKING AMONG BLACK ADOLESCENTS

The level of cognitive development influences decision-making in adolescence. Adolescents' choices to become involved in unprotected sexual encounters, their perception of the pregnancy risk, and their choice of options for dealing with the pregnancy are all related to their level of cognitive development. The fact that adolescents are very egocentric and have difficulty imagining that anyone else could really feel or experience what they are feeling influences their reasoning. Many poor, uneducated black adolescents living in depressed environments may be at more risk for errors in formal operations thinking during their teen years, since the development of formal operations thinking is dependent on schooling, individual experiences and cultural influences. Additional research on the influence of such environmental factors on the development of formal operations thought among low income black adolescents is clearly needed (Franklin 1987).

According to Schinke and colleagues (1978), female adolescents engage in a two-step decision-making process regarding their choice to engage in adolescent sexual activity and childbearing. Information gathering, the first step, is often based on the availability of information from schools, parents, peers, and others. Second, they must comprehend, store, and utilize the information. Many adolescents who have varied opportunities for achievement and positive feedback may weigh the costs and benefits of pregnancy and early childbearing and reject the idea, but many poor black youth find it difficult to see any way out of their social status, or they may have other teenage parents as role models for choosing this alternative.

Taborn (1987) found that most females experience menarche around age 12 and that for black girls, menarche seems to be highly correlated with the age at which sexual activity is initiated (Zelnick & Kantner, 1977). Because most adolescents initiate sexual activity about two years after reaching menarche, prevention and education programs should be directed at black girls especially during this period (Taborn, 1987).

Parental attitudes toward premarital sexual activity also influence the behavior of black adolescents. Researchers who focused on the influences of parental attitudes on the sexual permissiveness of black adolescent females (Johnson, 1972; Roebuck & McGhee, 1977) reported that married black parents tended to be much more conservative in their attitudes toward premarital sexual activity than unmarried black parents. Differences in socioeconomic status were not an influence.

Experiences with and attitudes toward education, and lack of home supervision, have also been identified as factors affecting early sexual involvement. Chilman (1978) found that adolescents who have a positive attitude toward education are less likely to engage in premarital sex, but that low-income adolescents with poor academic skills are less likely to have many options for achievement, which can make early parenthood more problematic for them. According to the Children's Defense Fund (1988), poor adolescents are four times more likely than adolescents with incomes above the poverty level to have inadequate academic skills.

Black adolescent mothers are more likely to have completed high school than white adolescent mothers. This may occur because black adolescent mothers are 2.6 times as likely as white adolescent mothers to be unmarried at the time of birth. Thus, after the birth occurs, they may have more incentive to complete their education in order to improve their chances for raising their children as single parents. This process, however, may require outside intervention in the form of monetary assistance.

Early sexual activity is often more pronounced among poor populations because of a lack of parental supervision at home (Chilman, 1978). Families with no father present, or families with marginal incomes, necessitate maternal employment, which may result in children being unsupervised for long periods at home. Chilman suggests that when children lack regular parental supervision, they become vulnerable to powerful biological drives and social pressures.

The use of contraception becomes another decision-point for adolescents. Since 1976, blacks have increased their use of contraceptives. Several factors have been cited in the literature accounting for the use or nonuse of contraceptives by blacks. For example, the mother's interest and support of birth control, and knowledge about causes of pregnancy have often served to encourage the daughter's use of contraceptives (Furstenberg, 1971; Smith, 1982).

Once pregnancy occurs, the teenager must decide whether to marry, have an abortion, place the child for adoption, or raise the child herself. Black adolescent mothers often do not marry the fathers of their babies because these fathers are sometimes too young to provide either financially or emotionally for their offspring (CDF, 1988). The unemployment rate for black adolescents hovers around 40 percent (McGhee, 1985). Other factors, such as incarceration and the high mortality rate of young black males in low-income areas, are also responsible for the low marital rate among black teenage mothers (Stengel, 1985).

Blacks are less likely to consider abortion due to religious beliefs and personal perceptions about abortion (Taborn, 1987), and among blacks adoption has never been used widely. Black adolescents generally choose either to raise their infants themselves or possibly to place the child informally with a close friend or relative (Musick et al., 1984). When they choose to parent the child, they often must rely on their own parents and other family members for help. The result can be added financially and emotional strains within the family. Black adolescents are also at great risk for having more than one child. According to the Child Welfare League of America (CWLA) study of two hundred primarily black adolescent mothers between 12 and 15 years old, these mothers were more likely to become pregnant again. These adolescent mothers may have resigned themselves to the role of single parent, since the lack of child care obviated consideration of other life options (Miller, 1984).

The need for preventive and interventive approaches for helping these adolescents in decision-making related to their sexuality before they become pregnant is clear. The foregoing studies show that unique contextual factors influence the choices that black adolescents make. Lack of control; inability to find success in either school or employment; feelings of hopelessness; low self-esteem; low-income status; lack of successful role models; and attitudes and beliefs about contraception, abortion, and adoption are all factors that put black adolescents at greater risk for early parenthood. Reaching black adolescent fathers is an important step in reducing the risk of repeat pregnancies and in serving young mothers and their infants.

REACHING BLACK ADOLESCENT FATHERS

Adolescent fathers are often overlooked in discussions of adolescent pregnancy. They are frequently viewed as irresponsible and having no interest in taking care of their children, but many young black fathers are eager to help their children. Unfortunately, though, they often have limited education and unequal access to the labor market, and therefore may have no employment or, if employed, have very low income. Whites, with or without education, often are more able than blacks to find an adequate job to support their families (CDF, 1988; Stengel, 1985).

Hendricks and Solomon (1987) studies found that almost all of 133 young first-time fathers expressed an interest in their child's future and indicated that they had had a positive, loving relationship with the child's mother. Unfortunately, the lack of jobs prevented them from taking any responsibility. If a social worker wants to reach this population of black fathers, teenage mothers must be motivated to encourage teenage fathers to participate in social work services provided for mothers and infants. For teenage fathers who cannot be reached in this manner, the worker may need to locate and engage them in natural settings where they spend time: recreation centers, schools, barber shops, pool halls, boys' clubs, and cultural awareness centers (Freeman, in press). Once they are engaged, the worker will need to have a good understanding of the client's background—knowledge about the plight of black men in America, knowledge of the cultural norms and values in the local community, and knowledge about the black father's family of origin—to assess and intervene.

The following steps should be taken [combine these goals with those on page 166]:

1. Develop age-specific goals and objectives for adolescent mothers and fathers. Consider their age and level of cognitive development, and the perceptions about their life options, in designing preventive and interventive programs.
2. Provide role models of successful black persons who grew up in low- or moderate-income families.
3. Recognize family stresses from living at home and additional social and economic stresses, and wherever possible involve these family members in treatment as well. Enhanced family support might enable young mothers and fathers to advance their education, obtain job training, and break the cycle of early parenthood.
4. Encourage adolescents to complete school and job training programs.
5. Teach problem solving skills to help males and females to more realistically consider options related to reproductive behavior and other important life domains. Increased skills in decision-making are likely to result in higher self-esteem and a sense of control over one's life.

THE ROLE OF THE SOCIAL WORKER

The social worker who provides services to black pregnant teenagers and adolescent parents has a unique opportunity. During adolescence, teenagers are in the process of revising many of their values and concerns related to life in general and are thus more vulnerable to other perspectives as they attempt to shape their own. Moreover, the unique influence of significant others in helping to shape the lives of black individuals, particularly before and during young adulthood, has been well documented (Hill, 1972; Manns, 1981). The social worker with black teenage parents can therefore become a significant other to such clients, or encourage the identification of existing or new significant others in the environment.

The Worker as a Significant Other

When worker serves as a significant other, the relationship should be recognized as a transitional one until other natural supports can be identified. The worker's premise should be that such resources or strengths either already exist within the client's environment or can be developed. It is important that an ecological perspective be used in assessing needs and exploring resources. The families of black pregnant teenagers and teenage parents are usually able to help with this and may be the first source of support. In other circumstances, however, support may have been withdrawn and the worker may need to assume the role of significant other temporarily. Note the following example:

Sixteen-year-old Rita had brought her 3-month-old son to a clinic for routine immunizations. She had been referred to the social worker when a medical intern noticed that she seemed unusually agitated when her infant cried during the examination. The social worker had known Rita and her family for several years through regular visits to the clinic and Rita's involvement in the worker's self-esteem group for adolescent girls. The worker, too, noted Rita's obvious agitation. As she talked, Rita continuously patted the baby on his back as he lay face down on her lap. The more she talked and patted the baby, the more restless both she and the baby seemed to be. Rita believed her parents were upset because she could not stop the baby from crying at night. The parents both worked long hours and seemed to resent the noise made by the baby, according to Rita, and her efforts to quiet him. When asked how she attempted to quiet the baby, Rita said she yelled a lot. The worker wondered if she ever felt like hitting the baby. Rita hung her head and said she had hit him once or twice, but not very hard. She then began to cry, still patting the baby, but not so lightly. It was all her parents' fault, she said, because she had wanted an abortion, and they and her boyfriend had convinced her to have the baby. Now Rita felt as if the parents didn't want her and the baby to be there. She *knew* she had no place else to go. She was still in high school, and had never worked other than as a part-time waitress. The worker asked about support from the boyfriend. Rita said that he had gone off to college in another town and she had only heard from him once since he had left.

In her assessment of the situation with Rita, the worker discovered that Rita believed she was all alone. Her friends were going on with their lives and could not understand why she was not able to date and go to school functions as much as she had before the baby came. The parents and other relatives were still upset with Rita for becoming pregnant and were shocked that she would even consider an abortion, which was a cultural taboo. According to Rita, their favorite saying was "You've made your bed, now you must lay in it." While the boyfriend was happy about having a son, he had been an outstanding student in high school and had lots of plans about *his* future, without necessarily including Rita and the baby in those plans. An older brother and sister were supportive, both emotionally and financially, but each lived in another town some distance away. There was only so much they could do from that far away, according to Rita.

Any attempts by the worker to involve family, neighbors, or other individuals in the community in problem-solving were resisted by Rita. Her obvious depression and potential for abusing her child were other major issues. The depression was affecting her school performance; her usually average grades were decreasing rapidly. Rita did not feel good about herself or her circumstances. She believed no one knew or cared how she felt, including her parents, with whom she had gotten along fairly well until her pregnancy. Rita needed someone to talk with about her life concerns, her view of the family conflicts and how they could be resolved, and the stress of being a new teenage parent. She needed to be linked with significant others in her environment whom she could trust, but at the time Rita felt she had been betrayed and rejected by those supports. Her hopeless view of her situation is not unusual (see, e.g., Ortiz and Bassoff, 1987, p. 405).

The worker asked if there were things she could do to help Rita, leading to a plan for the worker to take on the role of significant other. This step was taken with the goal of eventually relinking Rita with her natural supports, so it was important for the worker to not become a surrogate parent in the process. The work included meeting with Rita several days a week during the period of active crisis. Those sessions were focused primarily on helping Rita move out of her depression by developing opportunities for taking care of her own needs. Examples included going to a movie alone, going to a school football game with a friend after arranging for a neighbor to babysit, and having time alone at home after negotiating with her younger sister to care for the baby for an hour each afternoon. The social worker arranged for a nurse practitioner at the clinic to talk with Rita about how to take care of her baby, and then to meet with her weekly for a while to answer Rita's questions.

During treatment sessions with Rita, the worker helped her see the connections between her feelings of anger about having the baby and how she handled him, as well as between her feelings of rejection and how she interacted with family members. Just allowing Rita an opportunity to ventilate during sessions validated her feelings and helped her increase her sense of self-worth. Rita also became aware of her role in the family problems. After two months she was less depressed and more confident about her ability to care for the baby, but while things at home had improved, the basic problems still existed. The worker and Rita considered whether the worker should meet with Rita and her family at that time, or identify someone in the family or community who could mediate. Rita chose a family friend who was also an employment counselor to assume this role.

Rita met with the friend, Ms. Knight, several times and learned how to improve communications with her parents. The new perspective was helpful. For example, Ms. Knight pointed out that the parents were probably trying to encourage Rita to assume a more adult role. Ortiz and Bassoff (1987, pp. 402 and 405) found similar role conflicts within the families involved in such problems.

The worker continued to meet with Rita weekly to help her make use of her supports. For instance, as some of the family problems improved and her depression lessened, Rita became very concerned about the possibility of failing in school. The worker encouraged her to utilize family members and the family friend to brainstorm solutions. Ms. Knight linked Rita with a school counselor who interceded with her teachers and set up a plan for remediation. Rita's mother agreed to make dinner and keep the baby for a while each evening so Rita could study. In exchange, Rita agreed to prepare some of the family meals on weekends.

Ms. Knight continued to help Rita think specifically about her future career plans. Rita was interested in becoming a cosmetologist, and Ms. Knight helped her explore the requirements and eventually to enroll in a cosmotology program after her high school graduation. Thus, Ms. Knight was able to give Rita critical feedback on her ideas and supported her goals. Manns (1981) calls this process of socialization by black significant others "positive defining." Based on this bonding process between Rita and Ms. Knight, the worker's previously intense role with Rita lessened to an occasional supportive contact, and termination occurred at the end of four months.

The Worker as a Broker/Linker

Work with black teenage parents in other circumstances may not require that the worker assume the role of a significant other. In such cases, the worker's role may be that of broker or linker, after helping the client identify or acknowledge existing supports. While the worker-client relationship may be a close one, it will usually not require the intensity necessary in Rita's case. For instance:

> Darrell was a 17-year-old black high school senior who had indicated interest in becoming a peer counselor for the drug prevention groups in his school. He participated in one group series and seemed to be an excellent choice for the peer counseling training program, developed by students with the help of a social worker from a nearby mental health center. The worker's services at the school were part of the center's consultation and education program in this predominantly black urban community. When the social worker approached Darrell about beginning the training program, however, he said he was no longer interested. He turned on the worker angrily when asked why he had changed his mind. He said he did not have to do the groups if he did not want to, or be hassled by the worker about them.

After thinking about the conversation with Darrell, the worker felt he could not leave things as they were. When he saw Darrell in the hall a few days later at school, he asked if they could talk again for a few minutes. He mentioned that Darrell's reaction indicated there might be a misunderstanding between them and that he wanted to clear it up. It became obvious that Darrell was concerned about something else, and that it, rather than the peer training sessions, caused his angry reaction to the social worker. The worker urged Darrell to talk over what was troubling him with someone he could trust if he did not want to talk with the worker.

> The next week, Darrell asked to meet with the social worker. Darrell told him that his 15-year-old girlfriend was pregnant and that he did not know how to tell his mother. The girl and her family attended the same church as Darrell's family, and he felt his mother was certain to find out even if they did not tell her directly. He knew he could not take care of the young woman or the baby. And while he had not taken school very seriously in the past, he felt he should not drop out at that point because he was a senior. The social worker helped Darrell explore what was behind his fears about telling his family and how he felt about his impending parenthood. He admitted that part of him wanted to brag to his friends about the pregnancy and that part of him recognized that his mother might be disappointed in him. His parents were divorced, and he thought his father might be more understanding, though not condoning. Darrell's older brother had become a father the previous year, and Darrell thought his brother would definitely think he was becoming a man.
> With the worker's help in problem-solving, Darrell decided to tell his father first

and then to have the two of them tell the mother. He clarified with the worker what kind of help he needed from each of them. For instance, his father understood some of the stress he was under as a young black man trying to "make it," and his mother would point out what his responsibilities toward his girlfriend and the baby were. Both might be helpful in thinking through how he could finish school, a family priority. The worker also encouraged him to think about what he might learn from how his brother had handled his parenthood so far. The worker discussed the cultural dynamics involved in being one of a growing number of black teenage parents, and the consequences in terms of the future life-style his child might experience. That discussion was a beginning attempt to influence Darrell's view that his impending fatherhood was something to brag about to his friends.

Later, as the worker thought about the narrow focus of the drug prevention groups, he decided on a plan for asking Darrell and other students to evaluate the groups. He hoped they would be able to point out other issues related to drug prevention and their general process of growing up that could be included in the prevention groups. For instance, the worker wondered whether there were some common factors that affected whether adolescents in the community decided to use substances or to become teenage parents. Were there additional responses to those factors that made black teenagers equally at risk for other problems in the community? Might there be common strategies that could be used in the groups or in some other service to impact on those factors? Could the students brainstorm ideas about how to involve their parents, significant others, the school, community leaders, and uninvolved peers in problem-solving around those issues? The worker acknowledged that pursuing those questions would give a different meaning to the mental health center's consultation and education services. It could be a beginning step toward what they had envisioned as using the natural resources and strengths of that community.

DEVELOPMENTAL ISSUES

The developmental transition of adolescence, along with cultural dynamics, is the context for teenagers' decisions about sexual involvement, so it must be considered in conducting assessments and developing intervention plans. Each example in this chapter illustrates this point.

In Rita's situation, for example, the developmental issue of separating from parents is of primary importance, although other developmental tasks were also addressed in the work. Some of the "distance" experienced by Rita is attributable to the natural pulling away and holding on behavior typically exhibited by parents and teenagers. The process is compounded, however, by the premature role transition that has resulted from Rita's pregnancy (Bolton, 1980; Freeman, 1987). The worker's assessment and intervention strategies were appropriately focused on typical communication problems within the family and on what Rita perceived to be rejection by her parents due to the pregnancy. The natural separation process was facilitated further by the worker's becoming a significant other temporarily and having the client seek support outside the family in a culturally acceptable way.

Darrell was confronted primarily with developmental issues related to individual and group identity, including decisions about sexual involvement. His peer group identity supported sexual involvement and pride about his impending fatherhood, while his family's priority on education was in conflict with the consequences he was facing. The worker's strategies focused on helping Darrell identify significant others who could help with solving his immediate problem related to the pregnancy. The worker was also planning more effective developmental services to groups of black teenagers with similar identity conflicts and decision-making dilemmas by utilizing the natural resources in the community (Freeman, in press). Moreover, the worker attempted to address racial identity issues directly with Darrell by pointing out the particular consequences for the infants of black teenagers. The link between developmental and cultural issues can be further illustrated by a discussion of specific intervention strategies consistent with the worker's role, described above.

THE INTERVENTION PROCESS

The helper must operate from the broad-based perspective described here for the worker's role. This perspective utilizes an ecological orientation. The focus of practice is on the social process of interaction and the transactions between the black adolescent and the adolescent's environment. This transaction is best reflected in the person-in-situation paradigm (Chapter 5). Moreover, the perspective encourages multiple interventions within systems. Proponents of an ecological approach to helping describe the practitioner as standing at the interface between different systems. Interacting systems may include the adolescent and the school, the family of the adolescent and the school, or the community and the school. Germain and Gitterman (1980) and Meyer (1976) point out that from this position the practitioner is able to intervene on multiple levels. For example, he or she may work to develop social competence within the adolescent; work to enhance responsiveness of the schools and other community institutions and services to the needs and aspirations of this client population; and work individually or within a group context in responding to the needs of the adolescent, peers, partner, siblings, and parents (Logan et al., 1986).

Organizational Issues

The extent to which programs meet the service needs of the black at-risk and parenting adolescent is directly linked to several key factors related to agencies' policies and procedures and the worker's commitment and capacity to respond effectively to the needs of the adolescent client. The type of agency and the way the agency functions have an impact on the quality and degree of client involvement (Burt & Sonenstein, 1985; Logan & Freeman, 1988). Agencies view and respond to the concerns of the parenting adolescent at the individual level with little or no regard for family involvement in the services, and even the time spent with the individual adolescent "is limited by pressures of staffing, inadequate funds, and the numbers of teens who need services" (Forbush, 1981, p. 268).

Staffing pressures are generally complicated by two major concerns: (1) the agency's inability to recruit and retain black staff members and (2) the incongruence between the staff's practice frame of reference and the agency's orientation to service delivery. For example, the staff's practice frame of reference may be ecological, but the agency may utilize a medical model orientation to service delivery.

General Treatment Considerations

Treatment for the at-risk or parenting black adolescent requires a creative, flexible, imaginative worker who understands the social and cultural context of early childbearing in the black community. The following suggestions should guide the practitioner who works with such black adolescents:

1. The worker must move beyond the stereotypic thinking that black families accept out-of-wedlock pregnancies with less difficulty than other ethnic groups. Out-of-wedlock pregnancy is more the exception than the rule.

2. The adolescent's problems and needs must be conceptualized within a family context. The practitioner must expand the adolescent transactional field to include parents, siblings—especially younger brothers and sisters, grandparents, partners, and peers.

3. Because adolescents' attention is generally directed toward themselves, the worker must guard against assuming the role of surrogate parent. This would mitigate against pregnant or at-risk black adolescents who are generally lacking in strong basic skills, developing skills that are necessary for negotiating complex organizations and advocating for themselves.

4. Intervention must be conceptualized on a continuum from prevention to treatment to include a model of treatment that is threefold: primary, secondary, and tertiary.

Primary prevention includes a range of activities and programs designed to diminish or decrease the number of teenage pregnancies within a given at-risk group. These activities may include peer counseling groups and education programs in the schools, fraternal and religious organizations, community coalitions, and fund raising to support teen pregnancy prevention. According to the Children's Defense Fund (1988, p. 10), six areas are important "in bolstering the motivation and capacity of teens to prevent too-early pregnancy": (1) education and strong basic skills, (2) jobs, work-related skills building, and work, (3) a range of nonacademic opportunities for success, (4) family life education and life planning, (5) comprehensive adolescent health services, and (6) a national and community climate that makes preventing teen pregnancy a leading priority.

Secondary prevention involves early assessment and treatment of those already affected by the problem. The objective is to reduce (1) the incidence of first teenage pregnancies in the siblings of teenage parents and (2) the number of adolescent school dropouts as a result of pregnancy and parenting.

Tertiary Prevention involves efforts to decrease the number of teenage parents who become pregnant again after a first pregnancy. Essentially, tertiary prevention and treatment are the same.

5. Not unlike the general society, practitioners are also ambivalent about expectations regarding teenage sexual behavior, about the relationship between parents and teenagers. Governmental and agency policies, as well as the media, convey contradictory messages to adolescents and their families (Ooms, 1981). Helping professionals receive ambivalent messages about their roles and responsibilities in teenage sexuality, pregnancy, and parenting programs. These are areas that evoke intense feelings, attitudes, and values. Consider the following scenario:

> A practitioner who considered herself open-minded was assigned a black, pregnant 13-year-old. During the initial contact the practitioner had a strong transference reaction to the adolescent. The youngster reminded the practitioner of her daughter as well as of her own ambivalent feelings about teenage premarital sex.
>
> The adolescent lives with her parents and a younger sister (age 7) in an inner-city housing project. She is tall for her age and quite attractive. She is not considered a good student academically and has functioned between average and slightly below average. She has been seeing a 19-year-old boy, against her parents' wishes, for nearly two years. Her parents have conflicts and argue frequently over care and responsibility for her and her sister. The mother is extremely upset about the pregnancy and has suggested that it be terminated. The father has abdicated responsibility and views the girl's social and emotional needs as the mother's responsibility.

The practitioner in this situation is confronted with at least four kinds of value/ethical issues: (1) those related to the lack of congruence between her personal belief about adolescent sexual behavior and pregnancy, and the values espoused by the social work profession regarding client's self-determination; (2) those related to abortion as a form of birth control; (3) those concerned with sexuality in general, especially for the very young and unmarried; and (4) those related to the role of parent(s) in fostering responsible adolescent sexual behavior. These concerns created not only conflict for individual practitioners but also a great deal of dissension between community groups and service providers.

For the practitioner, personal beliefs and values often collide with the basic rights of client self-determination. These personal values may range from the belief that it is morally unacceptable for teenagers to engage in premarital sex and that they should be punished, to an acceptance of teenagers' rights to decide about sexual involvement and advocacy for comprehensive care and services. The practitioner must be alert to such potential value conflicts, which also become apparent as specific strategies are used to intervene in situations involving black adolescent parents.

Specific Treatment Strategies

Barbara Washington is described in the August 1986 issue of *Ebony* as a non-typical teenage mother, but Sara Markie may be considered a typical teenage mother. For Barbara, a 17-year-old senior at Manley High School on Chicago's west side, high school and motherhood coincided. She described her pregnancy as "sort of a mistake." According to the *Ebony* article, Barbara will enter Southern Illinois University with a 3.8 grade point average and a full four-year academic scholarship. It was further pointed out that though Barbara came from a household headed by a single parent and an impoverished background, unlike the statistics on most adolescent mothers across the country, she was not dropping out of school and having her second child before reaching 20 years of age. The characteristics defining Barbara as an achieving teenage mother are that she is a serious adult, determined to be successful, bright and motivated to do something with her life, sensitive to the needs of her baby, and supported by her family. On the other hand,

> Sara Markie is also 17 years old and from a household headed by a single parent and an impoverished background, but she is expecting her second child before the age of 20. The ecomap (see Figure 9.1) depicts Sara as experiencing either tenuous or somewhat stressful relationships with significant others as well as with various community agencies and institutions. The map further depicts an array of fragmented or underutilized services.
>
> Sara is the oldest of four children (see Figure 9.1): Dawn, 14; Cathy, 11; and Adam, 8. The other children are doing well academically, but Dawn has been exhibiting mood swings. Sara's parents have been separated for nine years. Her mother works in the housekeeping department at the local hospital.
>
> Sara started having sex at age 15, in part because of pressure from her boyfriend but also because of curiosity fueled by accounts of sexual experiences from her girlfriends. Sara's mother warned her about getting "in trouble." Sara's response was that she knew how to take care of herself, so when she became pregnant her mother was not only disappointed and hurt but also angry. She told Sara that she so much wanted her to stay in school and make something of herself and that her only chance would be to not have the baby. Sara's boyfriend advised her to have the baby, and her guidance counselor at school told her the ultimate decision about the baby was hers to make. Sara chose to have the baby and keep it. She continued living at home with her mother and kept seeing the baby's father. She is now four months pregnant with her second child.

In considering appropriate intervention strategies for working with Sara an important question would be: How might those strengths identified as characteristic of the achieving teenage mother become operationalized in Sara's life? In addition to adopting a strengths orientation, it is equally important to assume an approach that is broad-based and operates from a family systems context.

162

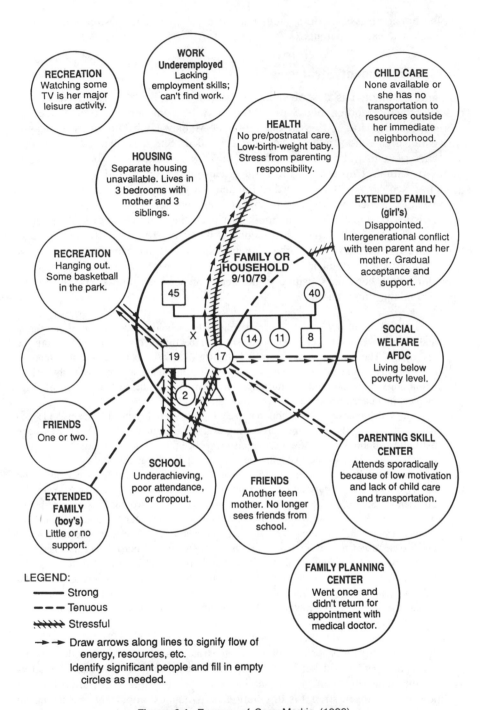

Figure 9.1. Ecomap of Sara Markie (1986)

Sara was referred to the parenting skills center by her worker and attended sporadically. She was then assigned, with several others, to a new social worker, who prepared for her initial contact with Sara by reviewing her records and noting the prior worker's assessment of Sara's situation:

Strengths:
1. Sara's family members care about each other.
2. Sara is devoted to her baby.
3. Sara is neat and smiles easily.
4. Sara has the emotional support of the baby's father.

Needs:
1. Child care.
2. Housing.
3. Prenatal care.
4. Parenting skills.
5. Family planning.
6. GED and vocational training.

The worker knew that she must consider certain practice guidelines:

1. Assume a flexible, broad-based approach in responding to the multiple potential needs identified in the case. Traditional approaches have the potential of joining with one aspect but alienating other aspects.
2. Be willing to provide not only information but also support and guidance through individual, group and family contacts. Individual and group contacts help adolescents explore options, listen to others' concerns, and bolster confidence and build self-esteem. Family involvement helps strengthening communication and securing uniform support as well as providing specific services to the adolescent parent and significant others.
3. Tolerate inconsistency in behaviors and appreciate social and cultural differences. This worker does not allow different values and personal priorities to keep her from sharing her thoughts with Sara about these differences. She remembers her ambivalence and hesitation about sharing her belief that getting an education was important as well as family planning. She eventually learned that the key was to help the adolescent to differentiate between someone's caring about them as a person and, at the same time, disapproving of self-destructive or negative behavior.
4. Avoid being triangulated between the adolescent and his or her family or organizations providing services to the adolescent.
5. Be able to reach out beyond the agency in providing services through peer outreach networks and networking and coordination with other professionals in the community, to help identify at-risk adolescents and plan and implement services. This will help avoid duplication of services, provide an interdisciplinary focus, and involve the lay community

(black churches, sororities/fraternities, and business leaders) (Logan & Freeman, 1988).

The worker's initial contact with Sara occurred through a prearranged *home visit*, which both gave Sara a feeling of security and allowed the worker to view Sara and the baby in a natural setting. During this visit, the worker used the *strengths-needs list* (Table 9.1) and the *ecomap* (Figure 9.1) to further assess Sara's needs and to begin establishing mutual goals. This contact also revealed that the relationship between the baby's father and Sara's mother was strained.

TABLE 9.1. STRENGTHS-NEEDS LIST FOR BLACK PREGNANT ADOLESCENTS

STRENGTHS are being defined here as the client's assets, significant others who are supportive, and available community resources.	**NEEDS** are being defined as what can be done, or what should be changed, and are stated positively in terms of what the client and worker could do to bring about change.
Strengths	**Needs**
Living Arrangements	
Where do you live? What do you like about it? Do you have enough space? What is the community like? How long have you lived there?	Is there anything that could make where you live more to your liking? What would you like to change about the way it looks?
Health	
How often do you see the gynecologist? Physically, are you having any problems? What do you do when you are not feeling well? Are you on a special diet?	How can you be stronger and healthier?
Social Support	
With whom in your family do you spend time? How often? Who in your family seems to care most about you? With which of your friends do you spend time? How often? Which of your friends seems to care most about you? Are you in contact with the baby's father? How often? Which family members or friends can you rely on to help you? What do you do with your family/friends? How often? Are you known to another social service agency?	Who in your family would you like to see more or hear from more? Which of your friends would you like to see more or hear from more? How often and in what capacity? Is there anything that your family or friends should do for you now? How do you see the baby's father helping? What has been your experience with other social service agencies? What would you like to do with other people? (Make suggestions from leisure time strengths list.)

TABLE 9.1. (Continued)

Leisure Time	
What do (did) you especially like to do? Do (did) you have any hobbies? What clubs or organizations have you belonged to? What do (did) you like to do on your school vacations or in your free time? How often do you do these things? With whom do you do them? Where do you do them? How long have you been doing them?	What would you like to do in your free time? Are there any hobbies or activities that you would like to do more? (Make suggestions from strengths list.) How much more?

Developmental Concerns	
How much do you know about caring for a baby? How will the baby change your life-style? Are you planning to continue dating the baby's father? Do you feel ready to live away from your family?	What do you need to care effectively for a baby? How might you balance caring for the baby with some time for yourself? Are you prepared to date others and practice safe sex?

Personal Characteristics	
What are you most proud of accomplishing? What makes you feel happy? What do you like most about yourself? What do others like most about you?	Who are your role models? What talents would you like to continue developing? This is what I have noticed is a strength for you: (e.g., friendliness, sense of humor, etc.).

Sara's mother had never liked the baby's father and saw him as a negative influence on Sara. However, he still visits Sara, but provides no financial support. As the ecomap reflects, he works sporadically. His most recent employment was at a local car wash.

After the initial contact, the worker and Sara agreed on the following, based on guidelines from the strengths-needs list:

1. There was much work to be done, and the best approach was for Sara and her entire family to be involved. In addition to the needs noted initially by the worker, the following concerns emerged:
   a. Prenatal care for the expected baby and postnatal care for the 2-year-old
   b. Sara's feelings of being overburdened with child care responsibilities
   c. Housing
   d. The relationship with the baby's father
   e. The strained communication between Sara and her mother
   f. The mercurial nature of Sara's second oldest sibling.
2. Areas of concern would be partialized with specific goals, and follow-up

plans. The idea was to start small and go slow, to encourage and foster a sense of competence and achievement in Sara.
3. Begin to explore options regarding future employment and completion of the necessary requirements for a high school diploma.

The practice principles presented in Sara's case are generalizable to all at-risk and parenting adolescents. The critical factors are that the practitioner [these goals should be combined with those on page 153]:

1. Genuinely like adolescents
2. Have a good understanding of their life cycle needs and the impact of social and cultural influences
3. Is able to motivate in a respectful, supportive way through role modeling, and other creative measures
4. Is able to transcend stereotypes and biases about "the black at-risk or pregnant adolescent" or "the black community" through self-awareness and an understanding of the black experience.

CONCLUSIONS

Adolescent parenthood remains a major problem for the black community because it disrupts the natural transition into young adulthood, disrupts educational goals and preparation for future employment, and is likely to lead to unstable interpersonal and intrapersonal relationships within and outside of the family of origin. These factors mitigate against adolescent parents being able to accept and effectively carry out parenting responsibilities, but they also create a high cost for society in terms of the costs of education, health care, and lost productivity.

REFERENCES

Battle, S. (Ed.) (1987). *The black adolescent parent.* New York: Haworth.

Bolton, F.C. (1980). *The pregnant adolescent: Problems of premature parenthood.* Beverly Hills, CA: Sage.

Boxill, N. (1987). How would you feel . . .? Clinical interviews with black adolescent mothers. In S.F. Battle (Ed.), *The black adolescent parent* (pp. 41–51). New York: Haworth.

Burt, M., & Sonenstein, F. (1985, Spring). Planning programs for pregnant teenagers. *Public Welfare, 42*(2):28–34.

Children's Defense Fund (CDF) Adolescent Pregnancy Prevention Clearinghouse. (1988, January–March). *Teenage pregnancy: An advocate's guide to the numbers.* Washington, DC: CDF.

Children's Defense Fund (CDF) Adolescent Pregnancy Prevention Clearinghouse. (1988, May). *Adolescent and young adult fathers: Problems and solutions.* Washington, DC: CDF.

Chilman, C. (1978). *Adolescent sexuality in a changing American society.* Washington, DC: Department of Health, Education, and Welfare.

Forbush, J. (1981). Adolescent parent programs and family involvement. In T. Ooms (Ed.), *Teenage pregnancy in a family context: Implications for policy* (pp. 254–276). Philadelphia, PA: Temple University Press.

Franklin, D. (1987). Black adolescent pregnancy: A literature review. In S.F. Battle (Ed.), *The black adolescent parent* (pp. 15–39). New York: Haworth.

Freeman, E.M. (1987, January). Interaction of pregnancy, loss, and developmental issues in adolescents. *Social Casework, 68*(1), 38–46.

Freeman, E.M. (in press). Adolescent fathers in urban communities: Exploring their needs and role in preventing pregnancy. *Social Work and Human Sexuality.*

Furstenberg, F., Jr. (1971). Birth control experiences among pregnant adolescents. *Social Problems, 19,* 192–203.

Germain, C., & Gitterman, A. (1980). *The life model of social work practice.* New York: Columbia University Press.

Hendricks, L., & Solomon, A. (1987). Reaching black male adolescent parents through nontraditional techniques. In S. F. Battle (Ed.), *The black adolescent parent* (pp. 111–124). New York: Haworth.

Hill, R. (1972). *The strengths of black families.* New York: Emerson Hall.

Johnson, L. (1972). *Premarital sex and family planning attitudes: A report of a pilot study in rural Georgia county.* Washington, DC: Department of Health, Education, and Welfare.

Logan, S., & Freeman, E. (1988). *Adolescent pregnancy programs: A training manual and technical assistance for service providers.* University of Kansas, Center for Black Leadership Development and Research, Lawrence, Kansas.

Logan, S., Freeman, E., & McRoy, R. (1986). *A comprehensive ecological approach to pregnant teenagers, their partners, and their families.* Paper presented at the National Association of Social Workers National Conference on Clinical Social Work, San Francisco, California.

Manns, W. (1981). Support systems of significant others in black families. In H. McAdoo (Ed.), *Black families.* Beverly Hills, CA: Sage.

McGhee, J. (1985). The black family today and tomorrow. In J. Williams (Ed.), *The state of black America, 1985.* Washington, DC: National Urban League.

Meyer, C. (1976). *Social work practice: The changing landscape* (2nd ed.). New York: Free Press.

Miller, S. (1984). Childbearing and children among the very young. *Children Today, 13*(3), 26–29.

Musick, J., Handler, A., & Waddill, K. (1984). Teens and adoption: A pregnancy resolution alternative? *Children Today, 13*(6), 24–29.

Not your typical teen mother: Chicago honor student balances books and her baby. *Ebony, 41*(10), 67–74.

Olson, L. (1980, July). Social and psychological correlates of pregnancy resolution among adolescent women: A review. *American Journal of Orthopsychiatry, 50* (3), 432–445.

Ooms, T. (Ed.). (1981). *Teenage pregnancy in a family context: Implications for policy* (pp. 254–276). Philadelphia, PA: Temple University Press.

Ortiz, E.T., & Bassoff, B. Z. (1987, September). Adolescent welfare mothers: Lost optimism and lowered expectations. *Social Casework, 68*(7), 400–405.

Pearlman, H.H. (1970). The problem-solving model in social casework. In R.W. Roberts & R.H. Nee (Eds.), *Theories of social casework* (pp. 129–180). Chicago: University of Chicago Press.

Pitman, K. (1986). *Adolescent pregnancy: Whose problem is it?* Washington, DC: Children's Defense Fund.

Roebuck, J., & McGhee, M. (1977). Attitudes toward premarital sex and sexual behavior among black high school girls. *Journal of Sex Research, 13*(2), 104–114.

Schinke, S., Gilchrist, L., & Small, R. (1978). Preventing unwanted adolescent pregnancy: A cognitive-behavioral approach. *American Journal of Orthopsychiatry, 1* (49), 81–88.

Smith, P. B., Weinman, M. L., & Mumford, D.M. (1982). Social affective factors associated with adolescent pregnancy. *Journal of School Health, 52*(2), 90–93.

Stengel, R. (1985, December 9). Children having children. *Time,* 78–83, 84, 87, 89–90.

Taborn, J. (1987). The black adolescent mother: Selected unique issues. In S.F. Battle (Ed.), *The black adolescent parent* (pp. 1–13). New York: Haworth.

Zelnik, M., & Kantner, J. (1977). Sexual and contraceptive experience of young unmarried women in the United States, 1976 and 1971. *Family Planning Perspectives, 9*(2), 55–71.

CHAPTER 10

Working with the Black Poor:
Implications for Effective Theoretical and Practice Approaches

Leon F. Williams,
Boston College

The rate of poverty and black family well-being have become almost synonymous—not because all black families are poor but because poverty and dependency status have had an impact on much of the black experience in the United States. Poverty is a critical factor in the lives of many blacks, and at the most global level it acts as a barometer to the general progress of all blacks in the United States. Continued poverty for a disproportionate number of black Americans dispels the American dream and precludes any premature celebration of black economic or political gains or achievements.

The black family and community are under greater stress than ever. Single-family units are on the increase. More and more black children are among the ranks of the poor; infant mortality rates are rising. Black men and young adult males are struggling to survive in a world of violence, drug addiction, alcoholism, homicide, and other evidences of despair and anomie produced by chronic societal neglect and structural unemployment. The black elderly are experiencing increased isolation and neglect.

The bottom stratum of the black community has compelling problems. The social disorganization, the lagging academic performance and high dropout rates for black students, the disturbing rate of black on black crime, and the alarming rate of early pregnancies among black teens mitigate against any form of progress (Hulbert, 1984; Loury, 1984). All these problems represent an assault on the overall institution of the black family. With few exceptions, black families are struggling for survival. This chapter focuses on the impact of poverty on black family life—the impact of economic and social welfare policies, the effects of chronic dependency, and the issues and implications for practice.

169

POVERTY AND ITS IMPLICATIONS

This chapter uses earnings, based on the guidelines developed by the federal government, as the absolute definition of poverty. In determining the number of families that are poor at any given point in time, one simply compares the total cash income of a family of any given size during a specific calendar year with the appropriate poverty line corresponding to a family of that size. The federal government does not adjust the poverty line to take into account changes in the real median income of families throughout the nation—only changes as measured by the U. S. Consumer Price Index (CPI).

When the median income of families is compared by family size and the poverty line, the plight of the poor is more readily understood. For example, the poverty line for a family of four was $10,000 in 1984. But the data reveal that the poverty line for a family of four was equal to only 34.1 percent of the median income of all families containing four persons in the United States during the year 1984. These ratios are sharply lower than those prevailing in 1964, when the official poverty line was first introduced. The poverty line for a nonfarm family of four in 1964 was $3,169, equivalent to nearly 42 percent of the four-person income for that year. Thus, the 1984 poverty line represents a lower fraction of the median income for families containing two, three, or four persons than it did twenty years ago. Current poverty in the United States represents a greater degree of relative deprivation for families in the 1980s than it did in prior years (Sum et al., 1986).

Structural Changes in the Family

During the past decade, the substantial increase in black female-headed households appears to have canceled out potential economic gains and has kept the black median income low (Rodgers, 1982), despite the general increase in income experienced by two-earner black families. The rise of female-headed households amounts to a revolutionary change in the structure of all families in America and probably represents an unmitigated disaster for the black community because it increases the number of vulnerable persons. The risk of poverty for a female-headed family is nearly five times that of families headed by a male or families in which an adult male is present (Goldberg & Kremen, 1986). In 1984, one in four families with children was a single-parent family: 20 percent of white children and 59 percent of black children lived in single-parent families, compared with 1970 figures of 10 percent and 36 respectively. The dramatic changes occurring in family structure are also reflected in the increasing numbers of babies born to unmarried mothers—currently more than 20 percent of all births. In 1982 some 15 percent of white mothers and 47 percent of black mothers were single (divorced, "spouse absent," or never married), compared with 8 percent and 31 percent in 1970 (see Chapter 9 for a detailed discussion).

Family Income

After experiencing steady growth between the decade 1969 to 1979, median family income has declined by 8.3 percent. The decline is probably due to the recession of 1981–82, which added 1.6 million persons to the poverty roll, and to the stricter 1981 budget and legislative changes, which added an additional 557,000 persons. At any rate, median income fell so much that the percentage change in that income for all families between 1969 and 1983 was a *minus* 8.6 percent. The average real family income among blacks fell a dramatic 5.3 percent from 1980 to 1983, representing the largest decline of any group (Rosen et al., 1987).

Progress in income and earnings among two-earner black families has been evident throughout the past decade. In families with two working parents, the average income of black families rose to 73 percent that of whites in 1978 to 84 percent in 1981 (Rosen et al., 1987). However, black labor force participation overall is below the labor force participation of whites because of an increase in the long-term unemployment. The bulk of the jobs held by blacks are in the job categories paying the lowest salaries. A study in 1987 by the National Committee on Pay Equity found that occupations with disproportionately high percentages of minority women have low average salaries. Minority women represent more than 25 percent of all nurses aides, sewing machine operators, and child care workers, and all these occupations have an average annual salary of less than $10,000. Another study showed that minorities and white women are concentrated in such low-paying jobs as baggage porter, farm worker, launderer, dressmaker, and dental assistant (National Association of Social Workers, 1987).

Employment

Blacks as a group experience lower levels of economic well-being than whites (Abbott, 1980; Gordon et al., 1982; Taylor & Chatters, 1986; U.S. Bureau of the Census, 1980). Racial differences in economic well-being are reflected in employment patterns and earnings. Abbott (1980) found that (controlling for education and occupation) blacks were still less likely to hold full-time, year-round jobs than whites. Among blacks who did hold such jobs, earnings were significantly lower than those of whites.

According to Taylor and Chatters (1986), even after controlling for education and labor market experiences, blacks have lower earnings than whites. Controlling for education, the earnings of black males 25 to 34 years of age were only 80 percent of their white counterparts, even though this cohort of young blacks is presumably in the best position to take advantage of increased economic opportunities. Recent gains in the economic condition of some blacks have had little impact upon the vast majority of the black population (Taylor & Chatters, 1986).

Education

The percentage of blacks completing high school and college continues to rise, but almost 750,000 black youth between the ages of 16 and 19 are currently classified as either alienated or disadvantaged. Their ranks continue to expand, in part because about 700,000 black youth drop out of high school or become chronic truants each year. As these young people leave school, they lose their link with the traditional vehicle that provides entry to the world of work—educational attainment (Stewart, 1986).

Health

The death rate among blacks is still significantly higher than that among whites, mainly because of the substandard environment in which they live (Rosen et al., 1987). According to McAdoo (1987), the death rate of older children and youth is clearly linked to the environment rather than to race. For inner-city youths, regardless of race, the leading cause of death is injury or violence. Anderson (1983) found that the infant mortality rate for nonwhites (he assumes the majority to be black) is 28.3 per 1,000, while the rate for whites is 15.8 per 1,000. There is a gradual progressive increase in the gap until age 65, when it begins to diminish and actually reverses itself if the black person lives until age 80. Anderson concludes that blacks die earlier and faster than whites. The risk of death from all causes (heart, stroke, cancer, homicide, accident, cirrhosis, diabetes) is higher for blacks than whites, except suicide (see Chapter 13).

Infant Mortality and Child Abuse

A critical index of group well-being is infant mortality. In 1983, the black infant mortality rate was twice as high as the white rate, 19.2 versus 9.7 per 1,000 live births (Rosen et al., 1987). This fact is dependent on socioeconomic factors: the dramatic increase in teenage rates of pregnancy and decrease in ongoing prenatal care; the higher incidence among this population of lower birth weight infants or premature births owing to poor health and nutrition in the mother; and the quality of medical care sought and received.

With regard to child abuse, whites are about two-thirds more likely than blacks to maltreat children, but a national incidence study indicated a nearly identical rate for blacks (11.5 percent per 1,000) and whites (10.5 percent per 1,000) for all forms of maltreatment. One can conclude that blacks are more likely to be reported for alleged maltreatment than whites, or that black family norms that permit spanking or slapping are more likely to be misinterpreted by white child welfare workers (Kinard, 1987). Factors associated with child abuse include socioeconomic status, unemployment, financial difficulties, housing and living conditions, family size, family structure, teenage parenting, and social isolation. All this should point to a higher incidence among poor blacks, but none of these factors has been proven to be characteristic of all child abuse situations. In sum, race or class does not predict child abuse, which can occur in any racial group or social strata (Kinard, 1987).

THE SOCIAL AND HISTORICAL CONTEXT OF BLACK POVERTY

Poverty has always been understood as a comparative relationship between segments and classes that are deprived of basic human needs (e.g., food, shelter, clothing, and medical care) and the secure and affluent segments within a certain social and economic order. It does relatively little good to advance an argument that compares and contrasts the family of a Puerto Rican welfare mother in the South Bronx with a family in Bangladesh or in Lagos, Nigeria, São Paulo, or Bombay. The black and Hispanic material realities must be judged against the backdrop of America's remarkable success in producing an unprecedented standard of living for the majority of its white population (Marable, 1983).

Black poverty is best understood within a historical and social context. Schermerhorn (1974) posited that there were "thresholds" of social systems, historical events where societies cross certain thresholds of social conditions that precipitate qualitative differences that affect entire fields of human activity. Such a threshold, he says, is like a sluice gate for social opportunities and does three things simultaneously: it shuts off some alternatives altogether, narrows other alternatives, and opens new ones. This social juncture or threshold also changes the rules by which the society conducts its business. Schermerhorn and others have suggested that the civil rights era and the subsequent Black Power revolution represented such a threshold, producing a crisis or disruption in the body politic that would cause significant changes in race relations in America. Declaring the period prior to the late 1960s the "B.C. era" (1900–68) or *Before the Crisis*, he named the subsequent period as the "A.D. era," or *After the Disruption*. According to Schermerhorn, the B.C. era was marked by assimilationism or Americanization, and the violent oppression of black persons of color who were then called Negroes, colored, and other less savory sobriquets. Successive waves of immigrants arrived, and popular opinion showed tolerance for European migrants only when they were willing to give up their language and customs. Even for the "Negro," assimilation was viewed as inevitable in the long run, and many black leaders opted for integration as a long-term goal—this being just one variant of assimilation (Schermerhorn, 1974).

Racism in the "B.C. Period"

The end of slavery and the influx of migrants from Europe converged with an economic reality—the rapidly expanding economy and demand for unskilled labor in nineteenth-century America. The B.C. period for European migrants represented a period of modest but solid economic gains, part of which was reflected in a substantial flight to working-class suburbs in the wake of black migration to adjacent areas. In the same period, only a tiny elite among the Negroes advanced with the economy; the great masses remained at the lowest occupational level, with many losing the little foothold they had as a result of lynching, segregation, and Jim Crowism in the south. Blacks did not enter the urban labor market until it was fairly well preempted by workers from abroad. They showed some advances during World War II, but they were not able to sustain those advances, partly because of widespread discrimination on the part of employers and organized labor, and partly for structural reasons. Technological changes eliminated unskilled and semi-skilled jobs (the very ones that gave European ethnics their start) at the rate of 35,000 jobs a week, or 2 million a year. The economy forged ahead by reason of increased productivity, which is a euphemism for job elimination at the bottom levels (Schermerhorn, 1974), where the bulk of black workers were to be found.

During the 1950s and 1960s, when the courts and Congress were enunciating new civil rights gains, federal promises raised the level of black expectations to new heights at a time when income levels were sinking and unemployment growing in the black community (Schermerhorn, 1974). But DeFleur and colleagues (1971) noted: "The very fact that the society has preached upward mobility so loudly and so long increases the bitterness and frustration of those who find themselves cut off from the good things upward mobility can bring and thus contributes to the tendency toward alienation and conflict" (p. 231).

These realities fed civil rights fervor throughout the 1950s and 1960s and led to three major pieces of social legislation prohibiting discrimination in employment, housing, and voting—the Voting Rights Act of 1965 and the Civil Rights Acts of 1964 and 1968. A number of legislated programs, including the limited War on Poverty, were increasingly oriented to black problems, but much of the payoff went to middle-class blacks (as, e.g., in hotel accommodations and government jobs), not to working-class blacks (Feagin, 1978).

Direct action against segregation and discrimination began in earnest in the north in the 1960s: boycotts, sit-ins, and mass demonstrations. Such groups as the Nation of Islam (Black Muslims) and the Congress of Racial Equality (CORE) came to the fore with the aim of promoting black pride and fighting discrimination. The latter accelerated protest campaigns against housing and employment discrimination (Feagin, 1978). Aggressively militant organizations oriented toward "black pride" and Black Power ideology, many of whom espoused Marxist and quasi-Marxist sentiments, grew in number, including the famous Black Panther Party. Pride and consciousness grew in all segments of the black community in the north, particularly among the young (Feagin & Hahn, 1973). The poor and working-class black Americans and college students took to the streets from the mid-1960s to the early 1970s, escalating from protests against oppression to collective violence. Nonviolent and violent strategies coexisted. Riots sometimes grew out of police action against nonviolent demonstrations, which were in turn a response to earlier police action.

The most common establishment response was increased repression, especially to quell ghetto riots, as exhibited by the millions of dollars spent on police forces (riot gear, water cannon, in some cases small tanks). Some attempts were made to cool down the ghettos with economic programs, but when this limited response faded the repressive forces remained. Co-optation of militant leaders into federal programs, coupled with repression and the killing or jailing of indigenous leaders, had by the mid-1970s produced another lull in the ongoing and cyclical history of black protest going back to slavery (Feagin, 1978).

Neo-Racism in the "A.D. Period"

The A.D. period (1969–present) is characterized by several phenomena: an increased conservatism and antiliberal bias in the body politic, represented by the ascendancy to the presidency of Republican Ronald Reagan; a stiffening of the resolve of white ethnic Europeans, and labor, in the face of putative black gains; an increase in societal narcissism and self-absorption, increased attacks on affirmative action programs; unprecedented prosperity in the white middle classes; and the fact of growing affluence among a segment of the black community that produced an ever widening income gap between the black poor and the black middle and upper classes. This latter fact produced an impoverished lower strata of the black community which has become a permanent poverty class, a group Glasgow (1981) calls the black "underclass." This permanent underclass is typified by hustling and hanging out. These are primarily 18- to 34-year-old black males who are unified by their common alienated condition. Gary and Leashore (1982) indicated that black men appear to be the major victims of modern racism.

Glasgow (1981) studied inner-city black youth in Los Angeles. He uses several criteria to distinguish the black "underclass" from lower-income blacks: an absence of intergenerational social mobility, the "lack of real opportunities to succeed," and widespread "anger and despair" from contact with mainstream institutions that almost imperceptibly and quite impersonally reject them (Marable, 1983).

There is indeed a growing underclass, or lower-class strata, which is disaffected and permanently barred from access to the American mainstream because of race. Theoretically, the existence of a black underclass represents a dangerous variation on the old ideological racism—a type of neo-racism that when taken to its logical extremes poses an even greater threat to the life chances of the black family. In the past, despite widespread discrimination and bigotry, the black community supported a large group of persons one could call the working poor, whose prospects for the future were generally good, barring catastrophe. These factors, and the intrinsic need to strive, helped black families experience steady upward social mobility in each generation over the past fifty years, but under neo-racism this trend has been curtailed (Williams & Diaz, 1987).

Racial and Poverty Politics in the 1980s

Prejudice and racism can no longer be counted on to serve the ends they once served. In the B.C. period, racism was tied to the subjugation and control of some human beings for the material wealth of a few others. The current (A.D.) period can be characterized as the *post–civil rights era*, operating within what is basically a service-oriented economy that requires a different set of skills as machines replace humans in the manufacturing process. American industry no longer requires unskilled labor. When jobs were plentiful and the smokestack industries thrived, American workers could at least grudgingly accede to black demands for jobs and equal employment opportunity. Blacks had moral leverage, if for no other reason than that they were the most lowly group in the labor force. Even with plentiful jobs, however, it was always understood the black workers would start at the bottom and would not openly compete for management level positions, such as shop steward, shift boss, or supervisor. With civil rights and the advent of affirmative action laws, blacks emerged as direct competitors for many of the higher status jobs held exclusively by whites. The result was a conservative backlash (Schermerhorn, 1974).

Theoretically, then, the target of opportunity for the dominant society in cooling down black community activism and rising expectations appears to be the highly visible but vulnerable group that has traditionally been the target of repression—black males. The evidence is there in significantly higher death rates, structural unemployment, and alienation and dislocation.

THE CAUSES OF BLACK POVERTY

Groups that have been subjected to oppression and exploitation throughout American history are overrepresented in the ranks of the poor (Rodgers, 1982). How important is race among the causes of poverty?

The most important mainstream theory is *orthodox economic theory*. This theory holds that each person is responsible for his or her own income (Gordon, 1972). Assuming perfect market competition and market equilibrium, this school of thought would have one believe that if a person's income is too low it is because that person's productivity is low. The ability of the individual worker determines his or her worth in the marketplace. The solution to poverty lies in higher productivity on the part of workers, which produces higher income. This idea is inherently at the core of job training programs for the poor. Structural poverty is also addressed by higher productivity. If all workers produce more, higher incomes and revenues will be the result. The subsequent prosperity *trickles down* to the lower strata to raise their overall standard of living. This view was prominent among advisers to the Reagan administration. In this explanation, poverty is the outcome of variations in natural ability—it places the blame for poverty mainly on the innate characteristics of the poor and takes on a distinctly racist overtone (Rodgers, 1982).

A second theory, the *culture of poverty thesis*, popularized by Oscar Lewis (1959), argues that the poor develop a deviant subculture with values and habits that are self-perpetuating and self-defeating. Some characteristics associated with this subculture are unemployment, underemployment, few savings, apathy, fatalism, violence, inability to defer gratification, and abandonment of the family by the father. Banfield (1968), Glazer and Moynihan (1963), and Moynihan (1965) altered the theory and put it to use in a conservative interpretation of the black poor as being socially and culturally deficient and lacking the means to overcome their plight, and poverty as being self-induced. The poor were considered unworthy of social assistance—another instance of blaming the victim (see also Lewis, 1959; Moynihan, 1965; and Rodgers, 1982).

Those left of center usually hold to a third theory, that of *dual labor markets*. In this theory there are two job markets, primary and secondary. In the primary market, employment is secure, compensation is good, and the possibility of salary increases and job advancement is strong. Millions of adults are trapped in the secondary sector, where employment is unstable, pay is low, prospects for promotion are nil, and unions are almost nonexistent. According to

Marxist theorists, the presence of a large secondary labor market means that their workers' labor is considered of low value. Productivity is in turn determined by the worker's job. A sharecropper would be more productive on an auto assembly line than in the fields (a low productivity job). Finally, according to this argument, one's job (productivity) is determined by one's class, so class division determines whether one will be in the primary or secondary sector. Poor people, by virtue of class, would have access only to the secondary market and thus to lower productivity and lower income (Rodgers, 1982).

The final theory gives race a prominent role. The *theory of institutional racism* owes its beginnings to the work of Knowles and Prewitt (1969) and has been elaborated on by Williams (1982), Feagin (1978), and Nasatir and Fernandez (1979). Essentially a structuralist-conflict theory, it attempts to explain the persistence of white domination and black subordination in the United States. Nasatir and Fernandez (1979) and Williams (1982) define racism as a cultural ideology that espouses the view that one race of people is inherently superior to another race. In the United States the white population has developed a cultural ideology that blacks are inherently inferior and whites have sufficient power and control of societal institutions to support this ideology. The institutional component of racism involves a system of exclusionary rules, procedures, and regulations that ultimately benefit white males. This process has resulted in the almost total barring of blacks and females from equal and full participation in society (Feagin, 1978; Nasatir & Fernandez, 1979; Williams, 1982).

In the poverty population are groups that are disproportionately persons of color—especially blacks, women, and traditionally discriminated-against persons. This suggests that race is a major factor in black poverty. As resources become scarce, scapegoats are sought and markets dwindle. Racism resurfaces to reallocate scarce resources and to protect the prerequisites of the dominant white society. In theory, the new era of racism is activist and played out under some peculiar rules. Open acts of racism and violence are decried (Uehling, 1987), but covert hostility is encouraged, and actions that challenge the fundamental basis for black entitlements are on the upswing—as are those that cut back governmental services benefiting blacks. Is this racism? Even blacks cannot agree, as is evidenced by the rise of such neo-conservative black thinkers as Glenn C. Loury and Thomas Sowell, who are challenging traditional black views on such issues as affirmative action (Loury, 1984; Sowell, 1983). The times are marked by great confusion as the old power base of racism erodes. Few targets of civil rights activity present themselves other than ambiguously, and the few that do are defended by relatively nice people who simply hold what are called honest disagreements in philosophy. Generally, the last and only frontier for black protest and activism exists in the plight of the poor, especially poor black children.

Black Families in Poverty

As of 1984, some 36.0 percent (9,490,000) of blacks were listed as being in poverty, and 45.5 percent (4,317,950) of them were children (Rosen et al.,

1987; McAdoo, 1987). As of 1984, black persons also accounted for 28 percent of the poverty population. From 1979 to 1983 the percentage of all people in poverty in the United States steadily increased (McAdoo, 1987). Even though the proportion of white and black families below poverty level had decreased by 1984, the poverty rate for all families was still the highest since 1966. In addition, more blacks (36 percent) were living in poverty by 1983 than at any time since 1966. Thus, the family as an economic unit has lost ground, and the black family even more so, considering the point at which they began (Hopps, 1987).

For the most oppressed and destitute sector of the permanently unemployed, social services and public welfare programs have provided little in the way of real additional income (Marable, 1983). They do, however, provide to those eligible with the essentials: shelter, electricity, heat, and sufficient food to stave off hunger. With growing gentrification, spiraling rental and housing costs, many of the black poor have found themselves among the growing millions counted as homeless.

Rural Poverty among Blacks

Poverty and disadvantage is not exclusively a black urban phenomenon. Even though most of America's poor are concentrated in metropolitan areas, 38 percent of all poor reside in nonmetropolitan areas (Martinez-Brawley, 1987). Persons of color who remain in rural areas are still among the poorest Americans; they suffer from ill health and malnutrition, high infant mortality rates, substandard housing, and inadequate job skills. Rural blacks have always been poor and a poorly served group in this country whose extremes of poverty have driven many into the even worse poverty conditions in central cities (Martinez-Brawley, 1983). Rural blacks tend to be the poorest of the poor. Concentrated in the south, they tend to also receive limited welfare benefits. The nonurban poor are primarily elderly, female family heads and their children, persons of color, and residents of the south (42 percent). Disproportionately represented are persons who generally cannot through their own efforts deal with their poverty— children, the aged, and female heads with small children and/or large numbers of children. A majority of these persons are black.

Federal Policies and the Black Poor

Poverty was rediscovered in America during the 1960 presidential campaign of John Kennedy. In 1963 Kennedy expanded the Food Commodity Program, initiated a pilot food stamp program, and ordered a full-scale attack on poverty. During the summer of 1963, Dr. Martin Luther King, Jr., led a demonstration of 200,000 people to Washington, D.C., in an attempt to focus the nation's attention on racism, unemployment, poverty, and hunger among black Americans. In this atmosphere, President Lyndon Johnson expanded on Kennedy's efforts by declaring a "War on Poverty," consisting of the Economic Opportunity Act of 1964. The coordinating office for the program was the Office of Economic Opportunity (OEO). The attack on poverty consisted of job and work experience programs and small-business loans. Becase it was underfinanced, the "war" was more like a skirmish (Rodgers, 1982). Representation from the poor was channeled through local CAP (community action program) agencies, designed to help the poor help themselves. Unfortunately, many problems were too enormous for the resources.

The discovery of widespread hunger and malnutrition and related diseases among blacks and other poor throughout America put pressure on Congress for welfare reforms and expansion. The leaders of the civil rights movement continued to demand new programs for the poor, while during the summers of 1965 to 1968 hundreds of riots erupted in American cities. Pressure from such activists as the National Welfare Rights Organization (NWRO) led by Dr. George Wiley, and riots in the streets, prompted Congress to establish a number of welfare programs in the 1960s and early 1970s—the Food Stamp Program (1964), Medicare and Medicaid (1965), and the Supplemental Security Income Program (1974) (Rodgers, 1982; Rosen et al., 1987; Wyers, 1987). By 1975, funding for all major programs had increased, and federal, state, and local governments were spending six times as much for cash and in-kind programs to aid the poor as in 1968 (Rodgers, 1982). The major programs affecting the black poor are cash assistance and means-tested programs (must show evidence of need), such as Aid to Families with Dependent Children (AFDC), Supplemental Security Income (SSI), General Assistance (GA), and food stamps, but there are other in-kind (noncash) programs as well.

Such programs are the "safety net" programs, designed to prevent low-income persons from falling into utter poverty and hopelessness. The biggest problem with the income maintenance programs is their piecemeal nature and lack of coordination and integration. They have an uneven effect on the recipients—some get more than is provided for, others get less, and this varies by state, region, and program. Developing an administrative technology to run a national system of income maintenance is also difficult. There are lost cases and overpayments (e.g., in the SSI program), and the complexity of different eligibility rules and benefits, both constantly subject to change, will clog the best computer systems and confuse the intended recipient of public largesse. Errors escalate with complexity and are increasingly becoming unacceptable (Austin, 1976).

Reacting to this dilemma and facing huge budget deficits, runaway inflation, unemployment, and a potent conservative mood, President Reagan pushed for reforms, which came in the form of the 1981 Omnibus Budget Reform Act (OBRA), intended to trim OASDI (Old Age Survivors, Disability, and Health Insurance), SSI, AFDC, and the food stamp program (Myers, 1987). The changes were immediate and dramatic. Means-tested programs, including AFDC and food stamps, show declining levels of expenditure, coverage, and benefits. SSI coverage was lower in 1984 than in the previous 1975–80 period. The share of all children receiving AFDC rose from 9 percent in 1970 to 12 percent in 1980, but fell to 11 percent in 1982. The result was directly attributable to changes in federal AFDC, which reduced eligibility for these programs (Rosen et al., 1987).

After 1981, the coverage of in-kind benefits—foods and nutrition, health care, and housing—was reduced. In 1982 some 40 percent of poor households received no in-kind benefits. Also in 1982, when the recession hit and the poverty rate rose, the number of households receiving means-tested benefits declined slightly, to 14.6 million. Food stamp and school lunch programs rose, but Medicaid recipients declined. In that year, Medicaid reached 39 percent of all poor households and half the poor households with children under 19. Food stamps reached 31 percent of female-headed households, 26 percent of black households, and 19 percent of Hispanic households (Rosen et al., 1987). A study estimated that fewer than one-third of all eligible people in 150 counties afflicted with severe hunger and malnutrition were receiving food stamps and that the total number of recipients dropped from 65 percent of those eligible in 1980 to 55 percent in 1984. The study also found hunger epidemic, affecting 20.0 million people who are hungry at least some part of each month, including 15.5 million officially poor who do not qualify for food stamps and 4.5 million near poor (Rosen et al., 1987). Because a disproportionate number of those in poverty are black, blacks assume a disproportionate share of the burden of poverty and are disproportionately affected by the budget reductions and program cuts of the 1980s.

THE ROLE OF THE SOCIAL WORKER

According to Michael Harrington's (1984) updated volume on poverty in America, the structure of poverty was created by people and must be changed by people. A critical element in the change process is the social work profession. The profession is entrenched in the social welfare system, which serves (or underserves) the poor and the disadvantaged (Kane, 1986). The present structure of social work is oriented toward an extreme form of private, personal therapy delivered by an entrepreneurial (autonomous) worker (Rosen et al., 1987). Trends since the 1970s suggest that as resources dwindle and as schools of social work gear up to respond to the needs of recruits who are interested in family counseling and individual psychotherapy, the profession will do even less to address the needs of persons of color and blacks. These recruits have shown a distaste for advocacy and for the case management and resource provision skills that have been traditional in working with the disadvantaged groups and the poor (Rubin & Johnson, 1984).

Theoretical Frameworks and Black Poverty

Social work practitioners have often assumed that practice principles learned within one medium are transferable to another medium and are generic in their application to persons of color (Lum, 1986), but we must seriously question this assumption. The factors having the greatest effect on poverty were those specifically targeted to unique dimensions of the poverty situation—for instance, the highly successful principle of "maximum feasible participation," the keystone of the War on Poverty programs, targeted isolation and alienation and the indexing of Social Security benefits, which dramatically reduced poverty among the elderly. And this happened *outside* the purview of social work, on the community level and within the political arena.

Social work has initiated and encouraged a variety of theories and/or frameworks for practice specifically for minorities. In the field of social work, there is a growing awareness that special knowledge and skills are necessary for work with these populations. The most prominent of those theories have been in the area of ethnicity and *ethnic-sensitive practice* and *cross-cultural practice* (Devore & Schlesinger, 1981; Jenkins, 1984; Lum, 1986). At the core of the ethnic-sensitive model of practice are some assumptions about ethnicity and ethnic groups that speak to a "kith and kin" ("my people") view of culture and suggest that there are distinct behaviors and patterns of behavior associated with common ancestry, national origin, and religion and/or race.

Ethnicity as a basis for minority practice is problematic, if for no other reason than that (1) when taken out of historical context and assumed to have independent explanatory power it fails to distinguish between so-called ethnic groups in reality, (2) it promotes and encourages dangerous ethnic stereotypes that can be used to the disadvantage of some groups, and (3) it promotes ethnocentric conflict of the "we" versus "they" variety (Steinberg, 1981). Lum (1986) observes that ethnic theories give us nothing new and are simply an effort to synthesize previous practice principles with ethnic principles. The result is incomplete models of practice relative to poverty populations and the black poor. Many aspects of the black experience in poverty, such as powerlessness, oppression, and discrimination, are left to inference (Lum, 1986).

Although the profession has in practice given attention to cultural or cross-cultural content, this content remains peripheral to the central aims of the profession, which are oriented to the white middle class. Cross-cultural practice relative to blacks has incorporated such concepts as power and empowerment, family strength and resilience, natural support networks, dual personality development, liberation, equality and parity, advocacy, and political and legal action, but none of these conceptualizations has led to systematic practice theories that are prescriptive (defining what should be done, with whom, differentially in cross-racial practice) or to eradication of poverty among lower-income black people. On the contrary, poverty has generally become more entrenched and in direct proportion to the number of cross-cultural theories propounded or proposed. This forces one to question the purpose for the theorizing. If it is not to actively intervene in fighting poverty, then is it a palliative to relieve the profession of any guilt or responsibility for the poor as it moves inexorably toward middle-class services? The bulk of the theories or theoretical models are of a direct practice nature and oriented to psychotherapy within a psychodynamic orientation relative to individuals, groups, or families. This is in direct contrast to what is known about poverty—its structural nature, and its scope, which requires large system changes of an economic and policy nature.

The literature on poverty reveals clear indications of the roles a social worker should adopt in order to work with impoverished black families. The most critical of these is advocacy, social action, and brokerage within systems and frameworks that are developmental and revolutionary (as in seeking a new paradigm or racial solution to an old problem), rather than evolutionary. The successful fulfilling of these roles assumes the worker has achieved a thorough knowledge of poverty and its causes, of black culture, of the society that serves as a context for the lives of impoverished blacks, and of a range of interventive strategies that can be used differentially in behalf of black impoverished families. Recent scholars of poverty or of black family theory have not been able to produce a body of micro- or macro-theory that is coherent, realistic, and effective.

The Power and Conflict Framework of Practice with the Black Poor

The changes in the black family structure, and the subsequent entrenchment of black poverty, are not a result of a dependence on welfare or of subcultural issues, as popularly believed. They are caused by lower marital fertility, increases in the rates of divorce and separation, general shifts in moral values attended by lowered or leveled aspirations, the early and irresponsible sexual activity of black youths, the fecundity of lower class black females, the reluctance to give children up for adoption outside the limited network of mother and daughter, delays in marriage, the imbalance in the ratio of men to women, and the high rates of illiteracy and unemployment of young black men, within the context of an uncaring and racially cynical society (Hill, 1971; MacLeod, 1987; McAdoo, 1987; Wilson & Neckerman, 1986). Those at the bottom strata of society appear to be evolving means for coping with and adapting to poverty that can be best described as normlessness—the state of being without norms or values and devoid of a conscious social goal or life purpose outside that of survival. Only in the "garbage cities" of South America and among the homeless children of Italy and the immigrant camps of Southeast Asia do we find similar phenomena.

These characteristics are the outcome of the impersonal workings of a social system with colonial roots. The dominant group in the United States, by virtue of its history of aggression toward persons of color, has forged a system of group relations that are conflict-ridden—based on power and conflict relations among groups. As a consequence, the poorest of poor blacks are the continuing victims in a social system that values them little either as competitors or as producers, because of their race and class position.

PRACTICE IMPLICATIONS

Having sought to distance itself from the poor, the social work profession has embarked on a course that threatens to lead it further from elements of practice that may have some bearing on poverty practice. Practice theorists tend to be lumpers—those who would seek common or generic elements in practice for all sorts of clients, a single practice suitable for all. Moreover, the trend has also been to create models of practice based on linear and/or structured process which require a great deal of uniformity among clientele. In this type of practice, A leads to B, leads to C, leads to D in sequence. These processes dictate how one performs in actual practice, and schools of social work spend the bulk of their time training students in the technique of applying them to unique and varying client situations. The practice process stages of Engagement, Assessment, Intervention, Evaluation, and Termination are essentially normative models of an action situation, involving well-motivated and culturally compatible clients who can truly benefit psychologically from verbal exchanges. But when such psychological gains are attended by external and environmental forces, such as the lack of food, shelter, education, power, and other indicators of social dislocation and distress, the process approach proves to be inadequate. For example, the initial contact between a worker and a poor black individual produces a set of contingencies. The worker's characteristics of culture, personality, race, training or education, social status, bureaucratic role, gender, family values, and own neediness interact with similar or dissimilar characteristics of the client and can result either in continued and mutually acceptable contact or in termination.

The effect of the process or action view of practice is that it eliminates social factors that do not fall within the framework. The social dimension of practice is defined by content (knowledge) and context (environment). Content refers to diagnosis or assessment, and knowledge; while context refers to the environment surrounding the practice situation (e.g., the current state of the economy, the availability of resources, discrimination, funding for social programs, the growth in the rates of teen pregnancy).

The current popular turn toward private practice and psychotherapy on both the psychological and the social level has supported a focus on personal feelings and privatization of services; the narrower the social worker's concerns and obligations, the greater the attention to process. However, the key to an effective "psychosocial" practice rests with a truer reading of cases, of situations, in which even intractable social conditions are factored into the assessment (Meyers, 1987). Consider the following case example:

CASE STUDY: MS. KENA TURNER, AGE 29

Ms. T. was admitted through the emergency ward to the maternity unit of a large metropolitan hospital. Her infant girl was born with ARC, testing positive for the AIDS virus.

A quiet, dark complected, thin, 29-year-old woman, Ms. T. seemed quite pleasant and agreeable—until one noticed that she agreed too readily, nodding and smiling with an off-putting kind of vacantness. Ms. T., who is black, has two sons: Derrod, age 13, and Guan, age 8. She says they are out on the streets, somewhere. She had left them in a vacant building when her pains started.

According to the worker who interviewed her, Ms. T. had never been married and is not on AFDC. She was living with the man who fathered her last child, who had been employed as a laundry worker in a large hospital. He lost his job, began going out in the evenings, and finally dropped from sight when Ms. T. was six months pregnant. "He used drugs, drank, and beat on me," she said. When she couldn't afford the rent and was evicted, she and the boys became transients, living with various people until they ended up in an abandoned building.

The boys are the product of liaisons with two different men, whereabouts unknown. Both boys have been out of school for the last year. Ms. T., who had difficulty filling out the medical consent forms given her by the nurse, does not read or write well. She says she finished the fifth grade and was once employed as a seamstress. The family has no relatives in the community, having come to the city from South Carolina to live with a girlfriend who has since vanished. Both of Ms. T.'s parents are deceased, and other family members are dispersed throughout various cities. There is no contact with any of them.

Ms. T. was seen by the social worker from the hospital social services unit. The short-term plans are to keep the infant in isolation and to help Ms. T. find housing for herself and the two boys. The long-term plan is to get her on AFDC.

The worker has little to work with in this situation. Although compliant, Ms. T. appears to have little self-esteem, little motivation, and few personal or external resources. The infant may not thrive, the boys are in the streets unsupervised and at great risk. This multiproblem situation is akin to that of a growing number of such families who are the current victims of the poverty and homelessness that plague many of our cities. By employing systems analysis, one can begin to assess the resources available in this situation:

1. Knowledge and skill and background in training of the worker
2. What personal resources Ms. T. brings to the situation
3. Community agencies and services
4. Agency policies, procedures, rules, regulations

The level and quality of knowledge the social worker brings to the situation is critical. No matter how well prepared a worker is, a multiproblem situation of such magnitude may tax the worker's limits, so that the client may be lost to the helping system. The ideal practice situation calls for a client with resilience, personal fortitude, intelligence, and a desire to succeed, which are temporarily blocked by current circumstances, but this problem situation is far from the ideal: a single homeless family, without income, which is under intense physical, social, and environmental stress and cut off from most sources of support. Intervention with this family must involve the development of natural support systems and the provision of social-emotional support within the context of a broad range of creative helping strategies. Traditional psychotherapy has been least successful with this type of situation, and macro-techniques alone would be inappropriate and misguided, given the immediacy of the family's needs.

The Failure of Ethnic and Cultural Perspectives

Black culture and identity are not resources that can be readily tapped by the worker or the family at this point. Cross-cultural perspectives appear to be of little immediate relevance. In fact, none of the indicators for successful intervention gleaned from the various theories of cross-cultural and interracial practice (e.g., innate rationality and intelligence, strong class or racial identity, family and communal ties and networks, cultural embeddedness, middle-class or working-class striving) are present in this situation. On the contrary, the worker is confronted with a raw human need of the most primitive kind, perhaps best characterized as survival. The members of this family are social outcasts, powerless to effect changes in their lives and circumstances without outside aid. Because social work theories and the subsequent interventions are biased toward the ideal, middle-class client (one with a requisite number of personal resources) in the ideal situation (wherein needed services are available), the prognosis for effective services being rendered to this type of impoverished family is extremely poor. The family has no personal resources, and there are no services that will enable this family to become self-sufficient.

INTERVENTION

Given differences in background and experience, one must assume that the worker and Ms. T. are basically alien to one another. They must first establish a relationship that will enable them to work cooperatively toward a common purpose. The initial contact must establish a style of working and communicating that is unique to this dyad; builds trust, confidence, and empathy; facilitates action; and preserves the dignity of Ms. T. and promotes in her an early sense of her own self-worth. The major purpose of the work in this phase is broader than simple assessment and calls for relationship-building, which involves an interweaving of both concrete tasks and psychological support that may involve activities as diverse as rescuing the boys from the street and reuniting the family, inviting Ms. T.'s cooperation in getting a juvenile officer to locate them, seeking information relative to emergency shelter for the family, and getting and sharing medical information about the infant in a manner that is understandable to Ms. T. If these things are done skillfully, Ms. T. will gain confidence in her ability to communicate, to make decisions, to understand and manage new information, and to engage in a positive and productive relationship with another adult. In this family development phase, the worker will have called upon various roles (clinician, broker, mediator, advocate, educator) that facilitate relationship-building, enhance the competence of the client in her role, and accomplish concrete tasks.

Suppose, then, the worker and Ms. T. are able to satisfy the initial needs of the family: the boys are located, the family is reunited, housing is found in a temporary shelter. With an address, the family is eligible for AFDC payments, the boys can be reenrolled in school, and the infant will remain in the hospital. However, can we assume that the family is connected to the right resources and that the worker can safely withdraw? The scope of the family's problems suggest otherwise, that many problems remain and others are likely to arise, that the family is moving into a phase in its development wherein it must begin to make critical life decisions from a position of relative security. But the family remains

powerless and is dependent on the resources afforded by various powerful agencies. Under the poverty practice analogy, the worker would recognize
that only the initial phase of family reconstruction had been achieved, that
without some outside agent (in this case, the worker) it is likely to deteriorate
further or to stabilize as chronic dependents. Aware of the nature of poverty and its intransigence, the worker should settle for no less than full and
autonomous functioning as a goal for the T. family. This means that they
will eventually become able to act on their own behalf, to have some countervailing power as they interact with complex and powerful agencies of social
control.

Because no single worker has the skill and knowledge to help all families
achieve autonomy, the concept of *synergy* (from social systems theory) that
involves increasing the energy in a single system by linking it to other systems,
becomes a useful one. The worker can actually extend his or her capacities as
service provider by enabling the family to get involved with other systems that
are naturally supportive in an environment and culture most suitable for the T.
family. Acting as case manager, the worker would help the family connect with
existing community groups (minority preferably) that are oriented to advocacy,
socialization, parenting, education, job training, and so on.

At this point, culture comes into play as a variable. If we assume the
exigencies of culture, that community and family networks and the feeling of
being a part of an affinity group is both healing and empowering, then it is
crucial that this family find itself "networked"—and the more so because this
was not a family with strong roots or ties to the black community or to any
community. The worker must help the family seek alternatives to indigenous
supportive networks, calling on knowledge of the functioning of the black
community and its skill at marshaling nontraditional resources.

Poverty Practice in the Context of Social Justice

The most serious deficiency of our current practice conceptions is that effective
helping is construed as a matter of a simple encounter—the skill and knowledge
of the worker joined to the personal resources of the client at a point in time. If
either of the actors is less than adequately prepared, termination or its
derivative—referral—usually ensues. But in terms of the realities of poverty in
the example of the T. family, the worker must be prepared to be at the center of
managing the case to the point where the family is able to function independently, giving rise to a number of encounters, each of which demands different
levels of skill: worker to client, worker to collateral, worker to worker, client to
agency bureaucracy. No single method will suffice, nor will a single role. In
fact, it is probably best to conceive of the practice situation in terms of role sets
commensurate with the tasks required to solve each problem. Table 10.1 drama-
tizes the ideal of role sets in relation to problems or tasks, although it does not
represent the full range of roles a social worker might assume in treating the
dysfunctional black family. With the exception of the task of *developmental
socialization,* most problems call for more than one set of roles. In addition,

many roles must be carried out simultaneously because problems may overlap. For example, just the goal of securing housing for the T. family will involve the worker as a broker, mediator, and advocate, and in a limited housing market the worker might act as a reformer—seeking to create new housing or pressing for housing alternatives. In the meantime, the individual problems of this family remain. The worker will continue to act as a clinician to this family, supporting and assisting the family in overcoming internalized stress, feelings of helplessness, and powerlessness, and working on the problem areas of resocialization, developmental socialization, and empowerment.

The integrated generalist approach comes closest to capturing the complexity of this situation. It includes role sets designed to respond to a broad range of client issues consistent with aims and purposes of the profession (Connaway & Gentry, 1988). This approach is preferred here only to the degree that this theoretical framework allows for flexibility because it is not bound to a particular method, to a class of clients, or to fields of practice. In the case management implications implicit in the various role sets, the worker is located solidly at the interface between the client and the environment. The process of intervention should account for intractable social conditions as well as for conditions easily overcome through technologies the worker possesses. Ideally, the worker should assume an ecological orientation and be proficient in knowledge of poverty and its effects, skilled in negotiating various systems and in applying role sets to particular problems, and capable of maintaining a realistic view of the complex of problems.

In the case of Ms. T., the goals of treatment should be self-sufficiency to the extent that the family is able to determine it. Working backward from this concept, one can establish with Ms. T. certain intermediate or short-term goals that constitute developmental phases that enable this family to achieve its long-term ideal. The developmental phases in this case are:

1. Reuniting the family
2. Securing housing and stabilizing the family
3. Securing financial assistance

TABLE 10.1. ROLES OF THE SOCIAL WORKER IN TREATING IMPOVERISHED BLACK FAMILIES

Problem	Role Set
Housing	Reformer, advocate, broker, mediator
Health care	Educator, advocate, broker, mediator
Financial assistance	Advocate, broker, mediator, reformer
Resocialization	Clinician, educator
Developmental socialization	Clinician
Empowerment	Social action, broker, advocate, reformer, mediator
Network/cultural	Educator, clinician

   4. Health care, psychological support, and clinical services
   5. Job training and/or education
   6. Child care
   7. Creation of quasi-familial support networks, and reimmersion into black
   community, possibly through the church or self-help groups or social
   action organizations
   8. Termination

One can envision this family as an evolving and developing system moving from marginality to immersion in a collectivity of affinity groups, the final outcome being the ability of the family to function from its own resources and on its own terms.

The more generic theories tend to abort the process at phase 3, when the client has been safely assigned to an agent of social control, such as the Department of Public Welfare. On the other hand, cross-cultural and interracial theories tend to emphasize phase 7 and to see this as a critical activity in all other phases. However, the focus is the same: the family as a microcosm, with work in its behalf evolving in stages that end with termination after successful connection with an agency of social control—thus falling far short of the objectives of social work, which is *the autonomous functioning of the family system.*

The principle of social justice should guide the nature of social work interventions. A client-centered and dignity-affirming basis should guide and ensure the extent and quality of the relationships established between social workers and those persons in poverty. Theoretical frameworks and modes of intervention should not become ends in themselves.

Practice Approach to Black Poverty

Poverty practice in general, and poverty practice as carried out specifically in behalf of minorities, is in shambles. Reductionism, incrementalism, linear thinking, and self-serving nostalgia have rendered the field incapable of taking a fresh look at poverty—aside from attempts to reform the welfare system, where increasingly fewer of the poor are to be found. A poverty practice aimed at reducing poverty and at aiding poor black families has as its social context the following:

   • Poverty remains a matter of insufficient income, and as such income
     redistribution is an important element in the eradication of poverty.
   • The income the poor receive is erratic, substandard, fraught with bureau-
     cratic waste and duplication, arbitrary, and the result of public attitudes
     that would force the poor into exploitative working conditions, with the
     assistance of a punitive welfare system.
   • The poor occupy a caste-like status in America. Many are doomed from

birth to perpetual poverty, unemployment, underemployment, and the approbation of their fellow citizens of higher class and different socioeconomic position.

- The primary issue in poverty is the plight of children, women, and youth, since it threatens the existence of the black family as a social unit.
- People in poverty adapt psychologically and socially to its miseries and accommodate to its excesses, but poverty is not inevitable.
- There are alternatives to poverty if and when we can adopt humane approaches that are universal, free of stigma, preventative, and based on the principle of a free, equal, and secure society for all.

A social work practice that would have a critical impact on poverty would have to prepare workers for a type of practice with the following attributes and within a broad-base ecological framework, as indicated:

1. The poverty worker would need both generic and specific skills of advocacy, social brokerage, outreach, education, monitoring, and counseling commensurate with a social generalist experienced in communication and engagement, evaluation and monitoring, and interorganizational dynamics.
2. Because individual approaches are severely limited in effectiveness, some knowledge and skill in group dynamics and the group as the core unit of intervention should be employed. These would be task and developmental groups and groups oriented toward rehabilitation, education, resocialization, and behavior change. The group would substitute for natural networks typical of more intact black families.
3. The outcome of practice must free persons to act autonomously and in their own interests through empowerment, self-help and networking, or family and community development approaches.
4. Interventions with the poor must be long-term, and micro, meso, and macro in scope, as well as individual and social. They must utilize a careful assessment strategy geared to each problem situation and working with clients to establish mutual priorities.
5. Service must be provided through a "close to the source" services strategy, perhaps out of community-controlled services centers separate and apart from established community mental health centers and branches of the Department of Public Welfare.
6. All sources of income distribution for the poor must be nationalized through a planning stream that emanates from a national agency created to eliminate poverty by producing housing, providing jobs and work training, public financing of minimum incomes, health care and nutrition services, and personal care. Poverty workers would be recruited and paid a *poverty dividend*, which would support both their training and their continued work in the community.
7. The proposed national agency would establish alternative training sites to train a coalition of workers for this newly emerging poverty field.

CONCLUSION

Poverty threatens the very foundations of black strength and resiliency—women, children and youth, and young black males, the essence of the future for the black family. Time, energy, talent, money, and commitment are necessary and require national leadership and a renewed effort to target and eradicate what has become a threatening circumstance for all Americans. The future of America's productivity, of old-age benefits and retirement, is bound closely to the fortunes of a generation of young people coming to their majority poorly educated, with higher-than-average rates of illiteracy, with no record of employment, and with values and attitudes that differ markedly from those that produced the economic miracles in the United States over the past several decades.

Social work can make a difference in black poverty, but instead has turned inward to private practice and individual psychotherapy. The field has little to offer the poor, either in basic theory or in practice technologies, and the black community must seek other alternatives.

REFERENCES

Abbott, J. (1980). Work experience and earnings of middle-aged black and white men, 1965–1971. *Social Security Bulletin, 43,* 16–34.

Anderson, J.R., Jr. (1983). The black experience with health care delivery. In A.E. Johnson (Ed.), *The black experience: Considerations for health and human services* (pp. 149–150). Davis, CA: International Dialogue Press.

Austin, D.M. (1976, Winter). Income maintenance programs: What next? *Urban and Social Change Review, 9*(1), 2.

Banfield, E. (1968). *The unheavenly city.* Boston, MA: Little, Brown.

Bell, I.P. (1968). *CORE and the strategy of nonviolence.* New York: Random House.

Bennett, L., Jr. (1966). *Confrontation: Black and white.* Baltimore, MD: Penguin.

Connaway, R.S., & Gentry, M.E.. (1988). *Social work practice.* Englewood Cliffs, NJ: Prentice-Hall.

DeFleur, M.L., D'Antonio, W.V., & DeFleur, L. B. (1971). *Sociology: Man in society.* Glenview, IL: Scott, Foresman.

Devore, W., & Schlesinger, E.G. (1981). *Ethnic sensitive social work practice.* St. Louis, MO: Mosby.

Feagin, J.R. (1978). *Racial and ethnic relations.* Englewood Cliffs, NJ: Prentice-Hall.

Feagin, J.R., & Hahn, H. (1973). *Ghetto revolts.* New York: Macmillan.

Gary, L.E., & Leashore, B.R. (1982). High-risk status of black men. *Social Work, 27*(1), 54–59.

Glasgow, D.G. (1981). *The black underclass: Poverty, unemployment, and the entrapment of ghetto youth.* New York: Vintage.

Glazer, N., & Moynihan, D.P. (1963). *Beyond the melting pot.* Cambridge, MA: Harvard University Press.

Goldberg, G., & Kremen, E. (1986). Feminization of poverty in seven industrialized nations: Only in America? *Social Policy, 17,* 3–14.

Gordon, D.M. (1972). *Theories of poverty and unemployment.* Lexington, MA: Lexington Books.

Gordon, H.A., Hamilton, C.A., & Tipps, H.C. (1982). *Unemployment and underemployment among blacks, Hispanics, and women.* Washington, DC: Clearinghouse.

Harrington, M. (1984). *The new American poverty.* New York: Holt, Rinehart & Winston.

Hill, R. (1971). *The strengths of black families.* New York: Emerson Hall.

Hopps, J.G. (1987). Minorities of color. In J. Atkins et al. (Eds.), *Encyclopedia of social work* (18th ed.) (pp. 161–171). Silver Spring, MD: National Association of Social Workers.

Hulbert, A. (1984, September 10). Children as parents. *New Republic, 69*, 20–25.

Jenkins, S. (1984). Ethics of ethnic concerns. In *Cross cultural issues: Impact on social work practice in health care, Conference Proceedings, May 17, 1984* (p. 7). New York: Columbia University School of Social Work.

Jones, L.E. (1987). Women. In J. Atkins et al. (Eds.), *Encyclopedia of social work* (18th ed.) (p. 874). Silver Spring, MD: National Association of Social Workers.

Kane, R. (1986). The future of social work. In W.E. Buffum (Ed.), *Charting the future of social work* (p. 11). Houston, TX: University of Houston Graduate School of Social Work.

Kinard, M.E. (1987). Child abuse and neglect. In J. Atkins et al. (Eds.), *Encyclopedia of Social Work* (18th ed.) (p. 226). Silver Spring, MD: National Association of Social Workers.

Knowles, L.L., & Prewitt, K. (Eds.) (1969). *Institutional racism in America.* Englewood Cliffs, NJ: Prentice-Hall.

Lewis, O. (1959). *La vida: A Puerto Rican family in the culture of poverty, San Juan and New York.* New York: Random House.

Loury, G.C. (1984, December 31). A new American dilemma: Racial politics, blacks and whites. *New Republic,* 14–18.

Lum, D. (1986). *Social work practice and people of color: A process-stage approach.* Monterey, CA: Sage.

MacLeod, J. (1987). *Ain't no making it: Leveled aspirations in a low-income neighborhood.* Boulder, CO: Westview.

Marable, M. (1983). *How capitalism underdeveloped black America.* Boston, MA: South End.

Martinez-Brawley, E.E. (1987). Rural social work. In J. Atkins et al. (Eds.), *Encyclopedia of Social Work* (18th ed.) (pp. 521–537). Silver Spring, MD: National Association of Social Workers.

McAdoo, H. P. (1987). Blacks. In Atkins et al. (Eds.), *Encyclopedia of social work* (18th ed.) (pp. 194–206). Silver Spring, MD: National Association of Social Workers.

Meyers, C.W. (1987, September–October). Content and process in social work practice: A new look at old issues. *Social Work, 32*(5), 401.

Moynihan, D.P. (1965). *The Negro family.* Washington, DC: Department of Labor.

Nasatir, D., & Fernandez, J.P. (1979). Use of log-linear and hierarchical models to study ethnic composition in a university. In K. Alvarez et al. (Eds.), *Discrimination in organizations* (pp. 270–288). San Francisco, CA: Jossey-Bass.

National Association of Social Workers. (1987, January). Public service drive to hit child poverty. *National Association of Social Workers News, 32*(1), p. 3.

National Association of Social Workers. (1987, April). Minorities filling low-paying jobs, new study shows. *National Association of Social Workers News, 32*(4), p. 11.

Neubeck, K.L., & Roach, J.L. (1981). *Racism and poverty politics.* In B.P. Bowser & R.G. Hunt (Eds.), *Impacts of racism on white Americans* (pp. 153–164). Beverly Hills, CA: Sage.

Reich, M. (1981). The economic impact in the postwar period. In B.P. Bowser & R.G. Hunt (Eds.), *Impacts of racism on white Americans* (pp. 165–176). Beverly Hills, CA: Sage.

Rodgers, H.R. (1982). *The cost of human neglect: America's welfare failure.* New York: Sharpe.

Rosen, S.M., Fanshel, D., & Lutz, M.E. (1987). Face of the nation 1987: Statistical supplement to J. Atkins et al. (Eds.), *Encyclopedia of Social Work* (pp. 13–17). Silver Spring, MD: National Association of Social Workers.

Rubin, A., & Johnson, P. (1984). Direct practice interests of entering MSW students. *Journal of Education for Social Work, 20*(2), 5–16.

Schermerhorn, R.A. (1974). Ethnicity in the perspective of the sociology of knowledge. *Ethnicity, 1*(1), 1–14.

Sowell, T. (1983). *The economics and politics of race: An international perspective.* New York: Morrow.

Steinberg, S. (1981). *The ethnic myth: Race, ethnicity, and class in America.* Boston, MA: Beacon.

Stewart, J. B. (1986, June 1). Education and work: Yesterday and tomorrow. *Black Issues in Higher Education, 20*(3), 20.

Sum, A.M., Harrington, P.E., Goedicke, W.B., & Vinson, R. (1986, Summer–Fall). Poverty amid renewed affluence. *New England Journal of Public Policy, (2),* 6–30.

Taylor, R.J., & Chatters, L.M. (1986). *Correlates of education, income, and poverty among elderly blacks.* Unpublished manuscript, Boston College Graduate School of Social Work, Chestnut Hill, MA.

Uehling, M.D. (1987, February). Oprah heads south. *Newsweek,* 67.

Williams, L.F. (1982). Measuring racism: An example from education. *Social Work, 27*(1), 111.

Williams, L. F., & Diaz, C. (1987). Family: Multigenerational. In J. Atkins et al. (Eds.), *Encyclopedia of Social Work* (18th ed.) (pp. 529–540). Silver Spring, MD: National Association of Social Workers.

Wilson, W., & Neckerman, R. (1986). Poverty and family structure: The widening gap between evidence and public policy issues. In S. Danzibar & D. Weinberg (Eds.), *The war on poverty: Taking stock of what worked and what did not.* Cambridge, MA: Harvard University Press.

Wyers, N.L. (1987). Income maintenance system. In J. Atkins et al. (Eds.), *Encyclopedia of Social Work* (18th ed.) (pp. 889–898). Silver Spring, MD: National Association of Social Workers.

CHAPTER 11

The Impact of Underemployment and Unemployment on the Quality of Black Family Life

James A. Moss, *Adelphi University*
George R. Lockhart, *Adelphi University*

Black unemployment, particularly black youth unemployment, has deepened in intensity and remained quantitatively unabated in the past eight to ten years (Moss, 1982). Freire (1985) speaks to the challenge that this problem area presents for both the black family and the social work profession: "The social worker who opts for change does not fear freedom. . . . She or he knows that all attempts at making radical transformation of society require a conscious organization of the oppressed and that this calls for a lucid vanguard. If this vanguard cannot be the 'proprietor' over others, by the same token it cannot be passive" (p. 4). Although the overall unemployment picture for both black and white Americans has improved since the end of the recession in 1982, relatively little change has occurred in the economically disadvantaged position of black Americans. A great deal of work still needs to be done in working toward strengthening black family life through confronting the problems of underemployment and unemployment. Social work is only beginning to recognize that unemployment is more a permanent phenomenon than a transient phenomenon, with major implications for social work practice (Macarov, 1988). This professional myopia also applies to the profession's interest and concerns with ethnicity. Lum's (1986) study revealed that leading social work practice theorists and texts have mentioned minorities and related areas only minimally.

Structural, social, cultural, and other factors also help account for employment disparities between blacks and whites, but the most glaring cause is race (see Chapter 2). The economic policies of the recent Reagan administration continued favoring the rich while worsening the conditions of the middle-class and the poor (Jacobs, 1987). Job discrimination policies from as early as 1686 (Higgenbotham, 1987) to the present have brought a disproportionate amount of suffering to blacks. Such major economic barriers have had a negative impact on the black families, individually and as units.

HISTORICAL BACKGROUND

At the beginning of the nineteenth century, black family heads-of-household were unskilled workers, and barely 9 percent were skilled artisans (Gutman, 1976). The pattern was similar in the 1950s. Unskilled and uneducated blacks were moving into northern industrial centers, where unemployment among young blacks was two and a half times that of young white men. The Kerner Report (1968) reminded us that the nation was rapidly moving into two societies, one white and one black and that "white society is deeply implicated in the ghetto. White institutions created it, white institutions maintain it, and white society condones it" (p. 2). In 1968, unemployment rates for black adults were twice that for white adults, with 40 percent of black youth unemployed, compared with 30 percent of white youth (Hill, 1978).

Many of today's inner-city blacks are the victims of a declining job market for semi-skilled or unskilled workers. The postindustrial United States in the ninth decade of the twentieth century contains a permanent generational jobless population. The depowerment of blacks, particularly black males, has transformed life in the black community and forced everything else to adapt to it. A recent National Urban League report (Swinton, 1987, p. 143), offers this assessment of the current employment situation for blacks:

1. In 1987, some 45.0 percent of the black population was unemployed, compared with 37.8 percent of the white population.
2. The employment picture is most dismal for black males over 20 and for black male teenagers. Black males over 20 are 11.4 percent more likely to be unemployed than white males over 20, and black teenagers are 48.9 percent more likely to be unemployed than white teenagers.
3. Black women are 1.8 percent more likely to be unemployed than white women.

The report also notes that all three groups have lost ground over the last two decades.

There are two long-standing explanations for the entrenchment and persistence of what has come to be regarded as a permanent, largely black and poor underclass. One view suggests that in the 1970s, following the War on Poverty, a new perception emerged that the quality of life for blacks had substantially improved. A second perception views the current circumstances of black life as deteriorating. These views tend to interact with the other forces that help maintain black unemployment.

FORCES AFFECTING BLACK UNEMPLOYMENT

There is little agreement on a single causal explanation for black unemployment. The interplay of a number of factors illuminates the issue, of which five will be summarized briefly: racial, economic, cultural, social, and psychological forces.

Racial and Economic Forces

Racial and economic forces are so closely intertwined that they are discussed together here. Unemployment is tied to the number of labor units available to meet the minimum requirements of production at the lowest available price. A surplus of labor is usually associated with a decrease in the price of labor, while a decrease in the labor supply is most often associated with an increase in the price of labor. Historically, blacks have been the most visible component in the labor force, the least educated, the most discriminated against, and the most exploited. As such, they have been the most consistent and permanent consignees into the surplus labor reserve.

The issue is then joined for blacks between capitalism's demand for the maximization of profits at the expense of the cost of labor, and the black man's demand for jobs and wages sufficient to meet the requirements for satisfying basic human needs. Thus, the dual factors of race and economic status are major structural impediments to the easing of unemployment among blacks.

Cultural Forces

Despite these historical circumstances, the American culture insists on believing that the problem resides within the black community itself. Some have suggested that genetic factors account for a perceived lack of intelligence, motivation, and sense of responsibility among blacks and that therein lies the root of persistent black unemployment. The majority society is reluctant to place the responsibility for black unemployment on institutional racism. Multiple systematic barriers to equal access to educational, political, social, and economic entitlements have been described as "circular reinforcing subsystems where powerlessness in one sector (for blacks) prevents significant participation in any others" (Jones, 1974, p. 2).

In a society that judges a person by the product of his or her labor, the nonproducing person is perceived as being of little value. Feelings of worthlessness, deriving from sources external to the individual, set in motion a self-fulfilling prophecy of failure and rejection within and across generations. However factually correct data concerning unemployment and underemployment are, more than half of all blacks are employed, do seek employment, are willing to work, and have historically been employed when work could be secured (Dewart, 1987).

Although unemployment among the black professional class is not viewed as quantitatively significant, underemployment plagues black professional men and women both. What has been described as the "glass ceiling" evokes feelings within this group similar to those that have been observed among the chronically unemployed. Richard Clarke (1988) documents the "invisible ceiling" operating against black professionals:

- Some 49 percent felt they had been treated and/or unfairly dealt with by their employer because of race.
- Some 44 percent believed they could not reach top management positions even if they worked extremely hard at it.
- Some 49 percent said hiring and advancement opportunities had become scarcer over the last five years, and only 29 percent felt things were better.

Swinton (1987) found that, within all occupational categories, black men and women earn less than their similarly educated white counterparts.

A recurring theme among black professional males is their strong self-depreciation. Subtle assaults on their professional competence, all too often accompanied by or expressed through threats of demotion or dismissal, take their toll on the self-esteem and self-worth of these men. Although trained in the best schools and working for large corporations, these men sometimes accept their employers' negative assessments of them as valid definitions of their level of competence. Where black professionals are victims of prolonged unemployment, feelings of failure and loss of identity are magnified. The situation of Gerald Smith, a 37-year-old black professional in the electronics industry, is an example:

> Mr. Smith had been unemployed for more than two years. He graduated from the most elite public college in New York City, where he earned a bachelor of science degree. He is 37 years old, neat in appearance, and engages in conversation easily. Mrs. Smith is a graduate nurse, and together they are the parents of two children: a son, 11, and a daughter, 6. From all indications this has been a good marriage, but they have been in family therapy for five months, having sought treatment because of the increasing stress within the family resulting from Mr. Smith's prolonged unemployment.
>
> The older child, Edward, has been diagnosed as learning disabled and is being educated in a special school at considerable expense to the family. Mr. Smith was a salesperson for a major electronics firm for thirteen years. He was transferred at his own request to another city because he hoped to place his son in a better educational facility. Shortly after relocating, he was terminated as excess personnel by his firm.
>
> During his unemployment, Mr. Smith has exchanged parental roles with his wife. He has assumed fully the housekeeping duties and child care responsibilities. Mrs. Smith is working double shifts as a nurse. The involuntary role shift is placing severe strains upon both husband and wife. Mr. Smith has been taking on temporary job assignments when they are available. Most recently, Mr. Smith went through extensive screening for employment on the sales staff of a major telephone company. He has just been notified that his application was rejected because of his "intermittent employment history."
>
> Mr. Smith is evidencing a deep sense of despair and hopelessness over ever securing another job in his field. He is finding it difficult to protect his family from his feelings of depression. Also, low self-esteem is introducing sexual strain upon the marriage. Mrs. Smith says, "If he doesn't get a job soon, it's over for us. I can't take any more."

Chronic and systemic unemployment and underemployment of black men and women are often rooted in cultural and racial misperceptions. For instance, Mr. Smith's most recent prospective employer seems to have assumed that his unemployment during the past two years indicates irresponsibility, a racial stereotype. His previous stable employment of thirteen years was ignored. Both the family's well-being and Mr. Smith's potential contribution to society suffer as a consequence.

Social Forces at Work

The costs of black unemployment and underemployment to the viability and validity of the social system are difficult to assess. These problems have an impact not only upon individuals but also upon the maintenance and stability of the black nuclear family. Legislation that keeps a mother and her children from receiving public assistance if there is an unemployed male in the house compounds the economic hardships facing the black family. The stresses of unemployment are devastating to the entire family system. It is a major social crisis as well as a financial crisis. For example, Keefe (1984) points out that unemployment rates do not indicate how many people are forced to move from full-time to part-time employment at well below their previous level of income, how many move from one temporary low-wage job to another; or how many become permanently discouraged from looking for employment at all. In addition, they do not reflect "the anxiety, depression, deprivation, lost opportunities, violence, insecurity, and anger people feel when their source of livelihood is severed and they lose control of a significant aspect of their environment" (Keefe, 1984).

The notion that all human beings have basic needs is deeply embedded in both the knowledge base and the value base of the social work profession (Towle, 1965). According to Maslow (1970), all human beings have the same basic needs which can be ordered as needs for physiological maintenance, physical and psychological security, love and belongingness, esteem and self-actualization. Within this context, the correlation between poverty and quality of life for black families is highlighted. For example, poverty is considered a more significant factor in infant mortality than the rates for traffic fatalities and suicide combined *(Black and White Children in America,* 1985). In the absence of primary care facilities offering prenatal and postnatal care, 18.0 per 1,000 black infants in New York City died in 1982, compared with 15.3 per 1,000 white infants (Community Service Society [CSS], 1986). These findings highlight the deficit in need satisfaction for all members of the black family.

The infants that do survive have minimal chances for a promising future. The birth mother, for example, is likely to be a teenager who is poor and the single head of a household. Such mothers are not entitled to any government assistance. They must depend on natural helpers in the immediate environment or private agencies. The fathers of such infants have also experienced a legacy of generational neglect and stigma (CSS, 1986). Wilkinson (1977) outlines the stigmatization process that cripples and distorts many black males throughout their developmental stages. The black father, often himself a teenager, may have been born into a single-parent family in which the father was either absent, only

peripherally present, or under stress. Like himself, his father may also be a high
school dropout and unemployed with few or no skills. However, within these
bleak situations many black families have attempted to reframe the devastation
that accompanies unemployment and to substitute a temporary low-wage job for
one that has been lost.

Infants of teenage parents are often born into a world bereft of significant
material, political, psychological, and social supports. According to the CSS
report (1986), poor New York City black children eligible for day care or some
other preschool program have a one in five chance of getting into such a
program. Above the preschool level, two out of three of these children will
attend "racially isolated" schools, three out of four will be enrolled in special
education classes, because their reading and computing skills are below grade
level, and some may be placed inappropriately and drop out before completing
high school. Only one out of nine black males will go on to college, while a
slightly higher number of black females will pursue higher education (one out of
eight) (CSS, 1986). A recent black high school graduate will be competing for
jobs with white elementary school graduates, and the recent black college graduate will earn as much as a white high school graduate.

Much data have been collapsed in the above profiles of an underserved
segment of black families, but they speak to the almost incalculable human
waste tolerated by society.

Psychological Forces at Work

For many black men, the world of work itself constitutes a delayed battleground
in their search for self-affirmation and self-esteem. The combined effects of
unemployment and unequal employment opportunities put blacks at risk for a
range of psychological and emotional problems that can have physical manifestations too. The recently unemployed often experience reactions similar to feelings of bereavement: grief, anger, guilt, feelings of loss, and a sense of losing
control over one's life. Practitioners also note that problem behaviors related to
stress (e.g., alcohol and child abuse) and stress-induced diseases accelerate with
unemployment.

IMPLICATIONS FOR SOCIAL WORK PRACTICE

Primary intervention is called for at both the macro-level and the micro-level.
However, interventions at the micro-level are necessarily reparative and should
be guided by an awareness that the larger environment has been experienced by
many blacks as hostile, historically exclusionary, and systemically pathological.
The norms that inform a linear assessment of effective coping are rooted in the
dominant culture's either/or view of events and behavior—a thing is either right
or wrong, acceptable or unacceptable, black or white. Such a view generates
misdiagnosis or an incomplete assessment and results in inappropriate interven-

tions (e.g., institutionalization, incarceration, overmedication). It is therefore imperative that assessment be individualized, culturally sensitive, and ecological.

Individualizing Family Assessments

The social worker must individualize and differentiate among black families. Enabling and empowering must take into account whether the black client's unemployment is chronic and characteristic, or current and episodic. Such distinctions will go a long way toward a realistic understanding of the impact of unemployment on individual and family functioning and may make clearer the coping and stress management capacities of the client.

The case of Mr. Smith indicates that assessment should identify the need to reestablish his self-esteem and supports and to redirect his previously successful coping strategies. The resulting intervention strategies can then be identified more effectively.

Intervention Strategies

Based on assessment, action (intervention) is directed to improving personal and environmental relationships by facilitating self-management of the internal world of feelings, perceptions, thoughts, values, motivations, and attitudes and helping people increase the responsiveness of the external world by intervening to modify maladaptive transactions in the person and in the environment (Germain & Gitterman, 1980). Interventions should thus be couched in an ecological or broad context and should be:

1. Supportive of strengths. (Black clients' self-initiated problem-solving efforts must be acknowledged and encouraged. Even when such efforts have been unsuccessful or only partially successful, they must be seen as valid attempts to cope. Their ego-syntonic value merits support enhancement.)
2. Directed to the immediacy of the client's concerns. (A venerable social work tenet is starting where the client is. Many black and other minority clients most often seek concrete help and are resistant to talk-oriented and insight counseling.)
3. Directed not only toward enabling clients to survive but also toward empowering them to function in a system that is itself often the source of pathology.

Specifically, micro- and macro-intervention strategies may also include:

1. An unemployed families support group. (In addition to addressing stress management, support groups may foster job-seeking skills.)
2. Informal consultants from among the unemployed or formerly unemployed. (In helping others, loss of identity and self-esteem may be enhanced.)

3. Social workers acting on behalf of the unemployed by joining coalitions of other service providers concerned about unemployment.

Role of the Social Worker

Social workers must assume a practical role in lending their voices and talents to the development of policies and programs that are responsive to the needs of the unemployed. The practice literature is noticeably short on minority-explicit content. Cooper (1973) cautions, "The worker must maintain sensitivity to the individual person before him or her, with all that person's unique desires, problems and needs"—as the worker should with any client. The worker must not treat "a culture carrier," nor can he or she be "colorblind." Cultural considerations are influenced by the social, economic, and political arena and are not static. Further, color is the predominant distinguishing factor of the black experience, and to deny its existence denies the validity of the client's ethnic being and some measure of his or her humanness. The social work truism that we must see the "whole person" is most important in the acknowledgment of blackness and in taking into account the omnipresence of "blackness" in the persona of every Afro-American. As used here, blackness conveys a kaleidoscope of experiences, alternatively oppressed or ascendant, prideful or burdensome, denied or proclaimed, but never absent. The Afro-American's response to blackness contains an array of coping strategies that move across a continuum from denial to commitment to action related to racial parity.

Being black affects how an individual or family unit perceives the world, and the reverse. Without exception, black clients have had some consistent life experiences that are unlike those of whites and quite similar to those of other blacks. These experiences, whether personal or historical group experiences, have helped determine the black client's individual feelings, thoughts, and behaviors just as significantly as early family experiences. When the pervasive centrality of this dynamic is internalized by the worker, the application of an ethnically sensitive practice will be relevant. All too often, cultural duality (if perceived at all) is erroneously perceived as "cultural deprivation" and inferiority.

The social worker must be prepared to accept and empathize with a black client's perspective and feelings of distrust and be willing to undefensively acknowledge any personal ignorance or stereotypical racist thinking the client may point out. To the extent that workers can present themselves as authentic and nondefensive in their roles with black clients, they may engender a climate of trust and honesty while modeling openness, risk-taking, and self-disclosure.

CONCLUSIONS

Black unemployment and underemployment are chronic and intergenerational phenomena for many blacks. Both race and economics have combined over historical time to assign an almost permanent and negative status to blacks in the surplus labor reserve. Black unemployment and underemployment have a structural base and structural consequences in and for the social system as well. Black males, and particularly black teenage males, are the population segment hardest hit by unemployment, but all members of black families, and all social levels, are affected.

The cultural definitions held by the dominant white majority have served more to assign inferior status and functional incompetence to blacks than genetic or social factors. Racial misperceptions have distorted the personality and self-concepts of blacks and deprived the society of the contributions of a significant segment of the nation's population.

Economic, political, psychological, and sociocultural forces all play inter-meshing roles in creating the conditions that foster and sustain unemployment. Social workers must engage in stronger advocacy for change in those concepts and behavior. There is little to be gained by repeating timeworn recommendations— for example, more skill training for blacks in the inner city, passing stronger full-employment legislation, or lowering the minimum wage. Any real solution to black unemployment must occur at the macro-system level. Micro-level inter-ventions must be secondary or tertiary.

There is no singularly different approach for working with black clients, but mental health practitioners must engage all of their clients' experiences. It is therefore important for the social work profession to take a proactive stance regarding Macarov's (1988) observations:

> Social workers will have to deal with people ready, willing and able to work for whom there simply are no jobs. . . . For many people, unemployment will be the norm. . . . Social workers will need to view unemployment . . . from a new perspective. They will have to learn to help clients have fulfilling lives, to engage in satisfying activities, not to feel stigmatized, and to maintain positive self-images, despite not being employed. (p. 24)

The worker must go beyond the unemployment problem and tune in to the individual who is hurting underneath. With keen self-awareness, sensitivity, and empathy, the worker will be able to make appropriate interventions.

REFERENCES

Black and white children in America: Key facts (1985). Washington, DC: Children's Defense Fund.

Clarke, R. (1988, June 22–28). Corporate America still resistant to change, expert says. *City Sun* (New York, NY), 25.

Community Service Society. (1986). Unpublished policy papers: Social Services (pp. 13, 15), Social Security (p. 2), Education (p. 10), Education and Training (p. 10), Health (p. 3).

Cooper, S. (1973). A look at the effects of racism on clinical work. *Social Casework, 54*, 76–84.

Dewart, J. (Ed.). (1987). *State of black America, 1987.* New York: National Urban League.

Freire, P. (1985). *The politics of education: Culture, power, and liberation.* South Hadley, MA: Bergin & Garvey.

Germain, C., & Gitterman, A. (1980). *The life model of social work practice.* New York: Columbia University Press.

Gutman, H. (1976). *The black family in slavery and in freedom.* New York: Oxford University Press.

Higgenbotham, A., Jr. (1978). *In the matter of color.* New York: Oxford.

Hill, R.B. (1978). *The illusion of black progress.* Washington, DC: National Urban League.

Jacobs, J. (1987). Black America 1987: An overview. In J. Dewart (Ed.), *State of black America, 1987* (pp. 1–2). New York: National Urban League.

Jones, T. (1974). Institutional racism in the United States. *Social Work, 19,* 2.

Keefe, T. (1984). The stresses of unemployment. *Social Work, 29*(3), 264–268.

Kerner Report. (1968). *Report of the National Advisory Commission on Civil Disorders.* New York: Bantam.

Lum, D. (1986). *Social work practice and people of color: A process-stage approach.* Monterey, CA: Brooks/Cole.

Macarov, D. (1988). Reevaluation of unemployment. *Social Work, 33,* 23–28.

Maslow, A. H. (1970). *Motivation and personality.* 2nd ed. New York: Harper & Row.

Moss, J.A. (1982). Unemployment among black youth: A policy dilemma. *Social Work, 27,* 47–52.

Swinton, D. (1988). Economic status of blacks 1987. In J. Dewart, (Ed.), *State of black America, 1987* (p. 143). New York: National Urban League.

Towle, C. (1965). *Common human needs.* Rev. ed. New York: National Association of Social Workers.

U.S. Bureau of the Census. (1980). *The social and economic status of the black population.* Washington, DC: Government Printing Office.

Wilkinson, (1977). *The stigmatization process: The politicization of the black male identity.* Chicago: Nelson Hall.

Wilson, W.J. (1986, December). Today's native sons. *Time,* 27.

CHAPTER 12

Culturally Sensitive Social Work Practice with Black Alcoholics and Their Families

Roosevelt Wright, Jr., *University of Texas at Arlington*
Barbara Lynn Kail, *University of Texas at Arlington*
Robert F. Creecy, *North Carolina Central University*

Alcohol abuse is a primary contributing factor to such social ills as family disruption, property destruction, lost production, poor health, and premature death. Its social and economic effects are debilitating and can be felt throughout American society (Hafen, 1977). Alcohol abusers and problem drinkers come from all classes, races, and income groups, but economic and social stressors from racism may make black Americans more likely than other groups to experience the most severe and negative consequences of alcohol abuse. The prevalence of problem drinking and alcohol dependency is considerably higher among blacks than among whites (Bailey et al., 1965) and blacks suffer disproportionately from alcohol-related health problems, and deaths (Gary, 1980; Herd, 1986; Williams, 1985). In addition, alcohol is linked to many of the domestic disputes, accidents, criminal assaults, homicides, and other conflicts in which blacks are involved (Harper, 1977; Herd, 1986; Watts & Wright, 1983).

Experts on alcohol and blacks conclude that alcohol abuse is the number-one health and social problem in the black community (Harper, 1977; Wright & Watts, 1985), so it is surprising that so little research exists on alcohol and black Americans. Only since the mid-1960s have a significant number of empirically based studies on alcohol and blacks become available (Watts & Wright, 1986). The use of other drugs by blacks is an equally important and complex problem, but the concern of this chapter is the problem of alcohol.

HISTORICAL PERSPECTIVES ON ALCOHOL USE AMONG BLACK AMERICANS

The use of alcoholic beverages by black Americans has deep historical roots, going back to precolonial times in West Africa, where the native beer played prominent roles in religious, economic, and social life (Herd, 1986; Herd, 1985; Umunna, 1967). The drinking of this beer took place primarily at ceremonies, feasts, and so forth (Heath, 1975), but excessive drinking was rare (Herd, 1985). During the early seventeenth century when blacks were brought to the American colonies, first as indentured servants and then as slaves, they found that the colonists had enacted measures aimed at preventing blacks from drinking (see Larkins, 1965). Such measures were based on the notion that blacks were too irresponsible to be trusted with the use of alcohol and also on the fear that blacks would be less accepting of the conditions of their servitude, more difficult to control, and prone to violence when inebriated (Lender & Martin, 1982). In the eighteenth century, all the slaveholding states prohibited or controlled the consumption of alcoholic beverages by blacks.

But slaves were sometimes allowed to drink. Slave masters often used alcohol to reward slaves for notable service, and other masters allowed slaves to drink on weekends or on special occasions. According to Frederick Douglass, the black abolitionist who grew up as a slave, "Slave holidays represent the most effective means in the hands of the slaveholder in keeping down the spirits of insurrection. Their object seemed to be to disgust their slaves with freedom by plunging them into the lowest depths of dissipation" (Lender & Martin, 1982, p. 28).

Although during the Civil War slaves found it easier to obtain alcohol, and some drank extensively, alcohol became less available in the south because much of it was used for war-related purposes (Larkins, 1965). After the Civil War ended in 1865 and the institution of slavery was dismantled, the extent to which excessive drinking and drunkenness continued to be features in the lifestyles of the newly freed slaves is unclear. Profuse drinking and public drunkenness were not uncommon in the ranks of ex-slaves (Wharton, 1947), but most former slaves practiced moderation (Stearns, 1872). Whatever the case, the drinking of alcoholic beverages in any amount by blacks was generally resented in most white communities. It was believed that liquor gave blacks a false sense of being equal or superior to whites, which was intolerable in the south (Whitener, 1945). Thus blacks, as a collective, exhibited comparatively low rates of alcohol use, drunkenness, and problems due to drinking. In this regard, Herd (1986) notes, "chronic drunkenness was so rare among blacks that they were thought to be physiologically immune from prolonged inebriety" (p. 77). During the reconstruction era, southern state legislatures in 1865 and 1866 enacted a series of prohibitive and harsh laws to define the status and rights of blacks and southern prohibition against alcohol use by blacks had become blatantly racist (Herd, 1986).

Despite recent improvements in the area of civil rights, blacks are still confronted by many blocked opportunities. As a result, a profound sense of discouragement, frustration, and social alienation exists among many black Americans, and because alcohol is now readily available in the contemporary black community, increasing numbers of black Americans engage in heavy drinking in an attempt to escape from these feelings (Cohen, 1982).

ALCOHOL USE AND ALCOHOLISM IN
THE CONTEMPORARY BLACK COMMUNITY

In marked contrast to earlier periods in this nation's history, current political and social efforts seem to be aimed at increasing rather than limiting accessibility to alcohol by blacks. For example, legal codes and laws that regulate the initiation, deployment, and operation of retail alcohol outlets and establishments in black communities are lax and poorly enforced. Such conditions have had a substantial impact on increasing alcohol availability and subsequently alcohol consumption in the black community (Harper & Dawkins, 1977).

Heavy or excessive drinking by blacks typically occurs on weekends, during special holidays, and (for those who are heavy drinkers) at various social events (Harper, 1976). Two important factors, presumably related to the institution of slavery, may have influenced contemporary black drinking practices. First, the permitted use of alcoholic beverages among slaves was traditionally associated with festive occasions (Heath, 1975). Alcohol became the reward for hard work, not merely a lubricant for social exchange but also an accompaniment to exhilaration and celebration. Second, restrained use of alcohol was irrelevant and inappropriate, and drunkenness on such occasions was the norm (Kelly, 1985). In addition, the current practice of heavy weekend drinking appears to be reinforced by the fact that pay checks are received on Friday afternoons, when persons are more likely to be able to purchase liquor.

Nationwide surveys of drinking patterns in the United States since the 1950s have included small subsamples of blacks that yield general data on black drinking patterns and problems (Herd, 1986). Cahalan and colleagues (1969), in a national survey, found that black men and white men varied little in drinking patterns. Roughly 30 percent of the men in both races abstained or drank infrequently, nearly 50 percent were in the light to moderate category, and about 20 percent of the men were heavy drinkers. Black women, however, differed significantly from white women both in their higher proportion of abstainers and in their higher rate of heavy drinkers. More recent surveys report blacks with higher rates of abstention and similar rates of heavy drinking, compared with whites (Rappaport et al., 1975; Clarke and Midanik, 1982). Clarke and Midanik (1982) found that white men had considerably higher rates of very heavy drinking than black men, while black women had higher rates of heavy consumption than white women, and that white men were twice as likely as black men to exhibit social problems as a result of drinking. Bailey and colleagues (1965) found that blacks, particularly black women, were subject to higher rates of alcoholism than whites. Echoing the findings of previous studies are studies by Weissman and colleagues (1980), Cahalan and Room (1974), Haberman and Sheinberg (1967), Robins and colleagues (1968), Sterne and Pittman (1972), and Wallack and Barrows (1981).

Thus, when drinking and drinking-related problems are examined in the black population, no consistent patterns of high alcohol consumption or high problem rates emerge for the group as a whole when compared to other racial groups. Drinking patterns appear to be heterogeneous and differ along lines observed in the general population.

ALCOHOLISM TREATMENT AND REHABILITATION

Those working with black alcohol abusers appear to take two philosophical approaches. One is that alcohol abuse and alcoholism should be treated on their own terms with little attention to race and sex, the other is that the historical and etiological patterns of alcoholism within the black community make it important that treatment be sensitive to ethnic and gender needs. We take the latter position in the following discussion.

Employee Assistance Programs

Employee Assistance Programs (EAPs) are corporate- and/or union-sponsored human service programs for alcoholism and other problems in the workplace. Referrals to EAPs can be made by supervisors, unions, peers, and by self-referral. EAPs provide information, problem evaluation and assessment, referral, and limited short-term treatment. But blacks are not likely to take advantage of EAPs (see Gray and Lanier, 1985), primarily because smaller companies generally cannot afford to staff EAPs and blacks are more likely than whites to work in smaller companies; blacks may be more reluctant to disclose their problems, especially to white treatment staff; and blacks may be referred for their problems at a later point in time, compared with whites, because supervisors may fear accusations of racial discrimination or may believe stereotypes about the commonness of black drinking problems.

Specialized Outpatient Clinics

The Yale Plan Clinics are the prototype of specialized outpatient clinics. Treatment includes a variety of methods and modalities. Ambulatory detoxification with the assistance of psychoactive drugs and disulfiram (antabuse) treatment are usually offered, and patients are encouraged to attend Alcoholics Anonymous meetings. The main treatment modality appears to be psychotherapy, both individual and group, addressed to personal conflicts that cause patients to abuse alcohol (Pattison, 1979). But this treatment assumes a degree of ongoing life functioning—clients are expected to have basic job skills, shelter, and food—which may pose a barrier to the black client whose lack of adequate social necessities, for example, might be due more to the nature of the local social and economic environment than to his or her disability.

Inpatient Detoxification and Inpatient Rehabilitation

There has been an increase in non-hospital-based detoxification, but such free-standing alcoholism detoxification wards can become revolving-door facilities if they are not linked directly to and are part of a comprehensive alcohol and rehabilitation program (Pattison, 1979).

One common inpatient rehabilitation model is the Hazelton Foundation in Minnesota (Bell & Evans, 1983), where clients stay three to six weeks and the orientation is nonmedical. The prohibitive cost of this type of treatment is a major barrier for the black abuser. Furthermore, black alcohol abusers, particularly adolescent abusers, may be in greater need of vocational rehabilitation and job-attaining skills. Halfway houses (residential treatment facilities) offer more structure, a longer period during which food and shelter are provided, and more extensive occupational training opportunities. Alcoholic black women with child care responsibilities, however, face numerous problems when asked to enter any residential treatment facility.

Alcoholics Anonymous

Alcoholics Anonymous (AA) is a major voluntary rehabilitation resource (Hudson 1985). The essential elements of AA are the sharing of common experiences, mutual acceptance of one another as human beings, and trusting in a "higher power" to aid in recovery. AA becomes the primary culture and reference group for those who become members. It serves as an extended kinship group characterized by common traditions, a shared world view, and shared principles, rights, and obligations. Some charge that AA promotes only mainstream white middle-class values and does not address drinking as a response to discrimination, poverty, unemployment, and violence (McRoy & Shorkey, 1985; Harper, 1976). But Hudson (1985) and Caldwell (1983) argue that AA is well suited to meeting the black alcohol abuser's unique needs because the spiritual fellowship and other elements of AA have a strong cultural affinity for black alcoholics.

A CULTURALLY SENSITIVE APPROACH: IMPLICATIONS FOR SOCIAL WORK PRACTICE

The social work practitioner working with a black alcohol abuser must be aware of treatment resources and their limitations for black families. He or she must also be culturally sensitive to issues stemming from the black experience and black culture. Lum (1986) suggests the following framework for social work practice with people of color, based on the following process-stages: contact, problem, identification, assessment, intervention and termination.

Contact

Basic to the contact phase is establishment of a relationship between client, the family, and worker. During this stage the worker gains an initial picture of the client's functioning and "presenting problem." A broad-based ecological perspective can help the practitioner understand the various systems involved in the client's decision to approach the agency and in the presenting problem. Moreover, systemic knowledge of the client's social environment, including the family, helps put alcohol use in a specific cultural context, that of the black community and the black experience. Such a systems-oriented perspective also can help determine when referral to another agency is in order.

Problem Identification

The main task during the problem identification stage is to define the problem and partialize it into clear and specific components. At this point the practitioner must be aware of the impact of race and/or ethnicity on the behavior of the client and other family members. An ecological approach that would include the race or ethnic group and the experiences surrounding race or ethnicity as one aspect of the problem is helpful.

Assessment: Selecting Goals and Developing Treatment Alternatives

During the assessment stage, the worker and client analyze the dynamic interactions between the client and the situation, assess the impact of the problem on the client system, identify the resources available for helping, and set specified treatment goals. The emphasis should be on identifying individual and familial strengths and delineating social support systems that can be used in problem resolution. An intrapsychic treatment model presumes that the problem(s) of the client stem from personal deficiency rather than from an interaction between individual or family concerns and institutional or societal issues, but an ecologically oriented social worker probably would be aware of more potential helping resources. Therefore, the goals and objectives agreed upon at this stage may be more appropriate, realistic, and attainable.

An initial, basic goal of alcohol treatment with blacks is retention in treatment. Practitioners must be aware of the organizational, professional, and environmental barriers to treatment and make specific efforts to overcome them (e.g., by providing child care for a black alcoholic mother who needs residential treatment, or by using creative outreach to involve a reluctant member of the alcoholic's family in the process). Goals related to excessive drinking behavior must be agreed upon and set clearly. Abstinence is the most viable and easily monitored goal in any alcohol treatment effort (Brisbane & Womble, 1985a, 1985b), but interest in treatment approaches that permit alternative drinking behaviors has been sparked in part by findings that a small percentage of treated alcohol abusers are reportedly able to return to moderate drinking without serious problems (*Alcohol and Health*, 1984). Social work practitioners and clients must distinguish between situations where abstinence is realistic and situations where it is not.

Several goal assessment and problem evaluation instruments are available: the Addiction Severity Index, Marlaff's Drinking Profile Questionnaire, and the Bowman Stern and Newton Volume Pattern Index of Alcohol Consumption

(Nathan & Lipscomb, 1979). Within this context, basic day-to-day survival goals must clearly be identified early in the treatment process. These may involve financial considerations, housing, occupation, the handling of situations involving discrimination, and child care. The McMaster Family Assessment Device (a sixty-item questionnaire to be filled out by the family), an ecomap, and the genogram may be useful in developing realistic survival goals for black alcohol abusers and their families.

As an overall goal, Ziter (1987) suggests black empowerment. Empowerment is defined as the recognition of indirect and direct blocks to power experienced by the black alcohol-abusing client and developing strategies for overcoming these blocks. Such a goal is particularly important for black clients, given their many negative life experiences in the larger white world. This goal also reinforces the need to involve the client, family, and other systems in setting goals and giving them the sense of power and responsibility for achieving the goals.

For all the goals set, it is important to involve the client in this process, to have multiple incremental goals, and to establish a timetable for attaining objectives associated with each goal and for points of reflection and monitoring throughout the treatment process.

Intervention and Termination

In the intervention and termination stages, a change strategy that will alter the interaction between the client and the problem environment is developed (Lum, 1986). Intervention strategies in social work practice are associated with a number of traditional schools of thought (psychodynamic, functional, problem-solving, crisis intervention, task centered, behavioral). No matter which strategy is used, a social worker with an ecological perspective may be more acutely sensitive to the different systems involved in a "problem" and will be able to incorporate a larger number of relevant systems in the treatment process.

Behavioral Approaches. Nathan and Lipscomb (1979) discuss behavioral approaches that might be potentially useful for blacks: chemical aversion, blood alcohol level discrimination training, contingency contracting, and broadspectrum behavioral approaches. Chemical aversion involves the pairing of drinking or scenes of drinking with chemically induced nausea and is typically implemented in a controlled inpatient setting. This technique may be most useful with alcohol abusers who are employed, have a higher income, are married, and are well motivated (*Alcohol and Health*, 1984; Nathan & Lipscomb, 1979). Blood alcohol level discrimination training attempts to train clients to discriminate among a range of intoxication levels and then maintain free drinking at moderate levels. Research suggests this might be a promising treatment (Nathan & Lipscomb, 1979). Contingency contracting is a highly developed and widely used technique in the alcohol field. It involves prior agreement by client and practitioner that performance of a desired behavior or modification-elimination of unwanted behavior will result in a reinforcing consequence. Formal contracts may even be documented in writing. The practitioner can focus on specific reeducation techniques to increase effectiveness in familial and vocational spheres. There may be fundamental gaps in knowledge about how to behave in the family or on the job which can be addressed through such contracts instead of focusing on achieving insight into the behavior or problems.

Broad-spectrum behavioral approaches tend to use the following basic elements in different sequences and proportions: aversive conditioning, behavioral assessment, assertiveness training, behavioral rehearsal to develop interpersonal skills, hypnosis, training in identification of problem situations, identification and evaluation of alternatives to drinking, and implementation of the chosen alternative behavior. These techniques are relatively effective (*Alcohol and Health*, 1984).

Individual and Group Dynamic Psychotherapy. There are several issues around counseling black alcohol abusers: (1) the issue of white and black counseling styles and black interpersonal styles, (2) the issue of the bicultural world the black lives in and the tensions this creates, and (3) the issue of spirituality in counseling black abusers. Effective counseling requires that the interpersonal styles of the social work practitioner and client should ideally match.

Bell and Evans (1983) identify several alcohol practitioner counseling styles. White practitioners may operate from a position of cultural ignorance, "color blindness," or cultural liberation, but only the last style will result in effective alcoholism counseling, allowing the white practitioner to express positive regard and honest confrontation across racial lines and encouraging positive expressions by the client about being black. Bell and Evans also suggest that black clients typically do better, and the treatment outcomes are more positive, when black clients are matched with black practitioners or therapists. Black alcohol treatment practitioners, for the most part, bring with them positive role modeling, ease in building empathy, shared life experiences, openness to honest confrontation, and a lack of fear and prejudice. The acculturated and assimilated black abuser, one who has rejected things black as inferior, would probably do better with a white practitioner, at least initially.

The issue of biculturism is relevant to the treatment of the black alcohol abusers. Black alcohol abusers live in two worlds, the black world and the white world. In negotiating between these two worlds, the abuser pays a price. Beverly (1975) suggests that treatment must include a clear perspective on the meaning of the black experience, the isolation of the positive behavioral components among black people that have fostered their survival, and the implications of counseling in a racist society. Effective counseling with the black alcohol abuser must include development of an improved self-image and pride in one's race, racial heritage, and culture (Harper, 1983; Lonesome, 1985).

Black spirituality can be a unique resource for the black alcohol abuser if used appropriately. In brief, spirituality is the belief that black people can reach out and call upon a "higher power" for solutions to their problems. Expressions of such spirituality are "It's in God's hands," "The problem is a punishment from God," "The church is my salvation." The black church, as an institution, provides an outlet for release of tensions and is a viable mental health resource in the black community (Knox, 1985).

Group therapy approaches may be crucial in treating black alcoholics; the presence of peer influences in a group context can often pierce denial and other maladaptive defenses (Lonesome, 1985). The group context also provides a sense of cohesion and racial group identity, a lessening of isolation, and less dependence on the clinical professional.

Family Treatment. The role of the black family system as a factor in the etiology of alcoholism is well documented (see, e.g., McRoy & Shorkey, 1985). Work with the family system will be needed in almost all cases for assessment, successful treatment, and continued sobriety of the alcoholic (Okpaku, 1985).

Based on what she refers to as the problem-centered systems therapy, Ziter (1987) presents a comprehensive model for involving family systems in the treatment of black alcohol abusers:

- Treatment is geared to six to twelve sessions.
- The family is an active collaborator, and the therapist is the catalyst, clarifier, and facilitator.
- Seven dimensions of family functioning are assessed.
- Treatment centers on specific problems in functioning, and steps taken to address these problems are mutually arrived at.

Ziter argues that for the black family the following modifications in this therapeutic approach should be made: (1) During assessment the family must take responsibility to foster empowerment; (2) assessment should focus on environmental obstacles; and (3) an ecomap may be used to identify sources of strain between the white world and the black world, as well as sources of family problems and potential supports. Moreover, treatment should emphasize rational problem-solving techniques for resolving bicultural tension and for developing an appreciation of survival techniques that work as well as those that are no longer functional.

Because black cultural and racial factors play a significant role in the recovery process, social work practitioners and others cannot be insensitive to their importance (Gary & Gary, 1985). Rogan (1986) clearly supports this perspective:

> Recovery [from alcohol abuse and alcoholism] is . . . an internal process that requires a psychological shift on the part of the client who is struggling to develop alternative coping mechanisms. Programs that help a client by fostering self-esteem and by encouraging clients to assume responsibility for their lives facilitate the psychological growth essential to ongoing sobriety. Programs that acknowledge all aspects of a person, including one's cultural and racial identity, are likely to foster a sense of self-pride that will assist a person through the journey to long-term sobriety. (p. 44)

Treatment Issues and Differential Assessment

The practitioner with an ecological perspective or framework must integrate information about specific approaches with what we know about the need for differential assessment across client situations. This will put the worker in a better position to make decisions on the following treatment issues that frequently arise when working with black alcoholics.

Hospitalization: General or Psychiatric. Pattison (1979) suggests general hospital admission when the patient is semiconscious or unconscious, hemorrhaging, at risk of serious withdrawal difficulties, convulsive, or jaundiced. Withdrawal from alcohol or polydrug abuse might also be an indication for at least admission to an inpatient detoxification setting if not a general hospital (Primm and Wesley, 1985). Admission to a psychiatric hospital is advisable when the client is clearly psychotic, severely depressed, or suicidal—in short, if there is a psychiatric disorder that necessitates hospitalization regardless of the alcohol use. However, Bell and colleagues (1985) warn that black alcohol patients with organic brain syndromes associated with alcoholism are often incorrectly diagnosed as schizophrenic. They caution the practitioner to be skeptical of a schizophrenic diagnosis in patients reporting a significant work history and affective bonding as adults and an onset of the illness after the age of 30.

Outpatient vs. Inpatient Admission to Alcohol Treatment Programs. Clients' retention of housing, job, and child care responsibilities would all suggest outpatient treatment as an initial therapeutic plan. Inpatient treatment is best suited for abusers who meet three or more of the following conditions: continued chronic alcohol abuse for two or more years; continued drinking despite previous treatment in other forms of alcoholism programs; continued drinking despite serious attempts to stop on his or her own; alcohol-related significant impairment in "life roles;" and signs of physical health impairments related to alcohol use (Lonesome, 1985).

Use of Pharmacotherapy. On a short-term basis there may be reason to use mild tranquilizers during the initial stages of detoxification. Antidepressants are not likely to be helpful because they take two to three weeks to reach adequate therapeutic blood levels; by that time alcohol-related depression will have ceased. Antabuse may be most helpful with alcoholics who have achieved a degree of social stability, including a stable family and work environment, and who are able to form therapeutic relationships with the dispensing physician or nurse. Programs that offer antabuse as a treatment option are likely to have a higher success rate (Becker, 1979; Pattison, 1979).

Termination and Aftercare Services. Social work practice trends on termination currently emphasize the importance of ongoing linkages to significant others, new activities, natural communities, and environmental resources. The task here is to maintain positive outcomes (i.e., sobriety or abstinence) by involving a variety of community linkages, significant others, and socializing agents, who impart positive feedback concerning the changes. For the black alcohol abuser this might include such institutions as the church, kinship systems, and employers. An ecological, culturally sensitive approach can help establish maintainable equilibrium among these different systems with the recovered alcoholic.

CASE STUDY: AN ECOLOGICAL APPROACH

John Starks is a 44-year-old unemployed and separated black male who was admitted to the alcohol dependency ward of a major urban hospital. In the initial session he was cooperative, alert, and verbal. Before admission he had been drinking one to two quarts of wine each day. During one of his recent drinking episodes, he tripped on some ice and broke his arm. After a discussion with Mr. Starks' family and his personal physician, he was formally admitted to the hospital for detoxification, treatment, and rehabilitation. At the time of his admission he was staying in the home of his elderly parents. In the past, Mr. Starks had received treatment for his alcoholism at several local mental health agencies in the black community. In the initial and subsequent sessions he denied having had any auditory or visual hallucinations, and he denied any desire to harm himself or anyone else.

Mr. Starks is the second oldest of eight children. His parents were strict disciplinarians yet loving. They do not approve of the use of alcohol by anyone. Mr. Starks feels that his parents and his siblings do not truly understand the reasons he is an alcoholic, that he drinks alcohol to escape from his family, marital, and employment problems. He does not feel able to openly and honestly discuss his alcohol dependency with his wife, children, or extended family network. Due to his long-term and chronic abuse of alcohol, his work and employment record can at best be described as irregular or sporadic. Soon after his discharge from the army in 1968, he was able to obtain episodic and short-term unskilled employment as a laborer. However, he was quickly terminated from his jobs due to his habitual dependence on alcohol.

Mr. Starks is currently separated from his wife of twenty-two years. The marriage produced two sons who are presently 17 and 15 years old. According to Mr. Starks, his inability to maintain full-time employment and his drinking were the primary reasons for his marital and family problems. Mr. Starks' wife and his sons are residing in another city with relatives. His contact with them since the separation has been infrequent.

Mr. Starks has had a long history of chronic alcohol abuse. He admitted having abused alcohol for more than twenty years, and during the past year he has been arrested and convicted of two DWI offenses. He was raised in a relatively restricted and religious home environment and has been unable to resolve the killing of Vietnamese soldiers during his military service. In addition, he feels that he has been unable to meet the expectations of his roles as a son, brother, husband, and father. He depends upon alcohol to relieve himself of his inadequate feelings about his manhood and self.

It is easy to fall into the trap of conceptualizing alcoholism as a biological or psychological problem idiosyncratic to the particular individual. An ecological perspective on intervention can help a person lead a full and satisfying life, sober and at peace with self, family, friends, and community.

The various familial and nonfamilial subsystems that can be affected by the alcohol abuse of an individual can be conceptually demonstrated by use of an ecomap model. An ecomap graphic depicts the causal linkages and interrelationships of several subsystems (Hartman, 1978). It provides a cross-sectional simulation and diagrammatic view of major systems currently involved in a particular behavioral or social problem, and it highlights the nature of the interfaces and points to conflicts to be mediated, bridges to be built, and resources to be mobilized in the treatment intervention process. Figure 12.1 depicts the ecomap for Mr. Starks. Solid lines intersected by short solid lines indicate the systems with which Mr. Starks has a stressful relationship. Of the nine identified ecosystems presently in Mr. Starks' life, six may be viewed as stressors that reinforce his uncontrollable and self-destructive drinking behavior. The three systems that are not identified as sources of stress are human service helping systems (the hospital's alcohol dependency ward, local mental health clinics, and Mr. Starks' personal physician). Because most of the ecosystems identified as stressors have evolved and endured as a direct result of Mr. Starks' excessive drinking, any

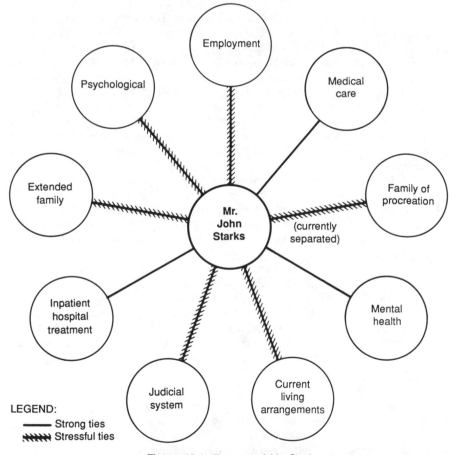

Figure 12.1. Ecomap of Mr. Starks

assessment and ultimate treatment strategy must recognize the influences that each ecosystem has upon the client and his problem drinking behavior.

The practitioner's treatment plan requires a full assessment of the damage Mr. Starks' excessive drinking did to the relationships with his nuclear family and the family of origin. This may mean involving the family in treatment on a time-limited basis, or having him initiate the discussions with them outside of treatment. In other situations where families are available and supportive, family counseling, family education, and appropriate referrals for family members to needed services are all essential. In addition, stability in Mr. Starks' employment ecosystem must be attained. The long-term need for job training, job placement and education should be mapped out.

The ecosystems would probably be delineated regardless of the race or ethnic origin of the client or practitioner. For many black clients, however, it is important to understand and intervene with other potentially important systems, including the rich sources of cultural support (i.e., churches, social and fraternal lodges, and community-based self-help groups).

Both black and nonblack practitioners have expressed doubts about raising the issues of racial, ethnic, and/or cultural identity in the therapeutic process, but it is clear that alcoholism involves alienation not only from self but also from one's family, peers, and cultural community. Thus, effective help for a black alcoholic involves systematic efforts to improve self-identity, self-esteem, and promote a sense of belonging rather than cultural alienation and estrangement. An ecological perspective allows for a rapid assessment of the presenting problem(s) and the areas of stress, suggests a possible prioritization of treatment goals and objectives, and identifies the presence and absence of important ecosystems that may need to be involved in the treatment and successful resolution of the presenting problem.

In all likelihood, alcohol abuse and alcoholism-related problems in the black community will continue to intensify. Effective approaches to alcoholism treatment must therefore simultaneously address both the issue of increasing consumption and the social, cultural, and psychological factors related to alcohol abuse that are unique to black Americans. Comprehensive treatment and rehabilitation programs based on culturally sensitive practice modalities will have the widest acceptance within the black community.

ALCOHOLISM PREVENTION IN A CULTURALLY SENSITIVE CONTEXT

Efforts to treat black problem drinkers and their families have always fallen short in terms of the number of individuals who require such treatment. Interventions cannot be the sole effort. The constant and increasing flow of blacks with alcohol and related problems into the health and social welfare system must be slowed at its source. Systematic and comprehensive prevention efforts have been neglected both by professionals and by federal funding, with treatment receiving an overwhelming share of attention and financial support, but this trend has been changing slowly. Miller and Nirenberg (1985) note: "Alcoholism prevention is being treated more seriously and an increasing number of clinicians and researchers are devoting their efforts to prevention. Advances are being made on both theoretical and practical grounds. As in any relatively new field information is growing rapidly" (p. 5).

Alcoholism prevention refers to steps that individuals and families, groups, organizations, and communities can take to ameliorate and eliminate harmful drinking practices (Wright & Watts, 1985). The reasons for stressing this particular conception of prevention are pragmatic and theoretical. Because the problems associated with alcoholism are so complex and highly interdependent, systematic and relevant efforts to prevent alcoholism require a conscious effort to develop general theories, knowledge, and practice skills that are comprehensive and interdisciplinary in nature.

Such approaches to the prevention of alcohol abuse and alcoholism in the black community have been derived primarily from the theoretical underpinnings of prevention models, such as the distribution-of-consumption model, the sociocultural model, and the social-psychological model (see Brunn et al., 1975; Harford et al., 1980; Heath, 1981; Jessor & Jessor, 1980; Schmidt, 1977; and Zucker, 1979). Heuristically, the underlying philosophies of these models demand that we conceptualize alcoholism prevention along a continuum: primary prevention would be seen as organized efforts to address the causes of excessive drinking or abuse, secondary prevention would involve preventing negative consequences of drinking with high-risk population groups, such as the elderly and adolescents; tertiary prevention (i.e., clinical intervention or treatment) would involve rehabilitation of problem drinkers from those negative consequences. Thus, prevention approaches would address many alcohol use issues and problems at several different levels. Tertiary prevention strategies are addressed elsewhere in this chapter. The following discussion takes a general approach to black alcoholism prevention at the primary and secondary levels because reliable data in this regard are largely absent (Dawkins, 1985; Watts & Wright, 1983).

Primary Prevention Strategies

Primary prevention strategies assume that the use of alcoholic beverages will continue to be an important part of the fabric of black residential life (Scott & Miranda, 1981). The aim is therefore to lessen both the frequency of abusive drinking and the severity of negative consequences (Room, 1980). A useful strategy might be development of specific programs that attempt to modify existing drinking norms or establish new normative prescriptions, values, and guidelines about drinking (Harper & Dawkins, 1977; Heath, 1976). For example, alcohol education programs could be used to train groups within the black community (middle-class people, young people, women) to be moderate and responsible drinkers and then serve as models of responsible drinking habits for others in the community. Education and modeling could also be initiated within a particular high-risk subgroup, such as adolescents.

Another primary strategy might be to develop programs that influence

alcohol consumption indirectly. For example, if we assume that individual deficiencies as well as social structural and environmental forces (e.g., racism,
poverty, feelings of oppression and powerlessness, low self-esteem, inadequate
interpersonal skills) contribute to alcohol abuse and alcoholism, then programs
that provide meaningful job training and education, develop appropriate adaptation and coping skills, increase opportunities for social competency and interaction, and improve the overall quality of life in the community would be
warranted. Such programs may enhance behavioral responses that are more
constructive than excessive drinking (Scott & Miranda, 1981; Wright & Watts,
1985).

Dealing directly with the availability of alcohol may also help alleviate
some reasons for abusive drinking. Some authors (Beauchamp, 1980; Dawkins
et al., 1979; Herd, 1986; Smart, 1980) suggest the establishment of local
community-based programs designed to lower rates of per capita alcohol consumption through such mechanisms as price controls, taxation, restriction in
number of alcohol outlets and hours of sale, and raising the legal age of alcohol
consumption.

Secondary Prevention Strategies

Secondary prevention strategies are alcohol-specific approaches that deal directly
with the drinking act itself and are geared toward preventing some of the
negative consequences of excessive drinking by modifying features of this act
related to abuse. Strategies developed to intervene at this level of drinking must
also deal with the difficult problem of gaining access to the alcohol-abusing
population. Individual abusers and groups at high risk for excessive drinking
may be located, for example, through child care, social service agencies, adult
day care centers, schools, indigenous community groups, grocery stores, beauty
shops, pool halls, liquor establishments, and work organizations employing large
numbers of blacks.

One important point of entry into the black community is through community-based providers of medical care services (e.g., physicians, nurses) or the
broader medical community. Providing alcohol education to medical care personnel may help increase identification and referral of abusers and their families to treatment and improve the ability of medical specialists to function as alcohol information disseminators in the local community. Strategies might also
include providing information regarding the effects of alcohol abuse and alcoholism (i.e., factual information regarding abuse and its management, and specific ways to overcome it and to change drinking patterns) to the broader black
community through, for example, television and radio, and especially black-oriented media and by making it available in community areas where black families tend to congregate.

Developing effective secondary strategies for blacks requires a thorough
understanding of their beliefs, traditions, values, needs, and culture. Blacks
themselves need to be involved in the processes that result in specific prevention
programs—for example, peer counseling programs can help prevent alcohol

abuse among adolescents (Spiegler, et al., 1985). The aims and goals of these programs should be established within the culture (Miller & Nirenberg, 1984). This is not to suggest that nonblacks should not participate, only that the guiding values should be be provided by blacks themselves. This is important for two reasons: (1) blacks can provide a cultural basis and natural helping strategies for programmatic developments, implementation, and operational decision-making and (2) their unique cultural values and traditions are accorded status that can increase the awareness, understanding, and sensitivity of nonblacks to the importance of the black cultural heritage. For this reason, the uniqueness of the black cultural environment must be appreciated.

Effective prevention strategies need to be not only multimodal but also multifaceted or ecological. Scott and Miranda (1981) recommend that prevention strategies be "designed to influence as much of the total environment as possible. Because alcohol use and abuse are intertwined with so many aspects of life (home, school, media, advertising, law, the economy, and the community), any strategy limited to a single element, such as home or school, can achieve only limited objectives" (p. 15).

CONCLUSIONS

Although the study of black alcohol abuse is in its infancy, it is escalating. At present, however, there is insufficient empirical evidence to support many of the conclusions concerning the etiology and consequences, treatment, or prevention of this problem. Still, important conclusions can be drawn regarding alcoholism among blacks and its treatment and prevention.

First, alcohol abuse is the number-one health problem and the number-one social problem among black Americans. It is both the cause and the result of numerous other problems, including poverty, unemployment, crime, familial disorganization, and marital disarray. Alcohol use is an integral part of the black cultural community and a convenient way to alleviate some of the anxieties and frustrations associated with the harsh realities of racism, discrimination, and oppression. Second, treatment of abusers must be based on an understanding of the quantitative and qualitative differences between blacks and other ethnic and cultural groups. Intervention and treatment programs must be tailored to the unique needs of blacks. Cultural sensitivity and genuine understanding on the part of treatment clinicians, especially white clinicians, is essential. Third, approaches to the prevention of black alcoholism must be comprehensive, multimodal, and ecological. Effective strategies need not necessarily relate specifically to drinking or to drinking problems.

Finally, a comprehensive treatment approach must involve prevention. Competition between alcohol treatment and prevention specialists has not been functional for the black community. Treatment efforts need to be viewed on a continuum with prevention efforts. If treatment is conceptualized along a continuum with prevention, many black alcohol issues and problems at different levels can be addressed simultaneously.

REFERENCES

Alcohol and health. (1984). Fifth special report to the U.S. Congress. (DHHS Publication No. ADM 84-1291). Washington, DC: Government Printing Office.

Bailey, M.B., Haberman, P.W., & Alksne, H. (1965). The epidemiology of alcoholism in an urban residential area. *Quarterly Journal of Studies on Alcoholism, 26*(1), 19–40.

Bailey, M., Haberman, P.W., & Sheinberg, J. (1965). *Distinctive characteristics of the alcoholic family.* New York: National Council on Alcoholism.

Beauchamp, D. (1980). *Beyond alcoholism: Alcohol and public policy and health policy.* Philadelphia, PA: Temple University Press.

Becker, C.E. (1979). Pharmacotherapy in the treatment of alcoholism. In J. Mendelsohn and N. Mello (Eds.), *The diagnosis and treatment of alcoholism* (pp. 283–303). New York: McGraw-Hill.

Bell, C.C., Thompson, J.P., Lewis, D., Ledd, J., Shears, M., & Thompson, B. (1985). Misdiagnosis of alcohol-related organic brain syndromes: Implications for treatment. *Alcoholism Treatment Quarterly, 2*(3–4), pp. 45–66.

Bell, P., & Evans, J. (1983). Counseling the black alcoholic client. In T. D. Watts and R. Wright (Eds.), *Black alcoholism: Toward a comprehensive understanding* (pp. 100–121). Springfield, IL: Thomas.

Beverly, C.C. (1975). Toward a model for counseling black alcoholics. *Journal of Non-White Concerns, 3,* 169–176.

Brisbane, F.L., & Womble, M. (1985a). Introduction. *Alcoholism Treatment Quarterly, 2*(3–4), 85–96.

Brisbane, F.L., & Womble, M. (1985b). *The treatment of black alcoholics.* New York: Haworth.

Bruun, K., Edwards, G., Lumio, M., Makela, K., Pan, L., Popham, R.E., Room, R., Schmidt, W., Skog, O. J., Sulkunen, P., & Osterberg, E. (1975). *Alcohol control policies in public health perspective, 25.* Helsinki: Finnish Foundation for Alcohol Studies.

Cahalan, D., Cisin, I., & Crossley, H. (1969). *American drinking practices.* New Brunswick, NJ: Rutgers Center for Alcohol Studies.

Cahalan, D., & Room, R. (1974). *Problem drinking among American men.* New Brunswick, NJ: Rutgers Center for Alcohol Studies.

Caldwell, F.J. (1983). Alcoholics Anonymous as a viable treatment resource for black alcoholics. In T. D. Watts and R. Wright (Eds.), *Black alcoholism: Toward a comprehensive understanding* (pp. 85–99). Springfield, IL: Thomas.

Clarke, W., & Midanik, L. (1982). Alcohol use and alcohol problems among U.S. adults: Results of the 1979 national survey. In *Alcohol consumption and related problems.* Alcohol and Health Monograph 1. (DHHS Publication No. ADM 82-1190). Washington, DC: Government Printing Office.

Cohen, S. (1982). *Methods of intervention. Prevention, intervention, and treatment: Concerns and models* (pp. 127–143). Alcohol and Health Monograph 3. Rockville, MD: National Institute on Alcohol Abuse and Alcoholism.

Coulter, E.M. (1947). *The South during reconstruction, 1865–1877.* Baton Rouge: Louisiana State University Press.

Dawkins, M. (1985, March 26–28). *Alcohol and blacks, 1974–1984: Review and update of the literature.* Unpublished paper presented at the 10th Anniversary Commemorative Symposium, Jackson State Interdisciplinary Alcohol Drug Studies Center, Jackson, Mississippi.

Dawkins, M.P., Farrell, W., & Johnson, J. (1979). Spatial patterns of alcohol outlets in the Washington, D.C., black community. *Proceedings of the Pennsylvania Academy of Science, 53,* 89–97.

Devore, W., & Schlesinger, E. (1981). *Ethnic sensitive social work practice.* St. Louis, MO: Mosby.

Gary, L.E. (1980). Role of alcohol and drug abuse in homicide. *Public Health Reports, 95*(6), 553–554.

Gary, L.E., & Gary, R.B. (1985). Treatment needs of black alcoholic women. *Alcoholism Treatment Quarterly, 2*(3–4), 97–114.

Gray, M., & Lanier, D. (1985). Designing employee assistance programs to meet the needs of black clients. *Alcoholism Treatment Quarterly, 2*(3–4), 85–96.

Haberman, P.W., & Sheinberg, J. (1967). Implicative drinking reported in a household survey: A corroborative note on subgroup differences. *Quarterly Journal of Studies on Alcohol, 28*(3), 538–543.

Hafen, B.Q. (1977). *Alcohol: The crutch that cripples.* New York: West.

Harford, T.C., Parker, D.A., & Light, L. (Eds.). (1980). *Normative approaches to the prevention of alcohol abuse and alcoholism* (pp. 37–46). Washington, DC: Government Printing Office.

Harper, F.D. (1976). *Alcohol abuse and black America.* Alexandria, VA: Douglass.

Harper, F.D. (1977). *Alcohol and blacks: An overview.* Washington, DC: Howard University School of Education.

Harper, F.D. (1983). Alcoholism treatment and black Americans: A review and analysis. In T.D. Watts & R. Wright (Eds.), *Black alcoholism: Toward a comprehensive understanding* (pp. 71–84). Springfield, IL: Thomas.

Harper, F.D., & Dawkins, M.P. (1977). Alcohol abuse in the black community. *The black scholar, 8*(6), 23–31.

Hartman, A. (1978). Diagrammatic assessment of family relationships. *Social Casework, 59*(8), 465–476.

Heath, D.A. (1975). A critical review of ethnographic studies of alcohol use. In R.J. Gibbins et al. (Eds.), *Research advances in alcohol and drug problems* (Vol. 2). New York: Wiley.

Heath, D.B. (1976). Anthropological perspectives on alcohol: An historical review. In M. W. Everett, J. O. Waddell, and D. B. Heath (Eds.), *Cross-cultural approaches to the study of alcohol: An interdisciplinary perspective* (pp. 42–101). The Hague: Mouton.

Heath, D.B. (1981). Cultural factors in alcohol research and treatment of drinking problems: Introduction. *Journal of Studies on Alcohol, 42* Supplement 9, 1–16.

Herd, D. (1985). Ambiguity in black drinking norms: An ethnohistorical interpretation. In L.A. Bennett and G. M. Ames (Eds.), *The American experience with alcohol: Contrasting cultural perspectives.* New York: Plenum.

Herd, D. (1986). A review of drinking patterns and alcohol problems among U.S. blacks. *Report of the Secretary's Task Force on Black and Minority Health* (pp. 77–132), Vol. 7 of Chemical Dependency and Diabetes. Washington, DC: Department of Health and Human Services.

Hudson, H. L. (1985). How and why Alcoholics Anonymous works for blacks. *Alcoholism Treatment Quarterly, 2*(3–4), 11–29.

Jessor, R., & Jessor, S. L. (1980). Toward a social-psychological perspective on the prevention of alcohol abuse. In T.C. Harford, D.A., Parker, & L. Light (Eds.), *Normative approaches to the prevention of alcohol abuse and alcoholism* (pp. 37–46). Washington, DC: Government Printing Office.

Kelly, J. (1985). Alcohol use and abuse among black youth. *Health Education, 16*(3), 27–29.

Knox, D.H. (1985). Spirituality: A tool in the assessment and treatment of black alcoholics and their families. *Alcoholism Treatment Quarterly, 2*(3–4), 31–43.

Larkins, J.R. (1965). *Alcohol and the Negro: Explosive issues.* Zebulon, NC: Record Publishers.

Lender, M.E., & Martin, J.K. (1982). *Drinking in America: A history.* New York: Free Press.

Lonesome, R. (1985). In-patient rehabilitation for the black alcoholic. *Alcoholism Treatment Quarterly, 2*(3–4), 67–83.

Lum, D. (1986). *Social work practice and people of color: A process-stage approach.* Monterey, CA: Brooks/Cole.

McRoy, R.G., & Shorkey, C.T. (1985). Alcohol use and abuse among blacks. In E.M. Freeman (Ed.), *Social work practice with clients who have alcohol problems* (pp. 202–213). Springfield, IL: Thomas.

Miller, P.M., & Nirenberg, T.D. (1984). *Prevention of alcohol abuse.* New York: Plenum.

Nathan, P.E., & Lipscomb, T.R. (1979). Behavior therapy and behavior modification in the treatment of alcoholism. In J. Mendelsohn & N. Mello (Eds.), *The diagnosis and treatment of alcoholism* (pp. 305–357). New York: McGraw-Hill.

Okpaku, S.O. (1985). State of the art on the multiply addicted: Treatment models for blacks. *Alcoholism Treatment Quarterly, 2*(3–4), 141–154.

Olson, S., & Gerstein, D. R. (1985). *Alcohol in America: Taking action to prevent abuse.* Panel on Alternative Policies Affecting the Prevention of Alcohol Abuse and Alcoholism, National Research Council. Washington, DC: National Academy Press.

Pattison, E.M. (1979). The selection of treatment modalities for the alcoholic patient. In J. Mendelsohn & N. Mello (Eds.), *The diagnosis and treatment of alcoholism* (pp. 125–227). New York: McGraw-Hill.

Primm, B.J., & Wesley, J.E. (1985). Treating the multiply addicted black alcoholic. *Alcoholism Treatment Quarterly, 2*(3–4), 155–178.

Rappaport, M., Labaw, P., & Williams, J. (1975). *The public evaluates the NIAAA public education program* (Vols. 1 and 2). Princeton, NJ: Opinion Research Corp.

Robins, L., Murphy, G.E., & Breckenridge, M. B. (1968). Drinking behavior of young urban Negro males. *Quarterly Journal of Studies on Alcoholism, 29*(3), 657–684.

Rogan, A. (1986). Recovery from alcoholism: Issues for blacks and Native American alcoholics. *Alcohol Health and Research World, 2*(1), 42–44.

Room, R. (1980). Concepts and strategies in the prevention of alcohol-related problems. *Contemporary Drug Problems, 9*, 9–48.

Scott, B., & Miranda, V. (1981). *A guidebook for planning alcohol prevention programs with black youth.* Rockville, MD: National Institute on Alcohol Abuse and Alcoholism.

Smart, R. (1980). Availability and the prevention of alcohol-related problems. In T. C. Harford, D. A. Parker, and L. Light (Eds.), *Normative approaches to the prevention of alcohol abuse and alcoholism* (pp. 123–146). Washington, DC: Government Printing Office.

Spiegler, D.L., Harford, T.C., & Freeman, E.M. (1985). An ecological perspective on alcohol use among adolescents: Implications for prevention. In E.M. Freeman (Ed.), *Social work practice with clients who have alcohol problems* (pp. 7–25). Springfield, IL: Thomas.

Stearns, C. (1872). *The black man of the South and the rebels.* New York: American News Co.

Sterne, M., & Pittman, D. (1972). *Drinking patterns in the ghetto* (Vols. 1 and 2). St. Louis, MO: Washington University, Social Science Institute.

Umunna, I. (1967). The drinking culture of a Nigerian community. *Quarterly Journal of Studies on Alcohol, 28*(1), 529–537.

Wallack, L., & Barrows, D. (1981). *Preventing alcohol problems in California: Evaluation of the Three Year Winners program.* Report prepared for the California Office of Alcoholism.

Watts, T.D., & Wright, R. (1983). *Black alcoholism: Toward a comprehensive understanding.* Springfield, IL: Thomas.

Watts, T.D., & Wright, R. (1986). *Black alcohol abuse and alcoholism: An annotated bibliography.* New York: Praeger.

Weissman, M.M., Meyers, J.K., & Harding, P.S. (1980). Prevalence and psychiatric heterogeneity of alcoholism in a United States urban community. *Journal of Studies on Alcohol, 41*(7), 672–681.

Wharton, V.L. (1947). *The Negro in Mississippi, 1865–1890.* Chapel Hill: University of North Carolina.

Whitener, D.J. (1945). *Prohibition in North Carolina.* Chapel Hill: University of North Carolina.

Williams, M. (1985). Blacks and alcoholism: Issues in the 1980s. In R. Wright & T.D. Watts (Eds.), *Prevention of black alcoholism: Issues and strategies.* Springfield, IL: Thomas.

Wright, R., Jr., & Watts, T.D. (Eds.). (1985). *Prevention of black alcoholism: Issues and strategies.* Springfield, IL: Thomas.

Ziter, M.L.P. (1987). Culturally sensitive treatment of black alcoholic families. *Social Work, 32*(2), 130–135.

Zucker, R.A. (1979). Developmental aspects of drinking through the adult years. In H.T. Blane & M.E. Chafetz (Eds.), *Youth, alcohol, and social policy.* New York: Plenum.

CHAPTER 13

The Older Person
in the Black Family

Marion L. Beaver,
University of Pittsburgh

The black elderly (or "older persons," age 65 and older) are not a homogeneous group and do not have a uniform set of experiences, but they have experienced collective discrimination all their lives. The National Urban League introduced the concept of "double jeopardy" to describe the life situation of elderly blacks (Hill, 1971). This term calls attention to the dual discrimination of ageism and racism experienced by older blacks. Other concepts emphasize even greater handicaps of elderly blacks. Jacquelyne Jackson (1985) added sexism to the jeopardies that confront older black women. She contends that older black women are more vulnerable and more disadvantaged than older black men. And the concept of "multiple hazards" was proposed by Inabel Lindsay (1975) to depict the hazards of income, housing, employment, and health situations of elderly blacks.

This chapter looks at demographic data pertaining to older blacks; addresses the unique survival patterns, problems, issues, and concerns affecting the black elderly; examines the gerontological theories; and discusses strategies for providing social work services to older black clients and their families.

DEMOGRAPHIC EXPERIENCE
OF OLDER BLACKS

The black elderly have substantially lower incomes than their white counterparts (*Aging America*, 1987–88). In 1986 the median income of black males age 65 and older ($6,757) was 56 percent that of white males of similar age ($12,131). Black women also had lower median incomes than their white counterparts.

Limited income is the most serious problem confronting many aging blacks. A significant proportion of blacks worked full-time all their lives for minimal wages and in menial jobs, generally without adequate fringe benefits related to retirement, so when they leave the labor force they frequently subsist at or below the poverty level. Black elderly women living alone had the highest poverty rates. In 1986, over half of all elderly black women (59.8 percent) had incomes below the poverty level.

The black elderly poor have had limited opportunities to escape poverty through the two most common means—a decent job and a good formal education. Approximately 6 percent of the black elderly have had no formal education, compared with only 2 percent found among older whites. Even among black elderly with formal schooling, only 17 percent completed high school, compared with 41 percent among the white elderly. Blacks reside almost exclusively in the oldest inner-city areas, where crime rates are high and neighborhoods are less attractive. About 96 percent of elderly blacks lived in households in the mid-1980s. Only 4.2 percent resided in group arrangements, such as nursing homes or boarding homes. Sharing a home with a grown child is a common arrangement.

Advancing age only compounds the multiple deprivations older black people face. Despite the demographic factors that affect the quality of life experienced by elderly blacks, many have developed valuable coping mechanisms.

HISTORICAL PERSPECTIVE

Black history in the United States has been dominated by the experience of slavery, and then by racism and discrimination (Perlmutter & Hall, 1985). In order to cope with the degradation to which they were subjected as slaves, black people developed systems of support, such as family, friends, benevolent societies, and the church. As it did during slavery, the church continues to play an important role in the lives of black people, particularly older blacks. A strong interdependence among generations also developed. Responsibility for the care of the elderly was worthy of note. To their advantage, intensive patterns of kinship interaction have survived among black people.

Black families headed by elderly couples tend to take relatives and/or nonrelatives—particularly children and younger persons—into their households (Kennedy, 1978). This practice has disadvantages as well as advantages. Multiperson households frequently result in overcrowded conditions, strain and tension between generations, and economic pressures and thwarted goals and aspirations of many family members. But the custom of taking in relatives and/or nonrelatives also strengthens black families. For instance, this practice led to personal involvement by family members in meeting the needs of others, a strengthening of emotional bonds, flexible family boundaries, and a willingness to share a cramped household. Most important, the practice led to an acceptance of and appreciation for the roles of elderly members.

Despite the differential treatment, discrimination, and a lack of personal and societal resources, the majority of black elderly are not lonely and unhappy.

They have developed coping strategies that have enabled them to survive in today's society.

THEORETICAL PERSPECTIVES
AND RESEARCH FINDINGS

Elderly black Americans have found ways to adjust to the most difficult situations that frequently confound many people, perhaps because of their experiences in coping with racism (Jackson, 1985, p. 146). For example, the meaning of widowhood, retirement, and poverty for the black elderly may be different from their meaning for the white elderly. One must therefore take into consideration the different life experiences to which blacks have been subjected all, rather than part of, their lives. However, "most theoretical orientations in gerontology—whether the central concept is 'disengagement,' 'activity,' 'continuity,' or 'development'—ignore or fail to treat sufficiently the historical differences between the majority culture and life in minority communities" (Rey, 1982, p. 192). Measures developed, validated, and standardized for one group (e.g., whites) frequently are inappropriate when applied to other groups (e.g., blacks) (Morgan & Bengston, 1976; Padillo, 1972; Russell, 1970; Colen and McNeely, 1983). Disengagement theory and activity theory are two of the best known theoretical formulations that are relatively useful for understanding the relationship between a society's social system and its older majority race members.

The architects of the *disengagement theory* are Elaine Cumming and William Henry (1961). The essence of the theory is that in preparation for death, as individuals age they begin to withdraw from society by giving up some of their social roles. The major criticism of the theory is that it is too simplistic; many individuals do not disengage and do not appear to suffer from continued engagement (Crandall, 1980).

George L. Maddox has been a major advocate of *activity theory*, which asserts that the more active an aged person is, the better his or her morale will be (Maddox, 1963), that successful aging consists of keeping active, remaining middle-aged (Crandall, 1980), and thereby remaining socially and psychologically fit. Some studies support activity theory (Havighurst, 1968; Rosow, 1967; Tallmer & Kutner, 1969), others do not (Lemon et al., 1972; see also Berghorn et al., 1978, p. 16). Arnold Rose (1965) proposed that the elderly live increasingly within the context of an aged subculture. They interact with each other more as they grow older, and much less with younger persons. Subcultures develop when certain members of a given category interact with one another more than they interact with persons in other categories. Some influences keep older people in contact with larger society and tend to minimize the development of an aged subculture: the mass media, continued employment, contacts with family, and an attitude of active resistance toward aging and toward participation in the aged subculture (Rose, 1965).

A number of personality theories describe and explain the psychological aspects of aging, but we will not discuss these here. Textbooks and articles on the life-cycle developmental process are also available (see, e.g., Bloom, 1980; Goldberg & Deutsch, 1977). Current theories are generally inadequate to explain the aging process among blacks: they ignore the significant cultural variables which are based on homogeneity among, within, and between groups, and they view the later life stage in isolation from the entire life continuum of a black person.

THE ROLE OF THE SOCIAL WORKER

Basic information about older black clients is essential for an understanding of the psychosocial consequences of aging and the social worker who is providing services to elderly blacks, but little is known about the processes of aging among blacks (Carter, 1972). Most data centers on vital statistics, social and economic conditions, and the effects of racism, not on the cultural life of this group, but more data on the cultural life of older blacks are becoming available. Black life and black experience encompass the rich history, heritage, culture, value orientations, hopes, and aspirations of its people. It is a philosophical stance, survival posture, and an organizing principle around which black life is understood and further developed. But while older blacks have as a group experienced a lifetime of social, psychological, and economic disadvantages in the form of inadequate housing, poor medical care, job discrimination, improper nutrition, and alienation in a hostile and exclusionary society, each person in the group has experienced these limitations in his or her own individual way.

Thus, the social worker must become proficient at individualizing all clients, regardless of racial or ethnic affiliation. Clients must be known by their own identifying bio-psycho-social characteristics, their role and status in their immediate society, their interaction with people around them, their modes of adaptation and of coping, their strengths and weaknesses, and their own uniqueness as a black person from all other black persons.

Factors essential for healthful growth and self-realization are the feelings of security that result largely from a sense of acceptance and belonging. In their communities, older blacks are generally accorded respect, dignity, and recognition, but outside the familiar environments and in interactions with whites, their behavior may be marked by caution. Many others have for years repressed the feelings of anger they have felt, but could not express, at having to endure the injustices discrimination. Often these same people present a seemingly happy facade to the outside world regardless of the seriousness of their situations. Nonetheless, these are learned responses that elderly blacks have acquired to enable them to deal with a racially hostile environment. Social workers, particularly white social workers, must realize that they may be regarded with suspicion by older black clients and must exercise restraint and give older black clients time to feel comfortable and less guarded in their presence. One setting in which older black clients feel more comfortable and secure is in their own homes, so the importance of working with older blacks in their own homes cannot be understated.

Older black clients have been coping and dealing with problematic situations all their lives, so when they are seen by a social worker they are at a stage in their lives where they are particularly vulnerable (advancing age compounds health and other problems), where inner and outer reserves are overtaxed, and where social interventions are needed to enhance their psychosocial functioning. Workers must see these clients as human beings with a range of feelings, attitudes, and coping abilities. In meeting the needs of the black elderly, it is also important to understand their underlying value system, the core of existence of all blacks that determines for them what is of considerable worth. Needs are gauged through values and are therefore accurate indicators of those values.

Social workers must be committed to the dignity and worth of every individual regardless of age, race, sex, or handicap. They must treat clients with respect. An obvious way to show respect is to address clients by the title of Mr., Mrs., or Miss and their last name (unless they insist on being addressed by their first name). Some older black men have frequently been called "boy" all their lives. It is difficult to assess the impact that this insult has had on the black man's pride, dignity, and self-worth.

INTERVENTION STRATEGIES
WITH OLDER BLACKS

If older blacks are to improve the quality of their lives, then social work intervention must initiate, arrange, or develop viable pathways to rectify some of the injustices black people have encountered during the course of their lives. The intent of practice in social work is to enable individuals to carry out their life tasks as defined by considerations of their age, the socioeconomic condition of their life, cultural, ethnic, and racial affiliations, and their particular problems or maladaptations (Meyer, 1976). It is to "seek out, develop, manage, and change environmental factors to create the optimum conditions for the individual to develop his capacities and interests" (Germain, 1973, p. 324).

Traditionally, the format for direct practice has been that of the client (individual, family, or group) engaged in face-to-face interpersonal contact with social workers. This face-to-face engagement is an important characteristic of most models of social work treatment. In this format many relational ingredients (i. e., transference, counter-transference, expression of feelings) can be played out during the professional encounter. In addition, most treatment models place prime importance on the "here and now" of the client's life and its immediate antecedents, on its current implications and effects on clients using their reasoning capacity to learn new patterns of behavior, and on involving clients in the total treatment process.

During the initial phase of treatment, the client should be perceived as an active, full participant, and the intent is to make himself or herself understood and to find out from the worker what the helping process is all about. Both tangibles and intangibles exhibit themselves during the initial phase. For example, the worker may provide some concrete services or make a referral, might engage the client in an ongoing therapeutic relationship, or might offer some general information about agency policy. Social work attitudes, the spirit in which the service is offered, a healthy respect for and understanding of racial and ethnic pluralism, and a commitment to basic social work values are all important during this phase.

Social workers must be aware that many older black clients whose priority is subsistence seek treatment as a last resort, often with only a vague sense of what "therapy" is all about. Many may be unaware that they can obtain relief by talking about their problems with social workers. In addition, many clients may seek symptom reduction as soon as possible; therefore as soon as they feel better and confidence returns, they may stop coming for treatment. Halpern (1973) asserts, "Telling the client that stopping his visits so soon will probably cause an early recurrence of the disturbance makes no impression on him. He feels better, so why keep going to a doctor?" (p. 135). Social workers must recognize that their contact with many black clients will be short-lived and that they may have only a short time to accomplish anything.

SOME EFFECTIVE HELPING STRATEGIES

The structure and cultural patterns of older black clients—their social class, value system, and style of life—often differ markedly from the social worker's. Further, older black clients bring to the therapeutic relationship a history of humiliating and abrasive contacts with whites, and it is reasonable to assume that this past is not shrugged off at the agency's door. Effective helping strategies must be employed by the social worker.

Listening

Effective listening in advancing toward better understanding is built on the cooperation of both the speaker and the listener (Schulman, 1974). The worker must be actively engaged in receiving, recording, and understanding the client's message. Good listening requires following carefully both what is said overtly and the latent undertones. It requires being expectantly attentive and receptive. Listening is a selective process in that we pick out from the many stimuli surrounding us those most fitted to our needs and purposes (Keltner, 1973). The task of the worker, then, is to observe and to record in his or her memory thousands of little signs and to remain aware of their delicate effects (Reik, 1971).

Schulman (1974) stresses that "competent listening presupposes a receptive state in which the client's glances, muscular twitches, gestures, and other bodily reactions as well as his tone of voice, his pauses, and his words are noted" (p. 121). In this state the worker is tuned in to what the client is saying and not anticipating what a client is going to say and therefore missing what is actually said.

Not being totally attentive to a client can have a negative effect on the client. "The empathic listener develops large eyes, big ears, a small mouth, and positive actions that reveal his interest and acceptance of the client" (Schulman, 1974, p. 121). Listening is the bridge between hearing and understanding. The worker's choice of words can tell the black elderly client that the worker is listening to and respectful of what the client is saying.

Assessment

After the client has related his or her concerns and responded to questions, he or she wants to be given feedback on how the worker perceives these problems, what the goals of treatment will be, what steps may be involved in the treatment process, and what the potential risks and gains are. At this point, the worker must think through the facts the client has presented in order to offer the client a professional opinion.

Other information useful for assessment may come from significant others who are part of the client's social network, both those with whom he or she has personal relationships, such as family and friends, and those within the more extended systems (Brill, 1973), such as social clubs, church, employment, and volunteer programs. The social worker must first ascertain what people are considered "family" and who lives in the home. Answers to the question "Whom do you depend on or go to for help when needed?" should disclose the significant persons in the support system. The client has a right to know what information is needed and to help decide which person(s) might be contacted. For instance, medical information is always essential in the case of the elderly, and contacts with other agencies, such as Social Security and multipurpose senior centers, may also be necessary.

Assessment and treatment too often hinge on white middle-class norms and values. Social workers must apply the assessment process to the situation and ethnic experience of older black people. For instance, assessment must consider black culture, the life-style of black people, the stage of development, previous adaptation, and the present situation. An assessment of the older person's social environment provides information about losses of intimate persons, income, independence, and social roles; the attitudes, feelings, and behaviors associated with those losses; and an understanding of how the individual has adjusted to the changes. In addition, the worker needs to gather information from the client and the family about family structure, housing, work or retirement, friendship patterns, income, social roles, and leisure activities and interests, to obtain valuable insights into how social factors contribute to the client's problems and how those factors can aid and support treatment (Butler & Lewis, 1982, p. 236).

Problem Finding

Out of the assessment process should come a definition of the problem about which the client is most concerned, the difficulty with which the client wants immediate help. It is the problem as the client perceives it, feels it, and experiences it that must first be worked on. Sometimes what the client sees as the problem and what the worker sees as the problem is different, though. For instance:

> Miss Sims, age 60, had been taking care of her mother, age 86, prior to the latter's hospitalization for chronic heart trouble. The mother is about to be released from the hospital and returned to the daughter's second-story apartment. Since her mother's hospitalization, Miss Sims has found employment as a secretary for a law firm. She likes her job a great deal and is torn between keeping it and giving it up to take care of her ailing mother. The worker believes the immediate need is to find a home health aide to come into the home while Miss Sims works. Miss Sims has become increasingly concerned about the effect her absence from the home during the day will have on her mother's recuperation.

Miss Sims must be given the kind of feedback that accurately sets priorities and goals as she sees them. Her immediate concern about leaving her mother in the care of someone else must be dealt with first if any progress is to be made in this case.

Goal Setting

Goal setting should be a mutual process with clients who are able to engage in the treatment process. The worker must discuss and share with the client his or her assessment and the proposed goals. The client must express his or her agreement with the goals or suggest how they might be modified. "The process of mutual goal setting with the black family" requires the worker "to assume an 'ecostructural' approach that considers a family's environment and community" (Ho, 1987, p. 201). The ecostructural reality frequently includes welfare, courts, schools, Medicaid, food stamps, and a variety of other supportive services. While an in-home health aide is clearly needed in the Sims' case, the worker may first have to deal with Miss Sims' feelings about leaving her mother in the care of someone else and with the cultural patterns among black families before dealing with any other realities in managing this issue. However, the worker may need to be actively involved in helping Miss Sims find an acceptable person to care for her mother—that is, the worker must take into consideration the Sims family in relation to the ecological environment. Some determination will need to be made about the kinds of significant resources that are available or unavailable to them to meet their ongoing needs.

Intervening in the Environment

Environmental conditions or systems most likely to impinge on older black families include the health care system (Medicare, Medicaid, etc.), Social Security, food stamps, transportation, and the legal system. Because these systems are integral components of the daily functioning of many older black families, social workers must be knowledgeable about social service systems and other help-providing agencies. They must also be willing to work collaboratively with a variety of service providers.

Public institutions have assumed responsibility for providing certain goods and services that neither older individuals nor their families are able to provide. An important part of commanding one's own life and destiny is the opportunity to be connected with those goods and services. Therefore, social work treatment models need to give more attention to the concept of resources and linkage systems as a basic aim of social work practice. Resources and linkage systems can connect people with goods and services and help them deal effectively with the complex arrangement of urban structures.

Social workers should link the older black client to resources that have maximum utility. For example, why give people better housing if their physical environment is too threatening for them to venture beyond their door? Other issues to be considered are: Is the population at risk actually getting the services? Are the services needed accessible? What linkage systems will most effectively connect the client with the resources? How can people be helped to develop and utilize their own internal resources? How can professionals make their encounter with older black clients more useful? Elderly black clients have been coping and dealing with crises all their lives, but they are now at a stage in life where their inner and outer reserves are depleted. Many have been denied equal access to goods and services. Social workers must initiate, arrange, or develop viable pathways to rectify this injustice.

THE OLDER BLACK PERSON AS CLIENT

The typical elderly black client has probably lived through numerous racially tinged events, has had to cope with severe gaps in environmental resources, has spent a lifetime giving services for family members and to white employers, and now needs services himself or herself. Engaged in this typical helping encounter is a young, white, well-educated, middle-class social worker functioning within the rules of the established system. She is perceived by the older black client to be in a position of power to grant or not to grant his or her needs.

The power and authority of the majority culture has deterred black people, particularly older blacks, from expressing how they feel and what they want. Reluctant to express their feelings and wants, they cope with their stressful situations by presenting a seemingly happy facade to the outside world. As a result, the very service that is needed may not be delivered or received, and the client may retreat once again to a stressful and/or hazardous situation. Consider the following example:

Mr. Andrews, a 71-year-old black man, was referred to the Public Welfare Department by a friend. He was accompanied by his 46-year-old daughter. Three weeks before coming to the agency, his wife of fifty years was hospitalized for diabetes mellitus. Mrs. Andrews, age 70, had diabetes most of her life, and her condition had become progressively worse with age. When hospitalized, she was forty pounds overweight. Prior to her hospitalization, she was advised by her doctor to go on a diet, but sticking to a strict regimen was difficult for her. About a week before Mrs. Andrews was hospitalized, she complained of such symptoms as numbness in her fingers, blurred vision, cramps in both legs, and dry mouth. Mr. Andrews immediately called the doctor, who wanted her brought to the hospital right away. Since his wife's hospitalization, Mr. Andrews managed to visit her at least two hours each day, which was difficult for him because he came directly from his part-time job as a janitor in a downtown store.

When he was informed that his wife would be released in about a week he was also advised that his wife's treatment regimen must include a proper diet, exercise, and insulin and that she would need the services of a visiting nurse, a physical therapist, and a homemaker. He was reluctant to accept homemaker services, be-cause he felt that he and his family could work something out, but the daughters have not been able to provide such care as preparation of meals and light house-keeping for their mother on a sustained basis except on weekends. Mr. Andrews does what he can for his wife, but the pressures of caring for her are becoming increasingly problematic. Mrs. Andrews is aware of how stressful caring for her has become for her husband and has encouraged him to apply for homemaker services. The family members agree that homemaker services would provide relief.

Mr. and Mrs. Andrews are currently receiving Supplemental Security Income (SSI) and Medicaid, and now Mr. Andrews has reluctantly agreed to apply for homemaker services even though he felt embarrassed and uncomfortable about it. After an hour, he was finally seen by an intake worker.

The worker, a white, middle-aged female, greeted Mr. Andrews in a brusque and formal manner. The tone of her voice was hostile and her facial expression was stern. In addition, she had a tendency to fidget anxiously with her watch through-out the interview.

She asked Mr. Andrews one question after another, and he felt almost as if he were on trial. He left the interview feeling dejected, angry, and hurt.

The complex factors—race, age, attitudes of the older black client toward the white worker, and attitudes of the white establishment toward the older black client—that converged during this brief encounter may never be known, but if treatment is to be successful, these factors must of necessity be dealt with.

Several cultural themes are the basis of survival for black families: strong kinship bonds among a variety of households; a high level of flexibility in family roles; strong work, education, and achievement orientation; and strong commitment to religious values and church participation (Hill, 1971). In addi-tion, the humanistic orientation and endurance of suffering must be recognized. In spite of the struggle for survival in a hostile society, "black family members have not lost sight of the value and the importance of concern for each other" (Ho, 1987, p. 182). The black humanistic orientation stresses person-to-person relationships and enables family members to band together in the best interests of a family member who has a problem. For example, Mr. Andrews had been actively involved in caring for his wife for some time, balancing his job and visiting his hospitalized wife. Only at the insistence of his daughter did Mr. Andrews agree to apply for homemaker services. In addition, it was unfortunate that Mr. Andrews had such a lengthy wait to see a social worker, but the fact that the worker did not acknowledge the lengthy wait and greeted Mr. Andrews in a harsh and disrespectful manner wiped out the humanistic elements that are so important in any treatment encounter.

Social workers can best obtain needed information by encouraging clients to talk freely, in their own words—not necessarily by asking a series of pointed questions. This is particularly important when there is a power differential between the worker and a client, including the elderly, blacks, and the poor. Unfortunately, the worker in the Andrews case put Mr. Andrews through a trying and humiliating process as if he were under investigation.

In the actual initial contact between the worker and Mr. Andrews, however, the worker showed little concern for Mr. Andrews' needs. She did not respond to him in a way that would indicate an interest, readiness, and willingness to help him. Workers demonstrate their interest in helping clients by focusing on their clients' problems, concerns, feelings, and reactions. This means that the worker should have listened carefully to Mr. Andrews' concerns and guided the interview along channels that seemed most appropriate to the situation. Because none of these things was done, it is difficult to assess the damage.

Mr. Andrews should have been encouraged to state in his own words why he had come to the agency. The following exchange illustrates what a more positive response to Mr. Andrews might have been:

> WORKER: Mr. Andrews, I am Robin Cummings. Your case has been as-
> signed to me for follow-up. I apologize for the long wait you had
> this morning. This has been a busier morning than usual.
> MR. ANDREWS: That's okay. We did expect that some waiting would be involved.
> WORKER: Could we begin by you telling me how I might be of some
> assistance to you and your family?

In another case situation, a medical social worker has an effective first interview with a 71-year-old black woman who is reluctant to schedule a needed operation because of concern about the care of her bedridden 75-year-old husband during the period of hospitalization:

> The social worker greeted the client warmly and introduced herself as Mrs. Parker. The client gave her name as Mrs. Butler. Mrs. Butler was offered a seat. Mrs. Butler haltingly told the worker that she was glad to have someone else besides her family and friends to talk to because she still didn't know what to do or where to start. The worker acknowledged that with so many things on her mind and with so many pulls in different directions, it isn't easy to know what's best to do.
>   Mrs. Butler breathed a sigh of relief as she wiped her brow. She mentioned that the weather outside was quite warm and that the heat makes it difficult for her to get around. The worker agreed that it was a hot day, and added that with so many things to think about, it makes it seem even hotter. "Oh, my, yes," Mrs. Butler stated, and told the worker that for a young person she seemed much smarter than her years. After a brief pause, Mrs. Butler asked the worker how old she was. The worker gave a direct answer of 33 years and waited for Mrs. Butler's response. "And where are you from?" "Chicago," answered the worker. "Is that where you went to school?" "No, I went to a school of social work in Pennsylvania." "How long have you been working?" "For about five years. But it seems you are very curious about my background. Why do you think that is?" "Oh, I don't know. I

guess I want to make sure I've come to the right place and to make sure I'm in good hands." The worker told Mrs. Butler she could understand how she felt and that it is important to see someone you have confidence in.

At that point the client opened up and started talking about her real concern. Mrs. Butler stated tearfully, "I know I'm supposed to have this operation, but I don't know what to do about my husband who is bedridden and has to be waited on hand and foot. My kids can't help because they're working and have families of their own—I mean, they come over whenever they can, and my friends come in and do for my husband some of the time, but most of the time I have to do everything."

The interview continued along positive lines, with the worker listening and expressing genuine concern and interest in Mrs. Butler's difficult situation. As Mrs. Butler continued to open up at her own pace, the worker was able to obtain other pertinent information. As a result, the worker was able to arrange for services such as a homemaker, meals-on-wheels, and senior companions. A follow-up home visit with the entire Butler family revealed that the Butlers' three adult children were willing to visit their father during evening hours, each taking turns for a week at a time. A neighbor arranged to stay each night with Mr. Butler during the week until his wife returned from the hospital, and a grandson agreed to come over on weekends. Needless to say, Mrs. Butler expressed relief over the plan. It involved much of her natural support system, as well as other services provided by agencies in the community. She was now free to concentrate on her own upcoming operation.

This example illustrates that a relationship with reciprocal respect allows for a more equal interchange between a worker and an elderly black client. There is a lot to be said about the importance of humanizing a relationship. One approach to humanizing the relationship with clients is to allow time for, in this case, older blacks to become acquainted with the worker. People who have been subjected to a lifetime of discrimination and oppression are reluctant to open up quickly and reveal personal details of their lives to anyone. Apparently, the experience of this worker sharing information about herself inspired the client's trust. Once a trusting relationship was established, Mrs. Butler was able to open up and talk about the things that concerned her.

Workers too can learn something from clients—and from their families. They can learn something about clients' past history, especially as it relates to racism and discrimination. They can better identify long-held feelings of rage, inadequacy, insecurity, and helplessness associated with these practices. They can develop a better understanding and appreciation of coping strategies that have enabled black people, especially the elderly, to survive in spite of racial injustices. They can also learn about the importance of the family to older blacks.

OLDER BLACK CITIZENS AND HELP-SEEKING

Most older people want to be independent; they must be closely involved in any decision-making about themselves (Butler & Lewis, 1982). The more older black clients are able to make decisions about their own lives, the better, and the less responsibility social workers will need to assume. This emphasis on decision-making among the black elderly can be operationalized through a number of important skills.

Many black families, especially the older members, are reluctant to seek help outside the family, relying heavily on extended family ties and church organizations during times of crisis. This practice of help-seeking is typical among all black families regardless of socioeconomic class (McAdoo, 1977). "Reliance on natural support systems produces fewer feelings of defeat, humiliation, and powerlessness" (Ho, 1987, p. 38).

Black families come for formal agency help as a last resort (Sue et al., 1974, p. 797). The underutilization of psychological help and family treatment by blacks is believed to be related to their general mistrust of social workers, especially nonblack social workers. In the example involving Mr. Andrews, it would be understandable if Mr. Andrews decided not to return to the agency. Some authors have noted that blacks drop out of treatment earlier and more frequently than whites because of earlier and negative experiences with helping professionals (Sue et al., 1974).

Many blacks prefer black social workers over nonblack social workers, but they also want a social worker who is competent, regardless of race (Sattler, 1977). Competent skills and techniques in work with older blacks must take into consideration the complexities of life, particularly family and community life, from a black perspective (Ho, 1987).

CONCLUSIONS

Older blacks vary considerably in their social situations and cultural characteristics, but most black elderly share a common vulnerability in their old age. "They are vulnerable because they are poor and because they have minority group status in a predominantly white culture." (Harbert & Ginsberg, 1979, p. 58). The relative deprivation of older blacks is a continuation of earlier patterns of discrimination in employment, housing, and education (Hess & Markson, 1980).

Existing social and psychological theories for older blacks do not shed enough light on the complexities of life among older blacks. Social workers need information about the processes of aging among blacks, the options that are available to them to improve the quality of life, the strengths of intergenerational ties and the sources of intergenerational strains, and the economic and social pressures that continue to shape the lives of older black people and their families.

Effective social work treatment with older black clients and their families requires that the social worker be sensitive, respectful, and understanding. Practice principles from various treatment modalities (individual and family) should be made culturally and ethnically specific, and social workers must demonstrate a genuine sensitivity to minority concerns in the assessment process.

Elderly people are still able to grow and to develop. By the time they reach old age, many people experience a number of successive losses for which treatment can be useful. However, many older black people are reluctant to seek help. When they do, social workers must express genuine interest, respect, and a willingness to help. In addition, they may have to make special efforts to reach the elderly to inform them of services that are available as well as to explain why they are entitled to such services. Finally, if the social worker is to help older blacks attain their maximum potential, they must first develop the personal qualities that are essential in helping all people to utilize their own strengths and resources.

REFERENCES

Aging America: Trends and projections, 1987–88 edition. Washington, DC: Department of Health.

Ary, D., Jacobs, L.C., & Razavieh, A. (1979). *Introduction to research in education* (3rd ed.). New York: Holt, Rinehart and Winston.

Beaver, M.L. (1983). *Human service practice with the elderly*. Englewood Cliffs, NJ: Prentice-Hall.

Berghorn, F.J., Schafer, D.E., Steere, G.H., & Wiseman, R. F. (1978). *The urban elderly: A study of life satisfaction*. Montclair, NJ: Allanheld, Osmun.

Bloom, M. (1980). *Life span development: Bases for preventive and interventive helping*. New York: Macmillan.

Brill, N. (1973). *Working with people: The helping process*. Philadelphia, PA: Lippincott.

Butler, R.N., & Lewis, M.I. (1982). *Aging and mental health* (3rd ed.). St. Louis, MO: Mosby.

Carter, J.H. (1972). Psychiatry, racism, and aging. *Journal of the American Geriatrics Society, 20*, 343–346.

Colen, J.N., & McNeely, R.L. (1983). Minority aging and knowledge in the social professions: Overview of a problem. In R.L. McNeely & J.N. Colen (Eds.), *Aging in minority groups* (pp. 15–23). Beverly Hills, CA: Sage.

Crandall, R. C. (1980). *Gerontology: A behavioral science approach*. Reading, MA: Addison-Wesley.

Cumming, E., & Henry, W. (1961). *Growing old: The process of disengagement*. New York: Basic Books.

Cummings, J. (1983, November 20). Breakup of black family imperils gains of decades. *New York Times*, A56.

Germain, C.B. (1973, June). An ecological perspective in casework practice. *Social Casework, 54*, 323–330.

Goldberg, S.R., & Deutsch, F. (1977). *Life-span: Individual and family development*. Monterey, CA: Brooks/Cole.

Hagestad, G. O. (1981). Problems and promises in the social psychology of intergenerational relations. In R.W. Fogel et al. (Eds.), *Aging: Stability and change in family life* (pp. 11–46). New York: Academic Press.

Halpern, E. F. (1973). *Survival: Black/white*. New York: Pergamon.

Harbert, A.S., & Ginsberg, L.H. (1979). *Human services for older adults: Concepts and skills*. Belmont, CA: Wadsworth.

Havighurst, R.J. (1968). Personality and patterns of aging. *Gerontologist, 8,* 20–23.

Hess, B.B., & Markson, E.W. (1980). *Aging and old age.* New York: Macmillan.

Hill, R.B. (1971). A profile of black aged. In J.J. Jackson (Ed.), *Proceedings of research conference on minority group aged in the south* (pp. 2–9). Durham, NC: Duke University Press.

Ho, M.K. (1987). *Family therapy with ethnic minorities.* Beverly Hills, CA: Sage.

Jackson, J.J. (1970). Aged Negroes: Their cultural departures from statistical stereotypes and rural-urban differences. *Gerontologist, 10,* 141.

Jackson, J.J. (1985). Aged black Americans: Double jeopardy re-examined. *Journal of Minority Aging, 10*(1), 25–61.

Kamerman, S. B., Dolgoff, R., Getzel, G., & Nelson, J. (1973). Knowledge for practice: Social science in social work. In A.J. Kahn (Ed.), *Shaping the new social work* (pp. 97–146). New York: Columbia University Press.

Keltner, J.W. (1973). *Elements of interpersonal communication.* Belmont, CA: Wadsworth.

Kennedy, C. E. (1978). *Human development: The adult years and aging.* New York: Macmillan.

Lemon, B.W., Bengston, V.L., & Peterson, J.A. (1972). An exploration of the activity of aging: Activity types and satisfaction among inmovers to a retirement community. *Journal of Gerontology, 27,* 511–523.

Lindsay, I.B. (1975). Coping capacities of the black aged. In *No longer young, the older woman in America* (pp. 89–94). Occasional Papers in Gerontology 11. Ann Arbor: Institute of Gerontology, University of Michigan, Wayne State University.

Maddox, G.L. (1963). Activity and morale: A longitudinal study of selected elderly subjects. *Social Forces, 42,* 195–204.

McAdoo, H. (1977). Family therapy in the black community. *Journal of the American Orthopsychiatric Association, 47,* 74–79.

Meyer, C.H. (1976). *Social work practice: The changing landscape* (2nd ed.). New York: Free Press.

Morgan, L. & Bengston, U. L. (1976). *Measuring perceptions of aging across social strata.* Paper presented at the Twenty-Ninth Annual Meeting of the Gerontological Society, New York, New York.

Padillo, A. (1972). Psychological research and the Mexican American. In M. Mangold (Ed.), *La causa chicana: The movement for justice* (pp. 65–77). New York: Family Service Association of America.

Perlmutter, M., & Hall, E. (1985). *Adult development and aging.* New York: Wiley.

Polansky, N.A. (1975). Theory construction and the scientific method. In N.A. Polansky (Ed.), *Social work research* (pp. 1–17). Chicago: University of Chicago Press.

Reik, T. (1971). *Listening with the third ear* (5th ed.). New York: Pyramid.

Rey, A. B. (1982). Activity and disengagement: Theoretical orientations in social gerontology and minority aging. In R.C. Manuel (Ed.), *Minority aging: Sociological and social psychological issues* (pp. 191–194). Westport, CT: Greenwood.

Rose, A.M. (1965). The subculture of the aging: A framework for research in social gerontology. In A.M. Rose & W. Peterson (Eds.), *Older people and their social worlds* (pp. 191–194). Philadelphia, PA: Davis.

Rosow, I. (1967). *Social integration of the aged.* New York: Free Press.

Russell, R.D. (1970). Black perceptions of guidance. *Personnel and Guidance Journal, 48,* 721–728.

Sattler, J. (1977). The effects of therapist-client racial similarity. In A. Gurman (Ed.), *Effective psychotherapy* (pp. 252–290). New York: Pergamon.

Schulman, E.D. (1974). *Intervention in human services.* St. Louis, MO: Mosby.

Sue, S., McKinney, H., Allen, D., & Hall, J. (1974). Delivery of community mental health services to black and white clients. *Journal of Consulting and Clinical Psychology, 42,* 794–801.

Tallmer, M., & Kutner, B. (1969). Disengagement and the stresses of aging. *Journal of Gerontology, 24,* 70–75.

U.S. Bureau of the Census. (1982). Current population reports, Series P-60, No. 745, *Money income of households, families, and persons in the United States.* Washington, DC: Government Printing Office.

U.S. Bureau of the Census. (1983). Current population reports, Series P-60, No. 745, *Money income and poverty status of families and persons in the United States.* Washington, DC: Government Printing Office.

Wirth, L. (1945). The problem of minority groups. In R. Linton (Ed.), *The science of man in the world crisis.* New York: Columbia University Press.

Younghusband, E. L. (1979). Foreword. In F.J. Turner (Ed.), *Social work treatment: Interlocking theoretical approaches* (pp. xiii–xiv). New York: Free Press.

CHAPTER 14

Blacks and the Health Care Delivery System:
Challenges and Prospects

Bernice Catherine O. Harper
Department of Health and Human Services, Washington, D.C.

Modern medicine is increasingly emphasizing the significance of social and emotional factors in relation to the etiology, treatment, and prevention of disease. An important element in medicine is the social component, which includes an understanding of the motivation of human behavior and the effect of environmental influences on the individual. However, biological and physiological changes also produce acute and chronic illnesses. The health status and quality of life enjoyed or not enjoyed by blacks has an impact on such disease states. For example, a physical disorder, such as high blood pressure or AIDS, is the sum of many conditions and the result of what is frequently a long chain of processes. There is rarely a single etiological factor, but rather a constellation of factors that affect the process and responses to a disease.

This chapter focuses on the black family and its relationship to modern health institutions, barriers encountered in negotiating the health care system, and strategies the social worker can use to respond to such health care needs in black families.

HISTORICAL PERSPECTIVE ON BLACKS AND THE HEALTH CARE SYSTEM

The historical perspective on blacks and health care is unalterably linked to the home, the black doctor, and the black family and rooted in slavery and the progress of health care experienced specifically by blacks. A segregated society fostered segregated health care facilities, so blacks have relied upon self-diagnosis and self-treatment at home. The current relationship between blacks and the health care delivery system has not improved much since the 1960s and early 1970s, when discrimination was blatant and overt in southern hospitals and more covert in the north (Sheham, 1973). The United States has a dual system of health care. One system is geared toward the upper and middle income groups, the other system toward the poor and minority groups. For the most part, the nation's health care facilities currently attempt to reflect the nation's progress in responding to the care and needs of all patients. The federal government's role as a purchaser of health care has greatly improved the conditions for blacks in health care. Yet much work remains to be done. And blacks must not lose sight of their own capacity and skills, as significant others, to care for ill family members. The strengths of such traditional natural helping should be retained, with the addition of the new service components created by Medicare, Medicaid, and the Catastrophic Health Insurance Coverage Act of 1988.

The following is a profile of the historical relationship between blacks and the health care delivery system:

- Blacks have always cared for the sick at home, yet it was never labeled "home care."
- Blacks have been dying at home and receiving care in the process, yet it was never called "hospice care."
- Blacks have relieved each other from the caring and curing processes, yet it was never seen as "respite care."
- Blacks have cared for each other in their homes, in their neighborhoods, and throughout their communities, yet it was never referred to as "volunteerism."

The helping and medical professions may collaborate with black families and the community to continue utilizing their traditional helping skills and talents and to gain new knowledge, and thereby add new ingredients and new dimensions to improved health care, to continuity of care, and to the quality and quantity of life.

THE COST OF HEALTH CARE

Chronic and acute illness relative to blacks must be considered in terms of the total health care delivery system and national health care costs. In 1986, the nation spent $458 billion on health care (Health Care Financing Administration [HCFA], 1987; Harper, 1987), a per capita expenditure of $1,837 and an increase of $127 over the 1985 figure. Hospital care continues to account for the largest share of health dollars. In 1986, hospital revenues amounted to 39 percent ($180 billion) of total health care spending. Physician services cost $92 billion and nursing home care cost $38 billion. The $63 billion spent for dental care, eyeglasses, and home health and other professional and medical services comprised about one-third of the category called "other professional services." Some $31 billion was spent for drugs and drug sundries.

Health Care Coverage

In 1986, blacks under the age of 65 were 1.6 times more likely than their white counterparts to lack health care coverage. Persons under 65 from families with less than $10,000 income a year were 5.7 times more likely than their counterparts from families in the $20,000–$35,000 income bracket to have no health insurance or coverage. During 1982, most Americans under 65 had some form of health care coverage, but 21.2 percent of blacks had no health coverage at all. Only 13.5 percent of whites lacked coverage (U.S. Department of Health and Human Services [DHHS], 1985).

Medicare

Enrollment in Medicare has risen steadily. In 1966 only 87 percent of nonwhite and 94 percent of white Medicare enrollees were covered by both hospital and supplemental medical insurance, but in 1980 some 98 percent of all enrollees were protected by both forms of coverage. Among the disabled Medicare enrollees, whites were more likely than nonwhites to be served (per 1,000 enrollees) under hospital insurance, supplemental medical insurance, or both. Disabled nonwhites were more likely to receive higher reimbursement, both per person and per enrollee, than the disabled whites in 1980.

In Toby's (1985) view, Medicare is substantially responsible for the decreasing disparity by race in the use of health services because if providers of Medicare discriminate against black Medicare enrollees they are not eligible for any Medicare reimbursement. Although premiums and co-payments might appear to be a disproportionately greater hardship for blacks than for whites, most states pay these for poor enrollees who are also Medicaid eligible. The quality of care Medicare enrollees received over the last twenty years has also improved significantly. The black elderly have also benefited tremendously from the rapid expansion of sophisticated medical technology. For instance, major progress has been achieved in life expectancy for the black elderly; more than two years have been added to their life span. Now the black elderly are facing more chronic conditions. But Medicare was simply never intended to deal with "custodial nursing home care." In fact, Section 1862 of the Social Security Act prohibits payments for "custodial care" (Toby, 1985).

Medicaid

Originally intended to provide medical services to low-income families, Medicaid has evolved over time into the largest third-party financer of long-term care in the United States. Total Medicaid benefits (including both federal and state shares) came to $44 billion in 1986, of which $16 billion was for nursing home care. In fiscal year 1985, some 21.8 million people received Medicaid benefits. Of that number, 2.5 percent received skilled nursing facility care and 3.8 percent received intermediate care facility services. This program is shifting its focus gradually from its reliance on institutional care to home and community-

based alternatives, and from the traditional fee-for-service system to more innovative payment schemes. The program is also beginning to expand to encompass
new groups of needy citizens. Congress approved a provision in the 1986
Consolidated Omnibus Budget Reconciliation Act that gives states latitude to
cover pregnant women and their children under age 5 with incomes up to 100
percent of the federal poverty line (Demkovich, 1987). Many states have already implemented this provision, and others are in the process of doing so.

Direct Patient Payments

In 1986, some $116 billion was spent for health care not covered by a third
party. For the most part, this money came from patients or their families
directly. The largest amounts of direct payments were for physician services,
drugs, and drug sundries, only then followed by spending for nursing home
care. It is not clear whether there are differences between black and white
families in the amount of direct payments made, but logically black families,
with a larger percentage living below poverty guidelines, would have a more
difficult time making such payments.

Demographic Change

Growth and changes in the population are other factors accounting for growth in
the level of health care spending. The largest impacts are expected to occur in
the next century, because health care use rises rapidly after about age 65 and the
aged population is expected to continue growing rapidly until the mid-1990s,
when a temporary slowing will set in as the small birth cohort of the 1930s
depression turn 65. By the year 2010, the postwar baby boom will reach
retirement age and the rapid growth of the aged population will resume until the
peak-year birth cohort (about 1970) reaches age 65 in 2035 (HCFA, 1987).

    The past, present, current, and projected costs of health care have tremen-
dous implications relative to black families. Good health is an important factor
in blacks being able to participate as productive members within their own
community as well as in the larger society.

UTILIZATION OF SERVICES

To what extent do health care costs affect utilization of services by black
families? Blacks have more difficulty entering the medical care system than
whites, and they express greater dissatisfaction with services. This may account
in part for why black Americans make fewer office visits to physicians than
whites do. Lack of access to care is especially relevant for those with chronic
cardiovascular diseases (Aday & Andersen, 1984) and may contribute to fewer
early diagnoses of coronary disease in blacks. On the average, blacks spent 8.2
days in the hospital in 1983, while whites spent 6.5 days per episode in the
same year. Blacks were less likely than whites to have had one or more

physician or dentist visits within the preceding twenty-four months but were more likely to have had one or more hospital episodes (James et al., 1984).

Patients from upper-income families and white patients were more likely than patients from lower-income families and blacks to seek medical care both in the physician's office or by telephone rather than from the hospital outpatient department. Blacks and low-income families experienced the greatest difficulty acquiring and regularly utilizing medical services for a variety of reasons: poor communication between the family and the doctor, lack of access, lack of knowledge regarding resources, insufficient money to pay for care, no transportation, and inadequate information relative to illnesses and diseases and referral to appropriate services (Sheham, 1973; DHHS, 1985).

Solutions to these problems and needs require a multifaceted approach. In addition to financing, and providing adequate and available facilities for the delivery of health care, attention must be focused on the quality of the relationship between the service provider and the black consumer of services. Similarly, any long-term improvement in the delivery of health care services to the black community must include not only preventive health care but also such basic human necessities as minimal levels of family income and improved housing and working conditions. Certain cultural factors must also be considered in helping black families use health care services effectively. Some of these factors manifest themselves in individual patterns, others are more observable in the patterns of black families in responses to acute and chronic illnesses. These factors may include spiritualism, communication styles, authority structure and compassion (*Health Education and the Black Community,* 1980).

THE IMPACT OF ACUTE AND CHRONIC ILLNESS

Certain acute and chronic illnesses—diabetes mellitus, cancer, cardiovascular and cerebrovascular disease, hypertension, sickle cell anemia, and AIDS—have had physical and emotional as well as social consequences for many blacks and their families.

Diabetes Mellitus

Diabetes mellitus was the seventh leading cause of death in the United States in 1980 and a major contributor to the disparity in health status between minorities and non-minorities (Drury et al., 1981). Diabetes as a health problem for blacks is increased by its association as a risk factor for other major diseases, including coronary heart disease and peripheral vascular disease. Complications include kidney failure, diseases of the eye, and vascular complications that result in amputations, and such complications are more frequent among the black population of diabetics when compared with their white counterparts. Thus, for the many blacks who have this incurable disease, employability, self-esteem, and the quality of social life may suffer.

Cancer

The American Cancer Society estimated that in 1986 some 472,000 persons would die from cancer. Of these, 53,000 would be black Americans, with some 145 black Americans dying from cancer each day. Blacks have had a higher cancer death rate than whites. It was further estimated that some 930,000 people would be diagnosed as having cancer and that of these about 93,000 will be black (American Cancer Society, 1986). Significantly higher incidences and mortality rates among blacks include such cancer sites as the lung, colon-rectum, prostate, and esophagus. Esophageal cancer has declined in whites but has risen rapidly in blacks (American Cancer Society, 1986). Such differential rates are attributed to hazardous employment conditions, diet, and a lack of preventive health care.

Cardiovascular and Cerebrovascular Disease

Heart disease and strokes cause more deaths, disability, and economic loss in the United States than any other chronic or acute disease and are the leading causes of days lost from work. The average annual death rates for heart disease are higher in black men and women under age 70 than in comparable whites. Under 45 years of age, the rates for blacks are higher than they are for whites, regardless of gender (Henderson & Savage, 1985; NCHS, 1965). Improvement of cardiovascular and general health in blacks should focus on such treatable and modifiable risk factors as hypertension, elevated blood cholesterol, cigarette smoking, diabetes mellitus, and obesity. Major socioeconomic differentials between blacks and whites also affect their respective life experiences, biological risk factor distributions, and access to medical care.

Hypertension

Hypertension is a major risk factor for heart disease and stroke. Mean blood pressure levels are greater in blacks than whites, with a marked excess of hypertension in blacks (Rowland & Roberts, 1982), but since 1960 there has been improvement (Cassell et al., 1971). High blood pressure has been related to residence in areas of high social stress and instability, as well as to coping styles, education, and high occupational stress and insecurity. Hypertension-associated mortality rates also show links with social instability. These relationships suggest that hypertension control in black communities can be improved by interventions that are not strictly biomedical but that increase levels of social support. Behavioral risk factors, such as diet, smoking patterns, and level of physical activity, are often part of cultural patterns grounded in the socio-economic circumstances associated with increased risk (*Report of Secretary's Task Force*, 1985).

Stroke and Hypertensive End-Stage Renal Disease

Strokes and stroke deaths are much higher among blacks than among whites. End-stage renal disease, resulting from hypertension, is more common in blacks than in whites (Easterling, 1977). Blacks with hypertension are at much greater risk of developing strokes and end-stage renal disease than whites, but blacks with hypertensive end-stage renal disease who receive dialysis treatment have a more favorable cardiovascular mortality outlook than whites who receive treatment, so it is important for blacks to utilize Medicare coverage for kidney dialysis in order to maximize their life span.

Sickle-Cell Anemia

Sickle-cell anemia is a hereditary disease, confined primarily to blacks but also affecting Mediterranean groups, where the abnormal hemoglobin is transmitted as a dominant trait (Krupp & Chatton, 1982). The individual with sickle-cell trait has inherited one gene that causes the formation of normal B chains and normal hemoglobin, and one gene that causes the formation of sickle-cell B chains, which results in sickle hemoglobin. The trait is estimated to affect one of every ten to twelve black Americans, or 8 to 10 percent of the American black population (Williams, 1977).

Sickle-cell anemia is usually diagnosed in childhood, but occasionally an individual will reach adulthood before a well-documented crisis develops. The painful clinical crisis consists of attacks of bone and joint pain or abdominal pain, sometimes fever lasting hours or days, and headaches, paralysis, and convulsions. Treatment is symptomatic. The frequency and severity of clinical manifestations vary greatly. Adults with sickle-cell anemia should be immunized against pneumococcal infection with Pneumovax. Bone marrow transplants are a potential new treatment. Prognosis is mixed: many patients die in childhood from cerebral hemorrhage or shock, others live beyond age 50. There is a tendency to progressive renal damage, and death from anemia may occur.

The greatest danger presented by sickle-cell trait is to the offspring of two carriers of the trait or to the offspring of one such carrier and a person with hemoglobin C trait or B thalassemia trait. Research is experimenting with correcting the actual genetic problem through gene therapy (Squires, 1987).

Acquired Immune Deficiency Syndrome (AIDS)

AIDS, the number-one infectious public health problem in the United States, is an important cause of excess death in minorities. AIDS stands for Acquired Immune Deficiency Syndrome. "Immune deficiency" means that the body loses its natural ability to protect itself against infections and illnesses (AIDS Foundation Houston, 1987), therefore the body deteriorates and becomes vulnerable to a number of opportunistic and serious illnesses that can result in death. A "syndrome" is a group of symptoms that appear in the body at the same time. In the case of AIDS, the person can develop rare and dangerous infections, such as parasitic pneumonia and a type of cancer known as Kaposi's sarcoma. AIDS is caused by a virus known as HIV. At one time it was thought that primarily white homosexual or bisexual men, intravenous drug users, and hemophiliacs were at high risk of getting AIDS, but we now know that the virus does not discriminate by race, age, sex, or sexual preference. Almost no one is completely safe from AIDS, so it is imperative not only to practice safe sex but also to have access to accurate information and regular medical checkups.

Adults are characteristically diagnosed late in the progression of the disease and most often die from opportunistic infections, such as unusual forms of pneumonia, meningitis, and rare cancers. An HIV-related condition of a seemingly less serious nature is called "AIDS-related complex" (ARC). It is unclear at this time how many of those with ARC will go on to develop AIDS.

Prevalence. Of the cases of AIDS reported in 1987 in the United States, 24,012 were white, 9,699 were black and 5,508 were Hispanic. Although a majority (61 percent) of these cases were whites, blacks and Hispanics contributed twice as many to the totals in terms of their percentage of the general population (Hopkins, 1987)—for instance, blacks, who comprise 12 percent of the U.S. population, constitute 24 percent of the AIDS cases.

Geographically, almost two-thirds of black and Hispanic adults who have AIDS live in New York, New Jersey, or Florida, versus 29.5 percent of white adult AIDS patients. But the real problem in terms of spread of the disease is from infected and infectious asymptomatic persons.

Symptoms of AIDS and Related Misconceptions. Many AIDS symptoms resemble those of other common illnesses:

- Fatigue or loss of appetite for one month or more
- Unexplained weight loss of ten pounds or more
- Fever of 100° F lasting one month or more
- Night sweats that come and go over several weeks
- Swollen and possibly painful glands on the sides of the neck, in the armpits, or in the groin, lasting a month or more
- Dry cough accompanied by fever and breathing difficulty, not caused by smoking, and lasting two weeks or more
- Diarrhea for two weeks or more, for no apparent reason
- White sores and spots, usually in the mouth, that gradually enlarge, lasting a month or more (AIDS Foundation Houston, 1987).

It is crucial to heed important differences in persons' understandings and perceptions about AIDS, HIV infection, and control measures in minority communities. Susan Blake at the American Red Cross national headquarters conducted a review of all published national public opinion polls on AIDS since 1983. A few areas indicate differences between responses of whites and those of other races:

1. *Minorities are more likely to have misconceptions about some alleged modes of transmission than whites.* In 1987, for instance, 12 percent of whites thought casual contact could result in AIDS, compared with 25 percent of minorities. These misconceptions need to be corrected.
2. *Many more minorities reported feeling vulnerable and/or concerned*

about AIDS. Some 32 percent of minorities polled in 1987 (versus 15 percent of whites) indicated concerns about AIDS. These fears are reality-based, but they need to be channeled into constructive action.

3. Another positive difference is a reportedly *higher level of interest in reading or watching programs about AIDS among minorities*. Some 64 percent of minorities said they would read an entire article or watch a program about AIDS, compared with 42 percent of whites in 1987.

4. *More blacks than whites report that they have changed their sexual behavior because of AIDS*. When asked in a 1986 poll whether they had altered their sexual behavior to protect themselves against AIDS, 4 percent of whites said yes, whereas 25 percent of minorities said yes. This change in behavior appears to have been in reference to limiting the number of sexual partners.

Action Programs and Control Activities. Several prevention and control activities funded by the Centers for Disease Control have been directed toward the black population. For example:

• Of the fifty-five AIDS Health Education/Risk Reduction Programs, twenty-one (38 percent) have targeted information services to black communities.
• The National Conference on AIDS in Minority Populations in the United States, another milestone in an effort to draw more attention to the AIDS problem, was held on August 8, 1987, to seek solutions, and to help mobilize the affected communities, (Hopkins, 1987).

Such programs are clearly needed to supplement programs aimed at the general population.

Children with AIDS. Some 54 percent of all AIDS cases under 13 years at the time of diagnosis are black, and 24 percent are Hispanic; thus, 78 percent of all children with AIDS are minorities (Hopkins, 1987). The dissimilarities between children and adults with AIDS go far beyond the obvious one of age (National Health Policy Forum, 1987). For instance, the clinical picture, transmission, and treatment of the disease are markedly different. The disease in children is generally characterized by the appearance of unusually severe infections without the presence of such predisposing factors as congenital immunodeficiency. Unlike adults, children with AIDS do not often succumb to rare, "opportunistic" infections, such as pneumonia, meningitis, and rare cancers. They are more likely to suffer from recurrent bacterial infections, persistent or recurrent oral thrush (a common mouth or throat infection), and chronic or recurrent diarrhea. Infected children may also demonstrate generalized enlargement of lymph nodes, failure to thrive, neurologic abnormalities, and developmental delays. Testing for HIV antibodies is extremely important in the pediatric population when there is suspicion of HIV infection. The majority of infected children acquire the virus in utero from their infected mothers who are drug users themselves or whose sexual partners have HIV infection. A much smaller number of children have contracted the disease through sexual abuse by an infected adult, by playing with a contaminated needle, by artificial insemination of the mother with AIDS contaminated semen, or by receiving a contaminated blood transfusion. More recent evidence also suggests possible transmission by HIV infection to infants by breast-feeding when the mother is infected. The majority of pediatric cases come from low-income families who lack the financial and social resources needed to provide even minimal care. The problem is magnified if one or both parents use drugs, for they frequently have limited and undependable resources, use health care services sporadically, and do not comply well with medical treatment. In many communities, the family support services necessary for home care of children whose families cannot or will not care for them are lacking, so the hospital must serve as the home and primary caretaker of children who could otherwise be cared for in the community.

AIDS is a family tragedy. The pain and stress experienced by families when they learn that a family member is suffering from AIDS is great. It is a disease that also "emotionally and psychologically affects the victim *and* the individuals who care for, love, and in many cases must literally nurse an emaciated body and confused frightened mind until death" (Blackwell, 1985, p. 54).

STRATEGIES OF INTERVENTION

The profession of social work is concerned with the dignity and rights of people. Essential ingredients of this constructive social work function relate to the issues of blacks and should be of far-reaching concern in program planning, health service delivery, and clinical practice with such families. Critical to this process is the manner in which tasks and roles of the social worker are conceptualized.

Tasks and Responsibilities in Health Care

In general, the social worker is expected to:

1. Accept the client first as a unique human being
2. Help the physician and other members of the health and social service team understand the significant social, cultural, and emotional factors related to a black client's health challenges
3. Assess social, cultural, and emotional factors in order to estimate the client's and family's capacity and potential to cope with challenges of daily living
4. Help the client and the family understand, accept, and follow recommendations
5. Provide services planned to restore clients to optimum social and health adjustment within their capacity

6. Assist clients and their families with unique personal and environmental difficulties that confront black families and that predispose them toward illness or interfere with obtaining maximum benefits from medical and health care

7. Utilize resources, to help clients resume life in the community or learn to live within their disability

The Role of the Social Worker

The role of the social worker in the health care field is sometimes equally divided between clinically related activities, such as helping individuals, families, and groups cope with a range of illnesses and disabilities, and case management activities, such as case finding, preadmission planning, and discharge planning; and outreach to high-risk situations. This role can be conceptualized on a continuum from that of mobilizer to that of facilitator (see Figure 14.1).

The following case illustrates the diversity and fluidity of the social worker's role:

Sally Buncum is a social worker at the Visiting Nurse's Association. Ms. Betty Thomas, her client, is a slightly overweight mother of seven children: Ned, 15; Rob, 13; Gloria, 8; 18-month-old triplets (Sam, Sara, and Sue), and one-month-old Seva. Ms. Thomas, feeling depressed after the birth of Seva, also suffers from diabetes and a heart murmur and is having a difficult time maintaining her diet. In addition to her health problems and being overburdened with child care and household responsibilities, she was having difficulty securing adequate housing. She had been scheduled to move into an apartment that was infested by rodents, and the plumbing was inoperable because the pipes had frozen and burst. The landlord ignored Ms. Thomas' request for necessary repairs before the family moved in.

The worker and Ms. Thomas identified the following needs in order of priority:

1. Secure adequate housing before the lease expires on the current dwelling— within the month
2. Explore options for respite care for Ms. Thomas
3. Arrange for the nurse to assess Ms. Thomas' nutritional needs and for a doctor to examine her related to the heart murmur and diabetes control
4. Explore the availability of parenting education classes

The worker assumed the role of collaborator, mediator, and advocate in working with the local public welfare office and the landlord to make the apartment ready for Ms. Thomas' move. The entire process so intrigued Ms. Thomas that she has discussed with the worker a desire to start a tenants' group in the building to assure that others do not have the same negative experience. With the worker's support, Ms. Thomas contacted several day care centers, only to learn that the triplets had to be 3 years old before they were eligible for day care services. In the meantime, arrangements were made to provide Ms. Thomas with homemaker services three times a week. In her role as facilitator and enabler, the worker helped Ms. Thomas

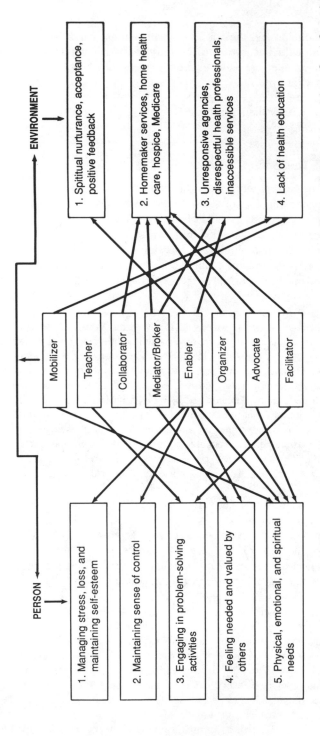

Figure 14.1. Role of the Social Worker in Helping the Client System Cope with Chronic and Acute Illness (Source: Adapted from Carel Germain, 1984.)

examine her ambivalence about weight and poor nutritional habits before referring her to the Health Department for nutritional consultation. Ms. Thomas was also referred to the Family Preservation Program's parenting class to deal with issues related to discipline, such as saying no to children and meaning it. The worker agreed to supplement Ms. Thomas' experience in the parenting class by teaching some specific skills regarding modification of children's unacceptable behaviors at home.

The role of the social worker in the broad health care field has also been directly affected by the first substantial revision of Medicare's Hospital Conditions of Participation since the inception of Medicare twenty-two years ago. These regulations added a new standard that provided for social work services as a part of the quality assurance provisions. The rationale is that social work services are closely linked with the overall quality of care provided in a hospital, a health maintenance organization (HMO), a home health care agency, or a rehabilitation facility, for example. The revised standards focus on medically related patient care services. For instance, they require the hospital to have an effective discharge planning program that facilitates provision of good follow-up care. It also requires the hospital to have an ongoing plan consistent with available services for medically related social work, and psychological and educational needs of patients. This standard will require a great deal of testing with accurate documentation, data collection, analysis of findings, and recommendations for future review and/or revision. It also opens the door for social workers to maximize assessment, care planning, and health educational needs of blacks relative to acute and chronic illnesses (Blanchard et al., 1988).

This change in role involves utilizing the natural resources of black families as well as the resources available through community agencies. However, a major concern for social workers, especially in inpatient settings, is that many referrals are delayed and sometimes may not occur prior to discharge on a Friday afternoon (Rehr & Berkman, 1973). This pattern must be changed. Irrespective of a client's ability to pay, there are some circumstances to which the social worker's response must be designed to change the system itself.

The Importance of a Comprehensive Assessment

A sound assessment is of utmost importance as the basis for effective helping. It provides the treatment team with relevant psychological, social, and cultural data needed for effective interprofessional intervention. When the black client with an acute or chronic illness and disability is assessed, the practitioner should consider the following factors:

1. The client's current and past life experiences
2. The client's beliefs, behavior, and family interaction, particularly those related to health
3. The impact of the illness on the family's overall functioning
4. The cultural background, including religious and spiritual perspective, of the client
5. The client's financial situation

The Client's Life Experiences. An effective care plan must be geared to the client's present situation—the here and now, with knowledge of the past and the anticipated future—from a physical, emotional, and mental health point of view. However, it is impossible to understand the client's current needs without an assessment of the total situation. This requires knowledge not only of the individual's past life experiences but also of the physical condition and natural history of the client's illness, the client's developmental stage in life, and the client's style of coping, which in blacks may be culturally determined. Essentially, the social worker should have knowledge about the client's fears, anxieties, frustrations, life goals, and aspirations, as well as the client's actions and reactions to the illness. With black clients, who have had negative historical and current experiences with the health care delivery system, it is important that the social worker's strategies of intervention focus on the client's perception of current needs, the illness, avoidance of seeking treatment, and the meaning of the illness, as well as the response to care, treatment, and management.

Beliefs, Behavior, and Family Interaction. The manner in which families respond to acute and chronic illness reflects their style of coping. The patterned behavior results from long-standing attitudes and beliefs about health, illness, and dying. Very often, "old wives' tales," folk medicine, and superstitions have a greater influence on the client's recovery than professional medical care (Kleinman et al., 1978; Sheham, 1973).

Helping professionals must understand the impact of chronic and acute illness on the family unit as well as on the individual. With respect to the individual, the concern is whether he or she feels secure, loved, and cared for. On the other hand, it is important to understand the family's coping and problem-solving techniques. For example, in coping with illness does the family, like many black families, engage in role reversals and home care as the treatment of choice?

The Family's Religious and Cultural Perspective. Family functioning is also influenced by its ways of being in the world, its feelings about wholeness, connectedness, and openness to the concept of a universal consciousness or supreme being (see Chapter 5). A family's cultural experiences influence not only its view of the role assumed by a sick family member, but also its perception of dying and death—for example, is this a leave-taking tantamount to going home, escaping from a world of pain, sorrow, and discrimination, or is it an anxiety-producing, fearful ordeal? Black culture is greatly influenced by religious heritage and spirituality, but it is important to understand the diversity within this context—meaning and practices will vary from client to client.

Financial Issues. The financial situation of the client will affect and reflect the type of medical, health, and social care, the place of care and follow-up care. Practitioners must have adequate knowledge of a client's financial situation to understand the family's level of survival, the ongoing continuity of care, and the quality and quantity of that care. This will help the practitioner intervene appropriately in making referrals for services.

According to Germain (1984), assessment is dynamic and ever-changing. It not only considers how personal, environmental, and cultural factors interact with illness, but is also concerned with stress level and available coping resources. Equally important, however, is the use of assessment to point up the need for intervention at the interpersonal as well as community level—specifically, the type of interventions that require advocacy, outreach, and organizing.

Advocacy, Outreach, and Community Involvement

An attitude of "What can I do as just one person?" in terms of intervention strategies is not uncommon among practitioners, but social workers can do a great deal by remaining involved at many levels of intervention (Germain, 1984; Sheham, 1973).

> A skilled nursing-facility administrator refused to admit a patient who was black. The home was qualified for Medicare payments and seemed eager to meet the needs of the patient, but when the administrator realized the patient was black she said, "We can't take him," and tore up the application. The social worker brought this to the attention of the director of social work, who in turn took it to the medical director of the hospital, and together they went to the state agency. In this situation the strategy was to use advocacy to encourage one system to influence another that withheld services to a black client. The sharing of such an experience with the supervisor and the administrator was necessary before action could be taken. It is also important to note that the worker is also conducting a community survey to determine why the nursing home is underutilized, although a previous community needs assessment had determined the service was needed. The worker is hypothesizing that some creative outreach will probably be necessary to encourage greater utilization of the nursing home services.

The above intervention was effective because it considered the overall situation—understanding the diseases to which black families are vulnerable and their natural histories, the integration of services, and the conflicts between policy and practice in a profession dedicated to helping disadvantaged members of society. Similarly, social workers must assume both leadership and advocacy roles in working with colleagues to improve health care for blacks and their families within an ecological context. This context bridges the psychological and environmental needs of families experiencing chronic and acute illnesses and encompasses the following intervention strategies, including advocacy within larger systems, the community, and the legislature:

1. Increasing personal awareness of aspects of the life-styles of black clients that are relevant to their health care, such as diet, and using that information to strengthen assessment and intervention

2. Developing programs in which members of the black community provide self-help services for negotiating the health care system, influencing legislation, increasing board and effective committee membership activities, etc.
3. Involving black families and the community in the design and implementation of services and individual care plans
4. Changing attitudes of other professionals that are barriers to adequate use of services through education, inducement, influence, and modeling strategies
5. Maximizing resource utilization for both natural and agency-based resources through outreach to the underserved and by lobbying to increase the allocations for preventive measures
6. Developing more relevant criteria for health care services to black clients on an ongoing basis, both formally in the form of research and informally

CONCLUSIONS

Specific, defined, and well-developed programs in black communities relative to employment, income, economic improvements, housing, and adequate social and mental health support systems, as well as appropriate governmental programs, will help break the current cycle of inadequate health care among blacks. In addition, knowledge and utilization of all known preventive methods to avoid acute, chronic, and terminal illnesses by making changes in life-styles, plus an understanding of the specific disease states that affect blacks, must become common in the black population.

Blacks must become more knowledgeable and cost-conscious in the area of health care; they must develop an appreciation of out-of-pocket costs and choices and begin to approach providers with an understanding of their rights to quality care and quality services. And there must be maximum utilization of all entitlements—Medicare, Medicaid, end-stage renal programs, hospice care, child care, senior centers, home care, nursing homes, and other resources. Professionals must leave no stone unturned in identifying gaps in services. If black researchers are not included in the cadre of research professionals studying health and social care, the true health care needs of blacks will remain undocumented, data will be skewed and unreliable, program planning will be inadequate, and outcome measures will be false and invalid.

REFERENCES

Aday, L.A., & Andersen, R.M. (1984). The national profile of access to medical care: Where do we stand? *American Journal of Public Health, 74*(13), 1331–1339.
AIDS Foundation Houston, Inc. (1987). *AIDS: It's a black problem, too.* Houston, TX: Author.

American Cancer Society. (1986). *Cancer facts and figures 1986 for minority Americans.* New York: Author.

Blackwell, M. (1985, August). AIDS in the family. *Essence, 16*(4), 54–56, 105.

Blanchard, L., Gill, G., & William, E. (1988). *Medicare documentation requirements for social workers in home health care.* Silver Spring, MD: National Association of Social Workers.

Cassell, J., Heyden, S., Bartel, A.G., Kaplan, B.H., Tyroler, H.A., Coroni, J.C., & Hames, C.G. (1971). Incidence of coronary heart disease by ethnic group, social class, and sex. *Archives of Internal Medicine, 128*(6), 901–906.

Demkovich, L. (1987, June). Medicaid directors face new challenges *Stateside.*

Drury, T., Harris, M., & Lipsett, L. (1981). *Health: United States, 1981. Prevalence and Management of Diabetes.* Washington, DC: Department of Health and Human Services.

Easterling, R.E. (1977). Racial factors in the incidence and causation of end-stage renal disease. *Transactions of the American Society for Artificial Internal Organs, 23,* 28–33.

Germain, C.B. (1984). *Social work practice in health care: An ecological perspective.* New York: Free Press.

Harper, B.C. (1987). *Social work in a competitive market: Who pays?* Unpublished manuscript, Colorado Public Health Association, Denver, Colorado.

Health Care Financing Administration. (1987, Summer). *National health expenditures, 1986–2000,* Vol. 8, No. 4, Office of Research and Demonstrations, U.S. Department of Health and Human Services. Baltimore, MD: Author.

Health education and the black community. (1980). Washington, DC: U.S. Department of Health and Human Services.

Henderson, M., & Savage, D.D. (1985). *Prevalence and incidence of ischemic heart disease in U.S. black and white populations.* Unpublished manuscript, Department of Health and Human Services Task Force on Black and Minority Health.

Hopkins, D. (1987, August 8). *Keynote address.* National Conference on AIDS in Minority Populations in the United States, Center for Disease Control, Atlanta, Georgia. Unpublished manuscript.

James, S.A., Wagner, E.H., Strogatz, D.S., Beresford, S.A.A., Kleinbaum, D.G., Williams, C.A., Cutchin, L.M., & Ibrahim, M.A. (1984). The Edgecombe County (NC) High Blood Pressure Control Program, II: Barriers to the use of medical care among hypertensives. *American Journal of Public Health, 74*(5), 468–472.

Kleinman, A., Eisenberg, L., & Good, B. (1978, February). Culture, illness, and care. *Annals of Internal Medicine, 88,* 251–288.

Krupp, M.A., & Chatton, M.J. (Eds). (1982). *Current medical diagnosis and treatment, 1982.* Los Altos, CA: Lange Medical Publications.

Medicare coverage of kidney dialysis and kidney transplant services: Medicare handbook, a Supplement. (1985). Department of Health and Human Services, Health Care Financing Administration. Publication No. HCFA 10128.

National Center for Health Statistics. (1965). *Coronary heart disease in adults.* U.S. NCHS Publication No. 1000, Series 11, No. 11. Washington, DC: Government Printing Office.

National Center for Health Statistics. (1984). Data on cardiovascular disease. Unpublished raw data.

National Health Policy Forum. (1987, April 6). *Children with AIDS: Education, health, and prevention issues.* Issue Brief No. 463. Washington, DC: George Washington University.

Rehr, H., & Berkman, G. (1973). Social service casefindings in the hospital: Its influence on the utilization of social services. *American Journal of Public Health, 63,* 857–862.

Report of the Secretary's Task Force on Black and Minority Health. (1985). Department of Health and Human Services.

Rowland, M., & Roberts, G. (1982). *Blood pressure levels and hypertension in persons ages 6–74 years: U.S. 1976–80.* DHHS Publication No. PHS 82-1250. Advance Data No. 84, Vital and Health Statistics. Hyattsville, MD: National Center for Health Statistics.

Sheham, M. (1973). *Blacks and American medical care.* Minneapolis: University of Minnesota Press.

Squires, S. (1987, September 29). Promising research on sickle-cell disease: Medical advances. *Washington Post,* 7.

Toby, W. (1985). *Medicare helps black elderly.* Paper presented at the annual meeting of the National Urban League, Washington, DC.

U.S. Department of Health and Human Services. (1985). *Compilation of the Social Security laws.* Washington, DC: Government Printing Office.

U.S. Department of Health and Human Services. (1985, August). Social characteristics of blacks. In *Report of the Secretary's Task Force on Black and Minority Health* (pp. 51–52). Washington, DC: Author.

U.S. Department of Health and Human Services. (1986). *Health Status of the Disadvantaged Chart Book.* Public Health Services. Health Resources and Services Administration. Bureau of Health Professions, Division of Disadvantaged Assistance. DHHS Publication No. (HRSA) HRS-P-DV86-2.

Williams, R.A. (Ed.). (1977). *Textbook of black-related diseases.* New York: McGraw-Hill.

PART 4

Research and Practice: Challenges and Opportunities

Part Four focuses on research issues and future practice concerns that are, in part, an outgrowth of the dynamic process of black family life. These research and practice issues focus attention not only on processes external to the family, but also on the interaction between external and intrafamilial processes.

Chapter 15 analyzes past and current research about black family functioning, draws implications for future practice, education, and research, and identifies gaps and biases in such research. The Epilogue looks at opportunities for the future, in curriculum, practice, and research. Ethical, methodologically sound, and ethnographic research on black families for relevant and unbiased knowledge-building about such families is the focus and the goal.

CHAPTER 15

Research and Practice Issues with Black Families

Billy J. Tidwell,
National Urban League, Inc.

One's prior values, beliefs, and predilections greatly determine one's understanding of social phenomena. They influence not only what one observes but also, and equally important, how one interprets those observations. Attributions of good or bad, functional or dysfunctional, normative or deviant, and similar value-laden distinctions largely reflect the predispositions of the observer. Research on the black family vividly illustrates the judgmental nature of social inquiry and the extent to which ostensibly empirical conclusions are contoured by preexisting philosophical, political, and cultural references (Nobles, 1978). Much of this research has projected a pejorative depiction of black family life and the institutional role of the family in the black community.

Scientific work on the black family has been highly instrumental in shaping popular sentiment, in developing public policy, and in formulating treatment modalities within the helping professions. The outcomes have largely been a disservice to the interests of black Americans. But the widespread concerns about the contemporary condition of the black family are unwarranted. Black families today experience a complex of adversities that urgently need to be relieved (Billingsley, 1987). However, positive intervention strategies for black families, in terms of both policy initiatives and professional practice, must derive from theory and research that is sounder than previous research. Above all, it is essential to achieve a more viable appreciation of black family functioning in relating to the broader sociopolitical context and the uniquenesses of the black experience.

The continuing lack of consensus regarding how to approach analysis of black families reflects both the complexity of the subject and the uncertainty of social science. Are black families in crisis? Frustrated and concerned about the prevalence of teenage pregnancy, drug abuse, youth crime, and other such problems in the black community, the broader public has become increasingly receptive to arguments that the black families are principally at fault. Explanations that denounce black families' functioning as a socializing agent and purveyor of positive social values have begun to appear. Even though the majority of black families function adequately under adverse circumstances, their resilience is often ignored or labeled as an individual strength rather than also a cultural or community strength. In the political environment a general conservatism concerning social issues is evident in unsympathetic attitudes toward black communities. The Reagan administration and its spokespersons consistently promulgated the view that the problems in black communities are the responsibility of blacks themselves and have little to do with the prevailing opportunity structure.

Theorists and researchers have a responsibility to represent the realities of black family life in contemporary American society accurately and fairly. The future well-being of black families and black communities, as well as the nation in general, could depend on the extent to which this is done. This chapter examines some crucial research issues pertaining to black families. The discussion includes an overview of the history of black families research, a review of selected theoretical and empirical work, a consideration of the role of social work practitioners in the study of black family life, and an assessment of implications for future practice, education, and research.

HISTORICAL OVERVIEW

The extended history of research on black families can be divided into several different periods, during which different types of research interests and orientations have been in the forefront (Myers, 1982; Staples, 1971).

Acculturation Orientation. Prior to 1950, the works of E. Franklin Frazier (1932a, 1932b, 1939) dominated the field. Frazier concluded that acculturation to the values and life-styles of mainstream society, spearheaded by families, was key to the advancement of black Americans. The acculturation thesis and its rationale informed a plethora of related investigations during the 1950s and early 1960s that concentrated on the adverse effects of economic deprivation on the organization and stability of black families and on the psychosocial development of their members (Clark, 1965; Moynihan, 1965; Rainwater, 1970). Such studies were linked by the primacy accorded culture and the deviations (defined as pathological) of black families from prevailing cultural norms.

The Victimization Period. The increasingly popular pathology notion precipitated a countervailing wave of studies, beginning in the late 1960s, by Scanzoni (1971), Willie (1970), Liebow (1967), and others. In particular, the controversial Moynihan (1965) report and its assertion that "at the heart of the deterioration of the fabric of Negro society is the deterioration of the Negro family" (p. 5) was vigorously challenged. Critics objected to the sweeping nature of Moynihan's conclusion and viewed it as an unfounded indictment of all black families, pressing the argument that observed differences in the behavioral characteristics of black and white families were attributable to differences in socioeconomic status and did not represent substantive or cultural distinctions. Thus, the black family was seen as "a victimized and less fortunate darker version of the white family" (Myers, 1982, p. 44). Although they repudiated the pathology thesis, the victimization theorists nonetheless accepted the premise that the viability of black families should be evaluated by the same criteria used to evaluate white families.

The Structuralist-Functionalist Period. An alternative orientation emerged during the late 1960s and early 1970s. Billingsley (1968), Staples (1971), Hill (1972), and Nobles (1978), among others, sought to reconceptualize black families in form and function. They ascribed legitimacy to the divergent patterns observed among black families, a legitimacy derived from the uniqueness of the black experience and its African genesis. This reconceptualization had far-reaching implications for the manner in which black families should be assessed and for the interpretation of empirical findings. According to Nobles' (1978) "Africanity" paradigm, "The combined 'continuation' of an intrinsic African (black) value system *and* its reaction to the cultural imperative of the wider American cultural milieu . . . determines the special features observable in black family life. The observable outcomes, therefore, must be interpreted in terms of: (1) the African nature or basis for 'behavior,' and (2) the American conditions which influence the development and/or expression of such behavior" (p. 685).

Research on black family functioning and related phenomena has recently been characterized by a more eclectic orientation. McAdoo (1978, 1981), Allen (1978), and Taylor and colleagues (1982) are representative of researchers whose refinements and qualifications of the cumulative knowledge base have provided important new insights, including a demonstrated link between the social connections of black individuals, their families, significant others, and the larger community. Extending the works of Billingsley (1968) and Nobles (1974), several researchers of black family life validated the extended family not only as an important and positive characteristic of black families but also as one closely linked to blacks' African heritage (Gutman, 1976; Sudarkasa, 1981; McAdoo, 1978). Billingsley's (1968) research also highlighted the importance of the mutual aid provided by the extended black family. McAdoo (1981, 1982), Rainwater (1970), Stack (1974), and others substantiated how social and mutual support and mutual aid have enabled black families to survive and grow in stressful environments.

Taylor and colleagues (1982) provided additional evidence regarding the prevalence of black social supports and extended families. Their national survey of black families consisted of 2,107 individuals and was a multistage probability sample. The characteristics of the sample were representative of black Americans in general. Most of the respondents reported that some form of family support was available to them, but those at the lowest level of incomes and education tended to report little or no family support and were likely to be isolated. Men and women reported equal levels of support, but the availability of support varied geographically. Respondents in the south reported greater frequency of help, while those in the northeast and north-central parts of the country reported little or no support. Overall, the findings on black families and strong, viable social support systems indicate that such linkages encourage healthy family functioning in terms of parenting responsibilities (Sparling & Lewis, 1981) and physical, emotional, and social adaptedness (Carter & Glick, 1970).

CURRENT PERSPECTIVES ON BLACK FAMILY RESEARCH

Three pivotal ideological perspectives can be extrapolated from the foregoing chronicle (Allen, 1978). One perspective defines black families as *culturally deviant*. It emphasizes differences between black families and white families and explains the characteristics of black families in terms of pathological deviations from preconceived norms. A second perspective views black families as *culturally equivalent*, legitimizing them as social units as long as their life-styles conform to "middle-class" standards. The third perspective treats black families as autonomous, *culturally variant* entities. They are understood as different, but nevertheless functional, family forms. The deviant/equivalent/variant typology is a useful and current framework within which to examine selected research and its influence.

Cultural-Deviance Perspective

The research that reflects a cultural deviance perspective largely represents elaborations on Frazier's (1939) early observations of the black family. According to Allen (1978), Frazier employed a "natural history" approach in an attempt to trace the evolution of black families from slavery to the urban centers of the north. In this vein, Frazier documented characteristics in the structure and functioning of black families that diverged from prevailing societal patterns. He drew attention to the disproportionate number of female-headed black families and promulgated the concept of "matriarchy," which stressed a negative and marginal role of the black male in familial affairs. Frazier inferred that such dysfunctional characteristics of black families were consequences of the slavery experience and the subsequent social, economic, and political deprivations blacks encountered, and he suggested that the well-being of blacks would improve as their common adversities were gradually overcome and black families approximated the idealized norm of the white middle-class family. In Frazier's view, assimilation of blacks into mainstream American life was the answer.

In later writings, however, Frazier (1957, 1962) pointedly addressed the cost of assimilation as a solution to the problems of black Americans. He lamented the prospect that blacks might lose positive qualities, such as their sense of collective identity and heritage in their quest to be part of the mainstream. This apprehension was supported by Frazier's (1957) observations on the black middle-class at that time, whose behaviors appeared to be exaggerated, superficial, and dysfunctional emulations of middle-class whites.

Frazier's principal legacy was his earlier emphasis on the structural and behavioral differences between black and white families, particularly as revealed in the characteristics used to describe lower-class blacks. In *The Negro Family: The Case for National Action,* Moynihan (1965) expands upon the differences between black and white families and provides the most influential articulation of the deviance/pathology viewpoint. His examination of secondary data, including census data, disclosed disproportionately high rates of illegitimate births, marital breakups, female-headed households, crime and delinquency in the black community, and a pronounced increase in welfare dependency. Even allowing for the negative effects of slavery, urbanization, and economic deprivation, Moynihan concluded that black families were deteriorating and, worse, that this circumstance accounted for the depressed condition of the black community generally. His findings were offered as further documentation of Frazier's concerns about the disorganization of black families and the emergence of a self-perpetuating "tangle of pathology" that required urgent action to reverse.

Staples (1971) pointed out that Moynihan's research had much more impact than other studies on black family life because it was released as an official government publication and because of the author's stature. As such, it was widely construed to represent a change in the government's attitude toward improving the status of black Americans.

Specifically, the report's findings and conclusions minimized changes in social policies to address the inequities in the social structure and the ameliorative strategies that were proposed. Black families were determined to be the major problem, rather than the oppressive external forces that impinge upon them.

Consistent with Frazier and Moynihan, Bernard (1966) traced the history of black family stability from 1880 to 1963 and related the problem of illegitimate births to a failure of blacks to internalize the marital norms of society and of black males to meet their paternal obligations. Indeed, a pervasive characteristic of pathology-oriented research on black families is the vilification and/or dismissal of the black male's contribution to the structural integrity of the family unit (Cazenave, 1981). By the same token, interest in the apparent deleterious consequences of female-headed families is a major preoccupation (e.g., Parker and Kleiner, 1966; Biller & Weiss, 1971; Hetherington, 1965; Scott, 1976).

The pathology perspective encompasses more than analyses of family structure and its consequences. It also addresses the internal dynamics of black family functioning. Rainwater's (1966, 1970) examination of the family's functional processes within a total community context is particularly noteworthy. Like Moynihan (1965), Rainwater (1966) postulates that the functional characteristics of black families grew out of the slavery experience and subsequent racial oppressions but took on a self-perpetuating character and thereby sustain the inferior status of blacks. In a study of black families, Rainwater observed the pervasiveness of dysfunctional norms, mores, and interactional patterns and concluded that premarital pregnancy was considered normative, that attitudes toward marriage and maintaining the marital union were lax, and that children were generally deprived of wholesome emotional and psychological inputs.

Cultural-Equivalence Perspective

Research advancing the deviancy/pathology viewpoint has been criticized because it failed to acknowledge the distinct cultural base underlying black family dynamics. However, what distinguishes that body of research from works that fall into the *cultural-equivalence* category is the issue of whether black families are qualitatively different from white families. Equivalence theorists argue that they are not, that the alleged deviant characteristics of black families are reactions to the realities of racial discrimination and economic deprivation, in the absence of which black families would approximate white middle-class norms. Rather than being pathological, then, black families are seen as effecting rational adaptations to their oppressive circumstances.

Scanzoni (1971) found that black families are stable, egalitarian, and functional vis-à-vis the white middle-class ideal. Based on a quantitative analysis of four hundred economically secure and insecure families, positive relationships between family patterns and measures of security were documented. Heiss (1975) obtained similar findings. Liebow (1967) and Willie (1976) employed qualitative approaches that supported the proposition that blacks in similar economic circumstances resemble their white counterparts.

Many equivalence-oriented scholars have taken issue with the black matriarchy arguments of Frazier (1939), Moynihan (1965), and others, which claimed that female-dominated households were the major source of family disorganization and pathology in lower-income black communities. Hyman and Reed (1969) and Tenhouten (1970) observed little difference between black and white families in patterns of female influence and found that in many cases female influence is more predominant in white families. Willie's (1976) case studies further revealed primarily egalitarian and therefore positive power relationships between black spouses in both working-class and middle-class families. He wrote: "Cooperation for survival is so basic in black working-class families that the relationship between husband and wife takes on an equalitarian character" (p. 63).

Arguments about the detrimental effects of being reared in a female-headed father-absent household have also been challenged. Duncan and Duncan (1969) found no evidence of intergenerational transmission of family instability, that current marital status was unrelated to the marital stability of the family of origin. Kriesberg (1967) showed that single mothers were more likely than married mothers to express educational aspirations for their children, and numerous studies contradict the suggestion that female-headed black families are inherently dysfunctional (Billingsley, 1969; Heiss, 1975; Hill, 1972).

Thus, research representing the cultural-equivalence perspective has sought to minimize the significance of observed differences between black and white families. Differences that do exist are explained by economic class factors and not in terms of qualitative cultural distinctions between blacks and whites. If the economic disadvantages are alleviated, the argument goes, black families exhibit the same structural and functional patterns as families that represent the idealized white middle-class norm. The cultural-equivalence perspective dominated the literature between 1965 and 1978 (Johnson, 1981).

Despite their vigorous defense, equivalence advocates tend not to impute any redeeming value to the differing structural and behavioral characteristics of black families. They support the need to change these characteristics, but stress the external forces that mitigate against this improvement, particularly with regard to blacks in lower socioeconomic positions. In other words, these theorists, in using a color-blind perspective, subscribe to the view that the viability and integrity of black families should be assessed within the same normative framework and by the same standards as the modal white family unit. This view begs a fundamental issue: To what extent should the characteristics of black families be recognized as legitimate and functional in their own right? This issue introduces a radically different perspective.

Cultural-Variance Perspective

This alternative perspective, that of cultural variance, is marked by (1) rejection of the notion of an ideal family type and a common culture across racial groups, (2) a focus on the strengths of black families, (3) an emphasis on continuities in the structure and functioning of black families in relation to the African heritage of black Americans, and (4) an illumination of the interplay between African-based family life-styles and the black experience in America. Nobles (1978) and Staples (1971) have been forceful exponents of the cultural-variance perspective and staunch critics of the normative approach to studying black families. In a highly regarded exposition on this subject, Staples (1971) wrote: "The black family cannot be explained by the use of normative social science models. . . . Rather than using a more objective approach and accepting the fact that black families are different and one must understand the way in which they live and try to understand their values and standards, . . . white values and standards have been imposed on the study of black family life" (p. 133).

A number of theorists and researchers have attempted to counteract the negative practice to which Staples refers. Billingsley (1968) pointed out that the black family has been a remarkably stable and resilient institution, many of whose alleged deficiencies have actually been sources of strength. Hill (1972) identified five strengths of black families associated with the internal dynamics of black family life: strong kinship bonds, strong work ethic, strong achievement orientation, strong religious orientation, and adaptability of family roles. The more recent work of Gary and colleagues (1983) also focused on the stability or strength characteristics of black two-parent and female-headed families. They explored the differentiating features and functional patterns of families perceived to be strong and found that strong black families (1) are stable, (2) have encountered problems and successfully resolved them with internal resources, and (3) are involved with their relatives, neighbors, and community organizations and seldom seek assistance with problems from persons outside the family.

Nobles (1978) stresses the special characteristics of black families as a result of their African heritage—their structural elasticity, child-centeredness, role interchangeability, and proclivity to network. Other analysts have highlighted the uniqueness and functionality of the extended kinship system of blacks, a phenomenon that is generally treated as a major cultural pattern that distinguishes blacks from whites (Billingsley, 1968; Stack, 1974; Hill, 1972; Hayes & Mendel, 1973). Hayes and Mendel (1973) found that the intensity and degree of interaction are greater among black extended families than among whites. Blacks interact with more of their kin, receive more assistance from them, and tend to have both a larger number and a wider variety of relatives living with them. Stack (1974) explains that the extended family is a necessity largely because blacks lack economic resources, so sharing is for survival and for improving the quality of life. McAdoo (1978) demonstrates that black extended kinship patterns occur across economic levels. In Nobles' (1978, 1974) view, these patterns have African roots and must therefore be understood as intrinsically cultural phenomena.

Thus, the most recent perspective on black families does not simply accept observed differences between blacks and whites; it conceptualizes these differences in terms of distinctive and functional attributes of black families. The cultural-variance perspective has become firmly ensconced in the cumulative body of theory and research on black families and is still developing.

Prospect for a New Approach to Research

Of the research within and across the three subclassifications reviewed above, several general observations can be made. First, there has been an excessive reliance on structural/functional analysis, which assumes that a family's behavioral patterns are dictated by the way it is organized. While there may be some validity to this assumption, which is based on European rather than African norms, the causal linkages between family structure and function are by no means so clear-cut. Thus, the structural/functional approach is hard-pressed to account for the differing functional characteristics of comparably organized family units as well as for the behavioral similarities of structurally different units. There is a dynamic aspect of family life that structural/functional theory tends to disregard or obscure.

Second, much of the research has been in the form of cross-sectional analysis, studying black families at one point in time, an approach that is ill-suited to understanding the changing, developmental nature of family life. It is unfortunate that the developmental perspective has been severely neglected (Engram, 1982; Myers, 1982), because the developmental framework "permits the study of changes in family roles as they are influenced by forces both external and internal to family units over time [and] incorporates variations generated by changes in the family composition" (Engram, 1982, p. 21). There is a great need for longitudinal research designs.

Third, the use of small, unrepresentative samples has been a major weakness of research on black families, and researchers have often shown little or no restraint in generalizing from white middle-class norms to their restricted study sample, or from the restricted sample to some larger population. In particular, there has been a widespread tendency to focus on a sample of low-income black families and draw conclusions about black families in general, a practice that fails to recognize the heterogeneity of black Americans. Equally objectionable is that samples of low-income black families are often compared with middle-class white families, thereby confusing the effects of class and race and reinforcing the assumption that all blacks are in the lower class. Inferences concerning the "deviancy" of the black family are predictable outcomes of these serious abuses of research methodology (Myers, 1982).

These and other methodological deficiencies must be corrected if a fuller, more accurate understanding of black family life is to be achieved, but the complexity of the subject matter makes it doubtful that a unified approach to studying black families will emerge soon. Although there will continue to be fundamental ideological disagreements, researchers who adopt different technical designs and conceptual frameworks must not promote as fact what is essentially an ideological position. The entrenched view that a given type of family is inherently superior is perhaps the most telling example. A viable family unit is determined by the interplay of different (internal and external) variables and cannot be reduced to a single ideal type. Moreover, the appreciation of the differences involved should be emphasized—and that is viewed as positive rather than negative.

A developmental approach to the study of black family life holds considerable promise. The developmental approach is broad-based and flexible. It can incorporate components of the interactional approaches, the structural-functional approaches, and other approaches as well. The Gutman (1975) study on black families may serve as an illustration of the usefulness of this approach: According to Allan (1978), Gutman was "able to view black family structure and process against the critical sociohistorical backdrops of slavery, emancipation and urbanization. Patterns of interpersonal relationships (e.g., husband-wife, sibling interaction) are detailed and in turn related to prevailing social conditions. Changes in the structural configuration of black families [were] interpreted in terms of variations in economic, social and political settings" (p. 124). This approach, with its broader ecological perspective and its appreciation for the influence of time as an important variable, is consistent with the emphasis of person-in-environment within social work and provides a useful foundation for exploring the implications for social work practice based on its utility.

IMPLICATIONS FOR SOCIAL WORK

Social work uses research data and analyses from the social sciences to clarify its mission, develop treatment strategies, and define appropriate targets and points of intervention. Research on black families and black community life has been an important part of the larger knowledge base social work has employed. The competing perspectives, differing assumptions, and inconsistent findings necessitate that future choices be exercised thoughtfully and in a way that minimizes the imposition of values that do not fully recognize the uniquenesses of the black experience.

Practice Guidelines

Social work practice based on the deviance/pathology paradigm of black family functioning will not effectively address problems that some black families experience. For example, this perspective would dictate that the practitioner define problems and needs in terms of individual pathology with little or no regard for the transaction between family, significant others, and the larger environment. The deviancy perspective overlooks certain attributes of black families, such as their strong kinship bonds, religious-spiritual orientation, parenting skills, and achievement orientation, which have played a critical role in enabling the family to cope with oppressive external forces and which therefore should be capitalized upon by the practitioner who seeks to assist with a given need.

Curriculum Development

Social work educators and practitioners must be aware of the myths, misconceptions, and distortions of black family life that have been generated by much of the literature. The curriculum for graduate and undergraduate schools of social work should focus on the following:

1. *Practice.*

- Conceptualization of problems and needs of black clients from a strengths perspective
- Skills necessary for intervening at the interface between person and environment, with focus on reinforcing existing assets, strengths, resources, and self-help efforts
- Social ties and their impact on the black individual's well-being, role performance, and parenting
- The impact of culture on the formation and resolution of particular problems and needs of the black family and community
- The adaptability of specific treatment approaches to black families
- The application of culture-specific approaches to concerns of black families

2. *Research.* The integration of research and practice with—

- An emphasis on the similarities between the practice process and the research process
- Specific client variables and worker variables that may positively or negatively affect the treatment encounter with black families
- Empirical examination of various bicultural approaches to prevention and treatment, factors affecting the low social service utilization

rates of blacks, and the incidence and rates for specific mental and physical disorders among blacks

3. *Practicum*. Operationalization of practice and research theory through—

- Continued examination of specific individual, family, and community needs, with the active input of those individuals in the needs assessment process
- Identification of coping strategies, unique attributes of blacks, communication styles, social change strategies at the level of face-to-face group system, organizational system, and community development
- Development of creative strategies to correct maladaptive personality development

These requirements imply a need for continuing self-assessment within the profession regarding biases related to its own value system through the process of internal and external review.

Future Research Initiatives

The social work practitioner is in a position to contribute to the knowledge on black family and community life through planful investigations. The need for more empirical work in this area on the part of the practitioner is long-standing (Briar, 1971). The practitioner-researcher must not approach the study with the preconceived notion that black family functioning is deviant and pathological. The framework within which the inquiry is pursued should take into account fully the peculiar realities that black people face and the efficacy with which they have confronted them.

The value of future research on the black family will be determined largely by (1) the extent to which its "unique features" are recognized and (2) how these characteristics are conceptualized based on universally applicable principles of family functioning. Of course, the methodological deficiencies of past research should also be rectified. Among other things, better sample designs and more longitudinal studies are needed.

The practice and education community have numerous opportunities to collaborate with black families and the black community in examining perceived problems, its styles and methods of problem-solving, and the dynamic processes that occur within the family units. For example, there is a great need for research on the impact of unemployment and underemployment on black family life and the community, and research that critically examines service opportunities and available resources and recommends programs, services, and policies that fill gaps in effective service delivery as well as reinforce existing strengths. Research could also focus on styles and methods of coping and problem-solving that account for the survival of poor and "working poor" black families. These major coping strategies could be transferable practice principles for other client groups experiencing similar problems. Research could also focus on the dynamic processes that occur within the family unit, including the impact of adolescent pregnancy and parenthood, family functioning and decision-making, and role performance in single-parent black families. The complexity of black family life cannot be adequately appreciated without more systematic attention to the internal dynamics that regulate and sustain it. Such examinations should be carried out within a developmental framework that allows changes in form or dynamics among intrafamilial factors to be analyzed over time.

CONCLUSIONS

Research on black family functioning has become an integral part of the social science literature. For the most part, the discussion has been destructive to black families, and only recently has it become constructive, as the traditional pejorative depictions of black families have been challenged and new insights have surfaced. We have yet to reach the point where black families are commonly evaluated on their own terms, largely because ideological disagreements do not readily lend themselves to definitive empirical resolutions and because the institutional biases that some researchers have embraced are difficult to identify and eliminate. Many issues concerning black families are inherent in matters of ideology and beliefs about what is desirable. In any case, there is a continuing need to challenge the presuppositions that give rise to denigrative analyses of black family and community life. Practitioners, educators, and social scientists who are concerned about promoting the well-being of black Americans have a critical role to play in this regard.

REFERENCES

Allen, W.R. (1978). The search for applicable theories of black family life. *Journal of Marriage and Family Life, 40*, 117–129.

Bernard, J. (1966). *Marriage and family among Negroes.* Englewood Cliffs, NJ: Prentice Hall.

Biller, H.B., & Weiss, S.D. (1971). The father-daughter relationship and the personality development of the female. *Journal of Genetic Psychology, 4*, 178–181.

Billingsley, A. (1968). *Black families in white America.* Englewood Cliffs, NJ: Prentice Hall.

Billingsley, A. (1969). Family functioning in the low-income black community. *Social Casework, 50*, 563–572.

Billingsley, A. (1987). Black families in a changing society. In J. Dewart (Ed.), *State of black America, 1987* (pp. 97–111). New York: National Urban League.

Briar, S. (1971). Family services and casework. In H.S. Maas (Ed.), *Research in the social services: A five-year review* (pp. 108–129). New York: National Association of Social Workers.

Carter, H., & Glick, P. (1970). Marriage and divorce: A social and economic study. American Public Health Association Vital and Health Statistics Monograph. Cambridge, MA: Harvard University Press.

Cazenave, N.A. (1981). Black men in America: The quest for manhood. In H.P. McAdoo (Ed.), *Black families* (pp. 176–185). Beverly Hills, CA: Sage.

Clark, K. (1965). *Dark ghetto.* New York: Harper & Row.

Duncan, B., & Duncan, O.D. (1969). Family stability and occupational success. *Social Problems, 16,* 273–285.

Engram, E. (1982). *Science, myth, reality: The black family in one-half century of research.* Westport, CT: Greenwood.

Frazier, E.F. (1932a). *The free Negro family.* Nashville, TN: Fisk University Press.

Frazier, E.F. (1932b). *The Negro family in Chicago.* Chicago: University of Chicago Press.

Frazier, E.F. (1939). *The Negro family in the United States.* Chicago: University of Chicago Press.

Frazier, E.F. (1957). *Black bourgeoisie.* Glencoe, IL: Free Press.

Frazier, E.F. (1962). The failure of the Negro intellectual. *Negro Digest, 30,* 214–222.

Gary, L.E., Beatty, L.A., Berry, G.L., & Price, M.D. (1983). *Stable black families final report.* Washington, DC: Howard University, Institute for Urban Affairs and Research.

Gutman, H. (1976). *The black family in slavery and freedom: 1750–1925.* New York: Random House.

Hayes, W., & Mendel, C.H. (1973). Extended kinship in black and white families. *Journal of Marriage and the Family, 35,* 51 57.

Heiss, J. (1975). *The case of the black family: A sociological inquiry.* New York: Columbia University Press.

Hetherington, E.M. (1965). A developmental study of the dominant parent on sex-role preference, identification, and imitation in children. *Journal of Personality and Social Psychology, 2,* 188.

Hill, R.B. (1972). *The strengths of black families.* New York: Emerson Hall.

Hyman, H.H., & Reed, S.J. (1969). Black matriarchy reconsidered: Evidence from secondary analysis of sample surveys. *Public Opinion Quarterly, 33,* 346–354.

Johnson, L.B. (1981). Perspectives on black family empirical research: 1965–1978. In H.P. McAdoo (Ed.), *Black families* (pp. 87–102). Beverly Hills, CA: Sage.

Kriesberg, L. (1967). Rearing children for educational achievement in fatherless families. *Journal of Marriage and the Family, 29,* 288–301.

Liebow, E. (1967). *Tally's corner.* Boston: Little, Brown.

McAdoo, H.P. (1978). Factors related to stability in upwardly mobile black families. *Journal of Marriage and the Family, 40,* 761–776.

McAdoo, H.P. (Ed.). (1981). *Black families.* Beverly Hills, CA: Sage.

McAdoo, H.P. (1982). Stress absorbing systems in black families. *Family Relations, 31,* 479–488.

Moynihan, D.P. (1965). *The Negro family: The case for national action.* Washington, DC: Department of Labor, Office of Policy Planning and Research.

Myers, H.F. (1982). Research on the Afro-American family: A critical review. In B.A. Bass, G.E. Wyatt, & G.J. Powell (Eds.), *The Afro-American family: Assessment, treatment, and research issues* (pp. 35–68). New York: Grune & Stratton.

Nobles, W.W. (1974). Africanity: Its role in black families. *Black Scholar, 5,* 10–17.

Nobles, W.W. (1978). Toward an empirical and theoretical framework for defining black families. *Journal of Marriage and the Family, 40,* 679–688.

Parker, S., & Kleiner, R. (1966). Characteristics of Negro mothers in single-headed households. *Journal of Marriage and the Family, 28,* 507–513.

Rainwater, L. (1966). Crucible of identity: The lower-class Negro family. *Daedalus, 95*, 172–216.

Rainwater, L. (1970). *Behind ghetto walls: Black families in a federal slum.* Chicago: Aldine.

Scanzoni, J.H. (1971). *The black family in modern society.* Boston: Allyn & Bacon.

Scott, P.B. (1976). Sex roles research and black families: Some comments on the literature. *Journal of Afro-American Issues, 4,* 349–361.

Sparling, J., & Lewis, J. (1981). *Information needs of parents with young children.* Washington, DC: Administration for Children, Youth, and Families.

Stack, C.B. (1974). *All our kin.* New York: Harper & Row.

Staples, R. (1971). Towards a sociology of the black family: A theoretical and methodological assessment. *Journal of Marriage and the Family, 33,* 119–138.

Sudarkasa, N. (1981). Interpreting the African heritage in Afro-American family organization. In H.P. McAdoo, (Ed.), *Black families* (pp. 23–36). Beverly Hills, CA: Sage.

Taylor, R.J., Jackson, J.S., & Quick, A.D. (1982). The frequency of social support among black Americans: Preliminary findings from the national survey of black Americans. *Urban Research Review, 8*(2), 1–4, 11.

Tenhouten, W. (1970). The black family: Myth and reality. *Journal of Psychiatry, 33,* 145–173.

Willie, C.V. (1970). *The family life of black people.* Columbus, OH: Merrill.

Willie, C.V. (1976). *A new look at black families.* Bayside, NY: General Hall.

Epilogue
Challenges and Opportunities: Future Practice and Research with Black Families

Sadye M. L. Logan, *University of Kansas*
Edith M. Freeman, *University of Kansas*
Ruth G. McRoy, *University of Texas at Austin*

In the past, social work practice was *done to* black families and their communities instead of *with them,* but new knowledge, improved skills, and advanced technologies have fostered more viable relationships between the helping professionals and consumers of services within the black communities. We are moving in the right direction.

CURRICULUM OPPORTUNITIES

The triad of social work curriculum in terms of policy, practice, and research must be made more relevant if it is to respond effectively to the challenge of future practice with black families. Practitioners and educators must be aware of and responsive to the interaction of intravenous drug use and the AIDS crisis when helping to prioritize the needs of black families, and the issues of homeless families, the increasingly differential effects from poverty and unemployment, and violence in schools must receive high priority in practice and in social work education. The impact on black family life is central, but such issues also affect families from other racial groups. A growing underclass has needs that must be addressed not only at social policy levels but also in the design of social service programs and in day-to-day interventions with those families.

PRACTICE OPPORTUNITIES

Social workers continue to be part of the front-line interdisciplinary professionals that will be helping families and communities address a range of problems and needs. Knowledge and skill building for practice in terms of those identified needs are therefore essential, as is the timing for preventing and diminishing the effects of those factors with families. Of course, as social workers struggle to respond effectively to traditional service commitments, they must also seek out innovative ways to respond to the needs of black families and communities. Some of these innovations may be agency initiated, others may result from joining forces with communities in implementing community initiated services. Agency initiated services are illustrated in one area of practice described as family preservation. This approach to working with families emphasizes family and community strengths, existing assets, resources, and self-help. Other agency initiated services are concerned with parent education and forms of family life education that focus on different types of problems-in-living.

Perhaps practice involvement at the community level is more challenging for social work practitioners than clinically oriented services. It is an area of practice where additional skills are needed and where the client system is quite large and diverse. As Wood (1978) points out, "There is a need to develop, refine and teach techniques of intervention in the social system such as broker-age, advocacy, confrontation, manipulation of systems, bargaining and negotiat-ing" (p. 346). Recognizing that, individually and personally, social workers serve on community boards and help to organize community service projects, it is also important that entire agencies establish linkages with those grassroot and self-help organizations in churches and nonsectarian settings. Some of these self-help innovations are concerned with economic development, community improvement, finding homes for institutionalized children, supporting single fathers and single mothers, and designing creative education programs to aid disadvantaged youths.

The movement of practitioners into the area of legislative advocacy and other types of political activities with and on behalf of at-risk and underserved groups within black communities is another challenge. To influence social policy that affects the poor and meets gaps in services, social workers must also possess special knowledge and skills in lobbying, testifying in legislative or public hearings, and coalition-building with consumer and professional interest groups (Mahaffey & Hanks, 1982).

RESEARCH OPPORTUNITIES

In responding to these practice demands of the future, social workers will continue to be in a position to identify the questions that future research on black families needs to address, to point out typical and potential biases in data, and to plan and implement research focused on those questions. For instance, research is needed on the vast majority of black families from all socioeconomic groups that *are* functional. What are their strengths, and how are those strengths used in handling normative life issues and unique stresses related to racial or cultural adjustment? What intergenerational processes positively affect the ability of those families to cope, and how are those coping skills passed from generation to generation? In troubled, dysfunctional black families, what interventions can be used effectively to resolve individual, familial, community, and large-system problems, and how can those outcomes be demonstrated? What is the role of the social worker in intervening with such families? How is the worker's role with black families different from his or her role with other families?

Practice principles must be generated carefully from research that is focused on these and other questions. To repeat the cycle of biased questions, biased research, and biased interpretations that already exist would be a disservice to future research that is based on such culturally relevant questions. Ethnographic studies, rather than survey research, may be a good beginning step in overturning the predetermined assumptions that some researchers have used in the past to shape their explorations. Bowman's (1983) cautionary note about research on black families is useful for ending this "look toward the future." He noted that in all circumstances prior to conducting research, "Blacks . . . from diverse backgrounds . . . should be organized to reality test further the hypotheses developed by researchers" (p. 24).

REFERENCES

Bowman, P.J. (1983). Significant involvement and functional relevance: Challenges to survey research. *Social Work Research and Abstracts,* 19 (4):21–26.

Mahaffey, M., & Hanks, J.W. (Eds.). (1982). *Practical politics: Social work and political responsibility.* Silver Springs, MD: National Association of Social Workers.

Wood, K.M. (1978, November). Casework effectiveness: A new look at the research evidence. *Social Work,* 437–458.

Author Index